THE POLITICS OF MULTIPLE BELONGING

DAMES

Dansk Center for Migration
og Etniske Studier

EUROPEAN RESEARCH CENTRE
ON MIGRATION & ETHNIC RELATIONS

The Politics of Multiple Belonging

Ethnicity and Nationalism in Europe and East Asia

Edited by

FLEMMING CHRISTIANSEN
University of Leeds, UK

ULF HEDETOFT
Aalborg University, Denmark

ASHGATE

Published by
Ashgate Publishing Limited
Gower House
Croft Road
Aldershot
Hants GU11 3HR
England

Ashgate Publishing Company
Suite 420
101 Cherry Street
Burlington, VT 05401-4405
USA

Ashgate website: http://www.ashgate.com

British Library Cataloguing in Publication Data
The politics of multiple belonging : ethnicity and
   nationalism in Europe and East Asia. - (Research in
   migration and ethnic relations series)
   1. Ethnicity - Europe 2. Ethnicity - East Asia
   3. Multiculturalism - Europe 4. Multiculturalism - East Asia
   5. Minorities - Europe - Social conditions 6. Minorities -
   East Asia - Social conditions
   I. Christiansen, Flemming II. Hedetoft, Ulf
   305.8'0094

Library of Congress Cataloging-in-Publication Data
The politics of multiple belonging : ethnicity and nationalism in Europe and East Asia /
edited by Flemming Christiansen and Ulf Hedetoft.
      p. cm. -- (Research in migration and ethnic relations series)
   Includes bibliographical references and index.
   ISBN 0-7546-4128-7
   1. Group identity. 2. Ethnicity--Europe. 3. Ethnicity--East Asia. 4. Nationalism--
Europe. 5. Nationalism--East Asia. 6. Globalization--Social aspects. I.
Christiansen, Flemming, 1954- II. Hedetoft, Ulf. III. Series.

   HM753.P65 2004
   305.8'0094--dc22

                                                                        2003028033

ISBN 0 7546 4128 7

Printed and bound by Athenaeum Press, Ltd.,
Gateshead, Tyne & Wear.

Contents

List of Figures   *vii*
List of Contributors   *viii*

Introduction   1
Flemming Christiansen and Ulf Hedetoft

PART I: TRENDS

1   Discourses and Images of Belonging: Migrants Between New Racism,
     Liberal Nationalism and Globalization   23
     Ulf Hedetoft

2   The Limits of Diversity: Community Beyond Unity and Difference   45
     Gerard Delanty

PART II: MIGRANTS AND BELONGING

3   Ethnic Migrant Minorities and Transnational Claims-Making in Europe:
     Opportunities and Constraints   61
     Virginie Guiraudon

4   Turkish Transnational Nationalism: How the 'Turks Abroad' Redefine
     Nationalism   77
     Riva Kastoryano

5   Looking Away from the Black Box: Economy and Organization in the
     Making of a Chinese Identity in Italy   93
     Luigi Tomba

6   Intermarriage and the Construction of Ethnic Identity:
     European Overseas Chinese Community Leaders' Marriage Ideals   109
     Xiujing Liang

PART III: BELONGING AND STATEHOOD

7   Language Belonging in the New Eastern Europe:
    The Politics of Inclusion and Exclusion   127
    Ray Taras

8   Putting Heritage and Identity into Place after Communism:
    Gdańsk, Riga, and Vilnius   147
    John Czaplicka

9   Between Doctrine and Belonging: The Official Language
    of Nation in China   167
    Flemming Christiansen

10 Marking Out Boundaries: Politics of Ethnic Identity
    in Southwest China   185
    Xiaolin Guo

PART IV: MULTICULTURAL BELONGING

11 No Joking Matter: The Multiple Identities of Belgium   207
    Georges van den Abbeele

12 Writing Indigenous Belonging: Ownership in the Construction
    of Identity in Japan   221
    Annette Skovsted Hansen

13 The Pan-Ethnic Movement of Taiwanese Aborigines and the Role
    of Elites in the Process of Ethnicity Formation   239
    Michael Rudolph

14 Identity Matters: The Case of the Singaporean Chinese   255
    Benedicte Brøgger

Index   *271*

List of Figures

Figure 8.1   Model of the Lower Palace   156
Figure 8.2   House of the Blackheads, photographed in 1999   157
Figure 9.1   A conceptual map of China in the world   181

List of Contributors

Georges van den Abbeele is Director of both the Davis Humanities Institute and the newly established Pacific Regional Humanities Center at the University of California at Davis, where he is also Professor of French and Humanities. He is the author of *Travel as Metaphor* and coeditor of *French Civilization and its Discontents: Nationalism, Colonialism, Race* (Rowman and Littlefield, 2003). He is currently working on theories of national identity with particular attention to the case of Belgium.

Benedicte Brøgger, Senior Researcher at the Work Research Institute, Oslo, Norway. Research director of the Enterprise Development and Innovation Group.

Flemming Christiansen, Senior Lecturer in Chinese Studies, University of Leeds, UK. Author of *Chinatown, Europe* (RoutledgeCurzon, 2003).

John Czaplicka is a Cultural Historian affiliated with Harvard University's Center for European Studies. His recent publications include an edited book, *Lviv: A City in the Crosscurrents of Culture* and, together with Blair Ruble, *Composing Urban Histories and the Constitution of Urban Identities* (both 2003). His current projects consider urban history and place-based identity in East Central Europe.

Gerard Delanty, Professor of Sociology, University of Liverpool, UK. His most recent book is *Community* (Routledge, 2003).

Virginie Guiraudon, Research Fellow at the French National Center for Scientific Research (CNRS). Member of the executive board of the European Union Studies Association and the editorial board of *Comparative European Politics*.

Xiaolin Guo, Lund University. Her research focuses on state and society. Her publications include articles in *The China Quarterly, The Journal of Peasant Studies*, and contributions to edited volumes.

Annette Skovsted Hansen, Assistant Professor of Japanese History at Aarhus University, Denmark.

Ulf Hedetoft, dr.phil., Professor of International Studies and Director of the Academy for Migration Studies in Denmark (AMID), Aalborg University. He has written widely on issues of nationalism, European integration and globalization, most recently in *The Postnational Self: Belonging and Identity* (co-edited with Mette Hjort; University of Minnesota Press, 2002) and *The Global Turn: National Encounters with the World* (Aalborg University Press, 2003).

Riva Kastoryano is a Senior Research Fellow at the CNRS (National Center for Scientific Research) and teaches at the Institute for Political Studies in Paris. Her work focuses on relationships between identity and states, on minority and community formation in Western democratic societies. Her most recent book is *La France, l'Allemagne et leurs Immigrés. Négocier l'identité* (Armand Colin, 1997), English translation *Negotiating Identities. States and Immigrants in France and Germany* (Princeton University Press, 2002). She is also the editor of *Quelle identité pour l'Europe? Le multiculturalisme à l'épreuve* (Presses de Sciences-Po, 1998); *Nationalismes en mutation en Méditerranée Orientale* (with A. Dieckhoff; Ed. du CNRS, 2002); *Staat – Schule – Ethnizität. Politische Sozialisation von Immigrantenkindern in vier europäischen Ländern* (with Werner Schiffauer, Gerd Baumann, and Steven Vertovec; Waxman Verlag, 2002).

Xiujing Liang currently teaches in East Asian Studies, the University of Leeds, UK.

Michael Rudolph, Institut für Ethnologie at Heidelberg University. Current research project on 'Dynamics and Efficacy of Ritual Performance and the Constitution of Socio-Cultural Identity in Taiwan and Morocco' within the Interdisciplinary Project *Dynamics of Ritual* at Heidelberg University. His most recent publication is 'The Quest for Difference vs the Wish to Assimilate: Taiwan's Aborigines and their Struggle for Cultural Survival in Times of Multiculturalism', in Paul R. Katz and Murray A. Rubinstein, *Religion and the Formation of Taiwanese Identities* (Palgrave, 2003).

Ray Taras is Professor of Political Science and Director of the World Literature Programme at Tulane University in New Orleans. He has recently published *Liberal and Illiberal Nationalisms* (Palgrave, 2002).

Luigi Tomba is a Political Scientist affiliated with the Contemporary China Centre and Department of Political and Social Change, Australian National University, Canberra. His most recent publications include *Paradoxes of Labour Reform: Chinese Labour Theory and Practice from Socialism to Market* (University of Hawaii Press and RoutledgeCurzon, 2002).

Introduction

Flemming Christiansen and Ulf Hedetoft

Belonging, Ethnicity and Nation

We often use terms like 'ethnicity' and 'nationalism' to label people's belonging to a state, territory, nation or community, frequently in a process of categorization which assumes or ascribes belongingness in such terms as essentialized, universally applicable, invariable and deterministic concepts.

This mode of thought and analysis has the Western nation state blueprint writ large all over. As the world became gradually ordered on the principle of national self-determination, according to which legitimate states originate in nations, nations are rooted in ethnicities, and convergences between states, nations and territories are the actual or desired state of affairs, people's primary 'belonging' became universally recognized as residing in their 'national identity' as the provenance and site of their individual and collective destiny. 'Politics of belonging' was coterminous with the politics of nation-building (often racially argued in no uncertain terms), cultural homogenization, minority assimilation and national defence, or, in other words, with the construction of 'imagined political communities' within national boundaries and the dissemination of this national principle (practically via the export of the superior qualities of 'nation xyz') worldwide, both by means of colonial rule and – later – as a weapon used by the colonized masses in their struggle to rid themselves of their colonizers.

Thus, 'belonging' was first politicized in and by the nation state context in a process of different interacting 'modernities', then essentialized (ahistorized) as 'natural identity' in a process of ascriptive discourse which has been a resounding success, with elites as well as masses across the globe.

In this sense there can be no doubt that the generalized categories described above contain a large measure of validity and explanatory value. However, they can also, depending on context, application, evaluative charge and extent of universalization, obscure more than they uncover and distort more than they clarify. Rashly used, and without proper regard for the present-day global context, they may blind us to the precise nature of different forms and processes of belonging, to how feelings of belonging are constructed and 'negotiated' in different political settings, to individual, local and regional variations in belonging, and to the interplay between highly different politics and strategies of belonging – from 'below' as well as from 'above'. This is particularly true in the current climate of contending and mutually contested 'politics of belonging', the multiple landscape of fast-changing, overlapping and porous identity constructions/debates which globalization in its many permutations has been instrumental in placing on the public and academic agenda, and which has highlighted the relative shortcomings of the Gellnerian assumptions about congruity between individual, nation and state (springing from a Central European context which has rarely – and certainly not until after the so-called 'end of the Cold War' – done anything but practically question them, except as Utopian ideals).[1] Increasingly, people across the world and across social divides have become prone to regenerating, constructing, and negotiating ethnic identities in a search for some measure of order, transparency and control of their lives; groups and individuals simultaneously play on a variety of identity registers; appeal to both the nation state and supranational bodies for recognition of individual and group rights; create organizations to promote ethnic and sub-ethnic identities and to represent group interests; use national and ethnic icons in business and construct ethnic business ideologies; while artists, philosophers and grassroots movements wrestle with civic and existentialist conundrums of identity, emerging configurations of belonging, and new nexuses of culture, space and politics – one of the problems being the moral foundations of belonging in the age of globalization, caught between the seemingly unethical nature of particularity (pointing toward a rejection of nationalism and racism and an acceptance of liberalism and cosmopolitanism) and the still-prevalent and ubiquitous sense of the superiority of one's own belonging (tending toward a reaffirmation of nationalism, localism and exceptionalism cf. Hedetoft, this volume).

The origins and circumstances of ethnicity and nationalism and the social and political contexts in which people construct their belonging(s) differ historically, from case to case, and from nation to nation. Thus, by focusing on the discrete and specific contextual features of these kinds of constructions, by shifting the focus away from ethnicity and nation as static categories to belonging as an act and a process, we are better able to capture the richness, nuance and variety of the social and political conditions under which people commit and entrust their loyalty to larger communities.

A central assumption underlying this volume is that belonging and the political forms and articulations it gives rise to are multidirectional and ambiguous (sometimes 'logically' contradictory), typified by increasingly mobile or at least internationally oriented/knowledgeable individuals appropriating and engaging in multiple belongings and political identities that transcend and to a degree (are intended to) challenge the labels of 'nationality' and 'ethnicity'. Belonging implies that individuals identify with a certain type of community and, conversely, that communities see and construct themselves as containers for individual belonging. Belonging thus works in two directions, embodying individual psychosocial agonies (like those of a young man in Singapore, exposed to a multitude of collective identities – cf. Brøgger, this volume) and the political construction of collective symbols for identification (like the appropriation of urban landscapes and languages for emerging nationalist statehood in Central Europe – cf.

---

1   Gellner (1983); Hall (1998).

Czaplicka, this volume). Further, belonging implies political competition between collectivities like nation states and migrant communities, where such groups, defined by their self-perception and possibly external ascription as ethnically separate entities, engage in making claims on the state in which they live while remaining culturally and socially tied to their place of 'origin'. Notions of 'multiculturalism', devised as much to exclude as to include 'alien' elements from the nation state, nevertheless widen the range of individuals' possibilities for identification and generally the 'opportunity structures' within which they may operate, thereby leading to new forms of inclusion that in effect run counter to the ideals of multicultural societies and threaten the cohesiveness of the nation state (Delanty in this volume). The political agency of indigenous peoples, for instance, gives substance and articulation to their senses of belonging, while using the subordinate status imposed on them to define their own – new, rather than 'primordial' or 'authentic' – collective identity in competition with the polity that constructed them.

In this sense the present volume intends to sketch both the conceptual and empirical intricacies of ethnic, national and transborder forms of belonging against the background of varying political and cultural configurations, disparate modernities and changing realities in – primarily – Europe and East Asia, attempting to understand change both in terms of 'domestic dynamics' and 'forces of globalization'. On the one hand, nationalism and modernization have developed very differently in these two parts of the world, having followed different (though clearly interactive and interrelated) historical paths and dynamics, and having resulted in regionally discrete patterns and permutations of culture, language and sovereignty – regionalism, nationalism and imperialism – and identity, citizenship and migration (Chow et al. 2001; Haratoonian 2000; Hedetoft and Hjort 2002; Mabry 1998; Said 1978; Schwartz 1993).

Processes of inclusion/exclusion have shaped up differently, as have discourses of homogeneity, ways of tying people and state together, the density of civic society, and the meanings of the separation between private and public. Finally, it is clear that, on this background, processes of globalization also have different impacts, have received different cultural and political responses in the two parts of the world and have therefore impinged somewhat differently on forms and perceptions of belonging.

On the other hand, however, these differentiating factors should not make us blind to the fact that they are all expressive forms of conceptually related structures and processes. However differently 'national' or 'ethnic' or 'local' belonging might shape up in Europe and East Asia, first, they are nevertheless manifestations of more universal patterns of reconfiguring, e.g. 'nationality' as a common notion of belonging and a point of spatial reference for groups and individuals in both parts of the world, faced with similar or comparable domestic and global forces of homogenization; and second, their regional commonalities are always punctured by significant regional diversity as well – national belonging in Denmark is not a carbon copy of national belonging in Belgium (Abbeele, this volume), nor is local belonging in Japan configured in the same way as local belonging in China (Skovsted Hansen; Guo, both in this volume).

We must not, therefore, fall into the trap of treating East Asian countries as little more than a bleak exception to the 'universal' (read Western) pattern, with implicit or explicit reference to its degree of estrangement from the European/ North American experience; nor should we assume, for that reason, that differences are unimportant and that it is wiser (possibly more politically correct) to collapse all manifestations of nation, identity and belonging into one undifferentiated pot. Both 'Western' and 'East Asian' experiences of belonging, uprootedness and exile must be viewed as a differentiated field to be explored, sensitively and in a nuanced manner, by reference to a context of general theoretical assumptions and ramifications – or, conversely, as empirical resources for drawing theoretical conclusions about the nature and direction of 'constructed belongingness' in the world order of the 21st century. Ethnic minorities in Europe, for instance, are constructed differently from national minorities in China in political, historical and cultural terms, and their dynamics diverge, but theories, concepts and analytical tools must be sufficiently spacious and comprehensive to be able to account for all such ethno-national configurations and their 'global' interaction, as special cases/reflections of more general processes.

The confrontation of multiform realities within a common set of conceptual reference points is conducive to a deepening and a strengthening of our understanding of issues of 'belonging' both in Europe and East Asia. Interesting and relevant areas that open themselves to exploration within this framework – and some of them are indeed the focus of theoretical and analytical investigation in this volume – are, for instance, whether and how the claims-making efforts of non-EU residents on European states and the European Union reflect back on their links with their 'home' countries? Does Islamic activism in Europe, shaped by the European context, have an impact on Muslim 'nationalities' in China? Does the European construction of an Oriental Other create political and economic niches/opportunities for diasporic groups from East Asia? The field also invites challenging comparisons: How do elites in European states and Japan juggle politically imposed ethnic homogeneity against the social reality of ethnic diversity? Could we see both China and EU-Europe as two contemporary forms of 'empire', and how should we in that case and on the background of two different historical trajectories explain the interaction between 'political nationalism' and 'ethnic belonging' in the two regions? How can we explain the differential meanings of core terms like 'nationalism', 'patriotism' and 'identity' (when translated into Chinese, these concepts carry different connotations than when they are used in English) in Europe and the Far East? And to what extent do political discourses and mass stereotypes of national belongingness and of the respective 'Western' and 'Eastern' Other frame and condition social integration and political interaction between European and Chinese communities, in Europe as well as in China? In recent years, scholarship has begun to address some of these issues. A volume by Daniel Chirot and Anthony Reid (1997) entitled *Essential Outsiders* has put a comparative perspective on the agenda, and works by Aihwa Ong (1997; 1999) have opened up an understanding of Chinese transnational citizens. These recent debates understand transnationalism as rooted in history, as a continuation of a long trajectory of modernization spurred on by global political forces. Transnational citizenship among overseas Chinese in Southeast Asia, one may argue, took shape partly due to racial discrimination by colonial regimes in French Indochina, British Malaya, and the Dutch Indies and the politics of the post-colonial states in the region and the pivotal role which a few of the overseas Chinese were able to play in the economies – different in each setting, but largely as a modernizing, capitalist class able to draw on contacts across borders. The exodus of Hong Kong capitalists to Vancouver and Toronto in the 1980s (Mitchell 1997), for example, transforming Canadian Chinatowns and pushing up residential property prices, can, of course, be perceived of both as a continuation of old patterns of migration inspired by the legacy of colonial rule, and as the emergence of a transnational bourgeoisie[2] acting within the new globalized economy. Indeed it is both, and it is probably impossible to make one clear distinction between the two perspectives.

This volume seeks to contribute to the field, focusing on the difference of ethnic and national belongings as they emerge in processes of political construction in Europe and East Asia. The individual contributions seek to lay bare these processes in particular settings, using a variety of cases. However, before we introduce the individual contributions, a few additional observations on core problems related to 'belonging' and 'multiplicity' as framing concepts for a new type of 'identity politics' worldwide are appropriate.

Belonging and Globalization

In their book entitled *Citizenship and Migration: Globalization and the Politics of Belonging*, Stephen Castles and Alistair Davidson (2000) argue that we are witnessing the beginnings of the 'end of national belonging' (which is simultaneously the title of the seventh chapter of their book). 'The context for a citizenship based on belonging to a single nation is being eroded' (Castles and Davidson 2000, p. 156), they contend, though the process of erosion and redefinition of citizenship 'in response to globalization' (ibid.) is uneven and impacts different nation states unevenly. However, even nation states that until recently were seen as extremely homogeneous, have been forced into realizing that they are now on the fast track toward becoming multiethnic societies. It is Castles and Davidson's core argument that this process is primarily driven by the characteristics of migratory patterns in the contemporary world, its 'rapidity' and 'its great variety...forcing the creation of a new layer of citizenship above that of the nation – the citizen who does not belong' (Castles and Davidson 2000, p. 157).

---

2   Mitchell (1997) calls them 'transnational cosmopolitans'.

The argument is compelling and no doubt contains more than a grain of truth (though other factors should be added to the picture given of new forms of citizenship: the movement of global elites, the impact of international human rights institutions, the lack of popular trust in national politicians worldwide, and much more). There are indications that the components of the traditional nation state compact are indeed becoming unhinged and, in the mental and practical horizon of elites as well as masses, decoupled from one another: 'nationality' from 'ethnicity', 'people' from 'state', 'citizenship' from 'belonging', even 'culture' (frequently global) from 'identity' (frequently sub-national). International migration weighs heavily into this picture, more perhaps as an effect of globalization than an independent cause (Hedetoft, this volume), but its significance is in any case immense. What is more doubtful is whether 'the citizen who does not belong' (a phrase carrying echoes of Marx's 'vaterlandslose Gesellen' as a concept capturing the objective interests of the proletariat) is the happiest way of describing this new dimension to the citizenship *problematique* and to understand the rationale and direction of multiculturalism (Delanty, this volume; Glazer 1996; Parekh 2000). In turn this is linked to the important question of the resilience and integrative potential of the national state – both as a site of structures of opportunities and a site of identity and belonging – to the way migrants (and other minority groups) cope with different kinds of belongingness; and to the more general question pertaining to the strategies of political elites and their chosen instruments for handling the challenge of globalization to their 'national' power, sovereignty and interests.[3] What all the groups involved – political elites, opinion leaders, ethno-national cores, national minorities, migrant organizations, NGOs, transnational institutions, 'homogeneous' as well as 'composite' polities etc. – seem to agree on is that 'multiculturalism' is a political issue, and not merely a question of cultural difference, diversity and multiplicity in strictly cultural and/or sociological terms. In other words, it is an issue which universally is being assessed in terms of its impact on the functionality, governability and loyalty structures of national societies, in terms of 'opportunity' or 'threat', 'potential' or 'problem', promises for more open, liberal-minded societies vs the risks it might pose to traditional ethnic solidarity structures as the underpinning of post-Second World War welfare states (Wolfe and Klausen 2000a; 2000b).

Champions of the liberal position contend that polities based on multiculturalism are not only feasible and workable, but humane and future-oriented too, guaranteeing the loyalty of diverse groups to the same overarching polity (Benhabib 1996; Kymlicka 2001; Tully 1995). Adherents to the homogeneous position counter that the most stable political regime is one based on a oneness of culture and ethnicity, that this is the only way to safeguard civic responsibility toward the state, and that minorities must be taught to assimilate to the dominant cultural premises (Miller 1996; Powell 1969; Smith 1996). For this view, belonging – like 'sovereignty' – is basically indivisible, and national

---

3   Giddens (2000); Hirst and Thompson (1996); Van Horne (1997).

allegiance is incompatible with a diversity of cultural practices. The liberal position (veering toward cosmopolitanism) refutes this objection by claiming that belonging consists of several layers, where some may well be directed toward a 'foreign cultural/religious setting' and others, more overtly political, toward the political culture and practices of the 'host country'. This is in fact the most democratic and efficient way of ensuring the loyalty and participation of minorities, they argue, where homogenizers insist that democracy and solidarity can only come to fruition on the basis of ethnically close-knit societies.

On the other hand, both positions are fraught with internal problems: Multiculturalists have difficulties defining the cultural limits of political entities, i.e. how much diversity a state can abide without falling apart, and how its constitutional basis and administrative practices may be orchestrated in such a way as to make multiculturalism a viable proposition and to safeguard a feeling of 'horizontal' solidarity as well as a commitment to shared values and a common future among its citizens (Bauböck 1994). And homogenizers – apart from confronting a world which makes their premises look more and more unrealistic, leading to a frequent denial of the obvious: that 'their' societies have already passed the point of no return to traditional homogeneity long ago – are hard put to it to define what 'cultural homogeneity' actually implies and how much difference this homogeneity can absorb without altering its basic characteristics – i.e. its degree of closure around itself.

What they usually agree on, as previously noted, is that multiculturalism and hence multiple belongingness is and should be a political/politicized matter, and hence subject to scrutiny, negotiation and construction within a traditional or novel framework defined by and within the nation state as the overarching arbiter of functionality, legitimacy and citizen/polity interaction. Whether – and how – 'culture' is significant in this context is a matter for these processes of endless contestation to decide. In this welter of identity negotiations and skirmishes about rightful belonging, however, at least four decisive elements stand out:

First, that 'multiculturalism' in all its various forms and guises (Delanty, this volume) is a codename for a particular, latter-day type of discursive identity politics conducted by traditional nationalists as well as 'postmodern' cosmopolitans and internationalizers. Multiculturalism has little if anything to do with the cultural properties of each component entity, nor with the 'encounter' and 'assimilability' of these cultures measured on the prima facie evidence of their cultural characteristics *per se* – rather the question is one of the functional benefits of multicultural societies for the political order and stability of a country. In other words, multiculturalism is what the word indicates: an 'ism' lodged between ideology, discourse and political instrumentalization. This is true even in those cases and for those theorizers and groups where multiculturalism turns into a near-essentialistic credo; arguments 'in favour' are always heavily functionalistic (order, well-being, benefits to the national economy, legitimacy, inevitability, democratic efficiency...) – unlike arguments for the maintenance of 'ethnic nationalism', which tend toward a discourse of fundamentalism, sacrality and the inescapability of a common identity – nationality for the sake of nationality – and hence are prone to getting immersed in tautological rhetoric. Multiculturalism (and hence the politics of multiple belonging) is thus a question of the cultural options and limits to national political regimes, and the ways in which these options and limits are being defined and redefined through the interaction between representatives of 'ethnic groups', 'national political institutions' and 'transnational processes'.

Second, that the terms on which this process of political identity contention is being carried on imply that traditional, core national 'indigenousness' is being squeezed from all sides: from liberal, outward-looking globalizers as well as from xenophobic, anti-immigrant political factions and movements; from anti-globalizing NGOs as well as from national political leaderships, who in the 'national interest' increasingly tend to compromise on national sovereignty; from immigrant and refugee organizations who not only symbolically embody the 'global threat' to traditional ways of life but insist on their right to their own cultural-political preferences; and from international human rights institutions which support such particularistic claims-making processes and hence seemingly help erode the ethnic bastions of the National by backing multiculturalist efforts and discourses.

This decoupling of national interest from ethnic identity is a paradox, since multiculturalism (much like the rationale behind liberal nationalism as well as European integration) is no more than the tip of a globalizing iceberg and pre-eminently one of the many attempts by supporters of the national idea to defend and retain the nation state in a context which is radically different from the mid-20th century (national boundaries being less rational, nationalism being less easy to legitimate, the nation state being less functional). The irony of political multiculturalism is that it is most accepted and legitimate when its protagonists (even as unlikely ones as former British Foreign Secretary Robin Cook in the run-up to the May 2001 General Election: 'Chicken Tikka Massala is now a true British national dish'[4] and so forth!) declare their multicultural ideal to be a novel integrative national paradigm, and thus attempt to defuse it as a political threat by on the one hand depoliticizing it and on the other treating it as a new and original container of loyalty to the nation state – the avenue toward a more contemporary and more mature form of citizenship and civic participation. This is why multiculturalism – apart from being highly suspect in 'homogeneous polities' – is both a method of inclusion and exclusion: minority cultures that do not conform to this recipe of 'unity-in-diversity' and differentiation between civic-political and ethno-cultural forms of identity and belonging are not part and parcel of the multicultural compact (cf. Black organizations in the USA, aboriginal organizations in Australia).

---

4   'Robin Cook's Chicken Tikka Massala Speech. Extracts from a Speech by the Foreign Secretary to the Social Market Foundation in London', *The Guardian*, 19 April 2001 (http://www.guardian.co.uk/Archive/Article/0,4273,4174096,00.html).

Third, that there are 'unintended consequences' of the overriding paradox, consequences which are not so easily handled and which do not conform to a single blueprint. In one sense, 'ethnic identity' (understood as coterminous with national belonging) has been estranged by the conflictual processes through which the nation state has attempted to adapt to and incorporate globalization. The immediate results are on the one hand multiculturalist strategies, on the other popular and political reactions intent on maintaining the stability and identity of the old order, and frequently blaming victims of globalization – unwelcome refugees and immigrants – for the disturbance of the peace.

But in another sense this is also an ethnic emancipation process, since it gives a multiplicity of politico-cultural actors far more latitude to (re)define and (re)configure their identity-as-interests and interests-as-identities, no longer constrained in the same way as hitherto by the national configuration. This process goes upward toward the creation of transnational interest/identity patterns (transnational NGOs, the EU, migrant organizations), but more frequently downward in a particularistic process of national or regional separatism (e.g. Central European states freeing themselves from the USSR); local 'subculturalization' (celebrated in a return to 'original cultures' worldwide and appropriated by tourist marketing ventures galore); or regionally based transborder identity constructions, like the Øresund project around Copenhagen in Denmark and Malmö in Southern Sweden.

For the individual migrant, his or her 'global' existence is vested in the multiple political construction and management of essentialized difference, for it is the ability to refer to several identities that matters. Transnational belonging, where the individual is able to use their ethnic belonging in two nations, is one possible form, often politicized, like in the case of Turkish immigrants in Germany and other parts of Europe (Kastoryano, this volume). The belonging to globally distributed networks of 'sub-cultural' or 'sub-ethnic' networks or communities is another – Chinese migrants construct organized bonds referring to sub-national units of regions and speech forms, and so have organizational frameworks that span many countries and provide political links with local governments in China; the 'sub-culturalization' – the seeking back to primeval bonds – in that sense provides the transnational belonging with even stronger globalizing power for the individual actor.

Fourth, do the processes of culturalist 'othering' we have seen in the post-Cold War period carve the world up in new provinces that negate both 'national belonging' and 'multiculturalism'? Where the Cold War mixed political ideology and military security in the creation of blocks, the 1990s saw 'world civilizations' emerge as the main blocks. The cultural subjugation of the East by the West as exposed by Edward Said (1978) was transposed into the 'clash' of civilizations competing for global dominance – the Christian, Islamic, 'Sinitic' and other lesser civilizations were all delinked from the nation states of the world and defined by their immutable cultural essence (Huntington 1996). Is the imagining of one's Other part of building the community? If that is so, is a truly global community possible? The Chinese relationship to the rest of the world, as discussed by Christiansen in this volume, maps out how 'othering' acts as a tool for China's global integration as a nation state. Although the idea of confronting civilizations in the world has some influence, it is possible that the transnational citizens of the world ignore it. They may subscribe to a range of cultures and engage in diverse communities without regarding the boundaries between the 'civilizations' as important. It is also most likely that nation states resist the gross classification into civilizations, some because their statehood is secular or at least non-confessional (and because these states, accordingly, cannot allow themselves to be associated with the labels used), others because their reality is multicultural, and yet others because the cultural labels fit oddly with the images these nation states project of themselves. A state like China, however, constructs its official discourse of nation in ways that, while rejecting the concept of the 'clash of civilizations', uses it to legitimize its own imagining of the other.

Do any of these different developments spell the 'end of national belonging' and create the 'citizen who does not belong', then? Hardly. Most immigrants as well as their 'ethnic' organizations – with the exception of self-pronounced expatriate, exiled political movements – publicly declare their sense of civic belonging to their new countries, emphasize their integrative purpose as well as the benefits thereof, clamour for multicultural policies, and vehemently maintain the position that 'ethnic background/roots' and 'political loyalty' are not contradictory entities. They may feel they belong in one place in a certain sense, and in another place in a different sense. This is the position of 'nested' and 'hybrid' identities. At the opposite end of the social spectrum, self-styled cosmopolitans – elites in business, sports, culture and entertainment – may want to see themselves as liberated from the constraints of national belonging, but at the end of the day even here nationality forms the psychological, social and political anchor of their existence and the secure moral ground on the basis of which they can construct their global identities (hence the apt coinage 'cosmopolitan nationalism', rather than just 'cosmopolitanism' *tout court*). Political elites, e.g. in Europe, have no doubt 'gone transnational' in the EU context, and some of them even support some kind of 'European identity' and the 'abolition of internal borders', but arguably all (or at least most) of these efforts are undertaken in the national interest of each member state – something which is abundantly clear in the case of the applicant countries from Central and Eastern Europe. Further, Schengen and related measures do not abolish borders, nor do they do away with the monitoring and control of immigration, but only, to some extent, with control at the borders. And as far as the recourse which citizen and resident groups increasingly take to international institutions (like the International Court of Human Rights), then such claims-making endeavours – though undoubtedly based on international rather than national normativities – ultimately aim at the vindication of the rights of legal persons in a given national context and in terms of their status as national citizens. The cultural promotion of localities (even if funded in part by transnational agencies) is most often done in the national as well as local interest and routinely receives the support of governments. And transborder, regional cooperative ventures are first and foremost driven by pragmatic, business-related considerations, and do not in any fundamental way challenge citizens' sense of national identity and belonging, though they may sometimes thrive on and abet the strengthening of supplementary regional feelings of spatial, cultural and historical attachment.

This is not to argue that the developments reviewed so far are inconsequential, but to place them in the appropriate relative perspective. If the end of national belonging is still way beyond the contemporary horizon, the truth component to the argument seems to be rather that current developments spell the beginnings of the end of a particular modality of national identity and belonging. National belonging is no longer universally regarded (and treated) as hegemonic, singular and morally beyond question. 'Multiple belonging' as well as politics and policies related thereto are imaginable and pursuable and as such are a real factor in many people's social, cultural and political lives. Norms and values of international/global provenance enter into the mental makeup and planning horizons of ever more people. A consequence of such developments is that the Other has become relativized, borders have started to appear less monumental and existentially defining, and the racial/ethnic components of national belonging have, if not disappeared, then at least emerged from the closet of organic assumptions and moved into the arena of cognitive debate and open contention. 'Banal nationalism' (Billig 1995) has become harder to maintain and cultivate. Belonging, in other words, is increasingly being handled as divisible, debatable and malleable.

'The citizen who does not belong', to return to Castles and Davidson's argument, is therefore to be understood as the citizen who feels (s)he belongs to multiple settings in different ways, whose sense of attachment is in a state of temporal and spatial constructedness, who is able to instrumentalize such individualized 'identity diversity' in and for their life trajectories, and who has shed the hegemonic assumptions of national identity as homogeneous, absolute and unchanging. This is still not by any means a description of the average citizen of today, but it is an actually existing habitus and approach to citizenship, which may well be a harbinger of what the future will bring.

There is little doubt that most of the new developments in the field of identity and belonging are a direct or indirect consequence of globalization (notwithstanding all the hype that the notion has given rise to, it should be recognized as a potent set of forces and processes in both politics, economics, identity studies and cultural affairs). There is even less doubt that the major driving force behind globalization is the Unites States, an 'immigrant country' of liberalism and entrepreneurship additionally blessed with a very specific configuration of belongingness, and the country of origin of both multiculturalism (in a specific format) and very vocal identity politics on the part of a multitude of social actors. The USA is not the specific geographical focus of this volume, but it is still worthwhile considering if the global phenomena pertaining to identity and belongingness structures which have been reviewed above imply that globalization not only constitutes the framing context and prime mover of these processes, but should also be considered a conduit for the global dissemination of 'Americanized' permutations of belonging.

At the level of simple descriptive comparison, there would seem to a number of interesting links between the two phenomena. For one thing, assimilationist 'melting pot' strategies of political identity have given way to multicultural, 'hyphenated' strategies – first in the USA, then in other places, some of which use the American model as an ideal frame of reference and justification (e.g. EU top-down strategies for a blend between national and European identity). For another, identity based on civic values and citizenship on *jus soli* principles (both part and parcel of liberal nationalism) have their main origin in the USA. Thirdly, the USA represents a 'postmodern' blend of mobility, individualism, bottom-up identity politics/claims-making strategies, acceptance of multiculturalism, and instrumentalist approaches to belonging, a blend which clearly resembles the permutations we have encountered more universally above. Finally, it is an important part of American foreign policy and global cultural export drives to promote these aspects of the American way of life as positive and worthy of imitation.

All of this is pertinent and valid. The specific causalities deserve more detailed scholarly attention, but it should be presumed that the similarities are more than coincidental and most likely are grounded in more general economic, social and political changes across the globe, which largely originate in the global impact of the USA and tend to be accompanied by similar cultural and identity-related 'reactions', while putting the 'homogeneous' model of belonging and citizenship in doubt. On the other hand it would be erroneous to reduce all the processes reviewed to a copycat version of American multiculturalism and thus to a single causality, as the specific contributions to this volume will testify. First, some instances constitute reaffirmations of the homogeneous model in modernized forms (like the recuperation of Central European sovereignties). Second, other instances of novel identity formations come about as reactions to and not emulations of American cultural influences (like the commonalities among anti-globalizing activists at world leader summits, who hardly notice the paradox that their transnational modes of (inter)action are no less expressive of globalizing processes than the policies and consequences they protest against).

Third, there is also a more fundamental distinction to be observed. The immigrant case may serve as exemplary illustration: The USA requires newly arrived (would-be) citizens to pledge an oath of allegiance to the American constitution and the US flag, while upholding an official discourse of multicultural liberalism and societal diversity. Thereafter, the former Mexican can refer to himself in blanket terms as a 'Hispanic American' (i.e. he came from a Spanish-speaking country but is now fully American – and wants to be, more likely than not). He can keep his religion, as long as it stays private and particular: religious pluralism, rather than a problem, is a *sine qua non* for America(ns), which/who would loathe the notion of an official state religion. Many European states, conversely, require no public pledge or similar displays of allegiance, but instead institute all manner of integration programmes (once their attempts to keep the newcomers out have failed), while upholding a discourse of national homogeneity and making it very hard for immigrants to acquire national citizenship at all. The immigrants (often refugees rather than economic migrants, as in the US case) on their part hang on, as best they can, to the cultural habits and religious ways of their countries of origin (e.g. arranged marriages), are constantly blamed for it (in countries which for historical reasons have practical difficulties respecting both the separation and – hence – fruitful interaction of Church and State, private and public domains), while nevertheless trying to 'integrate' socially, politically and economically in order practically to prove their credentials as residents who are more of a 'benefit' than a 'burden' to the welfare state in question (Bauböck 1994; Geddes 2000; Andreas and Snyder 2000).

The example demonstrates in a small way that the patterns and contexts of multiple belonging, not least their functional aspects, are clearly quite different (see further Hedetoft, this volume), not just in the sense that US multiculturalist strategies and discourses have proved much more successful in terms of integrating migrants into societal processes and on the labour market, but also in terms of generating a form of multiple identity, citizenship and belonging which almost automatically guarantees full commitment to the American nation, its founding constitutional values, and the absolute defence of its interests and integrity (Hall and Lindholm 1999).

Conversely, multiculturalism and the politics of multiple belonging in both Europe and East Asia are often to be seen as either emergency strategies for the maintenance of (some measure of) continued loyalty to a state or as a process of identity fragmentation – a separation between different senses and sites of belonging. In these contexts, belonging is 'divisible' in a transnational context where states are faced with a loss of absolute governmental control and borders are becoming less rigid therefore. Hence, the politics of multiple belonging in these kinds of settings illustrate the threat to the hegemony of the state/national identity, leaving a space open for individual and group-defined reinterpretations and supplements. In the USA the functionality is different: the multiplicity of cultures and the vehemence of identity politics form the backdrop for the maintenance of the hegemony of national identity – the pride in America – since this process of contention and negotiation is an integral, proactive part of what it means to be American. Other states or groups trying to adopt or imitate American forms of social identity and 'cohesiveness-in-diversity' are faced with the difficulty that in their settings and given their historical backgrounds, ethnic multiplicity is either foreign to the national political culture and the founding myths of the nation (say, Germany, France or Japan) or is very differently and often much more reactively configured (say, in the UK and Australia).

National identity in China provides a separate perspective on multiculturalism, for the statehood itself is built on the integration of 'national' minorities in the nation. The inclusion of the rich diversity of cultures and ethnic groups in China became an area of policy making, by which stereotypical and managed diversity became part of statehood and nationhood. Yet, the ethnic construction of Chineseness in the 1980s and 1990s that aims to include Hong Kong, Macau, Taiwan and the overseas Chinese reflects the assertion of a mainly Han Chinese culture, a culture that is broad and inclusive of the many local cultures, linguistic differences and traditions in China. Asserting a strong, uniform, multinational China serves one purpose in unifying the Chinese of the world, while the construction of local, regional, dialect-speaking and clan-based bonds allows the imagining of both the concrete home-village and the global presence of co-natives. In China, the 'emergency strategy' aimed at consolidating loyalty to the state in the 1980s and 1990s has been to reinforce the state's paternalistic role with an affective nationalism that resonates with Gellnerian ideals. At the same time, individuals assert their particularity within the larger nationalism, reinventing 'primeval' bonds of locality, dialect, lineage, and so on, or even inventing distinctiveness from the state in millenarian and pseudo-religious movements like the Falun Gong. The official invocation of nationalism, while inclusive *vis-à-vis* national minorities, has thus given individuals and sub-state communities a site for asserting separate identities.

The Chinese state claims national self-determination, autonomy and territorial integrity within the 'international community', but exile Tibetans in India, Uighur activists in Europe, and Falun Gong members in the USA and Europe appeal to the same 'international community' for recognition as fighters for Tibetan or East Turkestan independence, or as victims of human rights abuses. The Chinese political claim to territorial unity as a nation state, based on notions of ethnicity, aims to include the Mainland, Hong Kong, Macau and Taiwan into one statehood. The 'international community', China, China's sub-state entities and the parts of 'ethnic China' that are not governed by the Chinese state are divided by conflicting sets of norms. The parameters for belonging in China have shifted as the state-imposed categories of ascription began to change during the post-1978 Reforms; new focal points have arisen, where people in China belong beyond and in spite of the nation state. The Chinese nation state, as Christiansen describes in his contribution to the volume, seeks to restructure the legitimate scope of belonging through its public discourse.

Are we really talking about citizens who do not belong? Or are we talking about people who themselves choose where they belong, ignoring the prescriptions (and sometimes proscriptions) and predefined frameworks of belonging provided by the nation states? The answers can probably best be found in case studies of multiculturalism as it emerges from the interaction between states and people.

The case studies can also present us with the rich and diverse backgrounds and the variation in expression across the globe of ethnic, national, transnational, and multicultural themes. Although the manifestations differ, there is great similarity between different settings in Japan, China, Europe and in European states. Our search for credible and useful models to discuss these themes invariably brings us back to the dynamics presented by reality. Europe may seem so diverse and China and Japan so monolithic, but beneath the first impressions, complex dynamics thrive. To use two of the models presented by Delanty in this volume, China is both a melting pot and a pillarized society. The formally recognized and categorized minority nationalities are exemplary cases of successful pillarization; the Han majority is an exceptionally accomplished product of the 'melting pot', for it is an alloy composed of diverse linguistic groups, of people with different ethnic and social roots, and long histories of mutual feuds and strife, now regarded as a cultural and ethnic monolith hardly ever questioned. Both the pillars and the alloy have shifting political functions from which new dynamics emerge. Some of these dynamics link into other dynamics at work in Europe and globally.

Before we briefly introduce the individual contributions, it may be appropriate to ponder on one issue that only occurs indirectly and vaguely in this volume: silent protest. The silent protest against the state, which joined the Belgians across the divides (see van den Abbeele, this volume), resonates with similar popular sentiments occasionally seen; had the popular commiseration after Princess Diana's death a similar sense of unity and subdued protest? Did the popular moral empathy with the hunger strikers in Tiananmen Square in May 1989 (Pieke 1996) – irrespective of the later tragedy – convey the same feelings? Or later in 1989, the silent candlelight vigils that ultimately brought the GDR and the Berlin Wall down? Beyond the manicured and manipulated political agendas of belonging, there may be subtle currents of moral disgust and yearning for common decency among those in whose name politicians and officials play the ethnic and national cards. Was not the cry 'wir sind das Volk' (we are the people) from the 'citizens of the GDR' (*Bürger der DDR*) in those final days of 'really existing socialism' a moral effort to reclaim their identity that the system had so grotesquely misused? The fleeting manifestation of such sentiments may be very powerful (as witnessed in the media coverage), but the evocative strength evaporates as soon as it gains political direction or is turned into somebody's political capital.

The Contributions

Ulf Hedetoft's contribution maps out the meanings of belonging that emerge from migration, changes in the nation states and globalization. Belonging cuts through the limitations and divisions imposed by the nation states, ethnicity and other historical and political categories. 'Belonging', which used to belong to retrograde, nationalist and racist agendas, now indicates identity as it widens in response to globalization. 'Ethnics' themselves and politicians have captured 'belonging' and they use it in their processes of identity negotiation. Belonging, accordingly, turns common perceptions of identification upside down: rather than subsuming ourselves under one nation, in the global age we belong to the world by seeing it as a source of opportunities and a field of mobility where we can seek our fortune.

Gerard Delanty dissects the meaning of multiculturalism. This word, so often and so casually used in public debate, policy making, and legislation, is a catch-all term for a wide range of normative models for ethnic and cultural integration. Delanty examines these various models, seeking to place the role of multiculturalism within the emerging global world order. Multiculturalism as a policy ploy by governments to assert cultural difference with the aim to exclude 'non-native' groups is disintegrating, and ethnicity and cultural difference are increasingly becoming a field of multiple belongings of individuals.

Virginie Guiraudon takes issue with the idea that migrant groups in Europe seek to further their common interests at the level of the European Union's institutions. She argues that in spite of European integration and the increasingly equal access to universal rights across Europe (based, in part, on the ultimate recourse to European treaties and courts), citizenship and residence rights are still vested in the nation states. Examples of collective action on the rights of migrants, in particular relating to amnesties for illegal immigrants, demonstrate that even where such activities transcend national borders, they target EU member states. The parameters for ethnic belonging depend on the shifting political and institutional frameworks for citizenship: European citizenship only exists by virtue of the member states.

Riva Kastoryano debates how the Turkish communities in Europe, in particular in Germany, maintain their bonds with Turkey and at the same time carve out a significant role in the European institutions for multiculturalist policies in their home country. Their transnationalism and their recognition in the European host countries give them influence in Turkish politics, forcing controversial issues of belonging onto the national agenda. Various political and religious players in Turkey use the transnational institutions to further their own causes, while Turkish authorities seek to influence these trends.

Luigi Tomba's analysis of the emerging Chinese community in Italy is able to show the interrelated functions of culture, identity and economic organization in the formation of a community. The political economy of declining Italian enterprises that the Chinese give an extra lease of life by accepting lower returns on investment seems to be an important factor; the migrants entering as whole family units provides low-cost labour. The concomitant informality and closure of this economic enclave are habitually phrased in terms of 'tradition' and familism. Belonging, in Tomba's analysis of Chinese in Italy, is suspended between political economy and the collective belief in cultural separateness.

Xiujing Liang, in her examination of ideas about intermarriage among overseas Chinese leaders in Europe, provides an insight into how diasporic communities use ideas of marriage to distinguish themselves from host societies. Overseas Chinese community leaders' views on marriages between overseas Chinese and non-Chinese reflect a wide range of cultural perceptions and overlapping rationales that together form a moral condemnation of intermarriage. Behind the rejection of intermarriage lies not just an anxiety of cultural loss and assimilation, for community leaders' authority is partly sustained by their roles as patriarchs.

Ray Taras explores the role of language in the political construction of national belonging. The reclamation of national languages in the republics that gained independence after the fall of the USSR turned the tables on the political relationships with Russia in complex processes of identity politics. However, while language is central to national identity, it is also an important factor in globalization and development towards a new post-national world, where a *lingua franca* like Russian or English provides its speakers with an economic and political edge.

John Czaplicka explores how states, local authorities and citizens reshape cities and alter their historical narratives. The cases of Gdańsk, Vilnius and Riga, all seeking their identity following the collapse of the Soviet Union, show the efforts at providing identification points by (re-)constructing history and by erasing or ignoring traces of the 'Other'. To create an environment that fits new norms of belonging in post-communism, city planners avoid 'modernity' and use sepia-coloured photographs of historicist buildings that stood before the Second World War as a mental template for their urban reconstruction efforts.

Flemming Christiansen examines the official discourse on the Chinese nation that unfolded during the 1990s in vibrant debates on Chinese ethnicity and origins, which gained their own momentum. Christiansen's analysis focuses on how the authorities sought to set authoritative norms for discussing the national through the use of language.

Xiaolin Guo's chapter deals with the Chinese state delineation of ethnicity and its consequences. The historical parallels of state politics and ethnicity in the imperial period provide a useful setting for an understanding of the contentious issues of ethnicity and territory in the modern period. Guo's chapter provides insights into the interplay of primordial and instrumental expressions of ethnic identity which highlights important aspects of individual/group belonging. The future of the practice of ethnicity in China, as Guo argues, hinges on how the people identified as national minorities continue to interact with the state and how they themselves justify their roles in changing political and economic contexts.

Georges van den Abbeele examines the seeming impossibility of Belgium. The textbook perception of Belgium is that of two parts defined linguistically, socially, historically and so on as fundamentally different from each other and hostile to each other, only joined together through a royal household and immigrants who feel they have become 'Belgian' rather than Walloon or Flemish. Van den Abbeele debunks the myths of how Belgium is divided, demonstrating how the divisions have become a political playing field for politicians who have little regard for the real dividing lines in the country. What unites Belgians across all divides is disgust at the incompetence and venality of Belgian authorities. To be Belgian is thus to defy the official identity construction.

Annette Skovsted Hansen demonstrates how the writing about the Ainu people became an instrument for Japan's claim to modernity. Japan as a modern nation among other civilized nation states demanded the construction of an indigenous, primitive other. The Ainu, seeking to define their identity, face the dilemma inherent in the lack of their own written history: the sources to their past constitute an outside view, and development intrinsically means dissolution and absorption into the Japanese mainstream. It may be that a transnational, i.e. more global, perspective may provide a new way of writing Ainu history and belonging.

Michael Rudolph looks into the case of Taiwan's aborigines. Ignored by the Nationalist regime that sought to impose a single Chinese identity on the island's population, the aborigine elites gradually began to assert their separate identity. The democratization process since 1986 was followed by an effort to recapture the 'own', i.e. the use of their language and their original (non-Sinicized) names. The new identity was a pan-aborigine identity representing the many different ethnic or tribal divisions among the aborigines. Reconstructing aborigine identity was, so Rudolph argues, an elite matter, often silently opposed by aborigines not keen to embrace an identity associated with lower status and prejudice, but rather determined to use their Chinese names.

Finally, Benedicte Brøgger examines how the young Chinese man Andrew in Singapore belongs in the world. The ramifications of Singaporean society give Andrew many different identities. Andrew's multiple belongings arise out of his need to interact in the multicultural context of Singapore as a Chinese, as a Singaporean, as a Teochew and as a young man. His feeling of belonging is not to Singapore as a soil, for it is 'Malay'. Brøgger's contribution focuses our attention on how belonging exists as specific interaction between the individual, ethnic groups mutually negotiating their boundaries, state and nation. It also tells us that the multiple identities of the individual are often related to each other in a continuum, joined seamlessly in the individual as he or she navigates a variety of collectivities.

Works Cited

Andreas, Peter and Timothy Snyder (2000) *The Wall Around the West. State Borders and Immigration Controls in North America and Europe*. Lanham: Rowman and Littlefield.
Bauböck, Rainer (ed.) (1994) *From Aliens to Citizens. Redefining the Status of Immigrants in Europe*. Aldershot: Avebury.
Benhabib, Seyla (ed.) (1996) *Democracy and Difference*. Princeton, NJ: Princeton University Press.
Billig, Michael (1995) *Banal Nationalism*. London: Sage.
Castles, Stephen and Alistair Davidson (2000) *Citizenship and Migration: Globalization and the Politics of Belonging*. Houndsmills: Macmillan.
Chirot, Daniel and Anthony Reid (eds) (1997) *Essential Outsiders. Chinese and Jews in the Modern Transformation of Southeast Asia and Central Europe*. Seattle and London: University of Washington Press.
Chow, Kai-wing, Kevin Doak and Poshek Fu (eds) (2001) *Constructing Nationhood in Modern East Asia*. Ann Arbor: University of Michigan Press.
Geddes, Andrew (2000) *Immigration and European Integration*. Manchester: Manchester University Press.
Gellner, Ernest (1983) *Nations and Nationalism*. New York, NY: Cornell University Press.

Giddens, Anthony (2000) *Runaway World: How Globalization is Reshaping Our Lives*. London: Routledge.

Glazer, Nathan (1996) *We Are All Multiculturalists Now*. Cambridge, MA: Harvard University Press.

Hall, John A. (ed.) (1998) *The State of the Nation*. Cambridge: Cambridge University Press.

Hall, John A. and Charles Lindholm (1999) *Is America Breaking Apart?* Princeton, NJ: Princeton University Press.

Haratoonian, Harry (2000) *History's Disquiet*. New York, NY: Columbia University Press.

Hedetoft, Ulf and Mette Hjort (eds) (2002) *The Postnational Self: Belonging and Identity*. Minneapolis: University of Minnesota Press.

Hirst, Paul and Graham Thompson (1996) *Globalization in Question: The International Economy and the Possibilities of Governance*. London: Polity Press.

Huntington, Samuel P. (1996) *The Clash of Civilizations and the Remaking of World Order*. New York, NY: Simon & Schuster.

Kymlicka, Will (2001) *Politics in the Vernacular: Nationalism, Multiculturalism and Citizenship*. Oxford: Oxford University Press.

Mabry, Tristan J. (1998) 'Modernization, Nationalism and Islam: An Examination of Ernest Gellner's Writings on Muslim Society With Reference to Indonesia and Malaysia'. *Ethnic and Racial Studies*, 21:1 (January), 64-88.

Miller, David (1996) *On Nationality*. Oxford: Oxford University Press.

Mitchell, Katharyne (1997) 'Transnational Subjects: Constituting the Cultural Citizen in the Era of Pacific Rim Capital', in Aihwa Ong and Donald Nonini (eds), *Ungrounded Empires. The Cultural Politics of Modern Chinese Transnationalism*. London: Routledge, 228-256.

Ong, Aihwa (1997) 'Chinese Modernities: Narratives of Nation and of Capitalism', in Aihwa Ong and Donald Nonini (eds), *Ungrounded Empires. The Cultural Politics of Modern Chinese Transnationalism*. London: Routledge, 171-202.

Ong, Aihwa (1999) *Flexible Citizenship. The Cultural Logics of Transnationality*. Durham and London: Duke University Press.

Parekh, Bhikhu (2000) *Rethinking Multiculturalism. Cultural Diversity and Political Theory*. Houndsmills: Macmillan.

Pieke, Frank (1996) *The Extraordinary and the Ordinary. An Anthropological Study of Chinese Reform and the 1989 People's Movement in Beijing*. London: Kegan Paul International.

Powell, Enoch (1969) *Freedom and Reality*. London: Batsford.

Said, Edward W. (1978) *Orientalism. Western Conceptions of the Orient*. London: Routledge & Kegan Paul Ltd.

Schwartz, Benjamin E. (1993) 'Culture, Modernity, and Nationalism – Further Reflections'. *Daedalus* 122:3 (Summer) (Issue on Reconstructing Nations and States), 207-225.

Smith, Anthony D. (1996) *Nations and Nationalism in a Global Era*. London: Polity.

Tully, James (1995) *Strange Multiplicity. Constitutionalism in an Age of Diversity*. Cambridge: Cambridge University Press.

Van Horne, Winston A. (1997) *Global Convulsions. Race, Ethnicity, and Nationalism at the End of the Twentieth Century*. Albany, NY: State University of New York Press.

Wolfe, Alan and Jytte Klausen (2000a) 'Identity Politics and Contemporary Liberalism', in Karl Hinrichs et al. (eds), *Kontingenz und Krise*. Frankfurt am Main and New York: Campus Verlag, 79-101.

Wolfe, Alan and Jytte Klausen (2000b) 'Other People'. *Prospect*, December, 28-35.

PART I

TRENDS

Chapter 1

Discourses and Images of Belonging: Migrants Between New Racism, Liberal Nationalism and Globalization

Ulf Hedetoft

Introduction: Parameters and Objectives

Belonging and migration, like nationalism and globalization, might seem to be contradictory notions. This chapter intends to explore if (and how) this is indeed so. Whether belonging denotes roots, stasis and traditionalism in the context of bounded territoriality and national identity, whereas migration is linked to mobility, postmodernity and associated with porous borders and the insecurities attendant on globalization. Whether both belonging and migratory flows, in their global interaction, have acquired new meanings which call for new concepts, new ways of conceptualizing and explaining these phenomena. And how questions of belonging related to migration and migrants compare on the one hand with the global identity of contemporary travellers and cosmopolitans, and on the other different representatives of latter-day politics of identity. In terms of the ways such issues are pervasively addressed – both as problems and solutions to problems – in both public and academic debates, a notable change has undoubtedly set in compared with, say, 20 or 30 years ago. The most obvious change pertains to the ubiquitousness as well as legitimacy with which the notion of belonging is now universally applied in discussions about identity, ethnicity, nationality, citizenship, migration and multiculturalism – as a matter-of-course feature of an identity which is being constantly threatened; as a desirable objective; as an argument for minority groups making claims to autonomy or increased recognition; as part and parcel of political discourses either for or against multicultural societies; or as a notion dismissed by people – multicultural academics as well as global entrepreneurs – who perceive it as outdated and oppose ethnic-primordialist positions because humans have 'feet' rather than 'roots'.[1]

---

1   It is hard not to attach, in passing, a polemical comment to this faddish internationalist way of critiquing primordialism: 'Trees have roots, humans have feet!' Well, cows have feet too. What they do not have is mind, intelligence and consciousness to conceive of themselves with 'roots', nor do they have their very own politicians and opinion-leaders

In other words, whereas belonging used to be a notion almost exclusively used by right-wing racists intent on drawing a rigid line between their own national-natural and therefore 'organic' belonging 'here', and the Other who just as naturally belonged elsewhere and therefore *not* here (consequence: closed borders and repatriation), today it has developed into a broadly agenda- and debate-setting key concept. It has been colonized by all kinds of 'ethnic communities' and political factions as a central referent of identity and an important factor of identity negotiation in a context of rapid global change. Today, belonging is part of both mainstream discourse and of competing, alternative discourses, undoubtedly not in spite but because of this rapidly transforming context. In the process, some of the formerly ridiculed rightist positions have insidiously been taken over by much larger groups, though their normative status has, for the same reason, undergone a climate change.

Analytically, the concept of belonging must be situated in relation to four key parameters which in varying configurations are responsible for its relations to and importance for the identity politics of different groups. They are, in systematic order, (1) sources of belonging, (2) feelings of belonging, (3) ascriptions and constructions of belonging, (4) fluidities of belonging. Broadly speaking the site of (1) is locality and immediate familiarity, of (2) socio-psychological needs, identification with locality, and memory, of (3) nationalism and racisms, new and old, and of (4) globality and the cosmopolitan dream. The four build on and presuppose each other in this sequence. For instance, (2) cognitively and affectively orders the wellspring and conditions of belonging as categorized under (1) and hence entails an element of construction, in that feelings of belonging are never totally unmediated or entirely pure, but always pass through mental processing, personal and collective experiences, and the temporal distantiator and psychological filter of memory – all of which shape each individual's images and perceptions of belonging, giving them depth and value, and engendering the meaning they have for different persons. But, nevertheless, this element of constructedness is not socially, ethnically or politically predetermined and pre-structured, and there is no question of belongingness being the object of identity politics, being ascribed in fixed national categories from without, or being a contested issue of racist stereotypes or the politics of immigration and integration – like in (3). Likewise, the fluidities of global belonging are unimaginable except on the real-life background and normative assumptions of national constructions.

At this juncture, the following brief comments on each of the four sites must suffice.

(1) *Sources of belonging: locality and the familiar.* My basic presupposition is that belonging is rooted in place (rather than space, which is a much more abstract notion), familiarity, sensual experience, human interaction and local knowledge.

---

impressing their national rootedness on them, or – if they choose to use their 'feet' to move elsewhere – a corresponding set of people telling them that they don't belong and should get back to their 'roots' as fast as humanly possible.

These elements constitute the sources of homeness, its conditioning context, but they are not equivalent to nor do they automatically produce feelings of belonging, let alone identity. In other words, belonging is conditioned by social and psychological concreteness – persons, landscapes, sensory experiences and mental mappings of an immediate and familiar kind (often, but not invariably embedded in the formative years of childhood and adolescence). These are the materials, the building blocks of belonging. They are therefore the necessary conditions (but not the sufficient reasons) for feelings of belonging, homeness and related identity-producing processes – as well as for feelings of uprootedness, non-belonging and identity alienation in cases where these conditioning elements have been spiced by a dearth of human interaction, continuous spatial mobility, negative sensual impressions, and the like.

Feelings of belonging: identification and memory. Belonging as feeling is rooted in a positive identification with all or some of the above conditioning elements and the interiorization of them as determinants of homeness, self-identity and socio-psychological security. Feelings of belonging in this sense and on the level of immediacy do not have to be a conscious factor of identification; rather, belongingness plays itself out in terms of the satisfaction of needs, recognition by a specific community, participation in its cultural and social activities, and a shared horizon of ideas, knowledge, networks and topography. In this sense and at this point it is a category of practice rather than theory – it is unreflective, embedded. This kind of cultural belonging does not presuppose the existence of an Other, let alone a contradictory Other for its existence, viability and maintenance, and can co-exist with other factual forms of local belonging without problems or conflicts – because it is not/has not yet been politicized by nationalizing processes and interests. Hence it is this manifestation of belonging and identity that underlies Herder's theories of the non-exclusive nature of different cultural (read: national) spheres (Herder 1967/1774). On the other hand, in the course of individual histories, feelings of belonging will routinely begin to disengage themselves from this level of unreflected immediacy, as belonging becomes more conscious, as people move away from the sources of belonging, as belonging starts to become processed through and coloured by memory and by experiences, sensations and ideas encountered in other spheres and in different social contexts, and as varying forms of sentimentalism, mediated by distances of space and time, intervene between 'being' and 'belonging'. At this point belonging is losing its innocence – an affective construction process is underway, but belonging has not been transformed and instrumentalized by the nation state context and does not emerge as a discursive category and a political identity more or less forcefully *ascribed* to whole collectivities of people to the exclusion of others.

Ascriptions/constructions of belonging: nationalism and racism. In this compartment, belonging is collectively transformed into the modern, nation state-dependent form of identity, which collapses individual, cultural and political interpretations of identity; institutionalizes belonging in the form of passport, citizenship, socialization agencies and official, ethno-national versions of historical memory; draws boundaries of sovereignty between 'us' and 'them' (in the process producing exclusivist alterity forms); transforms concrete 'place' into abstract (imagined) 'territoriality'; and reinterprets familiarity as nationality and strangers as aliens – in other words, imposes homogeneity and ascribes belonging. Belonging in these forms is couched in organicist, frequently racist rhetoric, producing arguments and discourses about those who authentically belong and those who do not. On the other hand they would be impossible if they did not have 'sources' and 'feelings' of a truly authentic nature to build on (it is this fact that lends to primordialist notions of national identity an air of plausibility). These aspects of belonging will be developed in more detail below.

Fluidities of belonging: globalism and cosmopolitanism. Belonging as interpreted in the nation state context – ethnic, bounded, homogeneous, organic and unitary – has never been more than an ideal model, always practically contradicted by messy borders, migratory movements, ethnic minorities, dual citizenships and multicultural policies. Globalization has multiplied and strengthened such tendencies, by weakening the sovereign, autonomous nation state and also by means of transnational processes that create or facilitate porous, open borders, multiple forms of identity and belonging, or even borderless, virtual forms of belonging. Territoriality is becoming de-territorialized.[2] Identities, conceived as homogeneous, essentialized categories, are being contested, *inter alia* through more massive and qualitatively different forms of global migratory patterns. In the process a new ideal of homogeneity is emerging: belonging to the globe rather than the nation. Correspondingly, ideas of a world government, or at least world governance, are being floated and enjoy increased popularity, particularly among idealists of peace and justice. This is the contemporary cosmopolitan dream. Also these aspects of belonging will be addressed in more detail below, particularly the interaction between belonging, globalization and migratory processes.[3]

The next section will address issues related to nation states as sites of homeness and belonging, philosophical questions of normativity, and different 'models' of belonging in terms of national identity constructions. The following section will delve more deeply into forms of belonging in globalization, multiple homes, the belongingness of global elites, and the impact of globality on national belongingness. Then follows a section which examines different forms of transnational movers across borders with particular emphasis on transnational migration and related permutations of belonging and identity. The final section contains some concluding remarks on reasons and conditions for the added

---

2　In a sense also 'national identity' has an important element of de-territorialization. For more on this aspect, see the section 'Migrants, Travellers and Cosmopolitans' below.

3　See e.g. Bell (1999), Bromley (2000), Hudson and Réno (2000), Kymlicka (2001), Rapport and Dawson (1998), Skribis (2000), as well as the volume I have edited with Mette Hjort (see note 4) for interesting analyses of new forms of belonging in the context of nationalism, multiculturalism, migration and diaspora.

prominence and legitimacy of identity politics and questions of belonging in the contemporary debating climate surrounding issues of migration and globalization.

Home as Nation, Nation as Home[4]

In a thoughtful article, Judith Lichtenberg discusses the 'moral ambiguity of sources of identity based on belonging' (Lichtenberg 1999, p. 171), because belonging (meaning national belonging in this context) is both egalitarian and ascribed (i.e. not based on individual choice or accomplishment), and therefore in a certain sense clashes with liberal notions of the individual freedom to choose: 'there is also something "illiberal" in basing membership on something over which people have no control. This is, after all, part of the reason we condemn racism and other forms of prejudice and discrimination' (ibid.).

Later in the article, Lichtenberg resolves the ambiguity by abandoning all analytical and moral distinctions only to take note of the fact that

> (...)for most people cultural belonging is very important. It is hard to say a great deal about this in analytical (as opposed to poetic or literary) terms, perhaps because it is basically so very simple: for most of us, our native culture provides us with a sense of being at home in the world. (...) we can recognize the superior virtues of other cultures, but still feel the attachment bred of familiarity our own culture affords. The features of a culture that produce this sense of familiarity and well-being are its language and folkways, its sounds and smells, the innumerable subtle and, in the scheme of things, trivial customs and practices and ways of life we grow up with (ibid., p. 173). → *National belonging*

This account no doubt would meet with the approval of many, simply because it corresponds well both with commonsense perception and emotionally based *&* orientation: we feel we belong to our culture, because it constitutes a home of natural embeddedness and unthinking attachment – familiarity *tout court*. Somehow *cultural* it is beyond the grasp of analytical understanding, defies rationality, and has to be *belong* accepted for what it is. There is something alluringly attractive about this reference to the 'banality' of belonging, and it does have its merits. *useless*

1. For one thing it takes us beyond the most barren forms of dedication to the idea of a constitutional, totally rational form of patriotism and belonging (see Keitner 1999, and Yack 1999 for critiques of this notion). This is an idea which often overlooks the fact that national attachment and identity, in whatever form, are inconceivable and inexplicable without recourse to a certain measure of irrationality, emotionality, sentiment and unselfish dedication. All the apparently rational principles of government, citizens' rights and collective solidarity that are routinely invoked in discussions

---

4   This section and the next are substantially revised versions of my contribution to the introductory chapter of Hedetoft and Hjort (2002).

about civic nation(alism)s 'tend to say much more about the way in which we should order lives within *given* national communities than about why the boundaries of these communities should take one shape rather than another' (Yack 1999, p. 111, emphasis in original). National boundaries have never been drawn according to principles of rational argument or moral distinctions.

In one way, Lichtenberg's moral dilemma points us beyond such categorial confusion, by referring us back to the unreflected, emotive sources of belonging. However, in a different way it also retains it – as a loftier form of guilty conscience. For what kind of belonging is characterized by the normative paradox of a moral dilemma? Only that which on the one hand insists on all the concreteness and immediacy of familiar surroundings (see comments on 'sources' and 'feelings' in the first section) while transforming them into national culture, but on the other, in comparison with the supposed rationality of civic identity, is reminded of its non-liberal, ethnic and potentially racist nature.

The result is a dilemma of conscience where feeling and reflection, concretion and abstraction, personal predilection and civic responsibility cross swords. Lichtenberg interprets sources and feelings of belonging within the ambiguous (attractive yet scary) context of the National, on the background of (a) the shady history of ethnic nationalism and (b) the lures of liberal nationalism as well as cosmopolitan ideals; hence belonging becomes a moral question of far-reaching philosophical import. The suspicion that this might be a reflection not of a more general problem but of a particular political philosopher's pangs of conscience is worth considering, but should be tempered by the likely possibility that Lichtenberg only articulates, in a specific idiom, that belonging (like national identity) is losing its ethnic innocence and is becoming pervasively invaded by normative concerns of a liberal and heterogeneic nature – because it has become subjected to widespread public scrutiny and been cast in doubt by the relativization of nationalism and the participatory ideals of deliberative democracy characteristic of the latter part of the 20th century. As Seyla Benhabib has phrased the question: 'Whereas democracy is a form of life which rests on active consent and participation, citizenship is distributed according to passive criteria of belonging, such as birth on a given piece of land, and socialization in that country, or ethnic belonging to a people' (in Hedetoft and Hjort 2002, p. 102).[5]

---

5   This might be less of a contradiction than it appears to be. Citizens are expected to give active consent, but on the basis and in the framework of the political, cultural and territorial boundaries set to and by the national polity. In other words, democracy, though universal at the level of ideals, is bounded at the level of actual practice. Or in

2. In terms of popular identities, this distribution criterion (birthplace, ethnicity, the destiny of 'blood') is pervasively accepted and adopted by national citizens across the globe. In this sense, Lichtenberg rightly identifies the unconscious and very powerful nature of (national) belonging and some of the immediate objects of reference and justification most of us use when asked to explain our sense of home(sick)ness. In other words, in anthropological terms Lichtenberg's account faithfully reflects the organicist, pre-political dimension of feelings of belonging to a national *Gemeinschaft*. This dimension primarily springs from the fact that the nation state at the level of particularity bounds and organizes concrete places, local sites, urban architectures, regional landscapes and concretely rooted knowledges and memories of locales, as well as familiarities and engagements with these locales and the people inhabiting them (see Carter, Donald and Squires 1993; Czaplicka and Ruble, 2003; and Czaplicka, this volume). 'National space' and 'territoriality', in other words, are constructions that rest on what Czaplicka and Ruble call the 'archaeology of the local', including a sense of common history, common topographies, common genealogy. 'Space' is the reinvention of 'place' in the context of the National. All of this is 'instrumental to identity constitution' (my emphasis). On the other hand, they do not in themselves, and certainly not in the context of latter-day nationalism, constitute identity and belonging at the level of immediacy. Rather, nation states are political contexts that absorb and reorganize – through mechanisms of construction, ascription, generalization, socialization – these sources and feelings of belonging and homeness into the imagined communities of national cultures.

Lichtenberg's account of the moral dilemma overlooks or at least seriously downplays this process. Rather it tends to reify culture by assuming a direct, uncomplicated link between this concept and the concept of nation. The national element of culture is elided, the implicit argument being the following: cultures (as homogeneous units) produce nations which in turn engender strong feelings of attachment and belonging on account of the cultural homogeneity underpinning them. Culture equals nation equals home equals identity.[6] Thus cultures become native cultures, taken-for-granted and matter-of-course frames of reference and action. No matter how seductive the argument, it overlooks the fact that to the extent we can reasonably talk about cultural homogeneities in national terms (and often this is very

---

other words: there are limits to how active, in what spheres and in what ways citizens are encouraged and expected to be active. The dilemma, if there is one, consists in an increasing awareness, among citizens as well as academics, that 'rights' can be interpreted in a transnational as well as a national sense.

6   For a thorough critique of this proposition of homogeneity, see Hedetoft (1995) Part I, chapter V.

difficult), such homogeneity is the outcome rather than the cause of both historical processes and mental reconstructions; of oblivion as much as memory; of elite efforts to nationalize the masses in the transition from different kinds of Empire to an international order based on nation states; of selective perception in the process (which all individuals must go through) of forming a homogeneous image of their national communities (in spite of the fact that most nations are culturally and ethnically 'mongrel', as Giddens [1999, p. 131] calls them) and creating mental boundaries that match the borders of the state in which they live. Here the national education systems play an invaluable role.

In other words, this kind of explanation overlooks national belonging both in the form of Renan's 'daily plebiscite' (Renan 1882) and of the symbolic and historical construction of roots ('native culture') as identical with the limits of the national – in imperative, top-down, discursive terms *and* as popular transformations of such official discourse into second-order naturalness and axiomatic referentiality. In such terms, national belonging follows from neither nature nor culture in any simple forms – though this is how it is often experienced and more often articulated – but is the result of complex social and historical processes whereby the political, sovereign communities that we know as nation states reinvent themselves as pre-political, simplistic and ethnic, partly in the mirror of selective histories of glory, heroism and destiny, partly by drawing on anthropological paradigms of kinship, blood and territorial rootedness.

In these communities, therefore, it requires more than just legal citizenship really to belong and therefore to be a true native with a genuine and universally recognized nationality.[7] Features and images of the political (civic) and the pre-political (ethnic) community must merge in order for a nation state to be experienced and recognized as the authentic, cultural home of any individual living inside or outside its politically given borders. In other words, the state must appear as nation and the nation as ethno-culturally given and historically continuous. Identity and belonging must seem to derive organically from such pre-politically given homogeneity, though in the real world there is no such transparent, innocent and immediate relationship, and whatever cultural-national homogeneity there is,

---

7   This distinction between citizenship and nationality is one that not least coloured immigrants in old colonial states like Britain and France have been confronted with, e.g. in the forms of Powellism and LePenism. It was Enoch Powell, for instance, who in the 1960s talked about the 'legal fiction of British citizenship' as regards these people and further claimed that 'you do not become British by being born in Britain'. This is the credo that has since defined the ideologies of rightist nationalist movements in most European countries.

more often than not is the outcome of decades, sometimes centuries of cultural honing, ethnic mixing and social assimilation or exclusion.

One problem, of course, is that in spite of such long-standing efforts, frequently homogeneity amounts to little more than official discourse, a thin veneer of a common identity covering up the co-existence of a multiplicity of cultures and, sometimes, identities too (take, for instance, the cases of Belgium, the United Kingdom and Switzerland as different types of illustration of such scenarios). In this sense, most territorial states are not proper nation states, but 'multiethnic' in one way or another. Citizenship, culture and identity tend to part ways and to reassemble in new and multiple configurations of belonging. In the case of the United States, it has now even become the quasi-official credo to celebrate Americanness as multicultural and the USA as the prototype of an immigrant nation with ethnic roots all over the world and little common history to show for itself – a fact which for some bodes ill for the cohesion of the USA (e.g. Schlesinger 1992), but for others signals the strength of this (post)modern identity formation, which has managed to create unity out of diversity or where homogeneity is simply configured in ways that are different from what we have become wont to expect based on the European model of cultural exclusivism and ethnic cleansing (Hall and Lindholm 1999).

Where, in Europe, political communities pose as pre-political and ethnic, in the USA the situation is reversed: feelings of common ethnicity and organic solidarity, shaped no less arduously than in the rest of the world and drawing on a wealth of myths (of the West, of nature, of frontiers, of the self-made man, of golden opportunities, of war and heroism...), consistently pose as political or civic, ethnicity *eo ipso* being universally recognized and officially celebrated only in its plural form and as 'hyphenated' Americanness. But as Bernard Yack succinctly argues,

> (...) were Americans (...) to make citizenship contingent upon commitment to political principles instead of the mere accident of birth (to citizen parents or on American territory), they might become considerably more suspicious of their fellow citizens' declarations of political loyalty. Birthright citizenship can promote toleration precisely by removing the question of communal membership from the realm of choice and contention about political principles (1999, p. 116).

Though the avenues are different, the result is therefore much the same in the two kinds of nation states. Home as belonging to nation is a structured set of emotions and attitudes, shaped by an imagined oneness of political and pre-political, contemporary and historical, rational and cosmological orientations. And at least at the level of ideal blueprint (though far from always the actual state of affairs), this would seem to hold true for states in other regions of the world as well, in spite of the fact that the roads to the modernity of nationalism have been radically different (as have the results) in, say, Africa, Latin America, the Middle East and East Asia, where historical interactions of local history, impacts of colonization, independence, absorption/repulsion of Western cultures and ideas, and global processes have resulted in a multitude of particularistic permutations of identity, nationalism and belonging. Conversely, what ties them all together, whether in a democratic format or not, is the idea(l) of the National as an imagined oneness of state and nation, of 'civic' and 'ethnic', of past and present, of reason and affect. For instance, the PRC's 'one China policies' only make sense in this framework of national sovereignty, territorial integrity and historical legitimacy (which is also the universally acknowledged passport to recognition as a creditable entity by the international community). Liberal nationalism and internationalism, however open-minded, do not basically alter these facts, and even Western-based cosmopolitans – in spite of their assumption of belonging everywhere and nowhere in particular – arguably base their global outlook and interventionism on the confidence of embeddedness in particular national contexts and the possession of a national passport and national citizenship rights (Ignatieff 1993 and 1999).

Belonging in Globality: One Home or Many?

Nevertheless, globalization does spell significant changes in the cultural landscapes of belonging. Not because it supplants the nation state and the forms of homeness outlined so far, but because it changes the contexts (politically, culturally and geographically) for them, situates national identity and belonging differently, and superimposes itself on nationality as a novel frame of reference, values and consciousness, primarily for the globalized elites, but increasingly for ordinary citizens as well. In this context, notions of liberal and civic nationalism assume new implications. Their real news value lies less in the theoretical assumptions as such – which have been known and debated since the 19th century – and more in the widespread interest they have recently attracted, inside as well as outside academic circles.

The pervasiveness of this interest reflects two points worth noting: first, that the organicism and essentialism of national identities are no longer just taken for granted, but are being universally challenged by forces claiming forms of loyalty and allegiance that are not readily assimilable to the nation state context; and secondly, that this state of affairs has given rise to attempts to rescue the nation state – as 'civic', 'liberal', 'cosmopolitan' or whatever – by rethinking its basic parameters and proposing a rational trajectory (e.g. in the form of constitutional patriotism or sometimes even a political programme, as in the case of the European Union) for its practical transformation.

This double scenario reconfigures belonging. Wedges of uncertainty and impermanence are inserted into the imagined oneness of political and prepolitical orientations that underpins national identity. On the one hand, globality only constitutes belonging in the most flimsy and liminal of senses; on the other, nationality increasingly appears to be no longer a sufficient, though maybe still a necessary linchpin of belonging understood in terms of identity. This state of affairs, often compounded by new forms of individualism and migration, leads to cognitive and discursive reactions of different kinds: uprootedness, homesickness, affective alienation, attempts to retrace local knowledges and circles of immediate familiarity, or the construction of multiple homes and hybrid senses of belonging (in other words, new cosmopolitanisms or the advocacy of multicultural polity regimes) – though it might also imply reaffirmations of old-style nationalism in nostalgic, secessionist or new racist forms. In all events, it strengthens and reinvents the politics of identity as an increasingly transnational phenomenon, in the double sense of finding its way into all national contexts as a fairly uniform occurrence, and playing itself out as a substantively transnational politics of organization, platform and discourse.

Thus, the logical oxymoron of civic nationalism[8] and its pervasive popularity is a fairly precise reflection of a state of affairs where the nature and context of nationalism is being transformed by globalization. Where the age of nationalism and the nation state demanded that the political and the pre-political community, citizenship and ethnicity/identity, be imagined as one, the global era threatens to disaggregate the two, either by propagating a wholly rational kind of nationalism as the ideal end-goal while relegating *ethnic* nationalism to the dustheap of a belligerent history (or to less civilized parts of the world!); by transposing the political dimension of identity and loyalty to a supranational level (e.g. the EU, or some ideal cosmopolitan set-up) while conceding that people's ethnicity (or cultural identity) may remain nationally bound; or by building civic allegiances to the country one happens to live in while remaining ethnically tied to one's country of origin (the case of many Turks – or their descendants – resident in Germany, for instance).

Although examples of such cleavages have been around for many years, the difference today is that where they used to be exceptions, they are now more like the rule: all-pervasive, institutionally organized, and the subject of public and private debates. It is becoming widely acknowledged that hybrid identities, several homes and multiple attachments are a ubiquitous fact of life in most nation states. Where dual or multiple citizenship used to be seen as a remote and esoteric concern, relevant only to highly privileged elites, such issues are now widely debated (though not always condoned) in contexts pervasively described as multicultural. A cosmopolitan or a global citizen today is not to be recognized by the lack of passports (as was the case in the 19th century), but far more by the number of passports they can legitimately show for themselves – though in practice, the norm is still closer to one than one might expect.

---

8   The oxymoronic nature of the concept is nicely captured by Bernard Yack who argues that 'the idea of the civic nation defends the Enlightenment's liberal legacy by employing the very concept – that of the political community by voluntary association – whose plausibility has been undermined by the success of nationalism' (1999, p. 115).

From being conceived as a fact of nature, belonging has come to be treated as a property of the rational mind, as a particular kind of political activity, situating subjects between individual freedom, collective rights and negotiated identities, and confronting states with difficult choices between transnationalized policies and communicative strategies aimed at convincing their national populations of their primary belonging in and loyalty to their particular nation state. Increased mobility and virtual universes have added to this moveable feast of symbolically and deliberately constructing our roots as we go along.

We need, however, to observe a basic distinction inherent in the concept of belonging: there is a world of difference between imagining that the globe, like material possessions, memories and ideas, belongs to us (or rather, me) – and that we belong to the globe and globality. The images of home that we all carry around as regards national identity, and our linguistic way of speaking to them, are in the latter category. Here the question is: what national entity do we belong to? In our perceptions and conceptions of this type of homeness, we routinely objectify ourselves, make ourselves into a part and a property of a given nation state. We somehow adhere to it, are organically bound up with it, and spring from it, by virtue of birth, blood, race, history, culture or customs. In this sense, Lichtenberg's empathetic argument hits the nail on the head.

This is all very different in the case of images and discourses of global belonging. Here the world appears as a terrain of opportunities, mobility, networking, money-making and so forth: it turns into a means for the achievement of particular goals, and does not appear as the end-goal of ideal belonging and identity-formation, as roots. Potentially, the world is ours, it does not own us. It opens up possibilities but does not require sacrifices that we abide by because we belong to it. Or it allows us to cultivate myths and reveries of having our real roots elsewhere than where we happen to be, or of eventually finding real happiness somewhere else.

In such terms, the globe is a material and utopian tax haven, a site of (imagined) benefits, but very little belonging, in the sense this concept has been developed so far. Only in the cases of ardent universal religiosity, global environmentalism or the idealism of helping needy people on a global scale can we identify traces of an ideology of belonging to the globe, based in programmatic ideas of global responsibility. But even here the point of departure, more often than not, is a firm rootedness in a specific national identity, and the global position, including its cosmopolitan virtues, is ideologically rather than existentially defined.[9]

Thus, globalization – while certainly making inroads on the contexts and natural assumptions of national rootedness and homeness – does not offer a global substitute for them, despite much discourse to the contrary. The forms and perceptions of belonging that it engenders are, if not incompatible with those of the National, then at best their extension and complement. The new awareness of the

---

9   See Gubert (1999) for noteworthy contributions to the discussion of territorial belonging
    in the context of culture and ecological concerns.

difference between political and pre-political components of national identity that globalization and Europeanization have spawned has led to new configurations for the most globally minded, for whom nationality has come to represent their pre-political, ethnic, banal site of belonging, whereas globality or Europeanness have taken over as the main locus of their political orientations and identifications.[10] For the rest, belonging in globality is either a curse (globality as poverty, a threat to settled ways of life, rootlessness), a moderate blessing (globality as a means of getting help and support against repression) or an opportunity (globality as freedom and progress: the new land of opportunities); but in none of these cases is globality imagined as something people belong *to*. Though our home, understood as belonging to a specific nation state, may be open to the globe (liberal, tolerant, sensitive, multicultural), the globe is not our home. The semiotics of belonging spells different assumptions and implications in the two settings and the ever more crucial permutations that the interaction between them engenders.

Migrants, Travellers and Cosmopolitans: Fixity or Flux?

A consequence of these reflections is that we need to re-evaluate the kind of impact that globalization has on images and discourses of homeness and belonging in the context of transnational migration patterns. Where much sociological and anthropological reasoning, informed by postnational theorems, has recently tended to hypothesize that the fixity and homogeneity normally associated with national forms of belonging are being supplanted by flux, multiculturalism and indeterminate spatiality (identity becoming increasingly de-territorialized and home being found in movement *per se*) (e.g. Rapport and Dawson 1998), the argumentative gist of this chapter calls for caution based on discrete analytical distinctions.

First distinction: between migrancy and global movement.[11] This may seem odd, since obviously migrancy always involves movement, and often of a global/transnational kind. But the logic of migration is rarely, if ever, the flux of

---

10 For an interesting example of such interactions between matter-of-course national identity and self-proclaimed cosmopolitanism, see Michael Billig's analysis of the American nature of Richard Rorty's political philosophy, in Billig (1995) chapter 7.

11 The distinction used in the following between 'migrants' and 'cosmopolitans' is at this point analytically heuristic. Certain borderline cases do exist, particularly regarding certain types of entrepreneurial migrant workers who are adept at taking advantage of the opportunities presented by 'fluid borders'. This fact does not affect my main points, however, i.e. (1) that the binary distinction between architects and victims of globalization is cognitively necessary and normatively legitimate, and (2) that the majority of migrants, especially refugees and persons moving for purposes of 'family unification', do not find their identity or intrinsic purpose in the process of moving itself.

movement, but the attainment of a new fixity, a new spatially bounded rootedness. As a rule, migrants do not have moving between points as their purpose, but solely as a means to an end. Migrants do not find their identity in motion, in other words. They are not committed to an identity of fluid homes – mostly quite the reverse, in fact. This is true whether or not particular migrancies are more or less voluntary or more or less enforced. Globalization, in some format, may be the underlying reason and certainly the contextual framework for increased mobility and displacement of ever more people of the migrant kind, but globalization should not be mistaken as the identity-defining, de-territorializing *rationale* of migrants, neither individually nor collectively. In fact, the more massive the migration, the more emphatically migrants tend to search for new stable homes elsewhere. This is not to deny that migration comes with a vengeance in terms of identity, belonging and homeness, since old identities and memories of the places they came from, or have been told about, or are constantly reminded of by people and institutions in their new homes, stick in their minds and keep (co-)defining their sense of belonging – hence sentiments of exile, diaspora and multiple belongingness, and hence transnational forms of migrant organizations. But all of this must be conceptualized as consequences 'after the fact', and not as a jubilant embrace of a postnational condition. In this sense, migrants are victims of global processes, not their architects.

Second distinction: between migrants and movers. Where migrants move in order to resettle, movers move either for the temporary pleasure of movement (travellers, tourists) or because they *are* the architects of global processes and invest their money, careers and lifestyles in and on the global arena (cosmopolitan nomads of varying hue). This, as argued above, does not nullify the national point of departure of these privileged elites and symbolic analysts, although, unlike migrants, they do their utmost to delete any suspicion of national sentiments from their mental hard disk and behavioural currency. As a rule, they embrace and celebrate, if not transnationalism *tout court*, at least internationalism in the most liberal forms imaginable. Where the movement of migrants is finite, involving the abandonment of homes, networks and possessions, in favour of hoped-for replacements elsewhere in the world, the movement of cosmopolitan nomads is in principle infinite and continuous, incrementally adding homes, networks and possessions to the list, and for many constituting distinct lifestyles in their own right. Here, therefore, it makes sense to assume that movement is not just instrumental, a means to an end, but part of the overall teleology and identity of these global movers.

It makes sense, of course, that the architects of global processes should invest part of their identity make-up in the time/space compression that globalization carries in its wake. But this should not be allowed to confuse the overall picture: the general publics of this world, and the ever increasing masses of economic or political migrants, more often than not are on the fringes of these processes, and either do not move except for touristic purposes, or move only reluctantly and against their better judgement/desires. And international migration apart (often between third-world and first-world countries), labour mobility as a rule takes place within national boundaries (see e.g. the EU), where the national hub of belonging and homeness can be preserved intact. Ironically, the term mobile homes refers neither to that type of movement nor to the extravaganzas of cosmopolitan nomads, but is an often condescendingly applied term used to describe the life of marginalized sections of society who do not possess the wherewithal to rent or buy a proper home and who are therefore compelled to a life of constant movement between trailer parks that all look much the same. Movement and diversity do not necessarily go together, and de-territorialization is far from always a bliss – let alone an ideal that people practically and voluntarily pursue. Except in one form, paradoxically, i.e. that of national identity, which contrary to ordinary discourse possesses some of the characteristics of a de-territorialized identity form, though one that is not predicated on physical movement. (This point will be developed further below – under 'house and home'.)

Third distinction: between 'multicultural settings' and identity fixation. It is no doubt true that migration can result in the production or strengthening of ethnically plural communities, and also that processes of transvaluation in such communities can impact members' cultural horizons and individual profiles in the direction of hybridization – though this is a possibility rather than a necessity. However, in a sense, as has already been argued, all communities, including national ones, are pluri-ethnic, and what migratory processes do is primarily to foreground multiculturalism as the official codeword (and sometimes ideal) for the political and sociological handling of problems attendant on immigration within specific national settings. In this sense, most talk of multiculturalism is not just politicized from the outset, but furthermore presupposes the nation state and its national identity as the taken-for-granted framework and objective. In other words, forms of multiculturalism that are compatible with the nation state, which further integration and are useful as underpinnings of national loyalty, are acceptable and frequently advocated; forms that do not spell problems and are discouraged/opposed.

But this is also to say (assuming such a presumption is correct and realistic) that multiculturalism/hybridity are not *per se* antagonistic to the construction of fixed (national) identities – that there is neither a logical nor practical opposition between the two. This is consistent with the fact that cultures are not causally, deterministically related to identities in a one-to-one correlation. Further, hybridity is a very different thing from the outside and the inside perspective: for the observer it seems like a motley composite in constant motion, but from the subjective viewpoint (that of the possessor of a given identity at a given point in time) more probably like a relatively stable and fixed make-up (though the result of a number of identity choices and intersubjective 'negotiations'), emerging finally as 'character' or 'personality'. Here it is imperative rigidly to distinguish between the characteristics of a *milieu* in its totality and individual cultural and identity-related formations. Whereas the former might have the characteristics of a heterogeneous and arbitrarily concatenated mass of disparate elements, the latter normally do not – and when they do, nevertheless, there are signs of socio-psychological conflicts.

Multiculturalism is only a real problem for nation states when it has not been properly de-politicized on the level of public discourse and in the minds of citizens. In other words, cultural diversity must not by its constituent parts be interpreted as involving loyalty to other sovereigns (hence, demands for dual citizenship are rarely welcomed by national governments, though sometimes tolerated). Rather, the 'multicultural' individual should symbolically attest to his/her allegiance and genuine wish to belong to the host country. This does not guarantee full recognition, but is its necessary prerequisite.

However, although in principle hybridization and a fully fixed, stable, native sense of identification with the host country is not an unattainable ideal, and sometimes materializes too, contemporary migrant settlers (whether first or second generation) tend to practise this model of convergence in ways that are slightly different from a host-society blueprint, but at the same time one that is far removed from the 'identities-in-flux' hypotheses of globalists and also from the 'divided loyalty', moral-panic hysteria of receiving societies.

Modern migrants, as a rule (and of course there are exceptions), want to shape their own identities in such a way that they integrate sociologically and politically into the host societies and assume a 'host-society' identity on their own cultural premisses. For instance, they generally fail to see how the wearing of veils and the practice of Islam contravenes their adoption of a Danish identity, why the maintenance of networks organizing their ethnic claims and cultural adherence to their countries of origin is not compatible with belonging to Denmark, and why dual citizenship is anything more than a practical measure to facilitate their movement (as travellers, not migrants) between their old and new homes. The point here is not to assess whether such assumptions and expectations are realistic or contradictory, but to record that from these contemporary migrants' perspective (who have mostly abandoned the myth of return that was so prevalent 20 or 30 years ago), their many-sided sense of belonging does not run counter to their desire for integration and recognition as nationals in their new countries. What this amounts to in actual practice is an argument that new configurations between x-national identity and its cultural underpinnings are possible and desirable, and need not become politicized. Host societies, on the other hand, have a tendency to interpret precisely such new configurations as a potential threat to long-established traditions, ways of life and political cultures, and routinely react by transforming even the most innocuous identity-reshaping exercises into political problems – although the concrete form that such transformations take depends on the precise characteristics of the nation state in question.

Fourth distinction: between house and home. Questions of belonging – generally as well as in terms of migrancy – would be easy to settle if there existed an unproblematic relationship between 'house' and 'home' – if 'home' for people's imaginative lives was always and unquestionably where their house is located and where for that reason they have settled down or at least live (permanently or temporarily). The two terms, admittedly, are often used interchangeably, but the connection between their meanings is at best metonymic. 'House' is part of, sometimes the central part, of images of homeness and belonging (cf. the English adage 'my home is my castle'), but the cultural and political imaginary of 'home' covers a lot more – spatially and temporally – than the physical location of residence.

I return here to my point above relating to the de-territorial aspect of national identity. National belonging interpreted as 'home' is clearly distinct from 'house' or even 'locality' – it is abstract in Benedict Anderson's sense of imagined communities, since a lot of the national territory, population and history exists only as imagined, as spatially extended and temporally reinterpreted perceptions which far transcend the bounds of individually familiar or practically useful homeness in the sense of 'house' and its immediate surroundings. National identity is thus de-territorialized not in the sense that nation states do not have clear-cut spatial boundaries, but that these are not individually and naturally meaningful identity criteria, but – like 'collective national memory' – politically, culturally and historically orchestrated spaces, landscapes and locales, abstractions from the immediate life-world of individuals that are presented and often accepted as the limits of 'homeness', because they converge with the limits of political sovereignty.

However natural and organic this organization of the nation-as-home may seem, in fact it is not just a historical construction, but one in which territory is chiefly meaningful as a symbolic rather than physical entity.

Thus, 'home' even for the traditional national citizen is a dual concept: on the one hand it exists physically, as 'house' and 'locality', on the other as 'nation', in the de-territorialized sense set out above. The best example of this are the images of belonging of people who distinguish between their present physical but inauthentic 'home' and their 'real' national home, from which they are exiled, where they might never have been, whose language they speak badly or not at all, and which lives only in their fantasies, e.g. *Volksdeutsche* (Wolff 2000), or second- and third-generation immigrants who symbolically (and sometimes materially too) reconstruct their originary home where their house is, thus creating their very own virtual convergence in a process of mimicking the nation state blueprint (e.g. overseas Chinese communities in Europe).

This underlying national (European) ideal is that house, home, belonging and identity should be totally coterminous. It has already been argued how globalization tends toward separating these elements and questioning the absoluteness of national boundaries. Migration patterns, in one sense, contribute to the same process. What contemporary migrants do when they attempt to reorganize identities and forms of belonging is little more than taking advantage of the opportunity presented by such globalizing forces, but, it should be emphasized, also by the constructedness, contingency and variability of national identity.

The hyphenated model of American identity organizes and recognizes this model, based on the assumption that the core of identity is undivided loyalty to

American constitutional values, but that this can be orchestrated, individually or collectively, in a variety of ways, and that attendant forms of cultural belonging and homeness can be multiple as well. In Europe, on the other hand, states prefer to monitor not just the resultant identity in terms of its practicality and consequences, but, in spite of historical contingencies, also the preferred national configurations between identity, belonging and cultural resources (for that reason, in immigration matters they have great difficulties respecting their own constitutional principles, such as separation of Church and State and the concomitant freedom/privacy of religious belief). Homogeneity, both in spite of its abstractness/malleability and in spite of occasional rhetorical dedication to *European* diversity, is not up for grabs, citizenship comes with a price-tag, and identity in European states cannot be left to mostly unwelcome intruders to construct at their own convenience.

Concluding Observations

The Introduction discussed the issue of the ubiquitousness and legitimacy of belonging and the way in which the notion has increasingly come to occupy centre stage in contemporary identity politics – a fact reflected *inter alia* in the rapidly growing academic literature on the subject. In terms of pure analytical description, it is apparent that the popularity of the notion is intimately tied up with the 'postmodern' fluidities of borders and related phenomena of migration, globalization and interdependence; with the fact that the term has increasingly been adopted by ethnic/minority groups intent on confirming their (dual/multiple) feelings of belonging to a new polity and making ethnic claims on that background; and with the political discourses of host societies now finding the confidence to ideologically and rhetorically repossess their very own cultural and territorial framework of belonging and consequently to specify to newcomers which conditions they must meet in order to be accepted as (also) belonging.

These sub-themes indicate that the issue of belonging in its present-day configurations is both an articulation of globalization and a reactive, re-nationalizing response to it. If we add to this diagnosis the fact that issues and legitimacies of politics of belonging have become prominent since 1990 – the victory of the West euphemistically referred to as the end of the Cold War – a few additional comments are called for.

Globalization is a set of processes, transnational by nature, driven by economic interests, and primarily fathered by the USA, processes which basically regard the existence of national borders and national sovereignty as an obstacle and strives toward minimizing their role (with the exception of specific types of population movement). As a uniform and agenda-setting set of forces and discourses, it was, in a manner of speaking, set free by the victory of the West in the Cold War, since the global polarity and its ideological outgrowths until 1990 had set certain limits to how far, how fast and how freely Western market-forces, Western media and Western democratic values could impact the global stage. On the other hand, where the Cold War froze globalization, it simultaneously constrained manifestations of nationalism, and when it ended set free this ideological force as well.

In cultural terms, globalization is logically a leveller and homogenizer, though in the real-life world of transnational processes it comes up against a variety of counteracting influences and paradoxical consequences – partly because political and entrepreneurial globalizers are also, like ordinary citizens, embedded in nation state contexts and represent more or less obvious national interests and identities; partly because globalization in its immediate economic and social effects poses threats to handed-down ways and standards of life, material and psychological security etc. (though the threat varies from one global region and nation state to the next and obviously between different social classes too); and partly because the drive toward the establishment of new nation states and new nationalisms is part and parcel of the very same process.

The combination of the threat that globalization undoubtedly constitutes to established lifestyles and the fact that these lifestyles routinely become associated with the traditional political context and its traditional form of power execution, i.e. the nation state, accounts in general terms for the contemporary romantic return to the nation-as-home. However, it also provides a pointer to the universally negative/sceptical attitude among ethno-national citizenries toward the rise in immigration into their countries. For migration (including rising numbers of refugees, displaced persons, and other victims of ethno-national conflicts) – one of the many attendant phenomena of globalization – becomes symbolically singled out as the most prominent (humanly visible) threat factor and indeed as a cause rather than a consequence of all the (real or imagined) ills that globalization (and/or in some countries: Europeanization) implies for what is interpreted as citizens' national identity and their rightful scene of belonging. Thus, immigrants, like often before in world history, in a process of mass semiosis are penalized and stigmatized, or just barely accepted, for processes they have not created. Advocating multiculturalism in their new national homes naturally only makes things worse in the eyes of self-styled homogeneous societies; and political backing of such national egoism, from right to centre of the political spectrum, triggers a reversal of tolerance and liberalism back to overt racism and policies of exclusion. Belonging has been vindicated, having negotiated the path from conceptual outcast to guest of honour.

The irony and paradox is that the multicultural discourses of immigrant minorities and their champions around the world in the global era are doing little else, willy-nilly, than using as their role-model the discourses of ethnicity, minority positioning and related claims-making so prevalent on the domestic scene of the great globalizer, the melting pot of the USA. It is paradoxical because this type of multiculturalism works extremely well in the United States and is an integral part of the identity kit of most Americans. And it is ironic because once this model of identity/interest configuration is exported to other parts of the world (often by people critical of US culture), it immediately becomes politicized in a way which US citizens and the US polity would never have imagined in their wildest dreams.

The secret of American multiculturalism is that it plays itself out under an umbrella of confident and very homogeneous allegiance to shared values, shared goals and shared historical legends – in other words, a collective perception of manifest destiny which does not contradict but forms the very underpinning of American individualism and its optimal pursuit of happiness. Belonging in the USA implies wholesale acceptance of this very particular version of democratic nationalism – and proof of belonging resides less in passive oaths of allegiance than in the practical *success* citizens or groups of citizens can demonstrate in their business-related or political *practice*. Multiculturalism, diversity and ethnic claims-making make sense within this context, both as a means of constructing and projecting particularistic, socially competing cultural profiles, and as a platform for the expression of grievances and the vindication of group interests. In the latter sense they are, of course, 'political', but with the important proviso that the American model does not perceive specific ethnic claims (with the exception of Black militant organizations) or their reference to cultural diversity as a threat to the political identity of the USA. Hence they never, like in Europe, give rise to lofty political rhetoric in which the future and very soul of the country is apocalyptically orchestrated as threatened (by, for example, the influx of illegal Mexican agricultural labourers across the border).

This is not the place to enter into the many historical and cultural reasons for these differences and their links with the specifics of the US nation state in comparison with European, Asian and South American societies and polities. The point is merely to take note of the remarkable variation in the shape, dynamics and interpretation of multiculturalism and belonging, when on the one hand what appears to be near-identical models and discourses become reconfigured in their encounter with different national contexts and when, on the other, both practical and theoretical advocates of multicultural belonging, who take their explicit cue from US multiculturalism, underestimate both the degree of homogeneity in the States *and* the will and dedication of their own elites and compatriots to doggedly oppose this particular cultural export article of American-led globalization and rather stick with the home-grown variant of culture and belonging.

Works Cited

Bell, Vikki (ed.) (1999) *Performativity and Belonging*. London: Sage.
Benhabib, Seyla (2002) 'Citizens, Residents and Aliens in a Changing World: Political Membership in a Global Era', in Ulf Hedetoft and Mette Hjort (eds), *The Postnational Self. Belonging and Identity*. Minnesota: University of Minnesota Press, 85-120.
Billig, Michael (1995) *Banal Nationalism*. London: Sage.
Bromley, Roger (2000) *Narratives for a New Belonging*. Edinburgh: Edinburgh University Press.
Brubaker, Rogers (1996) *Nationalism Reframed*. Cambridge: Cambridge University Press.

Carter, Erica, James Donald and Judith Squires (eds) (1993) *Space and Place: Theories of Identity and Location*. London: Lawrence Wishart.

Czaplicka, John, and Blair Ruble (eds) (2003) *Composing Urban History and the Constitution of Civic Identities*. Baltimore: Johns Hopkins University Press.

Giddens, Anthony (1999) *The Third Way. The Renewal of Social Democracy*. Cambridge: Polity Press.

Gubert, Renzo (ed.) (1999) *Territorial Belonging Between Ecology and Culture*. Trento: University of Trento (Sociology Series).

Hall, John A. and Charles Lindholm (1999) *Is America Breaking Apart?* Princeton, NJ: Princeton University Press.

Hedetoft, Ulf (1995) *Signs of Nations*. Aldershot: Dartmouth.

Hedetoft, Ulf (1999) 'The Nation-state Meets the World'. *European Journal of Social Theory* 2 (1), 71-94.

Hedetoft, Ulf and Mette Hjort (eds) (2002) *The Postnational Self. Belonging and Identity*. Minnesota: University of Minnesota Press.

Herder, Johann Gottfried von (1967/1774) *Auch eine Philosophie der Geschichte zur Bildung der Menschheit*, in *Sämtliche Werke*, Band V. Hildesheim: Georg Olms Verlagsbuchhandlung.

Hudson, Robert and Fred Réno (eds) (2000) *Politics of Identity: Migrants and Minorities in Multicultural States*. Basingstoke: Macmillan.

Ignatieff, Michael (1993) *Blood & Belonging*. London: Chatto and Windus.

Ignatieff, Michael (1999) 'The Grandeur and Misery of Cosmopolitanism', paper presented to conference on *Reimagining Belonging*, Aalborg University, 6-8 May 1999.

Keitner, Chimène I. (1999) '"The False Promise" of Civic Nationalism'. *Millennium*, vol. 28, no. 2, 341-351.

Kymlicka, Will (2001) *Politics in the Vernacular: Nationalism, Multiculturalism and Citizenship*. Oxford: Oxford University Press.

Lichtenberg, Judith (1999) 'How Liberal Can Nationalism Be?', in Ronald Beiner (ed.) *Theorizing Nationalism*. New York, NY: State University of New York Press, 167-188.

Rapport, Nigel and Andrew Dawson (eds) (1998) *Migrants of Identity. Perceptions of 'Home' in a World of Movement*. Oxford: Berg.

Renan, Joseph Ernest (1882) 'Qu'est-ce qu'une nation?' [lecture at the Sorbonne], in *Discours et Conférences*. Paris: Calmann-Lévy, 1887.

Schlesinger, Arthur (1992) *The Disuniting of America*. Knoxville, Tenn.: Whittle Direct Books.

Skribis, Zlatko (2000) *Long-Distance Nationalism: Diasporas, Homelands and Identities*. Aldershot: Ashgate.

Weiler, Joseph (1997) 'Belonging in Europe – Eros and Civilization', paper presented to Nobel Symposium on *Nationalism and Internationalism in the Post-Cold War Order*, Stockholm, Sweden, 7-10 September.

Wolff, Stefan (2000) 'German Expellees and Their Organisations between *Heimat* and *Zuhause*. A Case Study of the Politics of Belonging', paper delivered to the conference 'Diversity within Unity', Lady Margaret Hall, Oxford, 2-6 August (mimeo).

Yack, Bernard (1999) 'The Myth of the Civic Nation', in Ronald Beiner (ed.), *Theorizing Nationalism*. New York, NY: State University of New York Press.

Chapter 2

The Limits of Diversity: Community Beyond Unity and Difference

Gerard Delanty

Introduction

We have become so accustomed to believing in the virtues of diversity that the term has lost meaning. It is not my aim to argue against the idea of diversity, but to ask what it might mean for late-modern, post-liberal societies, especially under the conditions of globalization and the rise of new anxieties about identity and belonging. As I shall try to show, many different positions argue for diversity and mean quite different things by it. Diversity is by no means a clear-cut concept and we may have reached a point at which it is changing its function and meaning: from being a rhetorical device to recognize the Other, it is becoming more and more a means of self-recognition for post-liberal societies in need of a new imaginary.

Multiculturalism emerged in the context of societies that did not experience major questioning of their national identities. In its inception, in the post-Second World War period in Europe (earlier in the case of the United States) it was formed out of societies that had to integrate, manage or accommodate exiles, immigrants, indigenous populations and other dislocated people who could be conveniently designated by groups; in a related sense, it also designated anti-racism and, in later practices, citizenship. Multiculturalism was a model of management rather than of genuine integration. Western multiculturalism, particularly in Western Europe, was always based on the assumption of liberal tolerance rather than of participation in citizenship. It was constructed on the assumption that there was a dominant cultural identity in the society to which ethnic groups had to adjust but to whom certain concessions could be made. It was never intended as a model for pursuing social equality or for addressing justice for individuals. Today it is a different matter: diversity has penetrated the cultural identity as a whole. Moreover, questions of tolerance have to be reconciled to problems of protecting individuals. Ironically, while there are more and more demands for group differences, it is more and more difficult to define exactly what constitutes a group.

Today, for a variety of reasons, most societies are undergoing significant shifts in their symbolic imaginaries and are drawing on the discourse of multiculturalism for a solution to problems that are in fact created by capitalism. Social fragmention is finding a cultural resonance in the language of diversity associated with multiculturalism. Multiculturalism in many cases is entering this new and uncertain territory to which it may be ill-equipped. In essence, my argument is that we need to move beyond the language of diversity which may be able, at least to a degree, to provide an alternative to false notions of unity and racism, but cannot provide a basis for new national identities/imaginaries and can even invoke divisiveness.

I shall try to make the case that the widespread concern with diversity is an expression of a crisis in community and signals a particular view of culture as a battlefield for post-liberal anxieties. My thesis is that in the contemporary discourse of multiculturalism a new anxiety is being created – the making of a society of strangers. To explore ways in which the social can be reinserted into culture will be the aim of the chapter.

Conceptions of Diversity

As a point of departure, I will outline some of the main conceptions of diversity that are implicit or explicit in discourses of diversity. To begin, there is the mainstream liberal conception of diversity, a position that in general is based on the virtue of tolerance of otherness and opposition to racism. The liberal position does not commit one to believing in the values of the Other, merely in respecting their otherness and tolerating different values (and especially when these values cannot be corrected – indeed the first inclination of the liberal will be to try to correct the erring ways of the Other). But when that strategy fails the liberal will tolerate, albeit without accepting, the Other whose values simply remain different, and often repugnant. The result can be a thin line between tolerance, disdain and indifference. With its origins in anthropology, which was the science devoted to cultural diversity, the liberal discovery of diversity was a reflection of the fact that alterity was to be contemplated at a safe distance. George Frazer, the founder of armchair anthropology, is reputed to have replied, in answer to the question if he ever met a primitive tribe, that the prospect would have appalled him. But today we are all members of tribes. The liberal attitude to diversity takes for granted a basic commitment of all people to fundamental values and broadly confines diversity to particular values that in general are non-public ones and confined to the private sphere. In this sense, multiculturalism was compatible with a wider commitment to civilizational understanding, which itself was a form of multiculturalism. Indeed, this is how another anthropologist, Claude Lévi-Strauss understood it when he used the term, the 'rainbow of human cultures'.

The liberal conception of diversity has been very influential and has been the basis of most versions of multiculturalism, for instance the view that minority groups must be allowed a degree of autonomy or the view that anti-racist policies must be created to facilitate their assimilation into the mainstream society. But it was not designed for much self-scrutiny or cultural critique.

The liberal conception of diversity no longer commands universal assent but has not dissipated. Perhaps because it was the expression of a kind of society that no longer exists, it has been partly challenged by new notions of diversity, which go far beyond the assumptions of classical liberal thought, and has itself crystallized into post-liberal anxieties, arising from an uncertainty as to who the We is, the fear that the line that divides racism and anti-racism can easily be crossed or that tolerance and indifference may not be too far removed (see Alperson 2002; Delanty 2003; Goldberg 1994; Kivisto 2002; Parekh 2000). The older liberal position assumed that the mainstream society was relatively homogeneous and it was only the incoming groups who were 'different' and had to be managed, or at least accommodated, in order to facilitate their eventual assimilation into a nationally delineated society; it also confined the idea of diversity to relatively minor cultural deviations from the values of the mainstream culture; and was not on the whole addressed to fundamental clashes of values. In many cases, the migrant groups were simply identified by religion and thus the only groups that could be recognized were religiously defined ethniticies.

The liberal conception of diversity has of course been modified by communitarianism, which holds that minority groups or large scale national groups must be granted special rights in order to compensate for social disadvantages. However, this communitarian position is largely a modification of liberalism rather than a departure from it, because there is still the basic assumption that there is a dominant social group whose values (national language, secularism, heritage, etc) must be privileged. Liberal communitarianism thus sets certain limits to the universal application of the principle of equal recognition (see Taylor 1994). It differs from mainstream or classical liberalism in the conviction that it is not enough merely to remove or reduce disadvantages, but it is necessary to empower minorities and positively recognize them. Within liberal thought itself several theorists have strenuously defended a limited conception of group rights on purely liberal grounds. In the most well-known version, Will Kymlicka argues that group rights can be defended for some kinds of national minorities such as indigenous minorities (who at the time of their incorporation into the state possessed a distinct cultural way of life and territory) but not for groups created by migration (who voluntarily gave up their cultural way of life and entered a new society). Kymlicka's arguments make only very limited concessions to diversity.

Kymlicka's very limited conception of liberal multiculuralism can be contrasted to a stronger communitarian liberal multiculturalism that does in fact resonate with policy developments in many countries. In several late/post-liberal societies, such as Canada and Australia, multiculturalism has become a national imaginary and with uncertain implications for indigenous and other minority groups. As Elizabeth Povinelli has argued in her book, *The Cunning of Recognition*, the confluence of liberalism and multiculturalism has in fact meant that culture must be mapped out in legal terms (Povinelli 2002). The achievement of liberal multiculturalism is also its greatest limit: recognition can only be a legal recognition. Although this is not a mark of the failure of liberal multiculturalism, it means that indigenous alterity is also forced to define itself in legal terms. The law is now the site where local languages, indigenous ways of life and memories are diverted into juridical languages, leading to an inevitable 'misrecognition'.

In addition to this communitarian modification of liberalism, three positions have defined themselves against the liberal stance and, as I shall argue, a fourth position has recently emerged in which the line between diversity and the legitimation of xenophobia is a thin one. Despite their differences, they are all the inheritors of liberalism and our current late/post-liberal position is very much shaped by the basic dilemmas of liberalism, namely the desire to recognize the Other while remaining suspicious of the values of the Other. In this contradiction the line between recognition and suspicion is a thin one. It is why multiculturalism generates a hyper-anxiety for contemporary societies.

Firstly, a radical communitarian conception of diversity can be identified which embraces relativism more fully than the older forms of liberalism. In contrast to the classical liberal stance it rejects a commitment to an underlying layer of values that are universal and, moreover, does not try to confine the accommodation of diversity to a dominant value system, as in, for example, Kymlicka, for whom special rights are to be confined only to large-scale groups (Kymlicka 1995). Diversity is radicalized to a point that, to cite Steven Lukes, liberal values are now only for liberals and cannibalism for cannibals (see Lukes 2003). In contrast to the orthodox liberal position, diversity is now extended into the public culture itself, and not as in liberalism confined to the private domain. It has become a tremendous legitimation of a particular kind of multiculturalism that abandons any belief in a mainstream culture. Diversity is now more than pluralism and necessitating a principle of tolerance and respect, but suggests the ultimate relativity of all values. In terms of multiculturalism it has led to the belief that all values are legitimate and that none should be privileged. Where the liberal suspends belief on the values s/he does not believe in, the radical communitarian or relativist proclaims to believe in everything, for all values are equal. In this conception, multiculturalism thus means the equal recognition of the values of all groups, none of which can claim ultimate validity. With the growing recognition of the need for a global perspective on culture, this position has become a solution for many organizations, such as UNESCO, which has adopted such a view of culture as diverse (Eriksen 2001).

Secondly, a position can be identified which shares much with radical communitarianism, but extends the latter's relativism into a rejection of the possibility of a valid foundation for all values. This might be termed the postmodern conception of diversity and which invokes a stronger scepticism than in the latter (which is not based on scepticism but ecumenism, the religious equivalent of the 'anything goes' argument, and which might also be called the ability to accept contradictory beliefs). Where radical communitarianism seeks the equal recognition of different forms of life, the postmodern position rejects all normative standards in a permanent incredulity to all master narratives. A tension has thus arisen between the belief that all values are equally valid and scepticism in the capacity of culture itself to generate valid standpoints. Thus for the postmodernist position, the admission of relativism must entail a scepticism of all of culture, including one's own. In this respect, the postmodern argument goes far beyond the assumptions of liberalism and all versions of communitarianism, which have been content with a politics of legal recognition. The kind of multiculturalism that corresponds to it will more likely be the reduction of multiculturalism to the expression of different points of view rather than the pursuit of an overall cultural goal or social inclusion. Its implications can point in the direction of Habermas' discourse ethics (not itself postmodern of course except in its acceptance of radical indeterminacy) or Rorty's postmodern, liberal pragmatism.

A third route out of liberalism does not remain within the universalism/ relativism divide typical of the previous two positions and places the emphasis more on multiplicity than on relativism. It might be termed simply 'cosmopolitan diversity'. In this view, diversity is not a problem as it is for radical communitarianism but a desirable condition and one that does not require either belief in a particular set of values or scepticism about the values of the other. Diversity *per se* now becomes desirable in its own right and does not need to be managed by multicultural policies. Reflecting a more positive view of the virtues of diversity, the cosmopolitan position marks an exit out of liberalism and seeks to regain a strand of unity that has been rejected by radical communitarianism, and which might be summed up in the phrase 'unity in diversity'. In this view of diversity we are all different and what makes us different is not just our different ethnicities but our expanding borders and horizons. As Romano Prodi has argued, all Europeans belong to a minority – it is all a matter of perspective. To adopt James Tully's phrase, there are only 'strange multiplicities' rather than homogeneous societies or cultural totalities (Tully 1995). This conception of diversity differs from the fixed categories of liberalism in recognizing that groups overlap and there are multiple loyalties in an age of permanent mobilities. The aim of multicultural policies that reflect this position will typically argue that multiculturalism is simply the promotion of diversity rather than the representation of different points of view or the reduction of inequalities. This is reflected in the main arena of postmodern multiculturalism, namely the cultural wars over the curriculum, where the aim is in fact often not just to present the view of the excluded Other, but to promote their values in a re-politicization of cultural discourse.

The concern with diversity, I have argued, reflects a growing uncertainty about the nature of culture and the role of values in late modern post-liberal society. Arising out of it is a certain unease or anxiety about the nature and purpose of multiculturalism – who is it exactly for? Is it to provide post-liberal societies with a new post-national imaginary? Or is it to provide groups with identities defined in terms of difference?

So far I have I tried to show that multiculturalism can mean quite different things depending on the conception of diversity that is invoked. Is the aim to reduce inequalities between different groups? Is the aim to promote diversity as a positive value? Is the aim the representation of different groups? Or is the aim to achieve integration or assimilation? These different goals reflect views about the desirability of diversity and the belief in unifying cultural values, but they also reflect different views as to what actually constitutes a social group in the first instance.

Before commenting on some of the implications of this turn to diversity and the demise of an older liberal multiculturalism and the rise of a new one, I would like to note that there is in fact another route out of liberalism which is ominous and suggests a view of diversity as adversity. In the extreme it is racism, but is more commonly the new respectability of xenophobia and the cultural politics of the small differences. Whether in the notorious thesis of the clash of civilizations, racism, the revanchism of the middle classes, extreme right-wing populism, we are hearing more and more about the dangers of diversity. The view of diversity at work here is more than soft relativism: it is adversity. Diversity in this discourse signifies a view of difference as entailing conflict and division. What is notable about this position is not the rejection of liberal values as such, but the deployment of liberalism for illiberal ends. This is an important point since what we often witness is the perversion of liberalism as in the argument that strict immigration laws are needed to keep non-Europeans out because they do not accept liberal values or the argument that ethnic groups should be kept apart in order to protect them from Western ways of life. This use of liberalism for illiberal ends is one of the most disturbing aspects of post-liberal anxieties (Wieviorka 1993).

Beyond Diversity: Rethinking Culture

The previous analysis showed how contested the idea of diversity is and that the language for debating diversity tends to make some highly problematic assumptions about the nature of social groups, culture and conflict.

The first point to be noted is that diversity exists on several levels of which ethnicity is only one. It is possible to speak of civilizational diversities (i.e. major cultural differences between the world civilizations), polynational diversity (the diversity of national cultures), regional diversity (largely within nation states). These are mostly geo-political diversities, but there is also a range of purely cultural diversities, of which ethnic ones are the most obvious. In addition, there are other kinds of diversities, such as those relating to gender and lifestyles, and one might also mention class and possibly generation. Finally, there are what might be simply called moral diversities, that is diverse conceptions of moral values, such as those relating to euthanasia, abortion, vegetarianism. It is questionable that ethnic diversities are the major expressions of cultural diversity, but certainly it is not at all evident that such forms of diversity amount to major cultural divisions. It is arguably the case that there are other kinds of diversity that are more divisive, such as divisions over the limits of life and death. In European societies, there is less ethnic diversity than in the US and in many Asian societies. The most recent British survey of social attitudes reports major lack of knowledge of the UK's ethnic composition. Indeed, it may also be suggested that conflict relating to genetic diversity may be a battlefield for politics in the future. My point is that virtually every cleavage in modern society is accompanied by a diverse and culturally mediated form of life.

Thus to speak of diversity is to refer to the obvious diversity of forms of life. But the notion of cultural diversity that entered political discourse today has tended to make certain assumptions about the nature of social groups, who are the carriers of diverse forms of life. Social groups, especially ethnic groups, are seen as coherent units that are defined by cultural values and packaged into symbolic wholes called collective identities (Brubaker 2002). Whether culture is ultimately what distinguishes a group is debatable, but what is problematic is the assumption that diversity refers to a fundamental divide between groups. This is to neglect the fact that diversity cuts into social groups and reflects the individualism of contemporary societies.

This, then, is the second point. Diversity should not be confined to the relation between groups, but must take into account the deeper nature of diversity and that many diversities in fact only refer to loosely defined cultural categories that are not underpinned by major cultural differences. In this sense, the third route out of liberalism is correct in arguing that social groups are overlapping and diversity is a reality *per se* and does not necessarily presuppose an underlying unity since groups are connected in many different ways. In the mosaic of group relations, diversity and unity are highly shifting terms referring to variable reference points.

A third problem is that diversity is generally equated with conflict and divisions. The border between diversity and divisiveness is increasingly discussed as if these terms meant the same. In fact, we have little evidence that diversity leads to major cultural incompatibilities. Despite the continued existence of essentialistic myths of national unity, the cultural accommodation of diversity in many societies is mostly an accomplished fact today. Nor does cultural diversity lead to an extreme and destructive relativism, as liberals fear. In actual practice, most cultures accommodate universalistic principles and, conversely, universalistic cultures – such as liberal and cosmopolitan values – are increasingly open to particularistic interpretations (Cowan et al. 2001). Ever since the anthropologist Ruth Benedict introduced the term in the 1930s, we are all cultural relativists today (Benedict 1935). The fact of difference and, more importantly, the accommodation of difference and the recognition of diversity is now widely accepted as a central part of democracy.

In sum, diversity is often exaggerated as a condition that undermines the possibility of any kind of unity. While liberalism maintains a basic commitment to the idea of a shared public domain, the three routes out of liberalism in different ways abandon this prospect. In place of unity, there are only different forms of life or, in the case of postmodern/cosmopolitanism, mixed or hybrid groups. While the communitarian postmodern and cosmopolitan stance offers an important corrective to liberalism, along with the other positions it retreats into a myth of diversity. The result of this embracing of diversity in contemporary thought and practice is that we are in danger of having nothing left to resist the increasingly vociferous xenophobic arguments.

In the remainder of this chapter I would like to discuss precisely this problem and to propose that the notion of diversity be subject to greater critical scrutiny. My thesis is that the major division in contemporary society is not culture as such and that there is more common ground than is commonly thought (see Smelser and Alexander 1999). We need to be wary of constructing a myth of cultural conflict and of groups locked in irreconcilable cultural identities. The defining feature of social groups is not difference. The idea of diversity has fed on a notion of symbolic difference which I believe is exaggerated and, more importantly, is falsely premised on a view of culture as divisive. The problem with diversity is that it does not problematize the idea of a social group, seeing only as the solution to the problem of liberalism a diversity of groups. While the cosmopolitan position offers a solution to many of the problems of liberalism, it too rests on a notion of diversity as the fundamental reality of the social bond. Whether diversity is positively embraced, as in postmodern and cosmopolitan conceptions, or regarded as a fundamental problem to be overcome, as in the xenophobic and authoritarian currents in contemporary society, we are still left with a problem, namely that of the possibility of society or even the possibility of social groups in the first instance. If diversity is the dominant social reality, how can community be possible?

One answer it would appear is that community is possible in the construction of difference and perhaps in the un-ending capacity to transcend all boundaries. This is the fashionable argument that is at present influential, inspired by postmodern and cosmopolitan arguments. In an age of diversities, nothing is secure and enduring. Belonging is transient, mobile and flexible and, so the argument goes, does not require locality or social reference points. Identities are fluid and mobile, and can be endlessly reinvented by their carriers who are not constrained by space and localities. I think this is the wrong response to the problem, since it exaggerates the other extreme, namely the capacity of cultural processes of invention to create forms of belonging and identity that can withstand the reality of social fragmentation. In making hybridity the norm, the perspective of the theorist and the perspective of the social actor are conflated. The reality is that social identities are relatively stable and the form groups take is very variable, depending on where they are located in the global processes. As Amit and Rapport have argued, what is often conflated here are personal networks with community and wider categorical identities (Amit and Rapport 2003). Undoubtedly the latter – Black, Irish, Chinese – can be imagined in many different and creative ways and which can be subversive of racism – but this is not necessarily translated into community as belonging in so far as this is experienced in everyday life. Moreover, networks are not made up of the same kind of relations of which communities are made. There is probably a point at which community as belonging cannot be extended without losing its very viability to sustain belonging.

The danger is that diversity is becoming a double legitimation of the social dislocations of globalization and a legitimation of cultural incommensurability. On the one side, the idea of diversity runs the risk of being an argument for the flexibility of capitalism, the view that people can be moved about without loss of identity because they can always invent – or 'imagine' – an identity. On the other side, there is the danger that the appeal to diversity strays into a xenophobic camp in which insiders are always to be distinguished from outsiders on the grounds of the latter's difference. Is there a way of avoiding these pitfalls and moving beyond the language of diversity to find an alternative foundation for multiculturalism? I think such a move would have to be one that goes beyond both diversity and unity, for the latter – the idea of a unitary national culture – is no substitute, for reasons we need not explore here (see Delanty 2001; 2003). However, a degree of common ground can be found in contemporary societies, notwithstanding their diverse constitution. Can people be equal and at the same time different (Touraine 2000)?

My argument is that the most important goal for multicultural societies today – and especially in Europe – is the creation of at least a language, if not more, for articulating community and that this needs to be more than the recognition of difference. By community I mean simply the experience of belonging in everyday life. Community is not merely a symbolically constructed reality but is also a lived reality and sustained by modes of belonging that do not consist of relations of difference but require social content.

Who needs community? It is not only a feature of ethnic minorities, but of all social groups and it is not a primarily cultural category. Community derives its force from belonging and belonging does not necessarily require cultural cohesiveness or a collective identity. Community beyond unity is also community beyond difference. The absence and even the denial of community is what sustains xenophobia. The new cultural politics of xenophobia breeds on the disappearance of community. The appeal to diversity alone will not be able to resist xenophobia since it is now precisely the language of diversity that is being used in the rhetoric of xenophobic discourse. The various forms of post-liberal multiculturalism in ascendancy today may be inadequate to this task.

In its concern with the recognition of the other, multiculturalism is becoming an expression of the deep uncertainty of the post-national subject's identity. The discourse of diversity in post-liberal multiculturalism expresses this uncertainty in the form of an anxiety about belonging and identity, which can never be fulfilled since the only terms it recognizes are those of radical alterity, terms that conflate fragmentation and difference.

Nor must we forget the fact that at least on the cultural level, the boundaries between social groups are more diffuse than previously. The implication for multiculturalism is that it is more and more difficult to demarcate ethnic groups and the boundary between ethnic groups and the majority culture is not always so clearly defined. This is not unconnected to the fact that today many immigrants are middle-class professionals (Ong 1999). There is also the crucially important factor of consumption and the reality of much unrecognized social integration, as

Steinberg has argued (Steinberg 1989). This thesis that the new multiculturalism has derived precisely from the success of the earlier models has also been more recently polemically re-stated by Russell Jacoby who argues that a myth of cultural difference has been created by academics who have applied the curriculum debates and the 'all is culture' philosophy to society, thus distorting the reality of widespread integration (Jacoby 1999). In the view of many there is the danger that multiculturalism is a form of cultural separation and also fails to solve the problem of reconciling tolerance of group differences with the need to protect individuals who wish to dissent from the groups (Eisenberg 1999).

Conclusion

The presuppositions of multicultural citizenship no longer exist. Migration is increasing worldwide and at a time when the developed world is becoming more concerned with exclusionary policies to restrict entry. With over 120 million immigrants worldwide and over 20 million refugees, the nation state is under pressure since the older model was not designed for such great numbers. As Sassen points out: 'Large-scale international migrations are highly conditioned and structured, embedded in complex economic, social, and ethnic networks. States may insist on treating immigration as the aggregate outcome of individual actions, but they cannot escape the consequences of those larger dynamics' (Sassen 1996, p. 75).

Western multiculturalism emerged on the basis of economic and social stability. Within the countries of the developed world multicultural citizenship has become unstable. Economic insecurity has risen, the welfare state is no longer able to absorb all kinds of social problems, and the cultural presuppositions of Western multiculturalism have been undermined by rising nationalism and the emergence of second and third generation immigrants who no longer share the same commitments of the first generation and are becoming more integrated in the mainstream society. Indeed, as Russell Jacoby argues, quoting Marcus Lee Hanson, claims about ethnic pluralism often derive from integrated immigrants who are reinventing the long lost roots of their grandparents: 'what the son wishes to forget the grandson wishes to remember' (quoted in Jacoby 1999, p. 48). Ironically, then, radical multiculturalism may be the product of assimilation, not its failure.

In sum, the size and status of immigrants have changed, undermining the established conceptions of multiculturalism. Moreover, it is increasingly difficult to say what is a cultural identity and what is a political identity. These are no longer separated in the way they once were as a result of pervasive de-differentiating processes. Along with the wider diffusion of the private and the public, cultural identities are coming more hybrid and political identities are less separated from cultural identity. While many ethnic groups retain their language, this is not a marker of cultural separation. The dominant groups in society have themselves been transformed by ethnic multiculturalism. Today cultural diversity rests less on ethnic heterogeneity – the pluralism of 'cultural forms of life' – than on the emergence of new subcultures based on class, gender, religion, and lifestyles shaped by consumption. That is, the ideology of ethnic diversity is no longer the basis of multiculturalism (Fischer 1999). Underlying all these modes of social action is a pronounced individuation in identity and values. Consequently, it is no longer evident exactly what constitutes a cultural group.

There is however one lesson for Europe to draw from the North American debate, in particular in Canada. It is that the problem of citizenship is not specifically a problem of ethnic multiculturalism. The Canadian model has much to offer European transnationalism, namely the need to solve polyethnicity along with the multinational and the growing diversity of the population. Only by divising a multi-tiered citizenship that is capable of responding to these three realities, will a genuinely democratic multiculturalism be possible. But beyond this the US and Canadian experience is limited. Communitarian and radical multiculturalism has generally been a response to either the problem of indigeneous populations or to race. In Europe, which does not have indigeneous populations of substantial significance, polyethnicity is the major issue and the problems its poses are less divisive for the population as a whole. Radical multiculuralism is possibly relevant as a temporary kind of policy, but not as a long-term solution. Strong communitarianism is pertinent on the transnational level of the European Union as a means of guaranteeing the survival of national cultures. Interculturalism is relevant, in particular in educational policy, but it has generally been held to be too weak to be of significance in enhancing social justice. Finally transnational multiculturalism is relevant in the case of de-territorial groups, such as the gypsy population. This would suggest that the most appropriate model for Europe is a deepening of liberal communitarianism supplemented with critical multiculturalism. In my view the way forward for Europe is to build on common ties rather than to create policies that can be divisive. Multiculturalism can no longer be posed in terms of migrants but must address all minority groups, including non-ethnic groups such as religious groups, linguistic groups and groups defined by social disadvantages (such as the elderly, the disabled). In this way, then, it is possible to combine the last models in the typology.

Western multiculturalism rested on the assumption that diversity lay primarily on the level of cultural identity and that this was largely shaped by the ethnic values of relatively homogeneous groups of immigrants who were quite separate from the dominant, national society. If we have reached the limits of multiculturalism today, it is because the assumption that ethnic groups are internally homogeneous and therefore distinct from the national community is no longer valid: cultural diversity has penetrated into the heart of the cultural ethos of society and has diluted the distinction between a prepolitical cultural identity and a neutral public culture that is the guarantee of the national community's identity. Multiculturalism today must reconcile itself to the reality of 'post-ethnicity' (Hollinger 1995). In short, the 'ethos of pluralization', to use William Connolly's term (1995), has penetrated into the political domain transforming the relationship between state and society. The implication of this is that common ground is to be found less on the level of culture – or even on the level of the political – than on the level of the social. Examples of this might be found in the wide acceptance of the value of education, support for ecological causes and the alleviation of suffering. In any case, the point is that the recognition of cultural difference does not automatically lead to social equality and frequently can be detrimental to it.

A democratic multiculturalism would be more attentive to the question of social issues. In particular in Europe, in the context of the post-nationalization, the American communitarian models may not be the most appropriate. While it is clear that many of the models inherited from the past are not suitable for the current situation, Europe has many traditions to draw from. One of the strengths of Europeanization is the apparent absence of a strong European identity rooted in cultural identity or in political identity (Delanty 1995). In my view this offers a space for the shaping of a new cultural model that might be appropriate for a democratic transnational multiculturalism. This would be one that sees culture as a medium of democratic dialogue in which diversity is not a limit to universalism. In this conception of multiculturalism, culture is a site of democratic explorations, translations and dialogue suspended between particularism and universalism. Multiculturalism should be more about relativizing identity rather than strengthening it. But it should not detract us from the reality that the problems it is attempting to deal with cannot be solved on cultural terms alone.

Works Cited

Alperson, Philip (ed.) (2002) *Diversity and Community*. Oxford: Blackwell.
Amit, Vered and Nigel Rapport (eds) (2003) *The Trouble with Community*. London: Pluto Press.
Barry, Brian (2002) *Culture and Equality: An Egalitarian Critique of Multiculturalism*. Cambridge, Mass.: Harvard University Press.
Benedict, Ruth (1935) *Patterns of Culture*. London: Routledge and Kegan Paul.
Brubaker, Rogers (2002) 'Ethnicity without Groups'. *Archives Européennes de Sociologie*, XLIII, 2, 163-89.
Brubaker, Rogers and Frederick Cooper (2000), 'Beyond "Identity"'. *Theory and Society*, 29, 1-47.
Connolly, William E. (1995) *The Ethos of Pluralization*. Minneapolis: University of Minnesota Press.
Cowan, Jane, Marie-Bénédicte Dembour and Richard A. Wilson (eds) (2001) *Culture and Rights: Anthropological Perspectives*. Cambridge: Cambridge University Press.
Delanty, Gerard (1995) *Inventing Europe: Idea, Identity, Reality*. New York: St Martin's Press/London: Macmillan.
Delanty, Gerard (2001) *Citizenship in a Global Age*. Buckingham: Open University Press.
Delanty, Gerard (2003) *Community*. London: Routledge.

Eisenberg, Avigail (1999) 'Cultural Pluralism Today', in Gary Browning et al. (eds), *Understanding Contemporary Society: Theories of the Present*. London: Sage.

Eriksen, T. H. (2001) 'Between Universalism and Relativism: A Critique of the UNESCO Concept of Culture', in Jane K. Cowan, Marie-Bénédicte Dembour and Richard A. Wilson (eds), *Culture and Rights: Anthropological Perspectives*. Cambridge: Cambridge University Press.

Fischer, Claude S. (1999) 'Uncommon Values, Diversity and Conflict in City Life', in N. Smelser and N. Alexander (eds), *Diversity and Its Discontents: Cultural Conflict and Common Ground in Contemporary American Society*. New Haven: Princeton University Press.

Goldberg, David Theo (ed.) (1994) *Multiculturalism: A Critical Reader*. Oxford: Blackwell.

Hollinger, David (1995) *Postethnic America: Beyond Multiculturalism*. New York: Basic Books.

Jacoby, Russell (1999) *The End of Utopia: Politics and Culture in an Age of Apathy*. New York: Basic Books.

Kivisto, Peter (2002) *Multiculturalism in a Global Society*. Oxford: Blackwell.

Kymlicka, Will (1995) *Multicultural Citizenship: A Liberal Theory of Minority Rights*. Oxford: Clarendon Press.

Kymlicka, Will and Wayne Norman (eds) (2001) *Citizenship in Diverse Societies*. Oxford: Oxford University Press.

Lukes, Steven (2003) *Liberals and Cannibals: The Implications of Diversity*. London: Verso.

Niethammer, Lutz (2000) *Kollektive Identität: Heimliche Quellen einer unheimlichen Konjunktur*. Hamburg: Rowohlt.

Ong, Aihwa (1999) *Flexible Citizenship: The Cultural Logics of Transnationality*. Durham: Duke University Press.

Parekh, Bhikhu (2000) *Rethinking Multiculturalism: Cultural Diversity and Political Theory*. London: Macmillan.

Povinelli, Elizabeth A. (2002) *The Cunning of Recognition: Indigenous Alterities and the Making of Australian Multiculturalism*. Durham: Duke University Press.

Sassen, Saskia (1996) *Losing Control: Sovereignty in an Age of Globalization*. New York: Columbia University Press.

Smelser, Neil and Jeff Alexander (eds) (1999) *Diversity and Its Discontents: Cultural Conflict and Common Ground in Contemporary American Society*. New Haven: Princeton University Press.

Steinberg, Stephen (1989) *The Ethnic Myth*. New York: Beacon.

Taylor, Charles (1994) 'The Politics of Recognition', in Amy Gutmann (ed), *Multiculturalism: Examining the Politics of Recognition*. Princeton, NJ: Princeton University Press.

Touraine, Alaine (2000) *Can We Live Together? Equal and Different*. Cambridge: Polity Press.

Tully, James (1995) *Strange Multiplicities: Constitutionalism in an Age of Diversity*. Cambridge: Cambridge University Press.

Wieviorka, Michel (1993) *Racisme et modernité*. Paris: La Décourerte.

PART II

MIGRANTS AND BELONGING

Chapter 3

Ethnic Migrant Minorities and Transnational Claims-Making in Europe: Opportunities and Constraints

Virginie Guiraudon

Minority ethnic groups – 'original' rather than 'immigrant' – have for a long time sought to enlist the help of foreign protectors beyond the empire or the nation state where they dwelled. Examples can be found in both Asia and Europe. This phenomenon has intensified and changed character with the development of international human rights legal instruments as well as transnational non-governmental actors.

Recent work in international relations has sought to analyze these developments.[1] Margaret Keck and Kathryn Sikkink in *Activists Beyond Borders* (1998) speak of a 'boomerang effect' whereby resource-poor groups in one country such as indigenous peoples achieve domestic change through the help of outside resource-rich actors, such as NGOs, third party states and international institutions.

Some empirical studies, however, suggest that one cannot generalize about the role of the global village in helping the tribal village. Deborah Yashar's (1998) work on indigenous movements in Latin America shows that they continue to be framed by domestic political opportunities and constraints. As Sidney Tarrow (1998a) has underlined, one should not underestimate the obstacles that domestic groups of various kinds face when seeking to develop the networks, construct the identities, and access the opportunities that give them leverage outside the state.

Concomitantly to this debate, sociologists such as Yasemin Soysal (1994) and Saskia Sassen (1996) have claimed that immigrant minorities have also benefited from the elaboration of an international human rights regime and the diffusion of norms that base state membership on residence and nationhood rather than nationality. Other studies (Joppke 1999; Hollifield 1998), including my own (Guiraudon 1997; 2000), have not found international norms/institutions to be the source of changes in foreigners' rights or citizenship paradigms. Constitutional

---

1   See, *inter alia*, Klotz (1995); della Porta, Kriesi and Rucht (1999); Risse, Ropp and Sikkink (1999).

norms upheld by activist national judiciaries have played a greater role in the evolution of foreigners' rights.

To pursue this debate in the context of this volume on belonging and diasporic identities, I would like to examine the matrix of incentives and constraints that underpin the transnational mobilization of immigrant ethnic minorities focusing on the European Union as the possible fulcrum and target for these groups. They stem both from the internal characteristics of migrant political mobilization and from supranational 'opportunity structures', which I will discuss in turn.

There are between 12 and 13 million non-EU nationals residing legally in the EU-15. They make up about four per cent of the total EU population while only 2.8 per cent of the world population are international migrants (OECD 2003). About a million and a half legal migrants arrive in the EU each year. Estimates on the number of unauthorized migrants in Europe vary. They suggest that between 10 and 15 per cent of migrants already present are illegal (about three million persons) and that each year anywhere between 120,000 and 500,000 foreigners enter Europe illegally every year (IOM 2000).

While they have access to social and civil rights, their rights to political participation are limited and they do not benefit from the right of free movement or from the political rights inscribed in the Treaty of Maastricht that apply exclusively to European citizens. The number of undocumented aliens has risen during the last decade following changes in asylum laws and procedures and the adoption of new laws on entry and stay, that took place as migrants continued to arrive from more varied destinations providing low-skilled and often illegal work. Moreover, immigrants and their descendants, although they may be EU citizens, still face a number of obstacles in the social sphere (housing, employment), as well as in the religious and political spheres. One may wonder how transnational contention creates an added value for these different groups and ask under what conditions they are able to seize opportunities at the EU level.

Opportunities and Constraints: Internal and External Resources for Contention

Immigrant minorities, in contrast to 'original' ethnic minorities seeking to claim rights, have a tendency to inscribe themselves within existing national paradigms of political participation even as they contest the latter perhaps because, unlike indigenous peoples, they must prove that they belong to the national community. Notwithstanding, their diasporic character may provide them with resources that are not available to 'original' ethnic groups that live in only one nation state, as opposed to other ethnic minorities such as those of Eastern Europe and the Balkans that live in several.

Recent instances of transnational mobilization by communities of migrant origin include that of some Moslem groups during the Rushdie affair and that of the Kurdish diaspora – and in reaction of Turks throughout Europe with prompting from Ankara – when Öcalan was held in Italy. In the fall of 2000, Kurdish inmates throughout Europe also engaged in synchronized hunger strikes, in solidarity with Kurds in Turkey, to be able to pursue political activities while incarcerated. While the mobilization around *The Satanic Verses* proved to be 'identity-constructing', the second spurred into action pre-existing ethnic self-understandings in well-structured diasporas with homeland ties and access to modern communication technologies like faxes, internet, and satellite TV in the liberal democracies where they have settled.

Studies that focus on the internal resources of migrant movements and the specificity of this minority may consider that transnational mobilization is a natural phenomenon for migrants. Migrants entertain transnational ties almost by definition as they operate socially, culturally but also politically in a 'transnational space' between their country of origin and the country of settlement. They also have links with fellow migrants in other sending countries whether these links stem from belonging to the same kin, national, religious, or political group (Cohen 1997; Hannerz 1996). A growing literature on transnational communities illustrated by the work of Alejandro Portes (1998) has insisted that modern communication technologies and cheaper air travel facilitate the maintenance of links across borders – even though such links are not new *per se*. Some of them have political ramifications (Levitt 1997). Case studies of Moslem or Turkish migrant social movement organizations in Europe also point to this phenomenon (Amiraux 1997; Ogelman 1998; Césari 1997).

Yet, in spite of having transnational ties, migrants do not necessarily have the material resources to operate at the European level as other lobbies or interest groups do. Moreover, this generally disenfranchised and socially disadvantaged group is also very divided, not only because it is made up of so many groups – a factor that can impede action coordination at the national level – but also because they pursue different agendas depending on the nation state where they have settled. As Riva Kastoryano (1996) has pointed out, the nation state has been the main structure or context within which migrant groups have been socialized but also their main interlocutor with which they have sought to 'negotiate their identities' as they contested prevailing notions of citizenship or political inclusion. In brief, a predisposition to maintain links across borders with one's community does not solve the 'Babel tower' problem that emerges when different ethnic groups operating in discrete national institutional contexts seek to coordinate their actions, define a common agenda, and find an Esperanto of contention. If we examine the external rather than internal resources of migrant minorities, we may consider with Yasemin Soysal that transnational collectivities and international institutions provide frames of reference for migrant groups. Arguments about the utilization of 'postnational' norms in the claims-making strategies of migrants in Europe have not gone unchallenged. A number of recent comparative studies have convincingly demonstrated the importance of national political contexts in shaping migrant political activism. Patrick Ireland's (1994) study of migrant mobilization in France and Switzerland showed that ethnic groups organize along different cleavages, make different claims, resort to different strategies in the two countries depending on the participatory channels (and citizenship rights) available in each nation state. Based on an event count analysis of a cross-section of British and German newspapers from 1990 to 1995, Ruud Koopmans and Paul Statham (1999) found little evidence supporting the 'postnational model' hypothesis. Less than one per cent of the protest events that they studied targeted EU institutions (0.5 per cent in Germany and none in Britain). The study points out that the main 'territorial frame of reference of minority claims-making on immigration and ethnic relations' remains the nation state (57.9 per cent of the German and 86 per cent of the English cases).

Finally, one may wonder whether the targets of migrant contention have moved beyond the nation state forcing them to adapt their strategies accordingly. The incentive to mobilize at the European level has been limited until very recently. The nation state has remained their main interlocutor on dispensing rights. Moreover, local governments (with some variation) have played a crucial role in bestowing social benefits and managing social programmes. Still, since the implementation of the Schengen agreement in 1990, the institutionalization of transgovernmental cooperation on justice and home affairs within the third pillar of the European Union in 1992, and more recently the Amsterdam Treaty provisions, there has been a shift in the location of decision making in the field of migration control to European sites. This could, in a similar way, relocate the locus of contention for migrant groups.

In summary, although, theoretically, there are reasons to believe that migrant ethnic minorities could and should mobilize at the European level, other equally tangible factors seem to indicate that the nation state is likely to remain the main locus and target of their action. It is therefore necessary to test the hypotheses that I have outlined.

Research Design

Has the European Union provided the 12 million non-EU migrants with opportunities to further their claims? It seems plausible since the European Commission and Parliament have tended to support initiatives in favour of migrant rights and integration and because the Court has sometimes consolidated the rights of third country nationals. EU organizations have supported migrants for reasons that stem from their own institutional *modus operandi* and telos: furthering the Treaty of Rome's four freedoms and the internal market, to name the obvious ones, and the expansion of their realm of competence. Quite apart from that, the legal and organizational framework of migration policy in the European Union provides material resources for social movement organizations and spaces where they can exert policy influence.

To answer these questions, I used a three-pronged research strategy. I first studied a grassroots movement, the *sans papiers* movement, to see whether they have developed into a transnational movement and whether the EU has served as a target for their campaigns. From this 'bottom-up' perspective, I turned to a 'top-down' approach by examining the two most prominent European migration-related initiatives of the last decade, the Starting Line Group and the Migrants' Forum. This allowed me to establish the characteristics of groups speaking on behalf of migrants who have seized upon EU opportunities. I also wanted to know whether the EU fostered transnational forms of political activism different from national repertoires of action. Successful EU initiatives in the migration field are led by international NGOs that are able to provide expert advice. Thirdly, given that my fieldwork uncovered a missing link between grassroots organizations and international (EU) institutions, I decided to scrutinize the few instances where both come into contact by analyzing direct EU Commission funding of migrant associations and pro-migrant initiatives. The EU Commission requires these organizations to operate transnationally to abide by the principle of subsidiarity. The effect of this emphasis has been to benefit a few groups, in particular pre-existing transnational networks. I am now conducting research at the sub-national level again to assess how migrants engaged in EU-sponsored local associations viewed 'Europe' and to understand the way that they rationalize their resorting to EU funding, focusing on associations based in the Lille area, and will outline tentative conclusions on this on-going complementary project regarding the notion of transnational belonging.

The Empirical Record

Protest Movements and Europe: The Case of the 'Sans-Papiers' Movement

Has the increasing 'Europeanization' of migration control and asylum policies and the convergence of policy goals led migrant grassroots movements to shift the target of their protests to supranational institutions? When the leading figure of the French *sans papiers* movement, Madjiguène Cissé, received the German human rights league award in Berlin in 1998, 'people' journalist Heribert Prantl stated: 'The *sans papiers* movement could play the role in the social and political history of the European Union that the Polish trade union Solidarnosc had in Eastern European history. The conflicts in which the *sans papiers* are involved exist throughout Europe'. A few months later, on 27 March 1999, a 'European demonstration for the rights and freedoms of foreigners' took place in Paris. Undocumented aliens groups, along with a dozen social movement organizations from other European countries, signed a call for an 'open Europe', the end of detention and expulsions of foreigners as well as the regularization of illegal aliens. Italian left-wing organizations were the most numerous and quickest to respond (Associazione Ya Basta, the Centri Sociali della Carta di Milano, the Movimento delle tute bianche, and Gli invisibili). They decided to occupy Italian trains to get to the border town of Vintimiglia, with a delegation of visa-less Albanians from

Valona and of asylum-seekers from Trieste before rallying into Paris on 'the train of free movement'. The 3,500 Italian, French and Albanian demonstrators aboard the train coming from Italy were turned back at the border as the French government closed the French-Italian border for several hours and suspended the implementation of the Schengen agreement that abolishes internal border controls for two days.

These events point to the transnational or European dimension of the protest movement that started when three hundred undocumented Africans occupied a church in Paris on 18 March 1996. Sidney Tarrow (1998a, p. 184) defines a transnational social movement as 'sustained contentious interactions with opponents – national or non-national – by connected networks of challengers organized across national boundaries'. It seems that, in fact, there are only sporadic international political exchanges as well as instances of cross-border diffusion through press coverage. Their website has served as a useful means of building an 'imagined community' for the movement and includes links to German, Spanish, Italian and Belgian organizations. Thousands of people have visited the commemorative multilingual page set up two days after the death of Sémira Adamu, a 20-year-old Nigerian asylum-seeker killed in September 1998 during a forced expulsion at Brussels airport who became the first 'European martyr' of the movement. In addition to these contacts abroad, the movement has given priority to cooperation with other domestic 'have-nots' movements (like those of the homeless and unemployed), and movements with similar repertoires for action (such as 'Act-Up') that belonged to a new 'cycle of contention' (Tarrow 1998a) in France during the 1990s. Also, the *sans papiers* have chosen French-specific frames rather than human rights frames. This need not have been the case. The slogan of the network of associations for the defence of undocumented aliens in Germany had clear universalizing overtones: 'Kein Mensch ist illegal' (no human is illegal) as did some of the initiatives to host deportable aliens in churches known as 'Asyl in der Kirche' (sanctuary in the church). The *sans papiers* have resorted to different arguments. Africans recalled their grandfathers and fathers who had died for France during the two world wars, arguing that the duties that their ancestors had fulfilled entailed rights for their descendants. This argument could not travel across the Rhine. *Sans papiers* were then given 'Republican godfathers (and godmothers)', French citizens who would help them with administrative procedures. Both the undocumented and the French sponsor received a *certificat de parrainage civil* that resembled a French identity card. The ceremony emphasized French obsessions with the upholding of 'Republican values', the same values that the current Minister of Interior calls upon to justify why 62,500 undocumented aliens will not be granted a residence permit.

Interviews with members of the movement involved in organizing occupations and demonstrations as well as my own observation of the Paris and Lille movements over the last two years suggests that the difficulty of sustaining a social movement in even one single country and of maintaining public interest seems to overwhelm the energies of movement leaders. Although Lille is half an hour away from Brussels, this has not prompted specific action by the local *sans papiers* movement in this city, Comité des Sans Papiers 59 (CSP 59), whose main objective remains the attraction of local and possibly national media attention. In the Paris area, the very 'multicultural' character of the undocumented who have been willing to participate in the movement's actions makes organizing the latter time-consuming as various *collectifs* have to be contacted and their number keeps growing. One activist, whom I asked about 'transnational' activities, answered by pointing out that getting the Chinese, the Turks and the Africans of the Tenth Arrondissement to agree to a meeting was 'transnational' enough for him and that he did not have the time to think beyond his city district.

The case of the *sans papiers* suggests that although 'fortress Europe' can serve as a target for groups across borders, nation-based frames of reference and limited resources limit the extent of transnational activity that a grassroots movement can engage in.

Pro-Migrant Contention in Brussels: Expert versus Representative Lobbies

There have been two major migration-related initiatives that involved the creation of a European activist network targeted at EU institutions: the European Union Migrants' Forum (EUMF) and the Starting Line Group (SLG). The Migrants' Forum was founded in 1991 by the European Commission acting upon an initiative of the European Parliament. It spoke for 130 migrant associations that hold an annual general assembly and every other year elect an executive board and executive committee (helped by a six-person staff in Brussels). In 1995, there was a 'support group' in each member state whose elected president also sat on the board.[2] In 1992, academic and NGO legal experts from six member states founded the Starting Line Group to draft an anti-discrimination article to be discussed during the 1996 Intergovernmental Conference that led to the signing of the Amsterdam Treaty. It now has 300 associated organizations that range from international NGOs to interest groups and associations. Its core group is made up of British and Dutch activists and there is a strong 'North European' bias to its membership. The European Union Migrants' Forum's experience demonstrates the difficulties that migrants face when trying to push for a common European agenda. The Starting Line Group initiative in the area of anti-discrimination shows that it is possible but the group is not made up of migrants and only indirectly serves their interests.

All studies of the Migrants' Forum point out numerous difficulties in finding common ground among the migrant lobby groups and in defining an agenda (Kastoryano 1994; Geddes 1998). The very word 'migrant' was problematic since many people of migrant origin are citizens of one of the member states. The

---

2   The Forum has been suspended since 2001 after an audit revealed financial mismanagement.

Migrants' Forum was very divided as different ethnic groups publicly expressed mutual antagonism. In particular the Turks and the Moroccans vied for control of the organization, with the Moroccans eventually winning out and giving the organization a francophone cast that sets it apart from the largely anglophone NGO-lobby world of Brussels. The Migrants' Forum's problems not only stemmed from the fact that migrants in Europe are made up of many different groups but also from the different agendas that depended on the nation states in which they had settled. In fact, the British Commission for Racial Equality preferred to create a parallel organization (SCORE, Standing Conference on Racial Equality in Europe), rather than join the Migrants' Forum, on the grounds that their system was the best and should not be diluted (Neveu 1994). Europhobia and a belief in the superiority of their anti-discrimination provisions combined to make the British opt out once again (Favell 2000).

In the Migrants' Forum, there were national groups for each member state and regional 'ethnic' groups grouping migrants of similar origin, but national groups from the EU's largest and most influential countries – the French and the German groups – dominated the discussion. The 'national groups' tended to reproduce the incorporation and citizenship models of their host countries, thereby making dialogue difficult. Migrants from Scandinavia and the Netherlands favour multicultural policies while those from France had internalized the assimilationist Republican model of integration. In countries such as Germany, statutory discrimination was still very much an agenda that unites migrant groups, whether they called for an easier access to citizenship, dual nationality, or for recognition of minority religions, while in others the emphasis was on non-statutory discrimination (e.g. in housing or hiring). Stemming in part from these differences, the modes of organization of migrants vary as well, from 'rainbow coalitions' to federated ethnic-based interest groups. They therefore not only have different claims but also different cultures of contention (Ruzza 1999).

Although it was the Commission that founded the Forum, it cooperates more closely with other networks – such as the Starting Line Group (SLG) – that better fit its model of expert input. At first, the group received support from well-established national agencies dedicated to anti-discrimination, such as the British Commission for Racial Equality (CRE) and the Dutch National Bureau against Racism (LBR) as well as from the small Brussels-based NGO now called the Migration Policy Group (MPG, formerly the Churches Commission for Migrants in Europe). The MPG had local knowledge and provided logistical help. The European Parliament endorsed its proposal for an anti-discrimination clause in 1993. By now, about 300 organizations (NGOs, INGOs, and social movement organizations, associations, and interest groups) are associated with the Starting Line Group.

Unlike the Migrants' Forum, the Starting Line has a vigorous leadership and a clear agenda that requires expert knowledge and therefore could gain approval by formal EU standards. The anti-discrimination clause project was reminiscent of the Equal Treatment Directive of 1976 and of Article 119 in a very Euro-correct way.

Leading up to the 1996 Intergovernmental Conference, before the revision of the treaty, EU institutions that had been accused of neglecting the 'democratic deficit' were receptive to initiatives that showed a gentler, kinder Europe or in any case had a social component that could inscribe themselves within the 'war on social exclusion', another keyword in the Commission's policy frames. The timing was therefore ripe for the SLG initiative. In the end, the SLG speaks on behalf of migrants' interests yet is very far removed from their grassroots organizations. Its relative success suggests that lobbies that propose expertise to EU institutions such as the Commission are more likely to be listened to than those that only claim legitimacy of origin in migrant communities.

The lack of a link between national and sub-national activists and Brussels-based NGOs was supported in my fieldwork in Brussels. The personal and organizational networks in which an NGO such as the Migration Policy Group evolves include INGOs, UN and OECD experts, American liberal think tanks and foundations such as the Carnegie Endowment for International Peace, as well as legal circles. They produce information for EU institutions and international forums more than they give information to groups from smaller national and local units. These international forums are also the locus where European NGOs find ideas to impute into the European context. This being so, they do not relay ideas or demands from grassroots organizations to Brussels; in Adrian Favell's (2000) terms, Brussels NGOs act as 'gatekeepers' for national and local social movement organizations, if only by choosing whom they help get EU funds or to whom they provide information.

Gaia Danese's (1998) study of migrant mobilization in Italy and Spain underlines the 'under-exploitation of European space'. The migrant groups that she interviewed either did not know about the Forum or other migration-related projects or, if they did, viewed them in a negative light. They criticized the 'Euro-centred vision' of the Forum as very 'far from migrants' real everyday needs' (Danese 1998, p. 723) and stated that the Forum did not provide them with practical information about Commission funding. This missing link between the grassroots and Brussels is key in understanding the lack of a 'boomerang effect' between resource-poor domestic groups and resource-rich international actors. It prompts us to turn to the actual funding strategy of the Commission authorities in charge of migrant integration.

Brussels Helps Those Who Help Themselves: EU Funding of Pro-migrant Associations

The Commission funds a number of migrant associations and their initiatives. The Directorate General for Employment and Social Affairs has been the main provider of capital since it finances projects against racism and xenophobia, actions in favour of migrant workers, free movement, and initiatives favouring the integration of refugees. In addition, it managed a budget of ECU 4.76 million allocated to fund local, national and European activities as part of the European Year of Racism (i.e. in 1997) and the budget has been rising every year since then – up to ECU 7 million in 1999 (Commission of the European Communities 1998). Finally, after the 1995 Barcelona Euro-Mediterranean conference, the Directorate for External Affairs opened a budget line called 'Medmigrations' which funds migrants' organizations registered in a EU state with partners in both their sending and receiving countries so as to foster 'co-development'. A 1995 report assessing 200 of the 560 projects on migrant integration that the Directorate for Employment and Social Affairs funded between 1991 and 1993 revealed that only 16 per cent were migrant-led (Commission of the European Communities 1995, p. 10). NGOs, churches, trade unions, and organizations involved in housing or education issues made up the rest of the beneficiaries. After 1995, the Commission laid down clearer criteria for support – including that of transnationality. The transnational NGOs that received funding before 1995 because they were better able to know about the funding opportunities were now funded because they were able to demonstrate their 'transnational' character.[3] With 2.6 per cent of the proposals, Brussels-based NGOs got 6.8 per cent of total funding, a clear success. Nevertheless, the small local projects that got funded before 1995 could no longer be financed. The report on the European Year Against Racism states that 28 per cent of the submitted proposals were rejected because they could not satisfy the 'transnationality' criterion (Commission of the European Communities 1998). Some migrant communities are far better placed than others to respond to the transnationality criterion that opens the Brussels bursary. For example, Moroccans' interest in their home countries was activated by the creation of associations that focused on cooperative ventures with Morocco (Migrations et Développement in France and Komitee Marokkaanse Abeiders in Nederland in the Netherlands). They could rely on the Moroccan opposition in Europe, which had maintained networks and contacts both there and in Morocco. When the Commission's Med project took shape, Moroccan associations with ties to the opposition networks were therefore much better placed than other national groups like the Malians and the Senegalese who had extensive contact in their home countries yet lacked the European connections or the political knowledge that the Moroccan opposition network had (Boussetta 1997).

To understand the dynamics behind the Commission's funding, one needs to examine the institutional logic of that institution.[4] In 1958, Unit D/4 'Free Movement of Workers, Migrant Integration and Antiracism' was created under the Directorate General for Employment and Social Affairs of the Commission to handle issues related to free movement of labour and situated within the Employment and Social Affairs directorate.

---

3   As an illustration, the Commission unit defines the organizations that qualify for funds
    within the framework of 'actions in favour of migrant workers' as follows: European
    NGOs, consultants for the Commission, and associations chosen in agreement with
    local, national authorities, and the Commission.
4   For a fuller discussion, see Guiraudon (2001).

Over the years, the unit became involved in matters relating to the integration of migrants and refugees and, since 1986, anti-racism. The head of the unit, Annette Bosscher, held her post for many years, compensating for the high turnover of her 20-member staff. European-based activists therefore had a faithful interlocutor, who, as it happens, firmly believed that European integration should go hand in hand with the integration of non-Europeans. The unit accordingly funds most of the migrant-related projects.[5] Yet, it has faced many challenges, often related to the very thin treaty basis for its actions. For its own survival and expansion, it had to adapt in creative ways. Once the European Court of Justice had ruled that cultural integration of migrants was no business of the EU, other bases of intervention had to be found. One consisted in jumping on the bandwagon of the EU war against 'social exclusion' (Article 137 of the Treaty of Amsterdam) as a justification for its actions. Many of the unit's policy documents insist that migrants and their descendants are prime victims of social exclusion and that non-governmental organizations know best how to fight it.[6] As member states became weary of the expansionist attitude and the bureaucracy of the Commission under the leadership of Jacques Delors, they jealously guarded the principle of 'subsidiarity': what can be best solved at the local or national level should be dealt with at that level. All units managing projects and proposing measures now had to tread softly and explain why they – and not national bureaucracies or local authorities – should intervene. This was also the case among the staff of the Directorate General for Employment and Social Affairs since, in the early 1990s, many of the funds that had been directed to the integration of migrants went to small local projects (Commission of the European Communities 1995). In this hostile atmosphere, where the Commission was also coming under fire for the opaqueness of funding procedures, the Unit D/4 under the Directorate General for Employment and Social Affairs needed to establish clear requirements that also showed the value added of EU funding. Its staff decided to include 'transnationality' – defined as projects involving the cooperation of multinational teams – as a criterion for receiving Commission funds. This stemmed from the legal constraints under which it had to operate; for without some underlying 'European' justification, member states could seek to annul programmes for non-respect of the subsidiarity principle before the European Court of Justice.

The promotion by Commission bureaucrats of non-governmental actors operating transnationally at the EU level must be understood as their creative way of responding to criticism from other institutions while expanding their realm of

---

5   The Unit administers about ECU 10 million for refugee integration, 6 million for migrants, and 5 million for anti-racism every year. On average, about two full-time members manage each area, the rest of the unit being made up of people handling the legal problems associated with free movement.

6   See, for instance, Guidelines on Preparatory Measures to Combat Social Exclusion that calls for the mobilization of the NGO community and for transnational initiatives (Brussels: CEC 1998).

allies and their spheres of action. 'Transnationality' served the first purpose and 'social inclusion' the second one. But the unintended consequence of this strategy has been that the groups most likely to benefit from this situation, rather than grassroots migrant's associations, were either pre-existing transnational networks or Brussels-based NGOs. The latter had the added advantage of being composed of British and Dutch activists who could draw upon their credentials and expertise in the area of anti-discrimination. EU institutions are reorganizing frequently as new treaties are adopted and European civil servants adapt their strategies to the mood of member states. The incentives and targets of European activists shift as well as they seize windows of opportunity (such as an intergovernmental conference or a bureaucratic reorganization). Those most likely to anticipate policy priorities and adapt to new organizational grids are elite-run Brussels-based NGOs such as the Migration Policy Group because of their know-how and personal contacts. For local and national-level groups, these changes are more difficult to know; and their actions remain embedded in national structures.

Back to the Micro-Level: European as a Default Identity for EU-Sponsored Associations

Notwithstanding the fact that EU institutions favour established transnational organizations and EU-based NGOs, the Commission also sponsors local associations that engage in cross-border projects. From a very preliminary study of such associations in Lille and Roubaix, it seems that their material and symbolic uses of 'Europe' respond to the same need or make up for the same 'deficit'. Materially, these associations looked for EU funds when municipalities refused to sponsor them under various pretexts (in one case, for example, the association ADICE was suspected of covering religious Moslem activities). This original constraint turned into an opportunity since the cross-border exchange projects that they had to devise and their European label distinguished them from the plethora of other associations catering for immigrant communities or providing social help to second generation youths. It provided them with a distinct identity as associations. Conversely, at the individual level, the members of these associations tend to refer to their being European as a supplement to their local identity and as an alternative to their being French since they do not feel recognized as French. Their idea of Europe, however, has little content, only consisting of a vague association of the concept with openness and tolerance. In this sense, it is a default identity and one to be mobilized defensively. Just as these associations sought EU funds to make up for the lack of local support, they seek a European identity for lack of a national one.

Conclusion

Mobilizing structures, framing processes and the sites of policy making are important in determining whether migrant movements are able and willing to invest in transnational activities targeted at the EU level. On the one hand, migrants are embedded in transnational social networks and could draw upon an emerging 'postnational' model of political membership that locates the basis of rights claims beyond the nation state. Moreover, the locus of decision making on entry and stay of third-country nationals is shifting to the EU level. On the other hand, divisions that stem from the national political and bureaucratic structures that have socialized migrants and determined on their organizational structures hinder their political activity across borders. The fate of the European Union Migrants' Forum, the Commission-sponsored consultative assembly, illustrates these difficulties. National paradigms of political inclusion still constitute the dominant frame of reference for migrant movements even as they seek to contest dominant definitions of the nation in the states in which they reside, as we saw with the French movement of undocumented aliens. Finally, the nation state remains the main source of (re)distributive policies, therefore a key target for demands. Whether one conceptualizes it as a structure, a reference, or a resource, the nation state is still relevant for migrant contention, making it difficult to develop a transnational agenda for European contention.

Works Cited

Amiraux, Valérie (1997) 'Turkish Islamic Associations in Germany and the Issue of European Citizenship', in Steven Vertovec and Ceri Peach (eds), *Islam in Europe: The Politics of Religion and Community*. London: Macmillan.

Bauböck, Rainer (1998) 'Sharing History and Future? Time Horizons of Democratic Membership in an Age of Migration'. *Constellations* 4, no. 3 (January 1998), 320-345.

Bauböck, Rainer (2000) 'Liberal Justifications for Ethnic Group Rights', in Christian Joppke and Steven Lukes (eds), *Multicultural Questions*. Oxford: Oxford University Press, 133-157.

Boussetta, Hassan (1997) 'Le nouveau partenariat euro-méditerranéen. Enjeux et perspectives pour les sociétés civiles et pour les communautés immigrés'. *Nouvelle Tribune* 15.

Brubaker, Rogers (1992) *Citizenship and Nationhood in France and Germany*. Cambridge, Mass.: Harvard University Press.

Césari, Jocelyne (1997) *Réseaux transnationaux entre l'Europe et le Maghreb*. Research report for DG-I. Brussels: European Commission.

Cohen, Robin (1997) *Global Diasporas*. Seattle: University of Washington Press.

Commission of the European Communities (1995) *Assistance Given to Migrant Associations*. Brussels: DG-V.

Commission of the European Communities (1998) *European Year Against Racism. Directory of Projects*. Brussels: DG-V.

Danese, Gaia (1998) 'Transnational Collective Action in Europe: The Case of Migrants in Italy and Spain'. *Journal of Ethnic and Migration Studies* 24(4), 715-733.

della Porta, Donatella, Hanspeter Kriesi and Dieter Rucht (1999) 'Social Movements in a Globalizing World: an Introduction', in Donatella della Porta, Hanspeter Kriesi and Dieter Rucht (eds), *Social Movements in a Globalizing World*. New York: St. Martin's Press.

Favell, Adrian (2000) 'L'Européanisation ou l'émergence du nouveau "champ politique": le cas de la politique d'immigration', in Virginie Guiraudon (ed.), *Sociologie de l'Europe: Mobilisations, élites et configurations institutionnelles*, special issue of *Cultures et Conflits* 38(9) (December), 153-185.

Forum des migrants (1995) *Statut*. Version adopted by the October 1995 General Assembly.

Geddes, Andrew (1998) 'The Representation of "Migrants'" interests in the European Union'. *Journal of Ethnic and Migration Studies* 24(4), 695-713.

Geertz, Clifford (1980) *Local Knowledge*. Princeton: Princeton University Press.

Guiraudon, Virginie (1997) *Policy Change Behind Gilded Doors: Explaining the Evolution of Aliens' Rights in Contemporary Western Europe*. PhD Dissertation. Cambridge Mass.: Harvard University.

Guiraudon, Virginie (1998) 'Citizenship Rights for Non-Citizens: France, Germany, and the Netherlands', in Christian Joppke (ed.), *Challenge to the Nation-State: Immigration and Citizenship in Western Europe and the United States*. Oxford: Oxford University Press, 272-318.

Guiraudon, Virginie (2000) 'European Courts and Foreigners' Rights: A Comparative Study of Norms Diffusion'. *International Migration Review* 34(4), 1088-1125.

Guiraudon, Virginie (2001) 'Weak Weapons of the Weak? Mobilizing around Migration at the EU-level', in Sidney Tarrow and Doug Imig (eds), *Contentious Europeans: Protest and Politics in an Emerging Polity*. New York: Rowman and Littlefield, 163-183.

Hannerz, Ulf (1996) *Transnational Connections. Culture, People, Places*. London: Routledge.

Hollifield, James F. (1998) 'Migration, Trade and the Nation-State: The Myth of Globalization'. *UCLA Journal of International Law and Foreign Affairs* 3/2: 595-636.

IOM (International Organization for Migration) (2000) *World Migration Report*. Geneva: IOM.

Ireland, Patrick (1994) *The Policy Challenge of Ethnic Diversity: Immigrant Politics in France and Switzerland*. Cambridge, Mass.: Harvard University Press.

Joppke, C. (1999) *Immigration and the Nation State: The United States, Germany and Great Britain*. New York: Oxford University Press.

Kastoryano, Riva (1994) 'Mobilisations des migrants en Europe: du national au transnational'. *Revue Européenne des Migrations Internationales*, 10(1), 169-181.

Kastoryano, Riva (1996) *La France, l'Allemagne et leurs immigrés: négocier l'identité*. Paris: Armand Colin.

Keck, Margaret and Kathryn Sikkink (1998) *Activists Beyond Borders. Advocacy Networks in International Politics*. Ithaca, NY: Cornell University Press.

Klotz, Audie, (1995) 'Norms Reconstituting Interests: Global Racial Equality and U.S. Sanctions Against South Africa'. *International Organization*, 49(3), 451-478.

Koopmans, Ruud and Paul Statham (1999) 'Challenging the Liberal Nation-State? Postnationalism, Multiculturalism, and the Collective Claims-Making of Migrants and Ethnic Minorities in Britain and Germany'. *American Journal of Sociology*, 105, 652-696.

Levitt, Peggy (1997) 'Transnationalizing Community Development: The Case of Migration Between Boston and the Dominican Republic'. *Non-profit and Voluntary Sector Quarterly*, 26(4), 509-526.

Neveu, Catherine (1994) 'Is "Black" an Exportable Category to Mainland Europe? Race and Citizenship in a European Context', in John Rex and Beatrice Drury (eds), *Ethnic Mobilisation in a Multicultural Europe*. Aldershot: Avebury.

OECD (Organization for Economic Cooperation and Development) (2003) *Trends in International Migration*. Annual report 2002. Paris: OECD.

Ogelman, Nedim (1998) 'Identity, Organizations, and the Transnational Political Opportunity Structure of Turkish-Origin Inhabitants in Germany'. Paper presented at the *Eleventh Conference of Europeanists*, Baltimore, MD, (February).

Portes, Alejandro (1998) 'Transnational Communities: Their Emergence and Significance in the Contemporary World System', in Roberto Patricio Korzeniewicz and William C. Smith (eds), *Latin America in the World Economy*. Westport, CT: Greenwood Press.

Risse, Thomas, Stephen Ropp and Kathryn Sikkink (eds) (1999) *The Power of Human Rights: International Norms and Domestic Change*. Cambridge: Cambridge University Press.

Ruzza, Carlo (1999) *Normal Protest: Social Movements and Institutional Activism*. Unpublished manuscript.

Sassen, Saskia (1996) *Losing Control: Sovereignty in an Age of Globalization*. New York: Columbia University Press.

Soysal, Yasemin (1994) *Limits of Citizenship*. Chicago: Chicago University Press.

Starting Line Group (1998) *Proposals for Legislative Measures to Combat Racism and the Promotion of Equal Opportunities*. Brussels: Migration Policy Group.

Tarrow, Sidney (1998a) *Power in Movement. Social Movements and Contentious Politics*. Second Edition. New York: Cambridge University Press.

Tarrow, Sidney (1998b) 'Fishnets, Internets, and Catnets: Globalization and Transnational Collective Action', in Michael Hanagan, Leslie Page Moch and Wayne Te Brake (eds), *Challenging Authority: The Historical Study of Contentious Politics*. Minneapolis and St. Paul: University of Minnesota Press.

Yashar, Deborah (1998) 'Citizenship Claims in Latin America: Parsing out the Role of Globalization'. Paper presented to the conference on *Citizenship Claims*, Harvard University Center for International Affairs (October).

Chapter 4

Turkish Transnational Nationalism: How the 'Turks Abroad' Redefine Nationalism

Riva Kastoryano

In November 1992, a week after the racist attacks in Mölln, during which five people of Turkish origin had been killed, a soccer competition fielded Türkiyem Sport (My Turkey sports club), a Berlin team composed of the offspring of Turkish immigrants, against a local team of 'Germans'. After the Turkish national anthem, those present in the stadium were called on to observe a minute's silence in commemoration of the victims of racism a week, a month or a year earlier. The match had hardly begun before the spectators, with radios pressed to their ears, began to shout in rhythms that did not necessarily correspond to the game they followed with their eyes, but rather reacted to the one they listened to on the wireless – another soccer match taking place in Turkey. With their eyes on the field in Berlin and their ears in Istanbul, the 'Berlin Turks' were present in two spaces at the same time, expressing the same feelings of victory and defeat. Their physical presence demonstrated their solidarity with Türkiyem Sport, while they lived Turkey in Berlin through the radio.

Also in Berlin, on 19 May 1998, an association called 'Atatürk's Thought' (Atatürkcü Düsünce dernegi) organized a ball to celebrate the inauguration of its Berlin branch. The date is not incidental. On 19 May 1919, Mustafa Kemal held his first 'speech' on national independence at Samsun (a town on the Black Sea coast),[1] a speech that he dedicated to the 'Turkish youth'. Since the foundation of the Republic on 19 May 1923, the 'Feast of Youth and Sport' has been celebrated in all Turkish towns every year with processions of schoolchildren.

In Berlin, just before the inauguration ball, one of the leaders drew attention to the fact that there was no organizational link between the association established in Berlin in 1997 and the organization of the same name established in Turkey in 1989. All the same, in contrast to associations preaching the virtues of integration, this organization announced its clear aim of defending the interests of Turkey. Its president defined Ankara as the centre and added that it was 'impossible to dissociate the Turks in Germany from Turkey'. It was necessary to 'remind the

---

1 See Parla (1991) for an analysis of political culture, based on Mustafa Kemal's speech.

Turks in Berlin, and the whole population of Berlin, that the Turkish state is secular'. He thus attacked Millî Görüş (National Vision), an organization linked organizationally to the Prosperity (Refah) Party that has been replaced by the Virtue (Fazilet) Party, in 1998 both representing political Islam in Turkey. National Vision has, since the 1980s, not only become the most important association among the immigrants in Germany, but also the most established in Europe with 28 branches joined together under the name European Organization of National Vision. The spokesperson of the association 'Atatürk's Thought' in Berlin declared that his association sees it as 'its duty to make the Turkish nation return to its Kemalist ideal'. He envisaged the establishment of a secular and republican school in Germany as a reaction to the Quran classes organized by Islamic organizations. In his speech, he rejected any 'fragmentation of the identity' that would allow the resurgence of the ethnic, linguistic, and regional bonds that had been oppressed since the foundation of the Turkish nation state and were today appearing as a political force both in Europe and Turkey.

 An abundance of events, speeches and symbols travel between Turkey and Europe. They demonstrate the existence of a transnational nationalism. It is a nationalism that finds expression and develops beyond and outside the borders of the state and its territory, and returns to arouse nationalist sentiments inside the country. This brings to mind studies on 'diasporic nationalism' or 'minority nationalism' that show the role played by such communities in the construction of the state (Cohen 1997). Transnational nationalism is different. It refers to a nation state that is independent, sovereign and has a defined territory. It either manifests itself through the nationalism of the state beyond its borders, or through the return to the country of origin of identities 're-appropriated' in the country of immigration.

 In the Turkish case, the extension of nationalism beyond its borders arises from the Turkish state's intervention in immigration through means of bilateral agreements or simply its support of organizations like 'Atatürk's Thought' that disseminate its ideology. It is within this dynamic scenario that the leader of the association in Berlin returns to the official discourse based on Kemalism – a nationalism until recently considered 'natural', which has, however, for some years now got into an increasingly defensive position due both to the growing influence of Islamic currents on political life and to the Kurdish movement in Turkey. After two movements – the integration of Islam in politics and the expansion of the Kurdish movement – have gained a foundation of legitimacy within political frameworks for identity enforced in the countries of immigration, they return to the national territory with the same claims for representation as in Europe. Their militant supporters base themselves on new forms of solidarity that reach from the local to the transnational, and that allow them to elevate the power relationships established by the usual economic and political rules of the game into the realm of the 'global system'. This is woven into the political projects and shows how the very understanding of nationalism undergoes changes in Turkey.

Identities regained during immigration appear as a reaction to the effort during the formation of the culturally and politically unitarian Turkish nation state to hide all cultural, ethnic and linguistic differences. Once transposed into the country of origin, such identities, which in most cases arose out of the relationship with the state of the country of immigration, give a new meaning to nationalism by drawing the state of origin into the same process of transnationalizing nationalism. Accordingly, nation is not defined in the same way for diasporas and for transnational nationalisms. Diasporas point to nations defined by ideals vested in past symbols and projects itself into the future with the same myth, while the nation of transnational nationalisms is in the throes of the interaction between the states of emigration and immigration. Put differently, the will in a diaspora to unite around a common project of state building is in transnationalism superseded by the manifestation and expression of difference. This diversity, furthermore, is 're-centred' in a process where supranational institutions recognize these identities and afford them legitimacy on the international stage.

Transnational nationalism thus points to the formation of a transnational community; it points to a transnational public space that favours mobilization and participation in several national spaces and closer relationships between Turkey and Europe, which are based on the circulation of ideas, norms, actions, and claims for recognition in different political spaces, owing to new actors emerging from immigration.

The Formation of a Transnational Community

More than four million people who have emigrated from Turkey presently live in Europe. Having arrived in great numbers since the 1960s following bilateral agreements between Turkey and European countries, in particular Germany, their migration was mainly economic. Their dispersion in different West European countries sets them apart from post-colonial migration. In contrast to the North African migrants in France and the populations from the Indian subcontinent in Great Britain, the Turkish migrants have settled across Europe, although the majority lives in Germany.[2] For Turkey they constitute a new social category: the Turks abroad. Circulating across different family, commercial and association networks, they link private and public spaces as well as economic and political spaces in Europe and between Turkey and Europe. This is how their new roles emerge.

The presence of populations sharing the same geographic, national and religious references in different national spaces has given rise to an elaboration of the diaspora concept, a concept of Greek origin that signifies dispersal. It has often been used to describe the dispersal of the Jews and later the Armenians and Palestinians; it refers to a mythical territory and often to an identity based on a

---

2   More than two million in Germany, 300,000 in France, 35,000 in the Netherlands, etc. (SOPEMI 1997).

common religion or a common language.[3] For the Turkish migrants, Stephanie de Tapia has developed the idea of a 'migrant circulation' to describe the migratory flows and to document the 'multitude of individual and family movements and the thousands of dislocations, which strengthen or weaken the presence of a "worker diaspora" that utilizes networks both of commercial, organizational, political and religious information and of strong state support' (de Tapia 1994).

The Turks abroad, in spite of their heterogeneous composition, refer to the state, i.e. the Turkish nation state, defined territorially. Their modes of organization, mobilization and participation reflect multiple belongings, both as migrants and in Turkey. The refinement of the commercial, family and organizational (based on regional identities and/or political ideologies) networks by introducing Turkey into Europe draws subtle borders of a transnational community.

The rise of such communities is a global phenomenon. Migrants participate in networks based on economic interests, cultural exchanges, social relationships and political allegiances. Migrants have lived simultaneously in multiple contexts for at least one or two generations, maintaining links with a real or 'imagined' community – their country of origin. Consequently, their belonging to such a 'community' is not a new phenomenon. It is its organizational dimension that is new – the establishment of networks and the formation of communities as well as their de-territorialized operation. The institutionalization of such communities requires the coordination of activities more often than not based on (objective and subjective) references and interests shared by the members of the transnational community. For several years now, their emergence has also been based on a 'context of globalization and economic uncertainty that facilitates the establishment of social relationships beyond national borders, relationships stimulated by growing mobility and the development of communications' (Rivera-Salgado 1999).

The emergence of transnational communities as a phenomenon follows on from the nation state. The emigration involved has the nation state as its reference, and the migrants who participate in the construction of the transnational communities do not refer to the territory of a 'mythical' state but to a territorial nation state from which they originate. However, the constituent elements of a transnational community's identity do not necessarily correspond to the 'official' identity displayed by its reference nation state; this holds true in the case of Turkey. It often takes the form of a 're-appropriation' of identity during migration – be it Kurdish, Turkish, Alevi, or Islamic – that transcends the territorial borders between Turkey and Europe.[4] Their formation has brought about new 'transnational actors' who have either appropriated or been designated the task of linking Turkey and Europe.

---

3   For an analysis of definitions and usage of the term diaspora, see Bruneau (1994).
4   The Kurds, by the way, represent an interesting case, combining a 'transnational community' and a 'diaspora'. In the Kurdish case, the notion of ethnicity refers to a 'national' definition within the Turkish territory, defined by a language, a history and a

These new political actors emerging from migration have reorganized their interests and identities, be they social, cultural, ethnic or political, around associations in most cases established with the support of the countries of residence in the name of a democracy increasingly scrupulous in recognizing difference. Some of these associations have replaced left-wing or right-wing, military or revolutionary, religious or ethnic organizations rooted in Turkey and conveyed into 'exile', which were oriented towards Turkey and regarded the Turkish state as their adversary. They were originally protest movements against politics conducted in Turkey, against its idea of the nation, and against its attitude to religion. In Europe these associations, financed by individuals, by political (opposition) parties in Turkey, or by international organizations, found room for action and expression of identity denied them in Turkey. As in the case of the Imams who were officially (i.e. within the framework of religious affairs) sent to Germany and France, once they had established themselves in a European country, they pulled together the brotherhoods, which are illegal in Turkey, but active in Europe, with a power of conviction and strength of mobilization greater than in Turkey.

Other associations have come about, often aided by the authorities of the countries of immigration, aimed at 'integrating' the Turks (and immigrants in general) in the countries of residence. Their activities are appreciated by Turkey and their representatives are regarded as the ideal interlocutors between the two countries. Yet other associations have sought to combine the two aspects (militant action directed against official Turkey and for integration in the country of immigration) in order to be convincing *vis-à-vis* all Turkish migrants. This is the case with Millî Görüş (National Vision), an association springing from the religious party (which is now called Fazilet).[5] However, taken as a whole, no matter whether the associations are derived from political groups already active in Turkey, result from a transformation of workers' movements in Turkey or in Europe, or stem from initiatives in the different countries of immigration, the discourse of their leaders has since the 1980s given particular weight to culture and identity, defined variably as a reflection of their ideological function: national identity, religious, ethnic, linguistic and regional identity, or political identity.

The creation of these associations spawns a fragmentation of identity and the expression of new allegiances. The claim for recognition of these identity fragments makes all the differences surge in the public sphere. However, these differences are not only voiced with regard to France or Germany, they also emerge inside the official representations of Turkey. Each particular trait is thus an element of distinction from which the new cleavages within the population originating in Turkey arise. It is within this division that ethnicity is invented and

---

territory. Their migrant organization is part of the transnational community as we have defined it through their reference to the Turkish state, but their mobilization comes close to classical diasporic movements, due to their aspiration to create a territorial state of their own.

5   The Fazilet was banished by the state in June 2001.

redefined, by way of defining oneself as Turk or Kurd, as Sunni or Alevi, or as originally from western or eastern Turkey.

The diversity does not question the structure of the community. To the contrary, the growing conflicts within the network signal the closure of the transnational community rather than its sunderance. Each division contributes to the formation of a 'community' that can be described as 'segmented', i.e. 'conflictual', and yet 'transnational'. The conflicting relationships and internal rivalries that make the individuals play the game paradoxically reinforce the crossed bonds of solidarity and arouse the identification with the 'transnational community' thus created. The links between such associations and their representatives in Turkey, in spite of their efforts to distance themselves from each other and in spite of their activities facilitating the 'integration' of Turkish families in French or German society, place the politically active migrants in relation to each other, determined by their membership of associations and their political and ethnic labels, but with one common reference – Turkey, be it geographically, socially, politically or culturally defined. This common denominator leads to the 'invention' of an ethnicity on which the transnational community is constructed in order to increase the influence of the constituent migrant identities, to influence Turkish political life with greater efficacy by sensitizing international opinion and the supranational institutions, and to ultimately redefine the nature of Turkey's political community.

The Turkish state, on its part, intervenes in the formation of this transnational community. It acts as its 'regulator'. It operates in the country of residence by means of 'mother-tongue' education. Even where this is part of the bilateral agreements with the various countries of immigration, the Turkish state in this way contributes to ensuring that populations of Turkish immigrant origin adhere to its national ideology, an ideology expressed in a Kemalist rhetoric and controlled by the Turkish state. It is as if it were aimed at maintaining the idea of a Turkish citizenry; however, this citizenry is outside Turkey's territorial bounds. It comes down to keeping the nation linked with its citizenry or conversely the citizenry linked with its nation, but in either case the belonging is de-territorialized.

This citizenry does not demand a common identity with the nation, but with the state. The nationalism of the transnational community is not homogeneous in respect of culture, ethnicity or even religion (Brubaker 1998). To the contrary, the tendency towards homogenization at the origin of the project to construct the Kemalist state and the Turkish nation is divided into its anthropological elements which have found political expression during migration. This evolution is due to integration policies of the countries of residence that directly affect the ways in which Turks are integrated in different European countries and on the emergence of a transnational European space, which through the complex interplay between nation states and supranational European institutions include Turkey in Europe. Identities that are 'marginal' in relation to the nation states, in effect, give rise to a new ethnic 'centralization' that is not any more defined by territory (Létourneau 1997).

The Emergence of a Transnational Space for Participation and Mobilization

Studies on the emergence of transnational communities emphasize post-colonial migration and the economic relationships the individuals maintain with their countries of origin. The transnational actors thus operate in two political spaces.[6] Within the context of the European Union, a 'transnational community' transcends the borders of the member states. Some networks arise from local initiatives in countries of immigration, others from the country of origin, and yet others are encouraged by supranational institutions such as the European Parliament or the European Commission. The intervention by supranational institutions places the transnational communities on a par with lobby groups that operate directly at the European level and define their activities as transnational (Smith, Chatfield and Pagnucco 1997).

The Turkish association networks are part of this 'spider's web' that extends across the European space. Their aspirations and activities are closely related to the project of the European Parliament which since 1986 has made funds available to immigrant organizations so that they can coordinate their activities. The 'Migrants' Forum' is a transnational structure that has sprung from this initiative. Although the Forum owes its formation to the European Union's budget policy, it aims to become 'a place where populations from outside the community established in Europe can express themselves and across which they can announce their claims and also disseminate information from European authorities' (Neveu 1994). It is mainly those associations whose activities are most supported by the welfare states of the member countries and whose leaders elaborate on a discourse of equality, human rights and universality that consider transnational mobilization as an effective way of fighting racism and xenophobia.[7] Since the creation of the Forum, Turkish associations have played an important role in it. They inserted themselves in the network through their ability to represent Turkish migration at the local, national, and indeed transnational – or European – levels, through the massive scale of their activities that have been recognized by public authorities, and through their forms of organization in federations of associations, as they mainly occur in Germany, that incorporate all ethnic, regional, religious, linguistic and ideological divisions.[8]

---

6 See Bash, Schiller and Blanc (1994); Cohen (1997); Gupta and Ferguson (1997); Hannerz (1996); Portes (1996); Levitt (1998); and Levitt (1997).
7 In 1990, 29 per cent of the respondents to a survey maintained that the rights of immigrants should be limited. By 1992, this number had risen to 34 per cent. Likewise, in 1992, 60 per cent accepted the arrival of Mediterranean migrants with certain restrictions, while only 46 per cent agreed in 1993. Eurobaromètre, December 1992.
8 Sixteen Turkish associations are presently represented in the Forum, of which ten are organized in federations of associations.

Apart from the 'immigrant' associations the Forum encourages the formation of 'national support groups' and 'regional support groups',[9] of which the former refer to member states and the latter to third countries, to which one should add the 'stateless' populations. It is within this framework that the Kurds find an institutional legitimacy in Europe.[10] This procedure that results from a policy of joined-up development in the countries of immigration comes down to including the countries of origin in the representation of the migrants in Europe and consequently provides populations originating in migration with a certain legitimation for action or rather for making claims based on their national, regional and ethnic belonging as well as on divisions of identity in the countries of origin. Like the claims relating to rights of abode, citizenship and protection from deportation that are directed at European institutions, the interests expressed in terms of the identities of populations constructed in immigration find scope for action within the European Union as a political space, thus leading to new forms and structures of representation and to new negotiations.

A transnational European political space thus emerges, embracing Turkey, and turning the latter into a source of identity and Europe into a source of legitimacy for mobilization and claims-making. The differences between European countries affect the modes of and strategies for the migrants' political participation. Their claims are woven into the total institutional framework of the countries of immigration, bringing to the fore how the organization and mobilization of the populations formed through Turkish immigration have been 'nationalized', thus showing that they conform to the rules of the game laid down by the states. Put differently, groups constituted in associations make use of the same tools as the authorities and national institutions when negotiating with the respective states about their collective rights and the recognition of their specific identities. However, the transnational networks also act directly *vis-à-vis* the supranational European institutions and constitute a challenge to the nation states. Europe is, in effect, becoming an open space for claiming interests and identities. At the same time it attracts populations that seek recognition for their identities and/or interests beyond the framework of the states. The immigrant populations approach this with the same right as other organizations – like professional or interest groups – that seek to influence national policies through action at the European level. This allows them to strengthen their representation both nationally and in Europe. Hence the evolution of new forms of solidarity that place themselves beyond the 'nationalization' of action by immigrant populations. It thus becomes apparent how

---

9   The regions are defined as the Maghreb (North Africa), Sub-Saharan Africa, Latin America, the Caribbean and Turkey. Although the regions are defined as groups of countries reflecting their geographic and cultural proximity, Turkey is represented as a region on its own.

10 The Kurds, who can only be identified through their self-definition, represent around 30 per cent of the Turkish immigrants, divided proportionally over the various European countries.

immigrant populations active in associations identify with a political body transcending national boundaries. Furthermore, such participation leads to the assertion of a citizenship one could term 'extra-territorial' (Kastoryano 1997), albeit an extra-territoriality in relation to the countries of residence rather than Turkey. It defines itself through the commitment to the formation of a European space,[11] and is carried out beyond national boundaries, where new solidarities take shape that include all the populations of Turkish immigrant origin in the different European countries.

This is also due to the very nature of the European Union, where the logic of supranationality has given shape to a transnational civil society within which networks (be they national, regional, religious or professional) compete and interact, thus making the fragmentation of the democratic societies apparent. The politicization of each of these networks has led to the formation of a transnational, de-nationalized public space.[12] This space also becomes a space where, thanks to the density of interactions between actors from different traditions, the groups and individuals who are active in forming boundary-transcending networks, transnational communities which can socialize politically. It also becomes a space where the same actors learn the trade of a new political culture that takes shape outside the nations and their institutions. It is a space of political participation, of identification beyond national societies, leading towards identification with a European society of third-country citizens resident in the member states. This dynamic, arising from political participation in several spaces at the same time and speeding up the interaction between different political value systems and cultures, forms the basis for transnational action, i.e. transnational nationalism.

Redefining Turkish Nationalism

The very idea of transnational nationalism arises from social, economic, cultural and political transfers between two or more spaces: the 'diasporic' space that recombines the actions of different political cultures, and the space of 'departure'. This implies reciprocal and interdependent influences. The Turkish immigrants circulate between these spaces, carrying political values and norms gained during migration, institutionalized in the framework of associations, and legitimized by European authorities. Such is the case of the Kurds. Through the voice of their militants, the Kurds seek recognition as a 'Kurdish community' of immigrants whose culture, history and language are distinct from the 'Turkish community'. This differentiation, which takes the form of a conflict between 'nationalisms' in Turkey, situates the Kurds as a 'minority' within a Turkish transnational community. Their demand for recognition shows how claims are not only pursued by migrants, but also by people claiming a dual minority status, as a minority

---

11 On citizenship as commitment and participation, see Leca (1987).
12 On this subject, see Appadurai (1996), Cohen (1997), and Laguerre (1998).

within a minority in Germany and as a minority in Turkey. Given that they have access to more political resources abroad than in Turkey, they bring their claims forward to the European Court of Human Rights, the Council of Europe, the European Court of Justice and the European Parliament, in order then to return to Turkey after having gained recognition as a 'minority' from a central power through official institutional representation.

Yet the concept of minority is ambiguous. It even causes uncertainty in defining legal forms of recognition (Decaux 1998). The definition proposed by the Convention on Human Rights is large: 'The term minority designates a group that is numerically smaller than the rest of the population and whose members are inspired by the will to preserve their culture, traditions, religion and language.'[13] For Turkey, the concept of minority was reserved for the old millet (religious communities). The Treaty of Lausanne in 1923 even afforded them a legal and political status, together with cultural privileges like the preservation of their languages and institutions (places of worship and community schools).[14] This status and concept does not apply to the populations subjected to the process of cultural, linguistic and indeed religious homogenization. Having been assimilated into the Turkish nation state by virtue of their belonging to Islam, the denomination of the majority, other Muslim populations (the brotherhoods, Alevis, or Kurds) do not enjoy any institutional representation. Their demands for recognition, especially when voiced by the brotherhoods whose organization and demands bring them in opposition to the national community, involve the Turkish state that follows the French example of centralization, republicanism and secularity. The claims cause new cleavages that become apparent in present-day Turkey – ethno-linguistic, religious and national rifts, whose emergence demonstrates the very contradictions in the formation of the nation state.

The deepest contradiction crystallizes around Islam. Its appearance as a political force in Turkey has, since 1997, given rise to a polemic that separates the nation into a 'secular' and a 'Muslim' part. Like in France, the headscarf has become a symbol and a tool for resistance against the state and for individual freedom, arousing passions both among religious and non-religious people. Furthermore, as an indisputable element of identity it questions the official identity's ability to mobilize, throwing doubt on its indefinite place in the 'national conscience' and on the institutions of the state. In Turkey the head scarf has, different from in France where it represents a minority religion, become a symbol of 'empowerment'. In reality, the fight against political Islam that seeks to mobilize passions and emotions against it leads to abundant explanations of its nature, spanning from the faith of the nation to the faith of the individual, from a collective culture to its recognition in the political life, and while intending to separate religion and politics, underlines the difficulty of defining a clear border between them.

---

13 Article 2 of the 1991 convention, cited by Sudre (1995, p. 156).
14 In 1926 the minorities (Greeks, Jews and Armenians) rejected these privileges.

The state, and indirectly the army, have now for several years declared war on political Islam in Turkey. The President of the Directorate of Religious Affairs (Diyanet), who has again been directly subordinate to the Prime Minister, assumes an increasingly important place in the public space thanks to his speeches that are relayed by the media as the voice of the supreme authority. As if the central power does not want to allow Islam to be 'monopolized' by the religious party, the official discourse frequently reiterates that '99.9 per cent of the Turkish population is Muslim and the state does not neglect Islam'. The association DITIB (Diyanet Isleri Türk Isciler Birligi), an organization in Europe that represents the Directorate of Religious Affairs within the consular network in the countries of immigration, has, through its task to disseminate an 'official Islam', had an effect on the content of nationalism. The Turkish state established the Diyanet throughout Europe in order to fight Islam as it has developed among the migrants with the introduction of Millî Görüş and the brotherhoods, to fight a 'dissident' Islam spread by political parties opposing the secular principles of the Republic. The secular state has thus explicitly introduced religion as an element of national identification, and has institutionalized it under the auspices of the consular network abroad. This development contributes to redefining Turkish nationalism outside and inside its borders.

The brotherhoods (*tarikat*), freed of their 'republican ban' among immigrants, have reappeared in Turkey as associations in civil society, corresponding to interest groups that play the political game. Their role in the re-establishment of internal power relationships within national politics and in determining the place of Islam as folk culture and belief is indisputable.[15]

The Alevis, on the other hand, re-entered national politics as the friends of the Republic, although this very Republic has lumped them together with the *tarikat* and consequently banned them from public space. Since the 1990s, their mobilization around associations and the visibility they have gained has sensitized public opinion and the political class to the historical, sociological and political realities of the Alevis. The whole Turkish population in particular pays attention to

---

15 This is at least the message of Fetullah Gülen, the leader of the Nurcu movement. For a deeper understanding of the brotherhood, see Serif Mardin (1989). Since the 1980s, its president, Fetullah Gülen, has preached the reconciliation of Islam with secularism and the importance thereof for defining 'Being Turkish' outside the national borders. The importance of his movement in media reports, public opinion, and also within the political class and among intellectuals is due to his schools, of which there are more than 400 across the world from Central Asia to Europe, with the aim of teaching Islam, but also the Turkish language as well as the language of the country where the school is situated. Even more importantly, at least in the national Turkish context, are his declarations on Turkish Islam, which have in particular during recent years made him a sort of 'negotiator of Turkish identity' in which the strength of the state, the nation and religion are joined together.

their belief system that is considered secret.[16] The question that arises from this is to what extent their integration into political life in Turkey and their visibility is linked to their image among migrants. Actually, the Alevi have, from the beginning, attracted the attention of the authorities in European cities due to their 'distance' from religion and Islamic worship. To what extent has their undogmatic representation of Islam among migrants and in Turkey, i.e. of a modern Islam, played a role in the change of attitude of the political class in Turkey short of official recognition? Or is it because the Alevis commit themselves to identifying with the secular state and, as a consequence of recognizing it, have become a way of fighting the ethnic and religious divisions in politics? In both cases, a parallel development outside and inside the national borders demonstrates the interdependence of these spaces and how they affect the redefinition of nationalism.

We are thus witnessing an inversion of the situation that implies a redefinition between political spaces and action. At the beginning of their immigration, the populations arriving from Turkey transformed the political and ideological cleavages and conflicts, which found expression in social classes in the European countries, by turning Europe into an extension of Turkish politics. Today, with their organizations recognized and legitimized in the European countries of residence, their mobilization in Turkey is a sign of a political transfer that gives a new content to both militant action and nationalist discourses in Turkey.

These transfers also take place in the cultural, economic and social spheres in two ways. They are amplified through new means of communication and in particular the dissemination by satellite television that has spread rapidly among Kurd, Turkish, Alevi or Sunnite families. In fact, the families live Turkey on a daily basis through the images transmitted by the 12 or 14 private and public channels (Gökalp, Kastoryano and de Tapia 1997). Apart from the obvious effects on the migrant societies, the broadcasts take place at the same time as the inhabitants of Turkey blur the link between territory and identity. The territory of belonging remains regional, the territory of reference becomes national/religious (albeit up for negotiation), and the territory of residence is French, German, Dutch or simply European.

These transfers integrate the Turkish state in the transnational community as a political, social or even economic actor. The Turkish state also develops its relations with social and cultural associations that have a local or national impact on the families and that present themselves as 'multicultural' and recognized as such by the various states of immigration. Taken together, their activities base themselves on the 'ethnic' definition of the group, a definition that seeks its foundation in a 'common nationality'. As if it were intent to contribute to depicting the ideal of a national community as a 'united community', the Turkish state places

---

16 It is interesting to note that since the 1980s, the representatives of the state as well as the members of successive governments have participated, with media coverage, in celebrations of pilgrimage that take place each year in August in Central Anatolia.

itself in relation to the various aspects of Turkish identity, be they national/religious or political. These attempts have as their aim to influence public opinion about the image of Turkey and to use it for a 'representation' of the Turks abroad as a 'community'. The political actors originating among Turkish immigrants to Europe respond to the attempts by the state with their efforts to form lobbies recognized by both countries, resting on the community organizations that have not only been defined by Turkish politics, but also situate themselves within the German system or oppose it. They react to all German government statements *vis-à-vis* Turkey and vice versa. Their power rests in their economic success. Having organized themselves as associations of Turkish business people in many regions, they seek to influence the national politics of the countries of residence and in Turkey.[17] By letting the economy serve politics, the increasing number of businessmen of Turkish origin have leverage to negotiate with public authorities in the two spaces. Similarly, they develop close relations with Turkish businessmen in Turkey, who have great influence on national politics and are also established in Brussels to influence the European Commission on matters related to Turkey's integration into the European Union. These aspects, taken together, contribute to the evolution of a nationalism that in reality becomes 'transnational', exactly as the nationalist movements that oppose it, like the Kurdish movement whose mobilization is European and transnational.

Conclusions

Transnationalism gives shape to present-day nationalism that differs from the highly territorialized nationalisms of the 19th and 20th centuries. The transnational communities are constructed around shared references and bring to the fore a feeling of belonging to a 'de-territorialized nation' with identity claims that are nourished by new expressions of nationalism. Together, this leads to a redefinition of the link between territory, nation and political space, challenging the nation state as a culturally and territorially defined political structure.

---

17 A report published in Belgium in 1991 estimates the value of the direct and indirect contribution to the economy by the Turks to be around 57 billion German Marks; the amount far exceeded the state's expenses on foreigners, which amounted to 16 billion German Marks. Among the 1.8 million Turks in Germany, there were, in 1992, 35,000 entrepreneurs, spanning from restaurateurs to industrialists who employed a total of 150,000 Turks and 75,000 Germans, whose trade figure amounted to 25 billion Marks and who, in 1991, had paid 1 billion Marks in taxes. See *Migrations News*, Brussels, December 1991, quoted in *The Economic and Political Impact of Turkish Migration in Germany*, Zentrum für Türkeistudien (March 1993). See also Zentrum für Türkeistudien, *Konsumgewohnheiten und wirtschaftliche Situation der türkischen Bevölkerung in der Budesrepublik Deutschland*, Essen (September 1992). The centre regularly publishes reports on enterprises owned by Turkish residents in Germany, including trade figures, employment numbers and tax payments.

This break-up without doubt weakens the Turkish state at a time when it negotiates its place on the international and more precisely the European stage. However, at the same time, in spite of its heterogeneity, segmented organization, and often conflicting internal relations, the emergence of a 'transnational community' can only act as a driving force behind political and social change in Turkey, due to the introduction of 'know-how' and democratic political values gained in the struggle for equal rights as migrants.

This means that transnationalism necessarily comes down to a double or multiple citizenship to the extent that it relates to several countries, i.e. at least two spaces for social, cultural, economic and political participation. Multiple citizenship in fact introduces different ways of conceiving of moral and political values in a community, including different concepts of civic duties imposed on those who live within these communities (Pickus 1998). Some even regard double citizenship as a source of 'democratic influence', as a means to apply Western democratic values in the country of origin (Spiro 1997).

Taking into account the interdependence gained between internal and external issues of nation states, as well as between the latter, the transnational communities constitute both a challenge to and an opportunity for Turkey. A challenge by virtue of their ability to negotiate its identity as a state, and an opportunity by virtue of the affirmation of its sovereignty and its integration in a general process of globalization. This is one of the paradoxes of transnationalism: while it questions the relevance of nation states as political, cultural and territorial units, transnationality reinforces the role of the states. The transnational activities, in short, aim to influence the states from the outside (Kastoryano 1997). This became clear through the claims of the transnational actors who sought to strengthen their representation at the European level, but whose practical aim was to arrive at recognition at the national level. It needs to be made clear that the militants, who are also the most active at the European level, imagine the state as the only 'adversary' they need to consider in the final analysis.

Works Cited

Appadurai Arjun (1996) *Modernity at Large: Cultural Dimensions of Globalisation.* Minneapolis: Minnesota University Press.
Bash, Linda, Nina G. Schiller and Christina S. Blanc (1994) *Nations Unbound. Transnational Projects, Postcolonial Predicaments and Deterritorialised Nation-States.* Fourth edition. Basel: Gordon Breach Publishers.
Brubaker, Rogers (1998) 'Myths and Misconceptions in the Study of Nationalism', in John A. Hall (ed.), *The State of the Nation. Ernest Gellner and the Theory of Nationalism.* Cambridge: Cambridge University Press, 273-301.
Bruneau, Michel (1994) 'Espaces et territoires de diasporas'. *L'Espace Géographique,* 23(1), 5-19.
Cohen, Robin (1997) *Global Diasporas. An Introduction.* Seattle: University of Washington Press.

Decaux, Emmanual (1998) 'Les nouveaux cadres du droit des minorités nationales en Europe', in Riva Kastoryano (ed.), *Quelle identité pour l'Europe? Le multiculturalisme à l'épreuve.* Paris: Presses de Sciences-Po, 125-143.

Gökalp, Altan, Riva Kastoryano and Stéphane de Tapia (1997) *L'immigration turque et kurde: La dynamique segmentaire, la nouvelle donne générationelle, et le nouvel ordre communicationel.* Report prepared for the FAS. Paris (January).

Gupta, Akil and John Ferguson (eds) (1997) *Culture, Power, Place.* Durham: Duke University Press.

Hannerz, Ulf (1996) *Transnational Connections. Culture, People, Places.* London: Routledge.

Kastoryano, Riva (1997) 'Participation transnationale et citoyenneté en Europe'. *Cultures et Conflits*, 28 (Winter), 59-75.

Laguerre, Michel (1998) *Diasporic Citizenship: Haitian Americans in Transnational America.* Basingstoke: Macmillan.

Leca, Jean (1987) 'Individualisme et citoyenneté', in Pierre Birnbaum and Jean Leca (eds), *Sur l'individualisme.* Paris: Presses de la FNSP.

Létourneau, Jocelyn (1997) 'Le liu (dit) de la nation: essai d'argumentation à partir d'exemples puisés au cas québécois'. *Revue Canadienne de Science Politique*, 30(1) (mars), 55-87.

Levitt, Peggy (1997) 'Transnationalizing Community Development: The Case of Migration Between Boston and the Dominican Republic'. *Nonprofit and Voluntary Sector Quarterly*, 26(4), 509-526.

Levitt, Peggy (1998) 'Local-Level Global Religion: The Case of U.S.-Dominican Migration'. *Journal for the Scientific Study of Religion*, 37(1), 74-89.

Mardin, Serif (1989) *Religion and Social Change in Turkey. The Case of Beddiuzzaman Said Nursi.* New York: SUNY Press.

Neveu, Catherine (1994) 'Citoyenneté ou racisme en Europe: Exceptionet complémentarité britanniques'. *Revue Européenne des Migrations Internationales.* 10(1), 95-109.

Parla, Taha (1991) *Nutuk,* Istanbul: Iletisim.

Pickus, Noach (1998) *Immigration and Citizenship in the 21st Century.* Littlefield: Rowma.

Portes, Alejandro (1996) 'Transnational Communities: Their Emergence and Significance in the Contemporary World System', in Roberto P. Korzeniewicz and William C. Smith (eds), *Latin America in the World Economy.* Westport, Conn.: Greenwood Press.

Rivera-Salgado, Caspar (1999) 'Mixtec Activism in Oaxacalifornia: Transborder Grassroats Political Strategies'. *American Behavioral Scientist*, 42 (9), 1439-1458.

Smith, Jackie, Charles Chatfield and Ron Pagnucco (eds) (1997) *Transnational Social Movements and Global Politics. Beyond the State.* Syracuse, NY: Syracuse University Press.

SOPEMI (1997) *Trends in International Migration.* Continuous Reporting System on Migration. Annual Report 1996. Paris: OECD.

Spiro, Peter J. (1997) 'Dual Nationality and the Meaning of Citizenship'. *Emory Law Journal*, 1411 (46).

Sudre, Fréderic (1995) *Droit international et européen de droits de l'homme.* Paris: PUF.

Tapia, Stéphane de (1994) 'L'Émigration turque: circulation migratoire et diaspora'. *L'Espace Géographique*, 23(1), 19-28.

Chapter 5

Looking Away from the Black Box: Economy and Organization in the Making of a Chinese Identity in Italy

Luigi Tomba

Collective Identities

The case of the Chinese migrants in Italy – and in particular of one mature community – presented in this chapter provides material for examining how migration processes and relationships with the receiving society help shape the cultural, economic and ethnic organization of the community, how this organization grows increasingly complex, how it adapts to a changing environment, and how it has potentially become a driving force in the shift from a hidden to an assertive identity, involving the issue of economic and social citizenship.

As a guide for this examination, I use one of the many possible definitions of 'home' for a displaced or migrant community – the organization of a physical and symbolic space where individual members subjectively belong. I am interested in the cultural mechanisms and symbolic forces that determine the cohesion of the community and the way the space is administered through these mechanisms. A re-created home (away from home) can, accordingly, also be the place and the network of interests and relationships where opportunities are created and protection is granted from or as an alternative to the external, receiving world.

I intend to bring the economic dimension and the developmental nature of migrant communities into the picture of 'identity-making' and I believe that the case of Chinese migrant communities is particularly significant in this respect. My idea is that, beyond all cultural elements, this 'home' is largely the result of a shared construction of 'patterns of regular doings' (Rapport and Dawson 1998), but that it evolves within a complex relationship with the receiving community and with the changing demands of the community. Home as a mutant construction identified by the place and social networks within which identity is constructed, confronted with an external 'non-home' world. In a migrant 'community', that is in a complex organizational form concerned with survival and affluence, collective identity is also the way social behaviours are made tolerable to the outside world in order to reduce cultural, economic and administrative pressure. Migration is not necessarily a community process, but in all relevant 'ethnic' migration it is a collective organizational phenomenon.

Are Chinese Migrants Different?

My interest in the social organization of Chinese migrants in Italy stems from my recent studies of informal labour organization in urban China. While investigating Chinese labour policy during the reform period, it became clear to me that the 'double track' presently advocated by Chinese policy makers for the domestic labour market in general terms tolerates informality and relies on the autonomous forms of organization of the outsiders in the lowest echelon of the market of economic opportunities (Tomba 2002). Since informality is also a major characteristic of Chinese migrant organization in Italy, a parallel between the organizational patterns of internal and international migration seemed to me the best way to evaluate how powerful and reproducible the specific governance model of 'economic' migration (or migration 'with the capital' *daizi liudong*) of the Chinese in different and international environments was (Tomba 1999).

This parallel – that intrinsically made a case for a cultural explanation of transnational migrant organizations – was made even more evident by the common geographic and cultural origins of the most mobile and business-oriented migrants inside China and in Italy, overwhelmingly from the Wenzhou area (Zhejiang). But are Chinese migrants really so different? Are their reactions, ambitions and forms of subsistence based on different presumptions? Or, rather, are their community lifestyles the result of a more flexible adaptation pattern based on the same practical conjectures as any other migrant's? I have argued elsewhere (Tomba 1999 and 2000) that migrant communities from Zhejiang Province (both within China and abroad) tend to be more selective in their migration projects and to put longer term developmental strategies to work than other migrants, thereby fundamentally contradicting the idea of a 'blind migration' (Ma and Xiang 1998), and differentiating themselves from the strategies of other ethnic groups in Italy and Europe (Tassinari and Tomba 1996). Apparently, for these migrants, 'belonging' to a local network-based community and respecting its developmental hierarchy is subjectively held as the only way to develop individual opportunities within the receiving society. Belonging to a 'home away from home' is a rational (and sometimes bitterly self-imposed) decision and the level of success and wealth of the existing community is a major motivation to take it as a target of the migration project.

The likelihood of overcoming the hardships of migration is, apparently, only seen within the networked community, together with a potential for upward social mobility. This is not to say that the community and its organizational patterns are highly conscious, concerned and caring structures whose only goal is the common good, and where the migrant only finds protection. Quite the contrary seems to be the case: the suffering experienced by migrants in their working histories, their financial dependence on a handful of usurers both back home and in the receiving place, and the high levels of competition within the ethnic community, testify to malpractices that are amplified rather than limited by the 'belonging', and are often made more tolerable only by the peculiar family structure of migration and business. The subjective vision of solidarity networks of the Chinese migrants is much more disenchanted than the one generally offered by the external observers. The community is built around the *tongxiang* identity that is around people coming from the same geographic environment, the county or even the village, rather than the province or the country. Chinese solidarity is an issue complicated by the existence of lower levels of network, based on kinship or common origin, and divided along the lines traditionally defined back in China (the difference between urban and rural dwellers, the boundaries set by different dialects or cultural levels, even family prestige). Although the myth of Chinese solidarity is largely defeated in day-to-day practice, it still exists in the shared interests of the community and in its way of creating and developing a collective identity.

Chinese Migrants in Italy

One of the few books on Chinese migrants in Italy was significantly entitled *Silent Immigration* (Campani et al. 1994). Different from other migrant groups, the Chinese in Italy chose an adaptation pattern that resulted in a narrow and hidden public identity. There are different reasons for this and the pattern seems to have changed rapidly in recent years. Significantly, Chinese migration to Italy targeted not only metropolitan areas. The settlements emerged also in the interstices of declining industrial areas or in small town peripheries, taking advantage of economic environments that were traditionally shaped to protect informal and family economic activities (Becattini 1987). This is the case, for example, in the industrial districts of central Italy, in particular in Tuscany, where small and medium-sized enterprises initially contracted out part of their production processes to Chinese craftsmen (Bortolotti 1992). The ability of the Chinese communities to organize economic activities in the cracks of a declining industrial society or in the niches left empty by the growing affluence of the receiving society was clear in Italy both in the initial years – when the boom of cheap catering in Italian cities led to the mushrooming of Chinese restaurants – and later, when the competitive crises of district-based textile and leather industries favoured the replacement of Italian home-working women with cheaper Chinese manual labour.

Chinese migration to Italy is not a new phenomenon, as Italy was known among Chinese in Europe as a host country even during the years of fascist racial laws of the late 1930s. The first Chinese had arrived mainly from France at the time of the first labour flow from the mainland during the first World War (Ma Mung 2000). Italy was however home to only 260 Chinese in 1955. The large influx of migrants did not begin until the mid-1980s. Between 1982 and 2000, the registered ethnic Chinese population rose from

3,500 to 47,000 (still a small presence if compared with other European countries), and most recent estimates put the Chinese at around 100,000.

The original productive structures of the Chinese community were built around autonomous workshops that based their accumulation strategies on self-exploitation. Almost all the Chinese living in Italy are originally from the Wenzhou area, and an overwhelming majority come from either Qingtian, Rui'an or Wencheng counties or Wenzhou municipality (although in recent years a limited number of Fujianese arrived to increase the complexity of Zhejiang-dominated settlements). This situation, the concentration within a relatively small and intensive economic environment, as well as the comparatively short tradition of migration flows to Italy, greatly enhanced the cohesion of the group and the reproduction of networks of relationship similar to those experienced in the home country. It also increased the exclusion of 'outsiders' (Chinese from other areas). This situation, as much as the necessity to resist the (albeit lower than in larger cities) cultural and administrative pressure, made the expression of a collective identity within the receiving society very difficult in the first phase.

These difficulties derived from both internal and external constraints, but also from the concerns (relevant in the individual choices but also shared within the groups) emerging from the activities undertaken in the 'ethnic economy'. In the initial years of the recent Chinese migration flow to Italy (around the mid-1980s), the construction of an identity aimed at functionally defining the community *vis-à-vis* the receiving society. The relationship with the receiving society was mainly dealt with in a collective manner and aimed at defending the difference, and at minimizing the exposure to local despotism and bureaucratic regulation. The Chinese/Zhejiang migrants thus sought their citizenship-like rights only within the community. Their potential for economic and social upward mobility was expressed within the 'Chinese' environment, rather than directly in the opportunities offered by the receiving society. In dealing with migrant enclaves in China, Solinger (1999) speculates about a quest for new forms of citizenship that are largely mediated by ethnic enclaves. While this applies more traditionally to the strictly administered and segmented Chinese urban society, we may surmise that it remains partly true in environments that are hostile in a different way.

Despite their preference for smaller towns and less competitive production markets, the Chinese in Italy have inclined towards ethnic marriage, family business, and internal labour markets. The productive (rather than commercial as in other European countries, Nyíri 1999) dimension of their economic organization has favoured this inclination. Informal production (long a local tradition also among Italians) needs to hide from local authorities while a commercial network needs visibility in the local market. This situation is changing, albeit on a scale that can barely be traced, mainly in those communities that display a more articulated and mature structure in terms of economic organization, educational and generational composition.

The idea of an 'internal identity' seems to call for a broader conception of 'social and economic citizenship', which can only be achieved through articulated administrative and political contacts with the host society. This quest for rights and citizenship, however, remains a collective rather than an individual effort and is mediated through the economically constructed community. The social demand for rights of the Chinese also evolves from their 'belonging' to established economic and cultural interests, and more from their identification within the category of *huaren* (ethnic Chinese), rather than with the general category of 'migrants'. Chinese rarely team up with other migrants to demand social rights, and they maintain their pride in being 'Chinese' rather than 'migrants' or 'Italians'. As noted by Ceccagno (1998), the Chinese are convinced that the image Italians have of China depends on their own condition and are therefore concerned about the degradation of their status. Long-term migration projects therefore do not necessarily lead to greater integration into the receiving society, but rather into the receiving ethnic network. When I met with a group of Chinese children in a school in Prato, they seemed to be much more impressed by the story that I had once personally seen President Jiang Zemin, than by any other of the questions I asked about their life in Italy. Notwithstanding such anecdotal evidence, it is not only a commonplace, but a relevant mechanism of belonging that Chinese regard themselves more as Chinese than as migrants, and that this determines not only their relationship with local society but also their choices and strategies.

The Chinese seem to utilize an established mechanism of self-identification when reacting to social and bureaucratic pressures, and to demand citizenship not for the individual but for their community and for its specific organizational forms. Especially in Prato, where a number of local public organizations and NGOs mediate the relationship between migrants and locals, the hardship experienced within the Chinese environment is generally a greater part of the individual grievances than the pressures they receive from local authorities. However, their belonging to an, albeit contradictory, network community (with a shared long-term migration project), remains the basis for the individual attainment of participation and of opportunities for economic upward mobility. In fact, these Chinese migrants differ from other migrants, assert their identity in different ways, and organize their interests in original forms. Nonetheless, this difference is puzzling: objectives and aspirations, push factors and rationale of migration are not as different from that of other migrants as is their organizational behaviour. The changing environment and the growing stratification within the community, however, opens a perspective for them to overcome this difference. It may create a space for the most 'specialized' migrants to achieve individual status through better access to services, language skills, labour markets, housing, education, thus potentially leading to the breakdown of the community-based defence, once the advantages to be obtained in the society at large become compatible with those gained within the community. In order to see how this seems to be happening let me introduce the case of Chinese migration in Prato.

The 'Prato Chinese': Interstice Identity

If we accept that migration is a rational decision, that collective migration is the result of economic, organizational and cultural synergies, and that chain migration signals the success of a migration strategy, then Tuscany and Prato have to be considered as the ideal economic cradle for a successful Chinese entrepreneurial community. The economic mechanism based on small and medium scale artisan production, subcontracting labour and house work, which formed the origin of Prato's success in the 1960s and 1970s, is the same that allowed the ethnic Chinese economy to flourish in the city and its outskirts. The city has a long tradition in the textile and leather industry. House workers have contributed to maintaining a low-cost labour environment, but the growing competition, the faster technological cycles and the demand for better compensation with the growth of economic affluence have reduced the profit margins. The Chinese have provided the sector with fresh air thanks to their proverbial ability to reduce labour-reproduction costs by living collectively and working non-stop. They thereby also fomented among locals the belief that labour markets were doped by their presence. Local unemployment was probably more due to general economic constraints than to the arrival of the Chinese, who, otherwise, in fact did 'profit' from the situation by extracting marginal wealth and limiting consumption. This system – that was typically based on the understanding of the economic environment and on the ability to adapt and survive – rapidly evolved, mainly from the beginning of the 1990s, into a more mature system of enterprises. It attracted not only people, but also capital both from Zhejiang and from other settlements of the Chinese diaspora. This movement of capital and people is evident in the dramatic increase of active enterprises owned by Chinese citizens in Prato: from 212 enterprises in 1992 to 1258 in 2000 (Comune di Prato 2001). The high 'death' rate of Chinese-owned enterprises and the predominance of individual (more than 90 per cent in 2000) rather than more complex forms of registered enterprises also testifies to the influence of the changing legal environment. Only in the 1990s did it become possible for non-EU citizens to work as individual entrepreneurs, and this new regulation increased greatly the possibility of attaining formal residence. Since then the entrepreneurial presence of the Chinese in Prato has increased steadily. The great majority – 1,146 active enterprises, according to the official census – are in the textile and clothing industry. Most are solely labour-intensive enterprises, but 48 of them are textile producers, evolving from knitwear to more complex and technological industrial processes such as spinning and weaving. They still overwhelmingly work for Italian subcontractors, but also begin to develop an independent network of commercial activities, both wholesale and retail (81 in 2000 – almost 70 per cent more than in 1999). Together with this commercial dimension a 'tertiary ethnic sector' is also emerging, including translation bureaus, intermediation agencies, real estate agents, public relations, construction, even transport (Comune di Prato 2001).

The growth of commercial activities is also accompanied by a further concentration of the ethnic image of the Chinese in the central area of the city. According to Ma Mung (1996), a similar process experienced in the evolution of the Zhejiang community in Paris reveals a phenomenon of 'territorialization' of identity. The appropriation of specific urban spaces would in this case be one of the forms by which the ethnic identity is being constructed *vis-à-vis* the receiving society. The entrepreneurial principle that leads to concentrated localization of ethnic enterprises gives birth, once the commercial network is extended, to a 'representation' of the Chinese identity. This also seems to apply in Prato (in the central and more commercial area of the city the Chinese are more than half of all foreign migrants and more than five per cent of the entire population), and the phenomenon is also helped by the 'emergence' of underground activities, but it is even clearer if we consider the growing number of Chinese setting up their shops in the centre of major Italian cities (Florence, Milan, Bologna and Naples in particular).

In the last three years, then, the Chinese economy in Prato has undergone a process of consolidation, one that is rather important for stabilizing the industrial potential of the ethnic economy, as only a small number of the active enterprises is older than four years! 720 of them are so-called 'artisan workshops' that typically employ less than 12 workers (a dimension that is characteristic of the extended household business) and enjoy special and privileged fiscal and administrative status thanks to the public regulations on supporting craftsmen activities. A bulk of solid enterprises, active during more than the last four years, is developing (142) and represents a guarantee that the local textile industry will be for a long time solidly influenced by the Chinese presence in the city and its surroundings. The registered Chinese population in Prato was 4,354 in 2000, with a significant increase of registrations in the last year (20 per cent).

Part of this increase is due to regularization (i.e. amnesties by which illegal immigrants are given legal right of abode) and newly born children rather than to new arrivals, and the trend of normalization of the Chinese community is continuing at a stable pace (one reliable estimate, however, put the total Chinese population at about three times that number). Almost 60 per cent of the registered population reached Prato (or was regularized) during the last four years. Two thirds of the 2000 population, also, migrated directly from China, while 20 per cent were born outside China (either in Italy or in other, mainly European, countries). Family migration, as expected, is still a characteristic of the Chinese population: the male/female ratio is close to one and more than half of the population in all age groups is married. This situation of Prato's Chinese economic settlement is indicative of the maturity rapidly reached by these migrants, and it opens the way for a more active role in the administration of the local economy. This role is still very difficult to achieve for practical reasons, including the difficulty of obtaining vital services from local providers such as financial institutions; the absence (despite a growing number of Chinese children attending Italian schools) of an established second generation that can act as go-between; the low level of self-representation of the Chinese, who are only now entering a phase where visibility is a 'plus' rather than a 'minus' in the construction of their relationship with the locality.

Things are, however, changing. The trend is clearly outlined by the transformation of economic activity along a path that goes from unskilled cheap labour towards full-fledged competition with local companies that in some cases give up their activities when faced with stiff competition from Chinese businesses. Chinese are sometimes taking over, but have to change strategies. When production was subcontracted, the only external relationship the Chinese had to maintain was with the contractor; in order to gain access to the local market, now, they are instead forced into the arena of commercial relations, into the much more complicated (economic and 'cultural') framework set by the local markets. Under this condition, looking back at one's own black box is not necessarily, or no longer, an advantage.

Shifting Strategies

Among the signs of these changes are the shifting organizational strategies and the emergence of Chinese private and public discourses. It is a sign of increasing stability and longer-term investment in the receiving territory that migrants prefer to provide their children with local education rather than mainly with that of the original country. Their evaluation of the importance of schooling and of the Italian system of education is fairly good, despite the many difficulties the Italian school faces when confronted with multicultural issues (Cellini et al. 2000). The number of children who join the family after receiving primary education back home is still high, but the opportunities for Chinese children to attend Italian schools are increasing. Chinese presence in Prato's primary and junior middle schools in the central area of the city (where the concentration of Chinese migrants is highest) is booming.

The 'second generation' has not yet reached working age and most of the Wenzhouese that arrived in Italy in the late 1980s have only managed to take their children along in recent years. The community, however, is investing heavily in the education of the children, who will in a few years overcome the lack of communication and interaction between China-born entrepreneurs, local institutions and existing commercial networks (children are already the members of the community that speak the best Italian and are sometimes utilized by the families as interpreters, especially when local authorities are involved). According to the parents who have children of school age, the choice of school is still determined by the availability of specifically Chinese-oriented services. In one middle school in central Prato, for example, one brave, self-taught Chinese-speaking Italian teacher organizes free extra Italian lessons for Chinese students, whereas most of the public schools do not provide similar courses. The school rapidly became a hot spot for Chinese children, most of whom have been brought in from China at school age and therefore need extra training to catch up with children of the same age. In this school children from ethnic Chinese families now constitute over one third of all the pupils. Interviews and research carried out by the local trade unions (Cellini, et al. 2000) also show that, although virtually no Chinese have attended university, the number who complete vocational secondary school is increasing significantly. However, bilingual Chinese remain an exception and most of the children I talked to still believe that Mandarin is more important for their everyday life than Italian.

The increasing interest toward public schools is, however, balanced by a generally low knowledge and use of other administrative structures. Everyone knows about the role and actions of the local police, on whose approval their residence permits depend; but only a small number know and utilize the services provided by official employment agencies. 'Internal' labour markets dominated by informal practices still prevail. Only trade unions and some of the NGOs, providing a less formal intervention in favour of labourers or less bureaucratic help, are considered as useful tools for their daily life. The knowledge of the Italian political reality is rather high if compared with that of other migrants – also thanks to the first published Chinese journals – but the interest is distant and curious. They only deem matters concerning their daily life and those of the Chinese migrant communities, such as new regulations on migration, changes in the fiscal regimes, etc., as interesting.

Participation in collective life outside of the working environment is still limited to the ethnic associations that tend to be led by an established elite, constituted by those who have either more economic power or longer migration experiences. The economic structure of interpersonal and family relations is reproduced within the associations. Their relevance in terms of contracting is still rather low and NGOs and other indigenous organizations can do much better in terms of presenting and obtaining support for initiatives in favour of the Chinese community. Nonetheless, associations are relevant tools for the relationship of the Chinese with their motherland representatives in Italy and for the creation of a cross-national network that produced some initiatives. In Florence, the PRC consulate was recently reactivated, in a new, larger and more functional building where Chinese can obtain all consular services they would otherwise get from the embassy in Rome. This is only one of the signs of the re-established link between Chinese authority and the entrepreneurial community. Chinese in Italy had long been looked at with suspicion by the Chinese authorities, who feared that they hid some sort of political opposition. But a pragmatic attitude toward the protection of Chinese investment abroad (including different agreements on mutually safeguarding investments between Italy and the PRC), has now moved the Chinese diplomats into the field of their compatriots' interests. This is not irrelevant in the apparent emergence of a more restive, assertive and public approach in the affirmation of their rights. This is partly also a consequence of the consolidation of economic interests, of the longer-term migration projects and of the growing stability of economic perspectives of the community. One fourth of the Chinese in

Prato declared in 1999 that their migration project is permanent, while two thirds have no direct plan to go back to China soon.

To turn the present situation to the advantage of this growing percentage of permanent migrants, the protection of their economic 'citizenship' has become necessary. The citizenship I define here is not identified with patterns of individual participation in political, social, or economic life. It is collective rather than individual, as it is not perceived as a tool for social mobility (which remains the major reason for a stable form of belonging to the community); it is a crucial passage in the relationship between the receiving system and informality and a step forward in the appropriation of the territory on the part of the communities; it is an 'ethnic' process in the sense that it devotes a great deal of energy to the affirmation of Chinese grievances ('we Chinese') rather than of social rights for all migrants. Paths of functional correlation between economic changes and identity similar to the one I suggest for Prato have been observed for other Chinese communities both in Asia and in Europe at earlier stages. Paris, which is considered to be the centre from which the major groups of the Zhejiang migrants started their colonization of the European *banlieu*, already experienced, for example, a dramatic growth of commercial activities between the two world wars (Ma Mung 2000). The long tradition of Zhejiangese trade in France and the large ethnic Chinese community of refugees from East Asian countries at war during the 1970s paint, however, a different picture from that of latecomer Italy. Nonetheless, as migration from Zhejiang to France also increased during the 1990s, the transformation observed for that country also reveals a trend toward greater autonomy of the commercial networks and a specific interest by the Chinese enterprises to target local markets directly rather than through indigenous traders (Ma Mung 2000).

In order to pursue their policy of autonomous commercialization, Chinese entrepreneurs from Prato and other central Italian communities also did not hesitate to move to other areas, both within Tuscany – Empoli and Arezzo (Tassinari and Tomba 1996) and to other peri-urban areas in southern Italy. Typically, for example, a group of Prato Chinese moved to the Vesuvian area in the Neapolitan periphery, where informality was the rule rather than the exception and where a flourishing trade of textiles and clothing was experiencing some difficulties due to third world low-price competition. In the Vesuvian belt, since the mid-1990s, the Chinese teamed up with local wholesalers to produce locally. The administrative pressure they found in the area was apparently lower than the one they had experienced in Prato, and the business relationship with local traders also helped them prosper. The small factories multiplied and are now estimated at above 400. Most of them have been registered but still rely on illegal labourers. By the end of the 1990s, the Chinese had established an autonomous retail network reaching into the city centre, and are now developing very fast in the commercial areas near the railway station. While Prato was the right place to start productive activities due to its specialized 'industrial district' qualities, Naples in particular offered an urban market that could be coupled with peripheral production to create a complex and complete economic system. The fact that Chinese from this area were the first to organize a national demonstration against police racism in March 2000 may give support to the argument that increased commercialization requires better visibility, and enhances the awareness of rights. Even more significantly, it is the demand for a right to an ethnic economy that leads to the emergence of a public discourse and of a more assertive stance. Differently from the general demands for individual social and political rights of non-EU migrants in Italy, Chinese demand the protection of their business environment and their rights to expand activities, as these (rather than the relationship to the local economies) remain the setting for their upward social mobility.

Emerging Discourses

One important element of this difficult transformation of social demands is the emergence of a public discourse produced by the Chinese communities, a discourse that remains limited to the Chinese language press and is therefore rather an internal, self-motivating, participatory tool than an instrument of integration or communication with the receiving society. Publishing in Chinese is a relatively new phenomenon in Italy. Three major journals are circulated among the Chinese communities and help to shape a public discourse of the Chinese presence in Italy.

Zhongyi Bao (Chinese Italian Newspaper) is a monthly bilingual publication, funded by an NGO active in Prato and the Florence area. Being edited by a joint Chinese-Italian board, it cannot be considered as a direct expression of the Chinese communities. It is, however, very popular among Chinese (it sells up to 5,000 copies), as it carries what is generally considered to be the most reliable (as it comes partially from Italians) information on regulations, visas, residence permits and on all which has to do with services offered to the Chinese community by local authorities and NGOs. This paper is also the only one to carry, on occasion, articles on sensitive issues in China, such as human rights violations (although mainly in the part of the journal published in Italian).

Xinhua Shibao (New China Times) is a two-year-old journal, under, it seems, the control of the official Xinhua News Agency. Its structure is reminiscent of PRC newspapers. International news is generally taken from Chinese language and mainland newspapers, local news from Italian newspapers, while news concerning the Chinese community in Italy is collected directly by journalists. This newspaper has the strongest nationalist flavour, endorsing the major issues back home (like the Taiwan policy, the reform policy, and China's Olympic pride), but devotes less space to the activity of the Chinese communities. News related to the issue of migration in Italy is generally prominent in the first pages, and attention is also given to local Chinese news (Zhejiang is a major topic, from economic development, via football results, to multiparous births). The number of copies printed for the whole of Italy varies greatly from issue to issue (between 3,000 and 10,000 approximately).

Ouhua Shibao (Europe-China Times) is older than the other newspapers, but still only three years old. It seems to be more deeply rooted in the Chinese community (not only in Italy) and it devotes much more attention to the activities of the communities and associations. It also has a more militant stance on migration-related issues and it is quite outspoken in favour of Chinese migrants *vis-à-vis* Italian authorities and police.

The changing environment and a more supportive attitude of the PRC authorities have contributed to make the discourse produced by these journals more assertive. This has been the result of a more uneasy attitude toward the Italian Government, that materializing, for example, on the occasion of the first public demonstration in Rome of about 2,000 mainly Campania-based[1] PRC migrants. Apparently, the protection granted by the Chinese diplomatic authorities is kept in much higher regard than the possibility of airing criticisms of the PRC, and this opportunity is among the determinants of an increasingly 'patriotic' taste in the Chinese language press. The characteristics of these emerging demands among migrants can be inferred from the articles that Chinese newspapers devoted to the demonstration. Despite differences in emphasis, both daily journals portrayed the demonstration – that brought together representatives from almost all Chinese associations in Italy from north and south – as a path-breaking event. Both published pictures from the public speeches by delegates of the communities, requesting the protection of their investment and of their work. The demonstration followed what leaflets described as 'a wave of unjustified racist deeds, arrest, interrogation and intrusions by the police into houses and factories' (*Ouhua Shibao* 4 April 2000).

This demonstration had also been accompanied in the previous editions of the journals by a series of anecdotes on Chinese unjustly harassed by police mistakes and by the complexity of regulations. The picture that the Chinese community wanted to provide to the outside world was a different one from that of colourful and lively migrants' demonstrations. The protesters carried their slogans in an orderly fashion and wore their best suits. Both journals reported on the 'costs' borne by demonstrators participating. *Ouhua*'s headline stated that the preparation of the event cost more than 47 million Italian Lire, while *Xinhua* emphasized that 1.6 million Lire was necessary to get all demonstrators on a public underground train to reach the demonstration site, and listed the names and donations of all the individual *laoban* (bosses) who had contributed to the fund raising. The exposition of the costs borne, which somehow gave 'face' to the demonstrators, was also intended to create a distance between general migrants and the Chinese. For the first time they had presented themselves as an economic entity (able to fund its public image) in the public space and as interested in establishing a public image *vis-à-vis* the central government and of the authority they are mostly confronted with in the area, the police. Also within the parade, they reproduced a model of public organization based on the *tongxianghui* (groups of same geographic origin)

---

1   Campania is the region of Naples.

to turn it into a political or pressure-oriented tool. Faced with the accusations of behaving improperly and hiding away their economic activities and of constituting an emerging mafia of Naples' *hinterland*, they reacted by displaying their willingness to emerge and claim their right to a peculiar (and quite clearly overexploitative and informal) business form. The emergence of a coherent public discourse remains a necessary requisite of the demand for citizenship. As individuals are still facing family and community constraints and are searching for opportunities for upward mobility within the community, an organization funded by the most successful and earlier migrants begins to take shape.

Conclusions

The idea of this chapter has been to present how migrant identities and the emergence of an insider-vs-outsider rationale (generally seen as a typical feature of Chinese 'identity') are sometimes, in some places and under certain circumstances, also a shared tool of individual and group affirmation within the local, receiving society. This 'identity as a strategy' changes under the pressure of relevant economic transformations of the environment and of the modification of its economic choices. The stories I presented here give evidence of a transforming social, political and economic identity affirmed through the collective. This does not mean that individual, family or small interest groups are irrelevant in the formation of a collective identity, but it does mean that 'hidden' or 'open' options are present and rationally undertaken by the Chinese in Italy, according to the necessities imposed by both internal and external constraints. This is due to reasons that have been observed in many other cases of Chinese migrant communities. One is surely the existence of kinship, family and local (*tongxiang*) networks, where some characteristics recur regularly. According to Fei Xiaotong they would be characterized by discontinuity, hierarchical and dyadic ties (of Confucian memory), uprightness, flexible morality, and moving boundaries (Fei Xiaotong 1992). Fei's cultural explanation does not contrast with the organisational understanding presented here: it emphasizes, for example, that there is no distinction, within the network, between the fundamental nature of the relationships (kinship or business, friendship or shared interests).

In the case presented here, the rationale of the network in shifting the fundamentals of identity and the demand for rights and citizenship is built around its ability to create opportunities for its members. The coherence they try to reach relies on the ability to exploit their internal resources (especially labour) despite the administrative pressure. To make a complex picture simple, we could say that when the advantage of a 'black box' organization is higher, the network's pressure toward informality and invisibility is highest, and the ability of the individuals to find alternative ways of making a living is at a minimum. However, when the network is faced with the problem of economic expansion, social entropy and organizational complexity, the 'black box' opens toward the external world. This does not lead to the break-up of the community. Quite the contrary, and even more so in an environment of limited cultural contacts with the receiving society, it searches for a collective, visible and positive identity in the face of other players (local markets, service providers, authorities). This assumption is one that accepts that there is a wisdom in the decision to migrate and to accept the self-imposed harshness, exploitation and informal hierarchy related to the migration experience. However it does not explain how this (presently only envisaged) process can be turned into a useful tool for the construction of a multicultural society and for the affirmation of Chinese social demands. Mainly because of the linguistic peculiarity of the Chinese, it takes much more time and is much more difficult for these migrants to penetrate the local society and to use it to their advantage than for migrants from English, French or Spanish-speaking countries (as is the case for the largest part of non-EU migrants to Italy).

A second generation in the making is therefore an important element of the evolution of an assertive identity. Also, Chinese migration – due to its family structure – makes the migrants' demand for public services much more complex than in other typical cases, where migration is individual (in Italy this is the case of north and central African migrant groups). These have long been provided within the communities, but a progressive formalization will probably create demands for Chinese-oriented services and will therefore make a more stable relationship with the host authorities necessary. The same thing could be said about the increasing complexity of the enterprise system. The increase in the number of enterprises not only reveals a more mature ethnic economy, but also envisages a more structured relationship with the local services (from financial to medical, transport, labour bureaus, etc.). Finally, the competitive advantage of cheap labour (still by far the most relevant 'plus' enjoyed by ethnic Chinese enterprises) is probably going to be insufficient to guarantee the increasing affluence of the shop-owners, and the challenges for Chinese businesses will come from the expansion into trading, with the consequences already mentioned. The tools for an 'open and collective' identity will most likely be the associations, whose number is growing in Italy but whose scope is still limited to internal organization. Another important element in the definition of a public demand is the support of the PRC authority that, especially after the entry of China into the WTO, is very likely to act resolutely in favour of its compatriots' investment.

Works Cited

Becattini, Giacomo (1987) 'Riflessioni sullo sviluppo socio-economico della Toscana', in Giorgio Mori (ed.), *La Toscana, Storia d'Italia. Le Regioni dall Unità a oggi*. Torino: Einaudi.

Bortolotti, Franco (1992) *Un distretto etnico? Le imprese cinesi della via Pistoiese*. Firenze: Istituto di Ricerca Economica e Sociale (IRES) Toscana.

Campani, Giovanna, Francesco Carchedi, and Alberto Tassinari (eds) (1994) *L'immigrazione silenziosa. Le comunità cinesi in Italia*. Turin: Fondazione Giovanni Agnelli.

Ceccagno, Antonella (1998) *Cinesi d'Italia. Storie in bilico tra due culture*. Rome: Manifesto Libri.

Cellini, Erika, Roberto Fideli and Roberto Pirami (2000) 'Multiculturalità e integrazione: primi risultati di una Ricerca sui Cinesi a Prato'. Paper presented to the Seminar on *Multicultural Integration*, Prato.

Comune di Prato, Centro Ricerche e Servizi per l'Immigrazione (2001) 'Analisi dei dati sulla popolazione immigrata'. Comune di Prato.

Farina, Patrizia et al. (eds) (1997) *Cina a Milano: famiglie, ambienti e lavori della popolazione cinese a Milano*. Milano: Associazione Interessi Metropolitani, Abitare Segesta.

Fei Xiaotong (1992) *From the Soil: The Foundation of Chinese Society*. Berkeley, Cal.: University of California Press.

Ma, Laurence J. C. and Xiang Biao (1998) 'Native Place, Migration and the Emergence of Peasant Enclaves in Beijing'. *The China Quarterly*, 155 (September) 546-581.

Ma Mung, Emmanuel (1996) 'Territorializzazione commerciale delle identit: i Cinesi a Parigi'. *La Critica Sociologica* 117, 64-77.

Ma Mung, Emmanuel (2000) *La diaspora Chinoise. Geographie d'une migration*. Paris: Oprhys.

Nyíri, Pál (1999) 'Chinese Organization in Hungary, 1989-1996: A Case Study in PRC Oriented Community Politics Overseas', in Frank Pieke and Hein Mallee (eds), *Internal and International Migration: Chinese Perspectives*. Richmond, Surrey: Curzon Press.

Rapport, Nigel and Andrew Dawson (eds) (1998) *Migrants of Identity: Perception of Home in a World of Movement*. Oxford: Berg.

Solinger, Dorothy J. (1999) *Contesting Citizenship in Urban China: Peasant Migrants, the State and the Logic of the Market*. Berkeley: University of California Press.

Tassinari, Alberto and Luigi Tomba (1996) 'Zhejiang-Pechino, Zhejiang-Firenze: due esperienze migratorie a confronto'. *La Critica Sociologica* 117, 27-38.

Tomba, Luigi (1999) 'Exporting the "Wenzhou Model" to Beijing and Florence: Labour and Economic Organization in Two Migrant Communities', in Frank Pieke and Hein Mallee (eds), *Internal and International Migration: Chinese Perspectives*. Richmond, Surrey: Curzon Press.

Tomba, Luigi (2002) *Paradoxes of Labour Reform: Chinese Labour Discourse and Urban Labour under Reform*. Richmond, Surrey: Curzon Press.

Chapter 6

Intermarriage and the Construction of Ethnic Identity: European Overseas Chinese Community Leaders' Marriage Ideals

Xiujing Liang

Introduction

When leaders of the European overseas Chinese community talk about the next generation's marriage, their prime concern is with the ethnic identity or race issue, that is to say whether one should marry a Chinese or a Westerner. The ideals they express often do not reflect their own practice or the spouse selection of their children, grandchildren or brothers and sisters. Neither do they necessarily coincide with the ideals of other (ordinary) overseas Chinese or their marriage behaviour. This chapter will examine the overseas Chinese leaders' identification structure by looking at how they talk about the next generation's marriage (mainly intermarriage) in two sets of interviews; their ideals, rationalizations, reasoning and anecdotes may illuminate an important aspect of their ethnic identity construction.[1] The aim of the analysis is to examine how the interviewees' marriage ideals are integrated in their discourse on ethnic and national belonging.

---

1   The analysis is based on two sets of interviews. One set of 25 structured interviews included a section exploring their views on the next generation's marriage, and another set of 65 semi-structured and open interviews included responses on intermarriage. All of the 25 interviews were with leaders (chairmen or vice-chairmen and -women) in pan-European overseas Chinese associations. Most of the 65 interviews were with leaders in overseas Chinese associations in European countries or spanning Europe. I will also use the discourse underlying 59 marriage announcements placed as advertisements in *Ouzhou Shibao-Nouvelles d'Europe* (Paris) between 1 January 1997 and 31 January 2000 to further illustrate the findings.

Intermarriage: What is in the Concept?

How important are the community leaders' marriage ideals for their ethnic identity? This issue aroused my interest when I discovered that their formulations on marriage focused on intermarriage. Why do they mind intermarriage? As overseas Chinese in Europe integrating with the host society, one might have expected them to regard intermarriage as a matter of course. However, the matter was sensitive. While they have the will to integrate with host society,[2] they do not welcome intermarriage. How can their discourse contain such a contradiction? Which factors influence their discourse about intermarriage and ethnic identity? What does 'intermarriage' mean? The term itself may reveal some possible explanation. It is, in fact, one of many terms for similar phenomena, like 'intermarriage', 'mixed marriage', 'interracial marriage', and 'exogamy'. The term normally signifies marriage across an ethnic boundary, where the spouses belong to different groups. Why this type of terminology? Why is it important to conceptualize marriage across ethnic groups? Why is the ethnic background of spouses considered as more than individual differences between two people? Why is there a presumption that ethnicity determines individual identity when it comes to marriage? Merton (1976) believes that intermarriage reflects social structures. The social boundary divides people into different groups, and limits their interaction across the boundary. When a marriage occurs between partners from different social groups it is considered special and referred to as 'intermarriage', 'mixed marriage' or 'interracial marriage'. These terms are not very clear, as their meaning depends on the social context and personal judgement. To make this point, Rosemary Breger and Rosanna Hill (1998) raised a question: if a Jew from Scotland marries a Jew from New York, is it an intermarriage or not? On the one hand, both are Jews, so they belong to the same ethnic group; on the other hand, however, their lifestyles diverge, and the different expectations of the mother and mother-in-law in such a marriage may wreck it.

If a member of an Anglican congregation in England marries a Catholic, it is no longer considered an intermarriage, while a marriage between a Protestant and Catholic in Northern Ireland would be. Historically, partners belonging to different races and religious communities were not allowed to marry, and some states also impose restrictions on the marriage of their citizens with non-citizens. Race segregation in the USA and South Africa produced such laws, and in particular orthodox Jewish communities and the Catholic Church for long periods banned marriage with partners who did not belong to one's own religion. In many multiethnic states (Singapore, Malaysia, Indonesia, etc.), intermarriage is an issue of much public policy and/or debate. In federal states in the USA where interracial marriages were illegal into the 1960s, they have become a measure of the success of racial integration.

---

2   On leadership discourse about 'integration', see Liang 2001a, pp. 172-173.

Intermarriage, therefore, seems to be an expression of how state and society negotiate the boundaries of social groups. If that is so, how are those boundaries created and upheld? Who imposes them? Why would individuals take them into account? It may be obvious that the boundaries shift over time, and that they are cast differently in different situations. It is also the case that the ethnic affiliation is only one among many qualities of an individual. Maybe, as Michèle Lamont (1992) points out, the symbolic boundaries between social groups are signals with which members of those groups indicate their membership. Sharing the evaluation of another person's (and by expansion, another group's) qualities is important for defining one's own status. The shared taste and cultural preferences one is raised in help define one's social position, as Bourdieu has pointed out in his work about taste as a social distinction (from which Lamont gains much inspiration). Attempts to cross the social boundary by an individual may trigger subtle mechanisms of exclusion. Upstarts, the new rich, class traitors and race minglers may in the collective judgement of their (former?) social group be regarded as immoral or dishonest, or as phoneys. Exclusion, however, is not, in the view of Lamont, a collective act, but an unintended consequence of aggregate behaviour within the upper middle class. The value systems that judge people of the 'other side' as dishonest, immoral, vulgar, uneducated or uncultured, however, are fluid, for the evaluations are situational and vested in individuals. It may seem difficult to transpose Lamont's findings to a discussion of overseas Chinese and the issue of intermarriage. However, as we will see, the mechanisms of exclusion are not that dissimilar. Is the problem of Chinese ethnicity similar to the issue of belonging to a social class defined by tastes and shared judgements? Perhaps there is a difference. For where the American men in Lamont's sample seemed to treasure more materialistic norms in their judgement, French men tended to use culture as a mark of distinction. We will observe that overseas Chinese leaders apply a range of competing considerations in their judgement, spanning cultural, family and material norms.

Marriage Ideals of Chinese Community Leaders

Key words signifying 'spouse' and 'marriage' in the 25 interviews collocate significantly with expressions for 'roots', 'integration', 'identification', 'culture', 'habit', 'family ideal', 'race', 'discrimination', 'community norms', and with antonymic pairs like 'tradition/openness' and 'Eastern/Western habits or lifestyles'. The data, therefore, led me to structure my exploration as follows: (1) marriage ideals and opinions on roots, integration, identification and the Chinese culture; (2) marriage values, lifestyle, family ideals and the community norms; (3) marriage ideals and issues of race and discrimination.

Roots, Integration, Identification and Chinese Culture

Seventeen of the 25 interviewees said that their ideal was that their children would marry a Chinese or, more generally, that people of the next generation would do so. Only four did not mind if their children were to marry a Westerner. They gave two main reasons. One was past experience. They said most mixed marriages of the past generation overseas Chinese migrants to Europe had been unsuccessful, so they wanted to avoid the next generation repeating the mistake. A famous Chinese leader in Italy is one example referred to; he had married an Italian lady and in his old days ended up in an unhappy situation. Compared with other leaders in Italy, who in their old age are blissfully surrounded by their caring families, sons and grandsons, he was alone and rejected (Int57). In this sense, 'to marry a Westerner' is almost synonymous with 'marriage failure'. The other reason was cultural difference. The Chinese share the same culture, customs and habits, so they can get on more easily. If one marries a Westerner who has a different culture and so on, it is very difficult to handle the two cultures within the family. One interviewee thought that it hurts if one has to give up one's own habits to accommodate the other. If it hurts, he argued, what's the point of marrying? (Leader24) The next generation's marriage is linked to Chinese culture issues. Chinese language schools and Chinese culture promotion in the overseas Chinese associations are given a role in partner selection. One said:

> I have four children. Now they have all grown up. [They] never thought of finding German girlfriends. So far, I think the Chinese language school is very useful for this purpose. I see their classmates make friends with each other now. I think many pupils in the Chinese language school will later marry each other. This has often happened (Int14-Yang).

One interviewee (Leader15) said that his son had originally identified himself as British, but after participating in a 'national salvation tour' to Taiwan, he identified himself as Chinese when he came back to England. Another (Leader18) said that when his son took part in the Chinese community activities, he exchanged his Western for a Chinese girlfriend. Interviewees agree that overseas Chinese community activities are useful for helping overseas Chinese youths to identity themselves as Chinese and to find a Chinese partner.

One interviewee said,

> As for us, coming from Kampuchea, generally speaking, all the overseas Chinese youths don't marry foreigners. Sometime [if you] can't find [a Chinese] here, [you] would like to take an aeroplane to Kampuchea [to find a Chinese spouse] (Int14-Chan).

Some interviewees said they would not intervene in their children's marriage, but would let them make their own decision; these interviewees only had a daughter, their children had already married a Westerner, or their children were still young.

Some said that they could more easily tolerate that a woman married a Westerner than that a man did so. Why? The explanation is:

> If a girl marries a foreigner, it is better. If [a man] marries a foreign girl, it means the wife is a foreigner; [the Chinese ethnicity] will be eliminated, because the mother's influence is greater than the father's. ...So basically, I do not hope for a mixed marriage (Leader18).

The worry of being assimilated is a crucial point. When the interviewees talked about the Chinese language education and cultural promotion, the point was not only to create a social network for young overseas Chinese, but also to provide opportunities for them to maintain Chinese culture, in order to identity themselves as Chinese.

> Like me, I could invite a teacher to teach him at home, but I did not do so. I pushed him here (the Chinese language school). My main target is not to let him study but to make friends [with Chinese], for our Chinese is not easy to learn. You learn four hours a week, and then you [forget it], you can only learn a small bit. [My] main target is to let him make friends. Chinese get together, when time goes by, his mind will absorb Chinese culture. So when he grows up, he will always remember his ancestors are Chinese (Int14-Chan).

Some interviewees said they worried that the next generation would be assimilated and lose their Chinese identity (e.g. Leader25).

The marriage opinions are also linked with the identity and integration issues, as well as with 'roots'. The question 'does the next generation's marriage intention influence their identity?' evoked affirmative answers. That is why they hope that their children do not marry non-Chinese. They regard the self-identification of young Chinese as an important element of their choice of spouse. If one is very Chinese, one may marry a Chinese, and if one is very occidental, one may marry a Westerner (Leader04). One thinks that if a foreigner wants to marry a Chinese woman it must be because she has Chinese culture and lifestyle (Leader04).

Most interviewees thought that the first overseas Chinese generation tended to 'sink their roots in foreign soil' because the next generation is married in the host country (Leader03, Leader23). The next generation will not 'return to the native soil', but 'sink the roots in the host country', especially if they marry a foreigner (Leader03). If a Chinese marries a Westerner, the Chinese is more likely to integrate with Western society, and give up the Chinese lifestyle, because it is common for Chinese always to suit others (Leader05). To part with the Chinese and marry a local French wife, may offer an opportunity to integrate into the host society. The worry is not about failure to integrate, but whether integration leads to the loss of their mother tongue (Leader08). One said his two children, a son and a daughter, married Westerners, 'I said, that is due to integration. That's for sure' (Int60). He regards intermarriage as an outcome of integration.

Marriage thus represents a worry among leaders of overseas Chinese associations that the Chinese assimilate and lose their culture.

Lifestyle, Family Ideal and Community Norms

The leaders' marriage opinions are mixed with their family ideal and lifestyle. One regards the personal lifestyle as a main reason to decide whether intermarriage is successful or not. If one wants to play cards with co-ethnic friends and the wife disapproves, the intermarriage may fail (Leader01).

Food is taken as a symbol of cultural difference. They prefer Chinese food and do not accept Western food. Language and attitudes to work are also issues. Most first generation overseas Chinese do not know European languages or have very poor fluency. They find it difficult to talk with Western family members and they feel uncomfortable with Westerners as members of their family. Some overseas Chinese said they could not accept a Western daughter-in-law or son-in-law because of the language. Other conflicts arise from attitudes to work. Some young overseas Chinese men divorce their Western wives because she objects to the Chinese husband working long hours and not spending enough time with her. Many overseas Chinese work in the catering business, with long working hours and hard work, and also need the family members to help. The Chinese do not think that a Westerner can do that.

Attitudes to the family also cause conflict. Many Chinese parents want their children to respect them, take care of them when they are old. They do not think a Westerner can do that. They think that in Western society, children have a greater distance to their parents especially after they have married. They do not expect their own children to behave like that.

The interviewees' understanding of the content of 'Chinese culture' mainly focused on three points: Chinese language, Chinese food and family norms. These three points are all linked with the next generation's marriage issue. In the interview material, the concept of 'family duty' (*xiao* – often translated as 'filial piety') is closely related to marriage. Some interviewees expect their children to continue to be 'dutiful' after they are married. If they fail to, it is because they have not chosen a good spouse (Leader02). If they have a Western spouse, it is believed to be the result of intermarriage. If the spouse is Chinese, it is thought to be because the young Chinese is too influenced by Western society, and has lost Chinese culture. Some interviewees think the parents should live with their married children (Leader02, Leader04). Some interviewees admitted they were being 'traditional' (*chuantong*) when they hoped their children would marry a Chinese.

One criticized the general objection to intermarriage with reference to his younger brother's marriage. His brother, younger by fifteen years, has been like a son to him. When his brother was going to marry a Westerner and asked his opinion, he asked the brother: are you sure? His brother gave an affirmative answer, so he agreed. He agreed for two reasons: (1) if he did not agree to the marriage, his brother may turn against him, breaking their brotherly affection, or doing something stupid; (2) he had to acknowledge that his brother is independent and has his own life, so he cannot interfere when his brother thinks it is right. Now the marriage has turned out well. To be able to take care of the family, the wife worked in a night-time nursery and did not take a daytime job (Leader06). This interviewee used this example to prove that a Western wife may be good and obey Chinese family virtues. Whether the spouse is Chinese or not, the measure of marital success is the maintenance of Chinese family values.

Do Chinese community norms also influence their members' marriage ideal? One interviewee talking about 'face' in the European overseas Chinese community, said:

> Many Chinese think their children must marry a Chinese. If their child found a white or differently coloured spouse, they would suddenly get into a rage, thinking they have lost face, it is totally unacceptable to them, they may even kill him/her. ...Many overseas Chinese are sensitive on this issue. They are too narrow-minded, so they cannot accept that their children intermarry or to take their mixed-blood grandchildren outside, seeing that as loss of face (Leader06).

Another said:

> I bring my little granddaughter outside, (she) always has a Chinese appearance. I bring her to China. If you take a half[-blooded] one along, they'll say, O, this hybrid. It doesn't sound nice does it? If they don't say it, they think it (Leader13).

Mixed marriages apparently infringe on the community norms, and these interviewees have internalized these norms.

The community concern with marriage is eminently illustrated by the habit of French overseas Chinese leaders to place marriage announcements in *Ouzhou Shibao – Nouvelles d'Europe*.[3] The announcements are placed by organizations (35 out of 59), companies (15 out of 59), or individuals (18 out of 59).[4] Individuals in most cases placed announcements in lieu of organizations or companies, and the format was to congratulate a leader of an organization with the marriage of his or her son or daughter.

The placement of marriage announcements (and their size and relative prominence) signals status in the community. The stylized and conventional format of these announcements may give an impression of marriage norms. The announcements concerned 39 different marriages, 25 congratulating with the son's marriage and 15 congratulating with the daughter's marriage. The sample is too small for us to be greatly concerned with the gender bias (it may be that a son's marriage is viewed as more significant than a daughter's, but it may just as well be

---

3   I have selected all the 59 marriage announcements that were placed in the period 1 January 1997-31 January 2000.

4   Eight of the advertisements were jointly placed by individuals and companies. The company category includes a substantial number placed by the newspaper itself.

a reflection of the accidental gender distribution of leaders' children who actually married in the period). In 74 per cent of the announcements of sons' marriages, the spouse was named, while this was only the case in 29 per cent of the announcements of daughters' marriages. In five cases of those where the spouse was named, he or she was non-Chinese (in one case Japanese). This trend of naming the spouse of the son, but not of the daughter, may indicate the habit of seeing the daughter as leaving the family, while the daughter-in-law enters the family. Among the congratulatory formulae used in the 20 different announcements of daughters' marriages, nine were 'the joy of finding home' (*yu gui zhi xi*), one was 'the celebration of finding home' (*yu gui zhi qing*), two were 'the celebration of leaving the chamber' (i.e. the parental home) (*chu ge zhi qing*), one was 'the joy of leaving the chamber' (*chu ge zhi xi*), while seven were gender-neutral. In addition to the congratulatory formulae, the announcements also contained a four- or eight-character well-wishing formula (in one case a poem), in 21 cases either 'eminent bond overseas' or 'eternal union of matching hearts'. Some of the well-wishing formulae indicated the gender role of the bride 'suitable for home and family', 'suitable for family and home', 'the door [of the in-law family] greets the bride', 'the bride goes to her home' and so on. Some reflected male-female complementarity, like 'a talented groom and a beautiful bride' and 'the [mythical male bird] and the phoenix in harmony'. Even though these ornamental formulae in most cases are devoid of any specific meaning, are used routinely and are incomprehensible to many of those who use them, they reflect a subliminal value system of complementary and fixed male and female roles. The one poem in the collection was:

> When sons and grandsons fill the ancestral hall, everything prospers. Respecting neighbours and kith and kin at peace. Continuing ancestral trades, sons inherit their fathers, strengthen their business and bring glory to their home.

This pastiche of lineage life (and a shrewd pun on the forenames of father and son) depicts a Confucian idyll of harmony and patrilinear descent. Even if the reality of life in France does not fulfil such dreams, it exists in the public ritual of marriage announcements. Although we do not know how many announcements refrain from naming the spouse because he or she is a non-Chinese, the ritual does not rely on the notion of endogamy. The well-wishing and congratulatory formulae in a couple of cases were manipulated to celebrate the non-Chinese bride or groom, like 'Eminent Sino-Japanese Bond'. What counts is the conformity with a constructed Confucian courtesy, congratulating the patriarch with his son or daughter's marriage, painting the picture of a stereotyped married life. The public role of the leader must be matched with his role as a patriarch. The size and number of announcements attached to any one marriage were a direct indication of social prowess. The top score was gained by the marriage of the youngest son of one of the most influential leaders; this marriage attracted six announcements, totalling 1.5 broadsheet pages (at a cost of somewhere between 15,000 and 20,000 FFR).

The second was gained by the marriage of another senior and influential leader's third son; this marriage attracted three announcements, of which one was a full broadsheet page, covering 1.3 broadsheet pages (at a similar cost).

It is understandable that 'miscegenation' and 'mixed marriages' may fit awkwardly into this social pattern, and may lead to loss of face.

Four leaders had married Western ladies. One's wife had died, one was divorced from his wife, and two of them lived with their wives and children. When I, in the course of the interviews, asked them about mixed marriages, they were all too ashamed to mention it. Even though they had Western wives, they had internalized the values of the community.

The interviewees seem to differ from most people in their marriage values. They did not talk about the matching of social and economic conditions, but focused on race, on the merits and demerits of marrying a Chinese or a Westerner. But these issues are mixed with each other:

Normally, the girls born and grown up here (in Europe) set high demands. So many girls marry late and cannot find a spouse. Because their demands are too high, they cannot easily find a husband. In Germany, and also in Paris, all face this problem. Some men find it difficult to marry a local overseas Chinese kid, so [they] prefer to go to Kampuchea [to marry] an overseas Chinese. [The overseas Chinese in Kampuchea] are willing to come to [Europe]. It is easy [to handle the marriage] (Int14-Chan).

The young men all go to Wenzhou to marry a wife. The girls are the same, go to Wenzhou to find a husband. Why can't [the young overseas Chinese] marry in a same country? Because they fancy different things (Int14).

Now there are more choices [for the young overseas Chinese]. Many of them go to their own country to find one. It also depends on the environment. If they get to know each other while they study together, or if they work in a restaurant, then it happens all by itself *(shunli chengzhang)*. It depends on the environment (Int14-Liang).

The Chinese traditional marriage values as expressed in 'be well-matched in social and economic status for marriage' *(mendang hudui)* and 'the man is clever and the woman is beautiful' *(nancai nümao)* seem to exist among the European overseas community, but have a specific significance. First, the 'be well-matched in social and economic status for marriage' means that the higher perceived status as overseas Chinese in Europe provides them with a better choice of spouses in China or Indochina. Not only is the number of potential spouses larger, but their own status means that spouses of a higher perceived quality (beauty, social status, age, working ability and so on) can be considered. Second, the virtues of the man are skills, knowledge and ability, while the woman must be beautiful. A 'vicious circle' has begun, where overseas Chinese men cannot aspire to overseas Chinese women and feel that they can have a better choice of more beautiful and younger women in China. The overseas Chinese women push out marriage, and due to the insufficient supply of suitable overseas Chinese spouses, they go back to China to marry.

There is a general claim that marriage with non-Chinese is on the decrease, 'because now it is easier to go home by aeroplane. At the same time there are many overseas Chinese [in Europe], so it is easier to find a spouse than before. In the past more [overseas Chinese] married a foreigner. Now [it] is less' (Int14-Man). Easier travel may be an important reason. However, overseas Chinese in Europe have gained status in China, and marriage migration has become a matter of status enhancement.

Race and Discrimination

Race and discrimination issues also relate to marriage. When the interviewees told about the earlier generation's mixed marriages, they mentioned that in the Second World War, many Western women preferred to live with Chinese men, because they could feed them. After the War, many of these women left them. Such anecdotes reflect a perception of racial discrimination: Western women cannot respect Chinese men, but are keen to use them. Interviewees talking about discrimination also gave another example: during the early period of Chinese migration to Europe, if a Chinese man walked in the street with his Western girlfriend or wife, he may be hit, attacked or abused; racial discrimination is considered an important part of the marriage issue (Int01). Interviewees married to a Westerner felt discriminated against by local people in Europe (Leader07). Some of them had very poor local language skills, but they preferred not to have their Western wife help them handle their business in the host country. One said that if he let his wife help him, local government officials would look down upon him and they may deliberately cause him trouble (Int15-Liang). Having their non-Chinese wives help them would also have caused loss of face *vis-à-vis* other Chinese, so racism came from two sides.

One interviewee said that he did not like Westerners, so he did not welcome intermarriage. But when he argued that the Chinese experience less discrimination than before, he said that the old overseas Chinese found it difficult to marry Western ladies, only women who had been prostitutes or widows would marry them. Now the young Western women with an education would marry Chinese men. That means that the Chinese status has risen (Leader14). He took intermarriage to symbolize the level of discrimination and the status of the overseas Chinese in the host country, and at the same time rejected it.

Constructing Belonging

Analyzing the interview data, I found that many issues are linked. The ideals of marriage among the overseas Chinese leaders, of course, were not one body of shared opinions and dogma, but were multidimensional and pointed in several directions. The ideals varied within a broader pattern of shared perceptions. While the individual was arguing within his or her own experience, the ideals expressed were premised on shared norms and perceptions.

At a fundamental level, the overseas Chinese community leader is a public person and is believed to embody and interpret 'Chinese values' (whatever they may be). His or her normative behaviour and opinions were likely to represent a will to sustain Chinese culture.

We have seen that aversion to assimilate was directly linked with the marriage issue, that inculcating Chinese values and teaching Chinese language to Chinese children served not only as a ploy to make them marry Chinese, but also as an instrument to protect family norms. 'Family duty', while originally a Confucian concept, is used casually to describe how a son should take care of his father in his old age. Superficial references to Confucian ideas are used to stereotype the role of the sexes and as emblems of a perfect world.

Foreign spouses can be included in this norm-set, but these are generally regarded as exceptional cases that deserve separate mention.

The dominant issue of the discourse is the preservation of Chinese culture. From this it follows that the marriage issue is set in a perspective of opposing norms: Western culture and lifestyle are opposed to Chinese culture and lifestyle, and 'family duty' is absent among Westerners. These norms are expressed in an 'us-them' dichotomy, using stereotyping.

Some of those who hold these views refer to themselves as 'conservative' (*baoshou*) or 'traditional' (*chuantong*) and imply that the opposite attitudes are 'liberal' (*kaifang*). Although the use of 'traditional' and 'conservative' suggests a different choice, an equally valid alternative, in reality it does not negate the main discourse. The conservative, traditional view is premised on the evaluation by the Chinese community leaders of marriage behaviour from the perspective of the Chinese/Western division. The criteria for evaluation are set by the discourse.

Success is measured by the fulfilment of Chinese cultural norms and family values. The discourse by default acclaims Chinese-Chinese marriages, as they are believed to fulfil these norms. If they do not, it is due to second generation assimilation and erosion of Chinese cultural knowledge.

The discourse discourages mixed marriages, as it believes them to fail. However, the discourse acclaims mixed marriages, as long as they fulfil Chinese norms. If they fail as marriages or do not fulfil Chinese norms, they prove the general inadequacy of mixed marriages.

If, hypothetically, a Chinese marries a foreigner and the marriage is a success by other standards than those of Chinese cultural norms and family values, and gains the spouses high status by norms other than those of the Chinese community, the marriage would probably be regarded as a failure, as it represents undue assimilation. Within the discourse it may be treated as an anomaly (with reference to individual circumstances that appear unusual), accepting some degree of success.

Social Status and Identity Construction

The value systems defining social status and identity construction come out well in the interviews. The mechanisms of exclusion are strong, and there is a clear sense of a division between 'us' and 'them'. In the following sections I will draw together some conclusions about the boundaries between the Chinese and other groups, and about how the individual negotiates boundary positions.

Boundaries and Groups

While the leaders talking about intermarriage seem convinced of the absolute and firm boundary between 'us' and 'them', their formulations reveal the changeable and shifting norms they apply.

Within the leadership discourse, what kind of marriage is regarded as 'internal' or 'welcome' and 'external' or 'unwelcome' depends on the particular context.

Generally speaking, the leaders do mind intermarriage, but some regard intermarriage with other Asians as better than with Westerners (i.e. white people). In the case of one leader (Leader13) already mentioned, he rejected intermarriage (with white people), because he did not want his grandchild to be mixed (in racial appearance), for it would cause him to lose face. Therefore, if the Chinese could not marry another Chinese, he preferred intermarriage with other Asian ethnic groups. Some did not express themselves in such blunt racial terms, but explained that other Asian ethnic groups are closer to the Chinese than the Westerners are, because their culture, food, habits and so on are similar to Chinese (Int51).

The reverse of this argument is where the interviewees noted cultural similarity across the race boundary. For example, several overseas Chinese leaders in Italy mentioned that Italian family norms are similar to Chinese family norms, such as the relationship between parents and children, as well as family cohesion (Int53). But they raised this with reference to social interaction with the host society, and totally unrelated to the issue of intermarriage.

We have seen how language is used both as an argument against intermarriage (because it blocks interaction within families) and as a tool to avoid intermarriage (by priming the young to socialize among Chinese in Chinese language schools). The argument is, when we look at the reality, rather vacuous. Chinese children may get to know each other in Chinese language schools, but they tend to speak the local European language with each other. Second or third generation Chinese marrying each other rarely speak Chinese with each other; they may not be able to speak it, or they do not use it as their first language.

I met several second generation Chinese in Germany, born and raised in Holland and now doing business in Germany. They married Chinese partners, but do not speak Chinese with their wives. They speak Dutch with each other, because they grew up in Holland and got used to speaking Dutch, although they also know Chinese. One told me that when they had a son, they decided to speak Chinese with him, because they wanted him to learn some Chinese, but between themselves, they feel unaccustomed to speaking Chinese (Int16). One leader in Italy told me that he was glad his children all married Chinese. When I asked him which language their children speak at home, he said: 'they couldn't speak the dialect well, they mainly speak Dutch', because they all grew up in Holland (Int56).

Food is a symbolic cultural difference between Chinese and Westerners, as well as a reason against intermarriage. But do all the overseas Chinese in Europe prefer Chinese food? What about the young Chinese? One leader in Denmark complained that young Chinese do not like Chinese food anymore, they 'only like burger, burger and burger' (Int10). One secretary in a French overseas Chinese community association complained that his family cuisine has become so complicated now, they cook Chinese dishes for themselves and Western food for their children, because the children do not eat the Chinese food. When I did the interviews, many leaders invited me for lunch. After lunch, they always asked me: 'would you like a cup of coffee?' When I said no, they still ordered the coffee for themselves, they explained they had become used to it. Why not tea, I thought; doesn't tea belong to Chinese culture? When I summarized the data from the interviews, the opinions on intermarriage began to form a coherent structure, but when I related the opinions to other expressions of ethnic identity, conflicting patterns became evident.

The interviewees tended not to distinguish between Chinese; most hope their children marry a Chinese, and do not mind which sub-ethnic group the spouse belongs to (Int56). Some leaders in Liverpool said the Toysanese did not marry the Hakkas in the past, they always went back to Taishan (or Hong Kong) to find a Toysanese spouse. But now, if only the Chinese marry Chinese, the parents think it is good enough (Int63). In terms of marriage, sub-ethnic group boundaries among the overseas Chinese community are invisible, but they are strongly present when they talk about their native place, fellow villagers, and native place associations (Liang 2001b).

The context or main theme often determines shifts in opinion, like in the case of sub-ethnic identity. The meaning, as used by the interviewees, of intermarriage shifts between marrying non-Chinese or just marrying non-Asians. In different periods, intermarriage, as already discussed, has different impacts on racial discrimination. The broader understanding of intermarriage may also change over time.

Given that the perceptions of intermarriage are not firmly set, the issue is an important factor in the continuous construction of ethnic identity.

Individual Experience and Group Norms

The leaders' marriage ideals often take a general form, and do not reflect their own or their family members' practice. They like to use others as examples to prove their opinion, and their ideas are divorced from the realities of any specific marriage (except when they use one as an anecdote); they infer from general issues such as language, food, family norms and lifestyle that such marriages must be unhappy or fail. They do not consider the individuals involved, who may have assimilated or integrated in the host society. They may even regard the loss of 'Chineseness' as a product of intermarriage (or going out with people from other ethnic groups); the term often used for Chinese who have lost their Chineseness, 'banana' (yellow skin and white inside), is part of a collective exclusion mechanism, a derogatory (and racist) term disapproving of ethnic 'dilution'. We have already discussed how the intermarriage issue is unrelated to the practice of the interviewees themselves. Cultural difference is one argument they use against intermarriage. As leaders of community associations (Liang 2001a, pp. 99-150), their expression has to be in line with the common discourse among leaders. Otherwise, they would not be accepted as leaders. In their personal situation, intermarriage may have a different significance, but their position as custodians of Chinese identity symbols forces them into adopting generalized views not reflecting their own or their families' experience. In the interviews, of course, they could not avoid referring to their personal practice, and they invariably struck a balance between the personal situation and the public discourse, regarding their personal practice as a special case. One of the interviewees (Leader06) who accepts intermarriage (because his brother is married to a non-Chinese), as we have seen, rationalizes it with the observation that the Western wife obeyed traditional Chinese family norms. Another interviewee (Leader01), who had married a Westerner, regarded himself as an exception, as a scholar with a special life-style. In his opinion, ordinary Chinese with a normal life-style may not be able to cope with intermarriage. He did not oppose the common opinion about the problems of intermarriage. Another Western-married interviewee (Int15-Liang), although persisting in his marriage with some success for several decades, never admits publicly to marital happiness, but rather uses it as a source of anecdotes on social discrimination and cultural conflict; for example, after he retired and closed his ten Chinese restaurants, he did not get a proper meal, for he does not like the Western food his wife puts on the table; his solution was to open a Chinese restaurant again. His strategy of dealing with the embarrassment of a happy marriage meant that nobody could challenge his Chineseness.

Personal experiences may conflict with the main discourse, and as personal circumstances differ widely, the individuals seek to explain their own cases in relation to the main discourse. The reinterpretation of the special cases confirm the main discourse, and the issue of intermarriage plays an important role in this.

Alienation or Maintaining Ethnic Identity

Some scholars (Kannan 1972; Richard 1991; Merton 1976) see intermarriage as a bridge for integration and assimilation among the different ethnic groups. Kannan (1972) used case studies to demonstrate that intermarriage has created inter-caste, inter-religious and interracial integration. Richard (1991) explores the relation between intermarriage and assimilation, and guides us to understand how marital assimilation has taken place.

While there can be no doubt that intermarriage may go hand in hand with ethnic integration and assimilation, the willingness to integrate and assimilate may be absent. I posed the question at the beginning, why overseas Chinese community leaders favour integration with the host society, but do not welcome intermarriage, if intermarriage may create social interaction between the different groups.

It is clear from the interviews that some would like to integrate with the host society, but did not want to assimilate, for they hope to keep their Chinese culture. Their logic was that integration means to integrate with the host society while maintaining Chinese culture and identity. Assimilation, conversely, means to integrate with the host society while losing Chinese culture and identity. In their opinion, due to racial or social exclusion, a person with Chinese blood cannot really be accepted by the host society, so the loss of Chinese culture would leave them with nothing (Liang 2001a, pp. 151-213). From this perspective, their worry about assimilation represents a fear of alienation.

While assimilation means that the Chinese embrace and live by the host society's cultural norms, they are not sure to be accepted by the host society, hence they are alienated. However, alienation works two ways, for losing the Chinese culture also alienates them from the Chinese community. This anxiety of cultural and identity loss is at the heart of the opposition to intermarriage. They worry that intermarriage causes the next generation to lose their Chinese culture, identity, and 'original' family relations that they know and understand.

The reasons they give against intermarriage tend not to be convincing (food, lifestyle, culture), especially when we look more closely at what they say and do; the reasons represent an anxiety that the Chinese family is invaded by another culture or becomes impure through the loss of Chinese culture; as parents they worry that their children will be alienated from themselves.

Some of the interviewees made distinctions between different forms of intermarriage, by saying it was easier to accept that a Chinese woman married a non-Chinese man than vice-versa. The reason was that a woman has more cultural influence on the children. If a Chinese man marries a non-Chinese woman, their children may more easily lose Chinese culture. Interestingly, this is in contrast to the Chinese tradition of lineage exogamy, where only male descent counted in terms of surname and heritage, and the original social or ethnic status of women was of minor importance if only they gave birth to male offspring. In spite of the fact that there are frequent references to the qualities of Confucian traditions, lineage norms seem to have been abandoned. There may be a fear that a non-Chinese woman would introduce a different culture into the son's family and thereby break the Chinese context of male descent. It may not be regarded as a great loss (in male descent terms) if a Chinese woman married out. If the relation between the father and the son is important, it would be worrying if it were alienated by influence from a different culture. Whatever the rationales, they are a mixture of cultural nurture, biological nature, and patrilinear ideology.

Mixed marriages are also associated with lost roots (Leader03), and with 'bamboo culture' (the subculture of young Chinese who belong neither here nor there) (Int63), even though this phenomenon is prevalent in all Chinese families with second and third generation youngsters.

We see a web of rationalizations of intermarriage that reflects ambivalence among community leaders. Some of them are suspended between the opinions they believe they must hold on behalf of their communities in order to claim to represent them and the practice of their families and themselves. Failure, immorality, abandonment of the family norms and many other aspects are used to mark out the boundary between 'them' and 'us', perhaps most importantly because intermarriage has become a symbol of transition from 'us' to 'them'. The cohesion of overseas Chinese community hinges on whether or not it is possible to uphold a distinction, a shared view of the Western 'Other' as immoral, phoney, shallow, uncultured, selfish, unfilial and so on. The issues of exclusion discussed by Lamont (1992) in a totally different context are relevant here, for the symbolic value of intermarriage as a transition from Chinese to Western is very strong, and the shared discourse of my interviewees reacts against it. The group's anxiety of alienation may be particularly prominent among leaders who derive their status from the shared identity of the group.

Works Cited

Breger, Rosemary and Rosanna Hill (1998) 'Introducing Mixed Marriages', in Rosemary Breger and Rosanna Hill (eds), *Cross-Cultural Marriage* (in the series Cross-Cultural Perspectives on Women). Oxford: Berg Publishers.

Kannan, Chirayil Thumbayil (1972) *Inter-Racial Marriages in London: A Comparative Study*. London: SW (Litho) Printers Ltd.

Lamont, Michèle (1992) *Money, Morals & Manners: The Culture of the French and the American Upper-Middle Class*. Chicago and London: The University of Chicago Press.

Liang, Xiujing (2001a) *Exploring the Ethnic Identity of Overseas Chinese Community Leaders in Europe*. Ph.D. thesis presented to the Faculty of Humanities, Aalborg University, Denmark.

Liang, Xiujing (2001b) 'Where is Homeland? Who is a Fellow Villager? Distributive Identities Among Overseas Chinese in Europe'. Center for International Studies, *SPIRIT. Discussion Paper* No. 18/2001. Aalborg: Aalborg University.

Merton, Robert K. (1976) *Sociological Ambivalence and Other Essays*. London: The Free Press.

Richard, Madeline A. (1991) *Ethnic Groups and Marital Choices*. Vancouver: UBC Press.

PART III

BELONGING AND STATEHOOD

Chapter 7

Language Belonging in the New Eastern Europe: The Politics of Inclusion and Exclusion

Ray Taras

Belonging to Blocs

A first lesson in belonging can begin with conceptualizing the changing place of states in post-Communist Europe. In order to understand which countries belong to Europe today, we need to superimpose the political upon the geographic (*The Economist* 2000, pp. 49-50). The enlargement of the European Union (EU) into Central and Eastern Europe in May 2004 is likely to put an end to the use of these adjectives or, at a minimum, it will shift what is 'Central' and 'Eastern' further east geographically. If in the 1980s Poland was classified as East European, in the 1990s it became Central European and, beginning in 2004, simply, and grandly, European. Periodizing Belarus in a similar way has it belonging to the Eurasian USSR, then to Eastern Europe and, after the latest round of EU enlargement, plausibly to Central Europe (Europe's geographic centre is indeed near Grodno, Belarus, so there is poetic justice to the lexiconical change).

This chapter examines politics and belonging in countries that were formerly Soviet republics, in the 1990s became independent East European states, and today are either EU member states or prospective ones. Their belonging in one way or another to Europe is just part of the problematic to be examined here. The principal focus is on how language policies have been designed in post-Communist states to enhance the National while still articulating the European. The simplest way to negotiate the two imperatives is to identify a group – by its speech as well as its political status – that is regarded as neither national nor European. For post-Communist elites in the region, the Russian diaspora in Eastern Europe fits that description. Before studying the relationship between political belonging and language, however, we will first look at the role of language, including Patois, in the making of nations in Europe and elsewhere.

Today's fluidity in belonging stands in sharp contrast with the ossification found in the communist era. Political belonging was highly formalized by successive Soviet leaders and was based on a system of international alliances that supposedly grouped together fraternal Marxist states. The ideological justification for alliance-belonging was well developed. From the official Marxist-Leninist perspective, the Sovietization project represented a civilizing mission designed to rescue and consolidate targeted nations, most of which were backward, agrarian, and in a few cases even nomadic. Whether it was Tuva, Turkistan, Kalmykia or Karelia, Sovietization was intentionally identified with post-colonialism – a historic irony since the USSR and the hegemonic nation at its core, Russia, had become the new colonial power.

The expansion of the Soviet bloc into Eastern Europe after 1945 gave Kremlin leaders an additional laboratory in which to test various means for overcoming primitive capitalism. Here Sovietization assumed the classic definition that it became known for – the effort undertaken by Russian Leninists to impose their political, economic, strategic, and cultural paradigm on non-Russians. The specific blueprints drawn up to Sovietize a nation included autocracy, central planning, militarization, and socialist realism. Yet, as we know, Sovietization was at least as efficient in degrading civilization in Eastern Europe and elsewhere as was primitive capitalism. This degradation was resisted through occasional insurrections, underground struggles, attempts to construct a civil society and, finally, national mobilization throughout the Soviet bloc. Marx's 'historic nations' – Poland and Hungary – led the charge, though others were perhaps ultimately more successful in de-Sovietizing themselves.

Since 1989, and perhaps even from a few years before then, nations that had been ruled by pro-Soviet worker parties began to demand national regeneration – nothing less. This process was dialectically connected to the prior Sovietization programme since regeneration is inseparable from and posits the play of degenerative processes weakening the preceding social formation. The early stage of transition in Eastern Europe – let us say the first five years after the democratic breakthrough and first competitive elections in 1989 – was marked, accordingly, by hybridity. In Homi Bhabha's use of the term, hybridity offers a neutral space that provides for overcoming 'grounds of opposition' where the newly constructed political object is 'neither the one nor the other' (Bhabha 1993, p. 25). This idea is crucial in understanding the ambiguous nature of belonging in post-Communist Europe after the collapse of the Soviet bloc.

Cultural theory has long recognized the importance of neutral space. Mikhail Bakhtin contended that 'consciousness awakens to independent ideological life precisely in a world of alien discourses surrounding it, and from which it cannot initially separate itself' (Bakhtin 1998, p. 534). This view provides an accurate depiction of social consciousness in the early years of transition in the former Soviet bloc. We can go further and apply literary theory's treatment of the border text to shed additional insight into the mechanisms of transition. According to Neil Larsen, 'the border text thinks, speaks and writes from the border itself. The polarisation is not only inverted but internalised' (Larsen 1991, p. xvi). Or again: 'we can situate ourselves at the extreme border, with a view towards the inside as well as to the outside, leaving an open space on either side of the periphery to dialogue with the text' (Dworkin y Mendez 1998, p. 10). Analytic insight is gained from occupying such a vantage point: 'Borders...may very well be the spaces that hold the answers to ongoing explorations of national and transnational identities' (Dworkin y Mendez 1998, p. 10). In short, observing political transitions from borders and neutral spaces is a valuable exercise.

Being anchored on the border – whether a temporal one such as between communist and democratic eras, or a spatial one as between East and West – also has praxeological implications. It stimulates dialogue and negotiation which can deepen the transition phase. Bhabha emphasized the primacy of negotiation over negation under conditions of hybridity. That is, the discursive temporality between two contradictory elements makes dialectical articulation possible. To be sure, he refers to negative polarities that inhibit negotiation, but these are usually benign and do not approach the notion of a 'negation of the negation' that Marx proposed in discussing the transition from capitalist social formation to socialism.

The recognition of the existence of contradictory elements, even polarities, by new (and sometimes not so new) political elites in post-Communist Europe furnishes a meeting point for their negotiation and then transition from them. From an empirical perspective, the gradual, incomplete process of de-Communization in East European states reflects their grounding in hybridity. An optimistic interpretation is that their elites recognize the value of de-territorializing the border between East and West, of transcending boundaries of language, class, and nationality. Ideally these elites should acknowledge that rebirth is impossible without a psychological link back to the years of degradation. In addition, negotiating the passage from Soviet hegemony to the freedom found in 'Western', European structures could deepen the transition if the polarity between the two is not articulated and made salient for all political and cultural undertakings. To be sure, if there had been oppression in the past there had to have been an oppressor. If there had been emancipation from Communist rule there had to be an emancipator. For the political transition to be profound and rich in texture, however, it becomes imperative for incoming political elites not to hold up stark contrasts, as for example between oppressive Russia and emancipatory America. Hybridity can be a transitional state's greatest asset.

In effect, what we are considering is a post-Communist state's encounter with an uncommon type of alterity – what it is not any more rather than what the post-Communist Other is. Though it is not highlighted very often, the temporal dimension of alterity is not new. Writing about a different continent, Carlos Fuentes theorized that if 'Latin America has now achieved an identity, then it must pass the test of living with alternativity...we must pass from nationalism to interdependence, but interdependence is senseless without a basis in independence. Only independent nations can become interdependent partners' (Fuentes 1998, p. 18). But Fuentes was concerned primarily about cultural identity rather than political independence. Cultural identity could not exist without an encounter with the Other. He underscored the importance of preserving 'your national or regional identity while testing it in the waters of alternativity. The Other defines our We. An isolated identity soon perishes; it can become folklore, mania, or specular theater...The Greeks survived by meeting the Other: Persia or Rome, victorious or defeated. The Aztecs succumbed because they could not imagine their own alternative: the European world' (Fuentes 1998, pp. 18-19).

It follows that Bhabha is right in pointing to the cultural (and we can add political) hybridity that serves as the 'in-between space that carries the meaning of culture' (and politics, too) (Bhabha 1993, p. 38). It is important to approach borders, then, both as critical constructs and as obstacles to negotiate. Have the governments of post-Communist nations in Europe really valued hybridity for all its uses? Or have they, after the first phase of transition (described more precisely as extrication from the Soviet bloc), chosen polarity? Having been located, for a short time at least, in the political, economic, and cultural borderlands of Europe, have the new states really promoted de-territorialization of Europe, or at least its reconfiguration? Or has the exercise been merely to locate oneself nationally in the other Europe? And, consistent with withdrawing from neutral space, has that involved introducing unambiguous markers of nationhood rather than more fluid transnational qualities? Only a country-by-country study can provide answers to these questions. This chapter does not do that but focuses instead on one of the most fundamental markers that is used to determine national identity – language. It reviews linguistic policies in selected 'East' European countries where multiple languages compete. Opportunities exist in much of post-Communist Europe for governments to adopt policies on language use that promote hybridity. But the proposition examined here is that constructing a unified linguistic community and entitling some individuals to belong to it while excluding others has been a priority for some of the smaller post-Communist states claiming they require regeneration.

The processes of language building and language belonging in former Communist nations are closely connected with (re)constructions of national identity. Unilingualism is the most straightforward method of fostering language belonging and, with it, national identity. It should be stressed that the unilingual paradigm is not the monopoly of post-Communist governments and can be encountered in 'Western' states such as France. Before reaching the conclusion that the rejection of linguistic hybridity and affirmation of language belonging are measures unique to post-Communist nations, we should consider the extent to which Western states have promoted a similar approach. And if they have, we may ask whether this can still be reconciled with liberal society, whether such states need not automatically be stigmatized as exclusionary and ethnocratic. Finally, the far-flung Russian diaspora scattered across former Soviet republics is at the centre of the controversy over language policy in Eastern Europe. Unilingualism as state policy has been aimed primarily at weakening its status in these post-Communist societies. Conversely the Russian-speaking diaspora, though its members who reside from Estonia to Kazakhstan may share few characteristics other than language spoken and association with the former hegemonic Soviet state, has in the process become marked off and defined by its own unilingualism. Membership in this diaspora is increasingly limited to people who are proficient in no language other than Russian. Language belonging has, therefore, drawn the contours for group politics in Eastern Europe for both titular and diaspora nations.

Language and the Making of the National

The ontology of nations has produced diametrically opposite conclusions on the connection between language and nation. The primordialist school claims that 'what you see is what you get': nations are the outgrowth of objective attributes, foremost among them language. By contrast, instrumentalists assert that 'nothing is what it seems': nations are largely fictitious constructs that may, with time, become reified. Languages are generally viewed as objective 'given' characteristics even though some have indeed had to be constructed when new states have been established, e.g. Norway early in the 20th century, Belarus and Bosnia at its end.

It is also paradoxical that language belonging has become more important at the start of the new century even as globalization, transnationality, and migration trends have strengthened. According to one study, 90 per cent of the world's languages are expected to disappear in the next hundred years, the vast majority of the victims the product of the spread of a few world languages, above all, English. Daniel Nettle and Suzanne Romaine have therefore made the case for 'biolinguistic diversity' – the promotion of both the world's ecosystems and of its cultures and languages (Nettle and Romaine 2000).

When studying the birth of nations, there is a natural inclination to search for breakthroughs in the adoption of a national language and the national culture it supposedly engenders. This is because the national history that we are taught invariably focuses on the linguistic breakthrough from the universal to the particular, from Latin to the vernacular, or some parallel process. Yet a tenuous relationship exists among language, culture, and nationhood. Up to when vernacular languages came widely into use, language was treated as a natural fact and not as a political or cultural determinant of nationhood. Its insignificant status was underscored when Arab invaders sweeping across the Mediterranean world at the end of the first millennium chose not to impose their language on conquered peoples. On the contrary, under the Caliphate of Omar ibn al-Khattab (634-635) Christians were forbidden from learning Arabic and Muslims forbidden from learning foreign languages. We know, of course, that despite these prohibitions the use of Arabic spread quickly thereafter and it became the *lingua franca* of much of the Mediterranean and Middle Eastern worlds by the 10th century.

In Europe significant progress in the emergence of national languages was recorded in the 14th and 15th centuries, which coincided with the rise of anti-ecclesiastical and national movements. But the ascendancy of the vernacular still had little political significance. In the Middle Ages some writers using the vernacular, like Christine de Pizan writing in French and Petrarch writing in Italian, drew stereotypes of their own nations and of others. But the construction of national stereotypes was humorous, mocking, and devoid of political subtexts. Dante never conceived of the political unity of Italy and even accepted that 'many nations and peoples use a more delightful and useful language than the Italian' (Lyttelton 1993, p. 92). In his youth four languages were used in his native Florence: Latin for scholarly works, French for literature, Provencal for aristocratic love songs, and Italian for democratic treatises. Politics, language, and nation were autonomous realms that were not dependent on each other for their survival.

Before the era of general primary education, identifying spoken 'national' languages was not a straightforward task since the 'National' was still an elusive concept. While more tangible and distinguishable, the literary idiom was confined to a narrow elite. According to Anderson (1990, p. 36), 'a particular script-language offered privileged access to ontological truth'. While administrative vernaculars were in use prior to the 16th century, Anderson (1990, p. 41) conjectured how 'nothing suggests that any deep-seated ideological, let alone proto-national, impulses underlay this vernacularization where it occurred'. It was print-capitalism that created 'languages-of-power', 'unified fields of exchange and communication', and 'that image of antiquity so central to the subjective idea of the nation' (Anderson 1990, pp. 44-45). For Marshall McLuhan (1962), the invention and spread of printing press technology produced a dramatic increase in literacy and with it triggered national and political awakenings. As languages pried open the public sphere, nations and their identities became feasible constructs.

The idea that language could serve as a determinant of nation was first expounded by Johann Gottfried Herder (see Barnard 1965). He referred to 'natural' cultural and linguistic communities even though the mythical language of the Volk, embodying its own special genius and unique contribution to civilization, had not yet come into existence. Anderson emphasized, therefore, that 'the convergence of capitalism and print technology on the fatal diversity of human language created the possibility of a new form of imagined community, which in its basic morphology set the stage for the modern nation' (Anderson 1990, p. 46).

The process of linguistic unification in European states was far from complete even on the eve of the French Revolution. In 1789, half of all Frenchmen could not speak French, for example. Only later were efforts undertaken to develop a standardized idiom out of a multiplicity of spoken dialects. Which dialect was chosen as the basis for a national language was often arbitrary, as it still was in some of the post-Soviet states that began nation-building only in the 1990s.

It is important to recognize that national language development has taken paths different in colonial and post-colonial situations from those in Europe after the 16th century. In the case of Bengal, celebrated for its literary achievements, the Bengali language only began to flourish in the mid-19th century when its 'bilingual elite makes it a cultural project to provide its mother tongue with the necessary linguistic equipment to enable it to become an adequate language for "modern" culture' (Chatterjee 1993, p. 7). Apart from establishing an institutional network of newspapers, publishing houses, and literary societies, a political motivation led the Bengali cultural elite to promote their language: 'The bilingual intelligentsia came to think of its own language as belonging to that inner domain of cultural identity, from which the colonial intruder had to be kept out; language therefore became a zone over which the nation first had to declare its sovereignty and then had to transform in order to make it adequate for the modern world' (Chatterjee 1993, p. 7).

Linguistic diversity in political societies remains common today, nowhere more so than in post-colonial states like India or Nigeria. Nations exist which have no living language of their own, for example, Scotland. By contrast the Swiss have four languages: versions of German, Italian, and French, plus Romanische. Continents exist which are dominated by just one language; most of Latin America shares one language, Spanish, while English dominates in most of North America. Linguistic engineering to change language preferences and shape political belonging is difficult to carry out in such circumstances. Moreover, if it is to be attempted at all, it has to target a population that is pre-political – children. There is one fundamental fact about language acquisition: 'The task of acquiring language is one for which the adult has lost most of her aptitude but one the child will perform with remarkable skill' (Moskowitz 1998, p. 529).

If the relationship between language and nation is tenuous, as has been argued here, efforts have recently been undertaken by both small and large nations alike to reinforce the connection between the two. This is true of the United States, where the debate on the role of English intensified early in the 1990s. It is true of Canada, where linguistic introspection began in the 1960s as part of defining Canadian identity. It is also true of former Soviet republics which, beginning in 1989, had to decide on official languages for the new states. It is also true of the new members of the EU in Central Europe which, in making the transition to democracy, also wanted to make a transition to a form of language and national belonging that would ostracize formerly dominant linguistic groups.

National Regeneration and Language Politicization

Why are the politics of language such a salient and contentious issue in many parts of the world today? One general reason is that language possesses aesthetic beauty in itself. As such, it merits protection and many of the world's governments have adopted interventionist policies to safeguard language. The Academie Francaise model has always been controversial but the most recent convert to it is Russian President Vladimir Putin, who was behind legislation enacted in May 2001 to keep the Russian language free of foreign words and to enforce its grammatical rules.

The importance of language also stems from the fact that it helps define the structure of political power in a society. J.G.A. Pocock (1971, p. 15) wrote: 'Men think by communicating language systems; these systems help constitute both their conceptual worlds and the authority structures, or social worlds, related to these'. The stakes over use of a particular language are therefore invariably high.

Closely related to this, language is an ideal instrument for determining political belonging. A given speech group can become transformed into an important political group when one of its resources – language – becomes elevated to a higher status. This may be the result of a native son assuming a national leadership role and politically rewarding his ethnic kin. Or it can be the recognition of a moral claim that the speech group has about either its threatened or indigenous status or even both. Thus, many Inuit languages in Canada are now treated as official languages in the legislative assemblies of the Yukon, Northwest, and Nunavut Territories. A second example: use of the Welsh language has traditionally been concentrated in certain parts of Wales, but after 1993 Welsh became 'national' across the principality, in part because of the moral superiority its use assures. In these circumstances belonging to a speech group can enhance political power, at times at the expense of a now-excluded language community (such as English speakers in northern Canada and Wales).

Yet another major reason why the politics of language have become so important today is that some languages are under threat, as we have just noted. Many aboriginal languages, in particular, have recently become extinct. In addition, the majority language spoken in a weak or formerly colonized (for our purposes Sovietized) state can come under threat. Threats to minority languages and the language of diasporas can be even more serious. The erosion of the status of a language constitutes an overlooked offshoot of the rise of nationalisms and the spread of globalization.

Theorists on nationalism and post-nationality concur that national identity is essentially multidimensional. In this view, the erosion of the status of a language in a given society should not be a cause for alarm since a group can compensate by embracing other markers of identity – intermarriage, food, and folk customs to identify the least convincing. Linguistic threat perceptions are based, it is claimed, on an exaggerated importance given to language belonging. Nevertheless, countless examples exist of the erosion of a group's language, thereby triggering a process that diminishes its culture to folkloric status and, eventually, destroying it altogether (e.g. Livonians, Rusyns). The converse principle – nurturing a language and the sense of belonging to it – is considered to be the most reliable way to protect a culture from extinction.

Creating a 'national' language where only 'minority' ones exist may prove as challenging a project as safeguarding languages at risk (Gurr 1993). In the context of Southeast Asia, Benedict Anderson (1990, p. 124) noted: 'No one has yet attempted to look at the language of contemporary Indonesia as an enterprise for the mastery of a gigantic cultural crisis, and a partly subconscious project for the assumption of "modernity" within the modalities of an autonomous and autochtonous social-political tradition'. The same may apply to certain parts of post-Communist Europe.

Let us reflect on Anderson's Indonesia. Writing about its most celebrated contemporary novelist, Pramoedya Ananta Toer, one reviewer observed: 'It's practically a law of literature that nation building produces epics; the passions and cataclysms unleashed by the birthing of a nation must find their way into heroic narratives, which run the gamut from *The Iliad* to *Doctor Zhivago*. The youngest of the world's major nations, Indonesia was created in the last days of 1949, when thirteen thousand six hundred and seventy-seven islands of the Southeast Asian archipelago gained their independence from Dutch colonial rule' (James 1996).

One would assume that a national epic would define and refine the national language. Indeed that is what Pramoedya achieved in his early novel, *The Fugitive*, which was one of the first accomplished works of literature written in Bahasa Indonesian, the dialect of Malay that was proclaimed the official language of the new nation. Just as the Homeric dialect helped formalize the concept of Greek-ness by welding together the various idioms of the Aegean, Bahasa Indonesian was one of the principal means for bringing about the unity (such as it is) of Indonesia, where more than six hundred languages are still spoken. Pramoedya never published a page in his native Javanese (James 1996).

Nevertheless, language belonging is central to an understanding of how new nations are forged and whether national unity will be achieved. Language is more tangible and less metaphysical than nation is and, consequently, it is a better indicator of identity. This is especially true in the study of non-Western peoples whose group belonging may otherwise appear to be impenetrable and esoteric, like the Uyghurs of China (Rudelson 1998).

Patois as Political Protest and Marker of Belonging

Distinguishing between language, dialect, and Patois, or even ascertaining who speaks a language in a way that assures belonging to a speech group, raises important questions about identities. Before searching for the causal arrow that leads from speech group to political group, the challenging exercise of determining what language belonging involves has to be undertaken. One scholar listed the possibilities that a national census would have to clarify:

> Sous la rubrique 'langue,' les récensements peuvent comprendre la langue maternelle, la langue d'usage la plus fréquemment utilisée (*Umgangssprache*) ou la langue de travail. Dans ce dernier cas, la langue dominante de la région ou du pays se trouve favorisée. Ernest Gellner...prétend que la langue de l'école maternelle détermine celle de la personne (Liebich 1997, p. 36).[1]

A commonly used strategy, often associated with colonial rule, to diminish the importance of a language community is to claim that it speaks in mere dialectic, or

---

1 'The "language" label may comprise the mother tongue, the language most often used in everyday interaction (*Umgangssprache*) or the working language. In this last case, the dominant language in the region or the country occupies a privileged position. Ernest Gellner...believes that the language spoken in the original family context determines the lanugage of a given individual' (Liebich 1997, p. 36).

Patois. The inference is that peoples speaking Patois are undeserving of a special linguistic status, display a flawed identity, and are pre-political. So let us look at an example of an identity being constructed precisely upon Patois.

Jamaica's greatest living poet is arguably Louise Bennett who, like Robert Burns, writes in native dialect. She justifies this in the following terms: 'some thought Jamaican English was vulgar, out-of-order language. It came out of the African heritage and at that time anything was bad: hair, skin colour, language, music. But I thought it was fascinating. Everything had a rhythm. It was the creation of the people' (Cadogan 2000). Her 1944 poem 'Bans o' Killing' (Bennett 1966) provided strong legitimation for the rise of Jamaican vernacular poetry.

> Y Meck me get it straight Mass Charlie
> For me no quite undastan,
> Yuh gwine kill all English dialect
> Or jus Jamaica one?
>
> Ef yuh dah-equal up wid English
> Language, den wha meck
> Yuh gwine go feel inferior, wen
> It come to dialect
>
> Ef yuh kean sing 'Linstead Market'
> An 'Wata come a me y'eye'
> Yu wi haffi tap sing 'Auld Land Syne'
> And 'Comin Thru de Rye'
>
> Dah language weh yuh proud o'
> Weh yuh hunour and respeck
> Po' Mass Charlie! Yuh noh know sey
> Dat it spring from dialect!

For Bennett, the real problem that those who despised Patois had was their denigration of everything African. Conversely, her effort was aimed at valuing Afro-Caribbean distinctiveness and advancing a self-definition for the group that was anchored in linguistic identity – not in cultural and linguistic boundaries defined by British colonizers. Mutabaruka, a dub poet following in her footsteps in the 1970s, tried further to reinforce respect for a national Patois while debunking those who poured scorn on this 'creation of the people'. His poem 'Miss Lou' (on a 1994 compact disc, 'Melanin Man') celebrates Bennett's contribution to the language's status and Afro-Caribbean identity in Jamaica:

> miss lou miss lou
> wi love yuh fi true
> wi love how yuh chat
> some nuh love dat miss lou
> miss lou miss lou

you heavy fi true
mi seh wi love wey yuh seh
wen yuh seh wey yuh seh
miss lou
mis lou yuh mek dem know
dat is from de base tings jamaica grow
dem use fi seh wi mus speak an' twang
but yuh mek wi proud seh wi a afrikan
now wi si dem a teach in schools
dat jamaica patwa is not fi fool
wen yuh chat is soun' suh sweet
an' all a jamaica jus a skin dem teeth
miss lou
miss lou miss lou wi love yuh fi true
wi love how yuh chat
a patwa dat

Patois and politics were of a piece. Mutabaruka (1998) elaborated on how words and language can be used to present distinct world views: 'when white people fight against white people they say it's WORLD war! I didn't involve in the war! I was in the Caribbean drinking coconut water and reggae music and you hear them say it's a WORLD war! But – you see: When the Africans kill the Africans you hear it's a TRIBAL war!' Mutabaruka urged Afro-Caribbeans to be masters of their self-definition. When asked, 'what can blacks learn from the white man?' he answers, 'We have learned enough now. We want to learn from ourselves now!' In another song he provocatively asserts: 'I doan have a colour problem/I si everything in black'.

Patois creates belonging to a speech group and plays a foundational role in shaping national and racial identities in many post-colonial societies. If respect for Patois is a pivotal moment in the de-colonization process, then proclaiming a national language has been central to the process of de-Sovietization in Eastern Europe. The debates on language policy that took place in several of these countries beginning in the late 1980s often paralleled the rhetoric of Mutabaruka: 'what can we Baltic peoples learn from the Russians? We have learned enough now. We want to learn from ourselves now!' That required, first and foremost, speaking and working in one's own language and enacting the legal framework to be able to do so.

Cementing Belonging: To Exclude or Include 'Foreign' Diasporas?

To pre-empt the emergence of multiple identities within an ethnically fragile state, its leaders are likely to discourage the use of multiple languages. One dimension of such a policy may be an attack on the rights of an unwelcome diaspora group. In Eastern Europe it is the Russians that have served this purpose. The main grievance against the language of the Russian diaspora is that it was the language of Sovietization. Nationalists in the new independent states – especially the smaller non-Slavic ones – believe that that is reason enough to dispense with it (Fouse 2000; Landau and Kellner-Heinkele 2001). The national elites in these states have opposed the principle of multiple identities because the composite includes the former colonizer. The Russian language has no place in independent, democratic, 'Western' Eastern Europe, the argument goes. Russians do not belong here.

Fear of the loss of national identity was fundamental in mobilizing Baltic peoples for independence in the late Soviet period. When independent Estonian, Latvian, and Lithuanian states were restored, nationalists proposed treating their Russian minorities (30, 34 and 9 per cent, respectively) in a way similar to Russia's treatment of minorities in the Soviet Union – as second-class citizens or, going one step further, as non-citizens. Lithuania, with only a small Russian minority, may be exceptional but otherwise 'In today's "ethnic democracies" of Estonia and Latvia, hard-line Baltic nationalists say that the only people who should be citizens are those whose families were citizens prior to the Soviet seizure of their country in 1940' (Rose 1997, p. 16).

If descent rather than place of birth, established residence, or language competence was used as the sole criterion for citizenship, then Russians in the Baltics would become a permanently disenfranchised group. To be sure close to 90 per cent of Russian speakers in the Baltics agreed in a 1995 survey that learning the national language was an obligation of residents in these countries (Rose 1997, p. 8). Partly because of such Russian goodwill, but in greater measure because of pressure from Western European states, which underscored the importance of a civic understanding of citizenship, as well as from the Russian Federation (Zevelev 2001), which threatened various sanctions if its 'beached diaspora' (Laitin 1998) was not accorded full rights, a more nuanced approach to Baltic citizenship emerged over time. This evolution in an understanding of belonging is best illustrated in the cases of Estonia and Latvia, where national elites were 'torn between their desire to join the European Union and their need to protect the culture and language of their own societies' (Johns 2002, p. 126).

Estonian policy had to take into account not just the size but the linguistic weight of the Russian minority: it constitutes over 80 per cent of the population in the urban northeastern part of the country (Raun 1991; Taagepera 1993). The 1989 State Language Law initiated a preference system favouring ethnic Estonians over others. It stipulated that government officials and public servants had to possess a working knowledge of Estonian. The 1992 Citizenship Law (amended slightly in 1995) made only Russians who could trace their origins to the interwar republic eligible for citizenship.

Citizenship could be obtained by fulfilling an Estonian language requirement. Its threshold seemed relatively low: 'An operational level of language competence for citizenship has been defined as the ability to use approximately 1500 words for everyday conversation. Examinees must have the ability to understand news and information items, converse about their family, read short texts, fill out a biographical questionnaire, and know some Estonian history and geography' (Chin and Kaiser 1996, p. 103). But as a Finno-Ugric language, Estonian is difficult for

Russians to master (of course, Russian is no easier for Estonians to learn), and there was a high failure rate among those who even made the attempt to pass the exam.

The 1993 Law on Aliens sought to reassure local Russians that, though officially stateless, they would be granted temporary Estonian residence permits. But the 1995 Language Law then placed limits on the special status of Russian in local administration. The best chance Russians had for a relaxation of language legislation was, paradoxically, in Estonia's accession into the EU. One of the three so-called Copenhagen conditions identified in 1993 as required for accession was the existence of stable political institutions, of the rule of law, and of a minority rights regime. When Estonia's application for membership was approved in another Copenhagen meeting, in December 2002, it was in great measure due to Estonia's language policy having been made 'linguistically correct'.

Similarly, Latvia began its resurrected statehood by following a 'Latvian first' policy. Its citizenship law, adopted in a more liberal form in 1994 after criticism from European bodies that it was too restrictive and exclusionary, included naturalization quotas, a Latvian language requirement, and a Latvian history exam. Another law even required native language competence to obtain employment in the private sector. There are greater linguistic similarities between Latvian and Russian than between Estonian and Russian. Nevertheless, 'Regarding Latvian language requirements, two Russian reporters wryly characterised the Latvians' real attitude toward integration as: "We don't need you to know the language; we just need you to know your place"' (Pettai 1996, p. 48).

International pressure convinced Latvian lawmakers to adopt a *jus soli* basis for citizenship in 1998. Naturalization windows and the language test were dropped, and citizenship was extended automatically to those born in independent Latvia. But the unilingual model of language building was not completely abandoned, and an important reason for this was that Latvian Russians seemed not to engage in the same level of protest against what they perceived as discriminatory laws compared to their counterparts in Estonia (*Minorities at Risk* website).

Other Soviet successor states located in Eastern Europe, notably Ukraine, opted for a 'dual-language' formula. Although not a truly bilingual policy, it is nevertheless accommodating towards the use of Russian and acknowledges the value of linguistic hybridization. This is an understandable approach in a closely-related East Slavic nation, and it also recognizes Ukraine's historic uniqueness in having been incorporated into the Russian Tsarist empire after 1654.

Ukraine is distinctive because of its make-up of three cultures and two languages, making belonging here more often multiple, nested, fluid, and situational than elsewhere in the region (Arel 1995; Kuzio 1996). Apart from the ethnic Russian minority which makes up about one fifth of the country's total population (the 1989 census reported 22 per cent as self-declared Russian while the 2001 census found only 17 per cent as self-identifying Russian), ethnic Ukrainians are subdivided into ukrainophones (40 per cent in 1989, up to 68 per cent in 2001) and russophones (33 and 15 per cent, respectively). In practice, this division into separate linguistic communities is largely spurious as pure ukrainophones or russophones are in the minority and are limited to particular regions in the country (Galicia for the first group, the Donbass and Crimea for the second). Accordingly, 'Although ethnically predominant, the core Ukrainian group is therefore in a linguistic minority' (Wilson 1996, p. 22).

While still a Soviet republic, Ukraine's parliament passed the Ukrainian Languages Law in 1989 making Ukrainian the titular – or official – language of the republic. Russian was recognized as the language of inter-ethnic communication. The Ukrainian dual language model also extended governmental status to other languages spoken in areas inhabited by non-Ukrainians. The 1991 declaration on the rights of nationalities guaranteed individuals – not groups – the right to use their native languages in all spheres of social life. The 1996 constitution changed the dual language model by affirming Ukrainian as the sole legal language of the state and substituting it for Russian as the language of inter-ethnic communication. Further, it now defined Russians as a national minority, thereby negating the concept of two founding nations in Ukraine. These changes may have been possible because of the absence of any real ethnic schism between Ukrainians and Russians. Moreover, the language battle did not seem worth fighting because the two East Slavic languages were so closely related to each other and enjoyed their uncontested spheres both in regional and cultural terms.

Yet another approach in the former Soviet republics is to adopt a policy of linguistic conflict-avoidance, or languages belonging. Moldova's 1989 language law designated neither Russian nor Romanian but Moldovan as the official language – a contrived solution since if Moldovan does exist as a distinct language, it is as a Romance rather than Slavic language. For a time in independent Moldova, Russian was described as a foreign language and Moldovan language testing of public servants was enacted. But the practice was suspended in 1994 when it became clear that the russophone minority (Russians and Ukrainians), which makes up one quarter of the total population, was not learning Romanian. Thus, even before a pro-Russian president took office in 1997, the Moldovan leadership sought to depoliticize language after the first nationalist wave subsided.

In sum, some East European states, particularly small ones, equated national regeneration with language belonging under a fairly strict unilingual regime. Their national elites stressed the need to defend fragile cultures living in the shadow of an imperial nation. The working assumption was that linguistic solitude was preferable to transitional bilingualism. While highly desirable in principle, bilingualism may occasionally conceal diglossia – 'a special form of bilingualism, where the state language is used mostly for "high" functions (such as trade, high culture, and contacts with state authorities), and the regional language is used for "low" functions (for intimacy, and for celebrations of folk culture)' (Laitin 1998, p. x).

Languages have market value and *lingua francas* rank among the highest. A hierarchy of languages in a small multilingual state is almost inevitable. The competition between languages is unequal when one is spoken by only several million people (as in the case of Baltic languages) and the other by several hundred million (as with Russian). Legislation can be enacted to secure the weaker, native one but it is unlikely that even that community's political and economic elite will choose to speak just that one language. They may support the passage of legislation that provides symbolic meaning to adhering to a language group. But their own social and economic practices are likely to reflect cosmopolitan values. Indeed, many members in the elite of the Baltic states embody extraordinary cosmopolitan trajectories – educated, professionally trained, and long-time residents in Western countries for whom English is their native tongue. The danger is, then, that a policy of unilingualism for the general population and a practice of multilingualism for elites will serve as a means of reinforcing existing relations of power.

Cementing belonging involves, therefore, selecting from a repertoire of language policies. Let us consider the case of a large multilingual state like Nigeria. Its political elites generally make an effort to speak all three major languages (Hausa, Igbo, Yoruba), along with English and their own native tongue when they originate in a minority group. If they have not learned all these languages themselves, they marry women who can complement the language requirements necessary for holding national office. Belonging in Nigeria entails such a polyglot background in its prospective politicians. In the process such elites come to belong globally as well.

Western Norms and Linguistic Regimes

Apart from pragmatic considerations, Western liberal thought would endorse affirmative action favouring a previously discriminated-against language, though not at the cost of excluding another one altogether from the repertoire. Liberalism would not acquiesce in the forced replacement of multiple identities by a unicultural one, nor in discriminatory policies aimed at minority or diaspora groups. Distinguishing between instrumental and non-instrumental language rights – which approximates the difference between social practices and symbolic meanings – can elucidate liberalism's nuanced stand on the issue:

The instrumental/non-instrumental divide distinguishes between, on the one hand, those language claims that aim at ensuring a person's capacity to enjoy a secure linguistic environment in her/his mother tongue and a linguistic group's fair chances of cultural self-reproduction which we could call language rights in a strict sense, and, on the other, those language claims that aim at ensuring that language is not an obstacle to the effective enjoyment of rights with a linguistic dimension, to the meaningful participation in public institutions and democratic process, and to the enjoyment of social and economic opportunities that require linguistic skills (Rubio-Marin 2003, p. 56).

To be sure, few legal assessments of language regimes are informed by principles of moral philosophy. Double standards are also occasionally discernible in Western critiques of linguistic policies adopted in Eastern Europe and elsewhere, and if they are employed at all the principles of liberalism are applied inconsistently. Representative of Western dissonance – and paternalism – is one analyst's deconstruction of prevailing attitudes to Czechs and Slovaks: 'When a

Czech identifies with his nation, he is considered to be a great patriot. But if a Slovak so much as identifies himself in a national way, the Czech political machinery labels him a nationalist and chauvinist' (Kirschbaum 1995, p. 260).

It is not just the historically-disadvantaged nations of Eastern Europe that encounter problems in obtaining support for non-instrumental, linguistic affirmative-action policies. Minority groups in Western liberal democracies have also faced difficulties in their efforts to foster language belonging. When it was first elected to power in Québec in 1976, one of the early measures taken by the nationalist Parti Québécois was to enact Bill 101, known as the Charter of the French Language. The act made French the language of work, business, and education in the province. The nationalists argued that only by making French both official and working language, to be used in schools, corporations, the professions, and on public signs, could it hope to survive the remorseless pressures of creeping anglicization (Taras 1987). The act was assimilationist in nature, seeking to francisize all immigrant children, and with Bill 101 Québec became *de facto* a unilingual province. Regular legal challenges to the Charter of the French Language by English-speaking groups have, ironically, kept the waning *indépendentistes* forces from disappearing altogether.

By contrast, the Welsh Language Act of 1993 represented a commitment to the principle that Welsh and English languages should be treated on the basis of equality. The act made Welsh and English official languages in Wales and the public were given the choice of using their preferred language when dealing with various public bodies in Wales. 'Recognising that English has in the past been considered by many to be the principal language of higher education, public administration and official communication, efforts shall be made to create conditions which facilitate the use of Welsh and to make it the natural choice of those who speak it' (University of Wales 2000, p. 5). In some aspects this measure was similar to Canada's 1969 Official Languages Act which declared French and English co-equal official languages and required that all federal services be available in each, at the client's choosing. But many English speakers in both Wales and Canada have regarded such linguistic democracy as a threat. The hegemony of their language would be undercut, they fear, and in the long term the prevalence of English might be eroded by the promotion of 'minority language' communities for particular regions.

As we have observed, languages have market value. Equal legal status for Welsh- and French-speakers in Britain and Canada does not change the fact that they remain economically at a disadvantage with English. Giving recognition to such languages for non-instrumental purposes is a minimal condition for ensuring their political belonging to a larger community. At the same time, even if efforts are made to instrumentalize such languages, they should not be treated as divisive to the extent that the rights of other language groups continue to be protected, if not necessarily prioritized.

Conclusions

A Canadian political scientist, Jean Laponce, skillfully framed the political debate about promoting language belonging: 'Should a state that is multilingual regret that fact or congratulate itself? Can a unilingual state better integrate its economy, mobilise its political system, develop and diffuse its culture?' (Laponce 1987, p. 94) His tentative conclusion was that 'it is unreasonable to give an answer without knowing which state is involved, or its objectives, its internal hierarchies, its attitudes, and, above all, the degree of reciprocal tolerance among its various social forces' (Laponce 1987, p. 94). Laponce's open-ended approach is a refreshing contrast to the dogma that asserts: 'Restrictive language legislation has bases which are linguistically, sociologically, psychologically, and probably morally questionable' (Harlig 1997, p. 480).

Several conclusions suggest themselves from the analysis undertaken in this chapter. First, language belonging is jealously micro-managed by the caretaker state. It is the most effective way to pre-empt the emergence of multiple identities in a state and to cement belonging to a posited political community. This holds true for yesterday's Eastern Europe, today's Central Europe, and contemporary Western democracies. While there may be a lack of enthusiasm for the languages of minorities and diasporas in both the post-Communist and Western worlds, governments have generally been deeply engaged in the crafting of language regimes, at the least as a preventive measure to avoid future conflict.

Second, if hybridity as we understand it is rare, encounters and dialogue with the Other are not. Again, this finding applies as much to Eastern and Central as to Western Europe. Policies on language and on language belonging are negotiated by state actors, nationalist leaders, minority and diaspora groups, and intergovernmental organizations. The normative regimes of many political systems have persuaded – even required – them to include the Other in their conception of belonging. In turn, scholars pay increasing attention to the role of the Other in national self-definition and belonging, To return to Fuentes' example, even most ultranationalists in economically developed countries accept the need to emulate classical Greek civilization and seek to engage the Other. The autistic Aztec approach finds few takers anywhere today.

This leads to a third conclusion. When a community prefers a national language, or even Patois, to a *lingua franca* (such as English or Russian), it is placing culture over economics. In today's world that choice rankles elites more than fears about exclusionary forms of identity. International normative regimes have advanced moral grounds for supporting diversity, usually hierarchically nested to favour the interests of the world's great powers. The main objective of these rights' regimes is to create hothouse conditions for globalization's further spread. Their understanding of the rational actor is based on economic calculus, not cultural preferences. Many leaders of the developing world critically noted the linkage between normative regimes and economic imperatives at the Millennial session of the United Nations.

Language is central to national identity, as it is to national economic development and prosperity. It is an important cog in the wheel of globalization and of a post-national, global identity. But language is first a national resource that is the cement of belonging to a particular community. It cannot be reduced to an instrumentality. As Francois Grin (2003) made clear, the argument in favour of linguistic diversity is nothing less than the defence of human rights.

Works Cited

Anderson, Benedict (1990) *Language and Power: Exploring Political Cultures in Indonesia*. Ithaca, NY: Cornell University Press.

Arel, Dominique (1995) 'Language Policies in Independent Ukraine: Towards One or Two State Languages'. *Nationalities Papers*, 23(3) (September), 597-624.

Bakhtin, Mikhail (1998) *Discourse in the Novel*. Reprinted in David H. Richter (ed.), *The Critical Tradition: Classic Texts and Contemporary Trends*. Boston: Bedford Books.

Barnard, Frederick Mechner (1965) *Herder's Social and Political Thought from the Enlightenment to Nationalism*. Oxford: Oxford University Press.

Bennett, Louise (1966) *Jamaica Labrish*. Kingston, Jamaica: Montrose.

Bhabha, Homi (1993) *The Location of Culture*. London: Routledge.

Cadogan, Garnette (2000) 'Dub Poetry as Nationalist Assertion'. March 2000, unpublished paper, Tulane University.

Chatterjee, Partha (1993) *The Nation and its Fragments: Colonial and Postcolonial Histories*. Princeton, NJ: Princeton University Press.

Chin, Jeff and Robert Kaiser (1996) *Russians as the New Minority: Ethnicity and Nationalism in the Soviet Successor States*. Boulder, CO: Westview Press.

Dworkin y Mendez, Kenya C. (1998) 'Beyond Indigenism and Marxism: The Deterritorialized Borders of Jose Maria Arguedas' Deep Rivers'. *South Eastern Latin Americanist*, XLII(1) (Summer), 1-12.

Economist, The (2000) 'Where is Central Europe?' (8-14 July), 49-50.

Fouse, Gary C. (2000) *The Languages of the Former Soviet Republics: Their History and Development*. Lanham, MD: University Press of America.

Fuentes, Carlos (1998) 'Prologue' to José Enrique Rodo, *Ariel*. Austin, TX: University of Texas Press.

Grin, Francois (2003) 'Diversity as Paradigm, Analytical Device, and Policy Goal', in Will Kymlicka and Alan Patten (eds), *Language Rights and Political Theory*. New York: Oxford University Press.

Gurr, Ted (1993) *Minorities At Risk: A Global View of Ethnopolitical Conflicts*. Washington, DC: United States Institute of Peace Press.

Harlig, Jeffrey (1997) 'National Consolidation versus European Integration: The Language Issue in Slovakia'. *Security Dialogue* 28:4 (December) 479-492.

James, Jamie (1996) 'The Indonesiad'. *The New Yorker* (27 May).

Johns, Michael (2002) 'Assessing Risk Assessment: A Baltic Test'. *Nationalism and Ethnic Politics*, 8, no. 1 (Spring), 105-128.

Kirschbaum, Stanislav (1995) *A History of Slovakia: The Struggle for Survival*. New York: St. Martin's Press.

Kuzio, Taras (1996) 'National Identity in Independent Ukraine: An Identity in Transition'. *Nationalism and Ethnic Politics*, 2, no. 4 (Winter), 582-608.

Kymlicka, Will, and Alan Patten (eds) (2003) *Language Rights and Political Theory*. New York: Oxford University Press.

Laitin, David, (1998) *Identity in Formation: the Russian-Speaking Populations in the Near Abroad*. Ithaca, NY: Cornell University Press.

Landau, Jacob M. and Barbara Kellner-Heinkele (2001) *Politics of Language in the Ex-Soviet Muslim States*. Ann Arbor, MI: University of Michigan Press.

Laponce, Jean A. (1987) *Languages and Their Territories*. Toronto: University of Toronto Press.

Larsen, Neil (1991) 'Foreword', in D. Emily Hicks, *Border Writing: the Multidimensional Text*. Minneapolis, MN: University of Minnesota Press.

Liebich, André (1997) *Les minorites nationales en Europe centrale et orientale*. Geneva: Georg Editeur.

Adrian Lyttelton (1993) 'The national question in Italy', in Mikulas Teich and Roy Porter (eds), *The National Question in Europe in Historical Context*. Cambridge: Cambridge University Press, 1993, 63-101.

McLuhan, Marshall (1962) *The Gutenberg Galaxy: The Making of Typographic Man*. Toronto: University of Toronto Press.

Minorities at Risk (no date) at www.bsos.umd.edu/cidcm/mar.

Moskowitz, Breyne Arlene (1998) 'The Acquisition of Language', in V.P. Clark, P.A. Escholz and A.F. Rosa (eds), *Language: Readings in Language and Culture*. Boston: Bedford/St. Martin's.

Mutabaruka (1998) 'Learning from Ourselves Now', at http://www.classical-reggae-interviews.org/mut-sup.htm.

Nettle, Daniel and Suzanne Romaine (2000) *Vanishing Voices: the Extinction of the World's Languages*. Oxford: Oxford University Press.

Pettai, Vello (1996) 'The Games of Ethnopolitics in Latvia'. *Post-Soviet Affairs*, 12(1), 40-50.

Pocock, J. G. A. (1971) *Politics, Language and Time: Essays on Political Thought and History*. New York: Atheneum.

Raun, Toivu (1991) *Estonia and the Estonians*. Stanford, CA: Hoover Institution Press.

Rose, Richard (1997) 'Baltic Trends: Studies in Co-operation, Conflict, Rights and Obligations'. (Centre for the Study of Public Policy, 288) Glasgow: University of Strathclyde.

Rubio-Marin, Ruth (2003) 'Language Rights: Exploring the Competing Rationales', in Will Kymlicka and Alan Patten (eds), *Language Rights and Political Theory*. New York: Oxford University Press.

Rudelson, Justin (1998) *Oasis Identities: Uyghur Nationalism along China's Silk Road*. New York: Columbia University Press.

Taagepera, Rein (1993) *Estonia*. Boulder, CO: Westview Press.

Taras, Ray (1987) 'Quebec's Language Laws and the Allophone Community: Toward a Morphology of Contemporary Quebec Society'. *Quebec Studies*, 5, 39-59.

University of Wales (2000) 'Language Scheme Prepared in Accordance with the Requirements of the Welsh Language Act 1993', Aberystwyth (26 January).

Wilson, Andrew (1996) *Ukrainian Nationalism in the 1990s: A Minority Faith*. Cambridge: Cambridge University Press.

Zevelev, Igor (2001) *Russia and its New Diasporas*. Washington, DC: United States Institute of Peace Press.

Chapter 8

Putting Heritage and Identity into Place after Communism: Gdańsk, Riga, and Vilnius

John Czaplicka

The logics of universalism and, more recently, modernization and globalization have sought to represent localized identities as historical, regressive characteristics, and have worked to undermine the old allegiances of place and community. But the burgeoning of identity politics, and now nationalism, reveal a clear resistance to such universalizing strategies.[1]

In some cases the process of recovering local heritage in East-Central Europe began as a mode of resistance to 'universalizing strategies' of Communist regimes. That process continues into the present and serves, on the one hand, as a means to revise an abridged history propagated by a highly centralized and oppressive state and, on the other, as a response to a transformed geopolitical situation. With the post-Communist devolution of authority from central to local governments and the enfranchisement of local populations, the reformulation of heritage is again more closely linked to the memory and imagination of the populace residing in cities such as Gdańsk, Riga and Vilnius.[2] In these cities state and municipal governments and interest groups are still changing street names, restoring and re-constructing buildings and monuments, and modifying urban structures in manners that *concretely* reaffirm 'old allegiances of place and community'. This transformation of physical heritage influences and is influenced by the evolution of place-based identities. At times commentators have seen a singular 'return of history' in this pattern of heritage transformation and identity constitution. But the 'burgeoning of identity politics', 'nationalism', and regionalism as well as the rush to integrate economically and politically into Europe have actually propelled *multiple* histories into place since around 1990.[3]

---

1 Carter, Donald and Squires (1993, p. ix).
2 Ilya Outekhine (2003) and Olga Sezneva (2003) map the role historical imagination has in reconstituting both local history and place-based identities.
3 See for example *Rückkehr der Geschichte* (1991) or *Die wiedergefundene Erinnerung/Die Verdrängte Geschichte in Osteuropa* (1992).

These histories are being contested and negotiated in a restored public and civic sphere, and they take form in the built heritage so elemental in determining how local populations identify – and identify with their hometowns. The following sketches out some tendencies in this complex process.

It is in the remnant historic districts of post-authoritarian cities that heritage transformation has been most evident. Their reinterpretation, restoration, and reconstruction have played an important role in recalling the history before the Communist 'interregnum' and in representing a chosen heritage conforming to the new civic order. These 'Old Towns' have become vehicles for the redefinition of the identity and character of each city. Historical ensembles in Vilnius and Riga are being completed to present an ostensibly more integral image of the past. In Gdańsk the reconstructed historic core is being expanded by buildings in a matching scale and style to complete a historic urban image set against the 'modernist' architecture associated with state socialism. In each city plans exist to complete historic structures by revealing the course of old city walls and streets, restoring historic scale and densities, and relating the cities with landscape elements such as rivers and canals. The remnant historical environments provide settings for various local, national, ethnic, regional, and European narratives. Remade to accentuate local peculiarities, the Old Towns also lend each city a specific character and offer the locals an opportunity to be proud of their *own history*. As they gain in significance, the property values of these urban cores have risen, and they have begun to attract new investments from businesses and the tourist industry.[4]

Coinciding with this refurbishing and new recognition of historic substance, monuments and memorials have been removed, built, restored, and reconstructed. Each city is transforming its commemorative topography to provide fix points for a changed, local self-understanding. The heralds of Communism's demise were the ubiquitous removal of its monuments from public spaces. In the period of transition from Communist to democratic governance contemporary events entered into that topography as sites were marked by relics of the recent political struggles. Near the Lithuanian Parliament building in Vilnius blocks of concrete used to barricade streets against Soviet tanks and armoured vehicles became an impromptu and messy, yet permanent memorial site to those who were killed in the transition from Communism to democracy. The sites in the Bastion Park of Riga where demonstrators were killed by Soviet security forces are now marked by simple boulders rolled into place. In Gdańsk in front of the shipyard gate where supporters of Solidarity strikers once gathered, a monument now rises to join a skyline of cranes. The new political actors are defining themselves for posterity by erecting monuments which have reconfigured constellations of memory and history and become themselves part of a built heritage.

---

4   For thoughts on the economics of world heritage preservation, see Georges Zouain (2001).

At the same time, older protagonists of history have been removed from the urban squares and streets because they conflict with new urban allegiances and identities. Representations of one national culture are discarded; those of another take their place. So, for example, Lithuanian authorities banished the monument to the Russian poet Pushkin from the centre of Vilnius to the forested hills on the periphery, while at the historical centre of the city a consortium of public and private interests erected a statue to the city's legendary Lithuanian founder, Grand Duke Gediminas. The Latvians of post-Communist Riga have resisted plans to resurrect the equestrian monument to Peter the Great with private funding, while at the same time they have employed scarce public funds to refurbish their Town Hall Square and reinstall the Germanic Roland. Changing historic orientations make certain cultural representations seem to *belong* in place, while others become *foreign*. One notes a shift in commemorative emphases in Gdańsk. The Solidarity monument dedicated to the shipyard workers who led the struggle against the Communist regime has superseded the memorials at nearby Central Post Office and at the destroyed fortress of the Westerplatte, which commemorate the heroic resistance of Poles against the Germans at the begin of the Second World War. Celebration and commemoration of local civic resistance supersede a national history of resistance and defeat exploited by the Communists.

Shifts in the constellations of monuments and memorials transform the urban narrative, recalling romantic legends of origins and ancestry, aspects of civic virtue, and significant historical events. Gediminas reclaims Vilnius for the Lithuanians by referring to mythic origins; Roland embodies a new civic autonomy while referring to an old; the Solidarity monument stands for the heroic struggle that led successfully to *local* self-determination. These set pieces play in narratives that have a significant role in the constitution of place-based identities. It does not matter that Vilnius had ceased to be a Lithuanian city for over four centuries until 1945 or that Roland was originally put in place by a German civic body that suppressed the local Latvians. The self-definition of a Polish Gdańsk allows its citizens to identify more closely with a city once populated mainly by Germans. Identity is constructed in the present. Heritage is a question of choice. Though very different in how and what they commemorate, Gediminas, Roland and Solidarity reassert the right of Lithuanians, Latvians and Poles to occupy and belong to their respective cities in which, historically, they had a tenuous hold – i.e. if belonging is defined in a modern ethnic-national sense.

In the Baltic States we note the changes in the contents of museums and the designation of historic sites. Some museums have been emptied out and refilled with objects to represent ethnic, religious, and national heritage. A Riga museum once dedicated to the role of Latvian military units in the Bolshevist revolution now houses exhibits documenting the Soviet and Nazi occupations of Latvia.[5] A new commemorative complex on Gediminas (formerly Lenin) Prospect in Vilnius

---

5 The museum was dedicated to the Red Riflemen, a military unit that served at one point as a sort of praetorian guard for Lenin.

tells the tragic story of Lithuanian insurgents and dissidents, who were tortured in the former KGB prison.[6] Historic populations, whose former presence had been ignored and obscured, are now being commemorated. At a site in Riga's Moscow suburb, a Soviet monument has given way to the excavated ruins of the Old Choral Synagogue burnt to the ground by the Nazis. The Jewish quarter in Vilnius, in part demolished by the Nazis and then eradicated under Stalin, is now marked by stone plaques. Jewish museums have opened in Riga and Vilnius to recall the significant historical contribution of Jews and to integrate them into the local heritage.[7] There are now even plans to rebuild the famous Great Synagogue of Vilnius, though there are not enough Jews left in Vilnius to fill it. The heritage of individual social, political, and cultural groups have been recognized by returning buildings to their original owners and uses, by marking them or the spaces where historic buildings once stood. After having served as concert halls, art galleries, or warehouses, churches have been re-consecrated, even if they have no contemporary congregation. This reclamation of built heritage is an offer to diverse religious and social groups, both historical and contemporary, to identify with sites in the city and with the city itself. Thus a sense of belonging is engendered.

Important in this pattern of (re-)identification is the changing of place names and symbols. Common public ancestry and a system of values are established and enter the everyday as streets and squares are renamed (Čaplinskas 2000; Hrytsak and Susak 2003). New allegiances are indicated as symbols associated with the old regime are removed from buildings, and new flags are hoisted. Other signs of the city's changing identity may be seen, for example, in the removal of Cyrillic script from the signage in Riga and Vilnius and its replacement by Latin script or in the predominant use of one language in traffic signs. These measures shift the understanding of cultural belonging and also demand a reorientation. Together the changes in the urban structure, symbolism, and place names generate complex and often contradictory historical topographies that support variable regional, ethnic, and national narratives. Not only do tourists and schoolchildren follow revised routes to inform themselves about the city's history, long-time residents have to adjust their understandings of their hometown and of themselves as landmarks, place names, and property values change. Some, like the Russians in Riga, may feel alienated from their new/old surroundings – may feel as if they no longer belong though their families have resided in the city for generations.

Accompanying the shift in the cultural-political conceptualization of a city projected through and influenced by changing patterns of commemoration, is the change in visual and conceptual orientation brought about by the insertion of new

---

6   The Museum of Genocide Victims was dedicated in 1992. The name refers to the genocide perpetrated against the Lithuanians and not the Jews.
7   In Vilnius the site of the Great Synagogue and the Jewish quarters of the city have been marked by commemorative plaques.

focal points and changes in urban structural configurations.[8] The physical and semiotic reorientations support particular characterizations of these cities. Riga, for example, is now celebrated by its residents and government as a Hanseatic city, a Baltic city, a city of Burghers, etc. And this is underlined in the rebuilding of the town hall square, the maintenance of the Old Town skyline, and plans to reconnect the Old City with the river. Such diffuse classifications related to these changes call forth particular historical *and* contemporary associations, justify an understanding of regional or cultural belonging, and provide an ideological platform for programmes of preservation or reconstruction. Corresponding narratives find their way into history books, guidebooks and tourist advertisements and become commonplace. The commonplace understandings are expressed simply. To claim that 'Riga was always a European city' is an understanding that has concrete causes and seeks concrete expression.

Transforming the Built Heritage: Historic Contexts

To understand heritage transformation in Riga, Vilnius, or Gdańsk one must review the 20th-century history of East-Central Europe, for the local heritage is composed in those cities very much as a reaction to the peculiarities of that history. After their illegal annexation by the Soviet Union in 1939, Lithuania and Latvia ceased to exist as sovereign states for over fifty years. Occupied by the Soviets, then by the Nazis, and then by the Soviets again, they were subject to exterior rule and definition. Mass murder of their Jews, deportation of various ethnic and political groups, emigration, and Russian-Soviet colonization changed the demographic mix in vast territories. Cities such as Vilnius, Gdańsk and Riga were depopulated and then repopulated. After the Second World War, in Riga and Vilnius the cultivation of local culture and heritage needed to be negotiated with Moscow, in Gdańsk with Warsaw. In varying ways, such political negotiations restricted local cultural self-determination, which was being undertaken by populations that had just arrived.

The post-Communist cultural definitions of belonging are complicated by changing ethnic-national contexts for these cities in the 20th century. Only after the Second World War does Gdańsk become a part of a Poland defined as an *ethnic-national* state (Smith 1998). Vilnius, at the same time, becomes the capital of a Lithuania incorporated into the Soviet Union, and Riga of a Latvia in the same state. Latvians constitute only a bare majority in their country (approximately 52 per cent in 1989) and are in a minority in Riga. Ethnic Lithuanians make up 85 per cent of the population of Lithuania, but they were in a very small minority (1-2 per cent) in

---

8   With reference to urban structures, see Lynch (1960). For the symbolism of urban narratives and description that relate closely to physical structure and commemorative practices, see Strauss (1961). Though many studies dealing with urban images have been published since, these two books remain touchstones.

Vilnius until the decimation and deportation of its Polish and Jewish residents during and following the Second World War. Against the background of Soviet occupation, Riga and Vilnius must be seen as post-colonial cities as well. Both Riga and Vilnius are capital cities of ethnically defined nations, which makes them the focus of restorative national representations even as they seek a 'return to Europe'. Multiple cultures resided in both cities before they became, in their respective ways, more homogenous, and both need to come to terms with the evident contributions of multiple cultures to their history. With all this in mind it seems logical that the residents of cities such as Riga and Vilnius would seek to reverse Russian Soviet cultural incursions through a reassertion of denied historical claims, visions, and imageries of place that recur to local, national, and European history.

A different situation existed in the Poland that emerged from post-war agreements, which redefined Polish national borders to eliminate the Eastern borderlands. This post-war Poland is an ethnically homogenous state, whose cities in the newly acquired Western territories ('recovered' territories) had been populated by Germans until their deportation and resettlement in the post-war period. With the normalization of German-Polish relations, mutual recognition of borders, and the end of Soviet domination, Poland, and especially cities such as Gdańsk, Szczecin and Wrocław, is beginning to redefine its historic relationship to Europe apart from the memory of the Second World War. The move of borders from East to West and the loss of large non-Polish ethnic minorities repositioned Poland to integrate into the Western sphere. The formerly German cities such as Gdańsk have a potential bridgehead function to the EU, especially through their regional connections and emerging regional identities.

Still, because of the wholesale ethnic cleansing, mass murder, deportation, and colonization, the problem of demographic shifts looms large over the whole project of composing the post-Communist heritage in cities such as Gdańsk, Riga and Vilnius. The ethnic Polish population that has replaced a largely ethnic German one in Gdańsk is confronted by a major question about how to respond to or to integrate aspects of the ethnic-German past into the urban heritage. The question is answered selectively according to the needs of the present. A mediaeval German burgher whose epitaph stands in St. Mary's Cathedral in Gdańsk and who fought against the domination of the Teutonic Knights can be easily integrated into a heritage of civic autonomy. The more general rejection of all things German, inspired by Nazi aggression and propagated further in the 'anti-fascist' mythologies of the Communist regime has now given way to a willingness to recognize German historical contributions even to the point of identifying German families that once lived in historic houses.[9]

As the new/historical capitals of Latvia and Lithuania, Riga and Vilnius have the charge to symbolize national-ethnic resurgence in their cultivation of urban

---

9   In March 2000 a commemorative plaque was dedicated by the parishioners of St. Joseph's Church to commemorate the East Prussian refugees locked in the church and set afire by the Red Army.

heritage. The incursions of Russian culture under the Soviets were less defining in Vilnius than in Riga. The Lithuanians of Vilnius, transplanted to the city after the war, grapple rather with the long and illustrious history of Polish and Jewish presence in the city. For the Poles the city came to be intimately associated with a romantic nationalism through, for example, the work of the poets Adam Mickiewicz and Julius Słowacki. For the Jews Vilnius was the 'Jerusalem of Lithuania' and a base for Jewish Enlightenment, secularization, and socialism. Despite the historical significance of Vilnius for both Poles and Jews, they are no longer significant producers of culture and identity within the city itself. For many if not most Lithuanians, Vilnius is simply the historical capital of Lithuania no matter who resided there. They identify with a historic capital devoid of its historic population of Poles and Jews.

Gdańsk, Riga and Vilnius are cities in need of what Jörn Rüsen has called multi-perspectival history. In Riga and Vilnius resentment and a lingering fear of an economic and political threat from the East somewhat hinders the acceptance of Russians as part of the local heritage. In Vilnius, Lithuanians still do not recognize the role of Polish culture. The complicity of Latvians and Lithuanians in the destruction of the Jewish communities complicates the recognition of that rich heritage, as does the status of Latvians and Lithuanian themselves as (competing) victims of war and occupation. The tendency is still toward exclusionary patterns of historical representation focused on a singular ethnic-national group.

Transforming the Local History and Heritage: Trends

At a truly local level, the return of municipal self-determination in all the cities under consideration supports alternative historical representations that focus on regional and local distinctions beyond the sphere of ethnic-national definitions. Thus Hanseatic, Baltic, Burgher, religious, and European aspects of urban heritage are cultivated in preservationist strategies emphasizing the uniqueness of these cities in a way that supports civic consciousness and local pride. To say 'I am from Riga' (or 'Vilnius' or 'Gdańsk') means something quite different now than it did during the Soviet period, because different historic understanding of a place of origin and belonging has changed.

Each city is promoting its local heritage to demonstrate the historical affinities with the (old) West. As Poland, Latvia and Lithuania are integrated into NATO and prepare to accede to the European Union, the built heritage of these cities has become a vehicle for geopolitical repositioning and the constitution of regional and supranational senses of belonging. The propagation of a 'European' heritage also offers a means to overcome the still perceived divide between East and West. That sense of belonging to Europe maintained more privately during the Soviet period has become a public good. That Gdańsk, Riga and Vilnius look like European cities is and was a commonly shared perception. During the Soviet period a Russian going to Riga or Vilnius spoke of going to 'Europe' or of going to the 'near abroad'.[10] Gdańsk, on the sea, in the 'recovered' territories, and far from Warsaw in the minds of many of its residents, presented the image of a Baltic/ Hanseatic city. Walking through the historic districts of these cities, their residents are able to concretely apprehend their belonging to a renewed Europe. Public cultivation of the historic substance in these cities goes hand in hand with the maintenance and renewal of shared identities and cultural values.

For is there any other way to understand the extensive Jugendstil architecture of Riga, the panoply of Baroque churches and Renaissance arcades in Vilnius, or the brick Gothic churches and mannered Burgher houses of Gdańsk, than to see them as an extension of a more general European culture associated with the West? Is Jugendstil of Riga with its local variations, not the fashionable style of a turn-of-the-century European bourgeoisie? Even the peculiar elements of Latvian National Romanticism which mark many of the buildings built around 1900, relate Riga to Budapest, Prague, Cracow or Lviv, where similar elements derived from folk cultures were incorporated into façades. And do the Baroque churches and Renaissance arcades of Vilnius not exhibit Catholic influences and the employ of Italian architects in the service of the Counter-Reformation? Is it not the form and colouration of buildings more typical of Southern Europe that make Vilnius seem the southernmost North European city? Cannot one recognize the Hanseatic heritage in the ornate Burgher houses of Gdańsk that might well have stood in Lübeck or Antwerp? Does such structural evidence not situate these cities firmly within the broader European cultural sphere? The form, styles, and materials of place retain their valence as historical and cultural signifiers and as a means for representing the distinct identity of place and engendering an identity with place.

Beyond the politics of identity, the historical substance in these cities that survived the Second World War and the Communist regimes, is now seen as a resource for the tourist industry. With their revaluation, the old towns of Vilnius and Riga are being gentrified and commercialized.[11] UNESCO has declared Riga and Vilnius World Heritage Cities,[12] lending them recognition as sites of world cultural significance while underlining their uniqueness. Though the revaluation of distinct historical structures has been continuous in Gdańsk since the Second World War and had already begun under Communist regimes in Riga and Vilnius by the 1970s, the devolution of the responsibilities for historic preservation from central to local authorities has intensified it. Historical preservation is now intricately allied with a public and politically propagated reassertion of place-based identities and a renewed sense of regional 'belonging'.

---

10 This common impression in part derived from the later incorporation of these cities into the Soviet Union and in part to their historical-cultural and religious affiliations.

11 Interviews with the chief city planner Andris Roze in Riga, July 2000 and with members of the Old Town Renewal Agency in Vilnius, June 2000.

12 The historic centre of Vilnius became a World Heritage site in 1994, while the historic center of Riga was awarded that status in 1997. Gdańsk's application for the status was unsuccessful.

This recovery of history in place is also driven and complicated by the deep sense of loss felt by the populations of these cities, who believe the Communist interregnum interrupted urban development.[13] From this perspective parts of the city developed under Communist rule seem inauthentic and imposed. Thus the project of recovering the urban past in Gdańsk, Riga and Vilnius also involves a radical project of cultural-historical dissociation from the Communist era.[14] The redefinition of heritage thus appears as much reactionary as revolutionary.

Each public instance of this transformation in the built heritage of cities evolves a complex play of political legitimization, identity politics, historical and archaeological research, international recognition, and economics. Each may involve years of negotiation, fund raising, and successive reinterpretations, and each relates to an extant complex constellation of commemorative devices and built heritage, whose hierarchies and focal points shift with the addition or subtraction of individual elements. The following only attempts to identify typical instances of transformation in each city.

A National Symbol and a Civic Landmark: Historical Scale

In October 2000, the outgoing Lithuanian Parliament dominated by Conservatives and Christian Democrats hastily passed a law and appropriated the funds to initiate the reconstruction of the Lower Palace in the lower castle complex, perhaps the most important architectural representation of the historic Grand Duchy of Lithuania. The proponents of the reconstruction generally understood the historic castle as a Lithuanian national symbol that fell into disrepair after being damaged in a Russian siege of the city during the 17th century and was ultimately destroyed circa 1800, while Lithuania was under Russian suzerainty.[15] Archaeological excavations that began in 1989 during the period of *perestroika* unearthed the palace foundations, some architectural fragments, and numerous artefacts, which evince a broad European influence on the building of this structure. Though the actual appearance of the palace can only be vaguely reconstructed from old drawings, engravings, and paintings, many supporters – including the former President of Lithuania – pleaded for a historic 'replica' to be built (see Figure 8.1).

---

13 'Nostalgia' might be the appropriate word, but its meanings are too complex and suggest a wish to return to the past, whereby the more sober reconstructionists of these cities only want the past and the character of the present city recognized. See Svetlana Boym (2001).

14 Though many of them, and especially those engaged in city administration, design, and architecture, were once proponents of that very scheme.

15 The Grand Duchy of Lithuania had been administered from this palace, which embodies that historic state and housed legends about its rulers.

Figure 8.1 Model of the Lower Palace

Photographed by Jurgita Remeityte

In the contemporary Lithuanian state the palace may serve to symbolize the era before 'foreigners' ruled in Vilnius and transmit the legacy of the Grand Duchy of Lithuania and Lithuanian-Polish Commonwealth, the largest state in Europe at one time. However, interviews with Napoleonas Kitkuaskas and Vytautas Urbanivicius, the directors of the excavation site and rebuilding project, and with Edmundas Kulkauskas of the 'Castle Society' indicate that the palace is a *national* symbol embodying the continuity in Lithuanian presence in Vilnius. The project directors seem unconcerned that the external appearance of the palace can only be gleaned vaguely from the structural remains and pictorial representations and that no representations of the palace interior are extant to guide them in its reconstruction. Projected as a national-historical symbol and meant to firmly foot the genealogy of a nation in place, they ignore larger questions of historical authenticity in content *and* form.

In its style and its history, the Lower Palace relates Vilnius to a broader (Western) European civilization and culture and was the seat of rulers in a composite state of multiple nationalities. After the Treaty of Lublin in 1569 which replaced the personal union of Polish and Lithuanian kings by a constitutional union of states, Polish became the language of administration and culture (Snyder 2003) and was thus probably the *lingua franca* within the palace walls. Lithuanian gentry living and passing through the palace were, for the most part, acculturated as Poles by the end of the 16th century. Ironically, the Wawel Castle in Cracow may have served as a model for the original Lower Palace and is being used as a model in the reconstruction. The palace's significance within contemporary Lithuania can either be nationalistically limited and historically false or can help revive the broader European heritage of a city cast in the mould of distinct but convergent cultures.

Figure 8.2 House of the Blackheads, photographed in 1999

Photographed by John Czaplicka

In 1999 the City of Riga reasserted another type of genealogy in place by reconstructing the House of the Blackheads, a landmark building at the centre of Old Riga destroyed in the Second World War, whose ruins were removed during the Soviet occupation (see Figure 8.2). Historically the building had first served as the seat of a mediaeval guild and the fraternity of the Blackheads, an organization of unmarried merchants. The main hall of the building was also used for various civic activities and festive public ceremonies. Renowned for the beauty of its architecture, sculptural decoration, and the collections it contained, it was a central landmark of the Old Town. The replica of this landmark civic structure derives its appearance from many extant historical photographs as well as from plans and extensive research. With better documentation than the projected palace in Vilnius, the Latvians have produced a fair simulacrum of the historic building both in its interior and exterior if not in their use of materials or construction techniques. The style and multiple symbolic elements of the replica recall the formative Hanseatic and Germanic contributions to the city (Krastins 2000; Sparitis 2003) and serves to emphasize the city's belonging to 'Europe'. It restores the configuration of the Town Hall Square, the historic civic centre of Riga.

The reconstructed House of the Blackheads reverses the Soviet decision to restlessly remove the landmark's ruins and the Soviet disdain for anything conveying the German and bourgeois past of Riga. Considered together with the reinstated statue of Roland before it and the new town hall being built on the foundations of a demolished Soviet structure across from it, the House of the Blackheads projects a historic image of civic identity and autonomy while recurring to a 'European' heritage.[16]

In Gdańsk, where the Hanseatic, Baltic and Germanic heritage of the city is also experiencing a revival, the most contemporary extension of the Old Town exhibits a postmodernist style largely influenced by Hanseatic and Wilhelmenian historicism. After the Second World War the 19th-century style was avoided by the first generation of Polish engineers and architects reconstructing the city, because it was seen as too 'German' or simply too ugly. Now the historicist style has come into vogue especially after the publication of a book on 'Old Gdańsk' containing sepia-colored photographs of historicist buildings, presenting an image of the historical city that not only contrasts the Communist 'modernism' but also with the stylistically select reconstruction of the city after the Second World War.[17] For the major architect involved in the contemporary reconstruction of Old Gdańsk the ornate and historicist Wilhelmenian central train station is the most beautiful building in the city.[18] The newfound appreciation of this style would indicate that the political aversion to anything that recalled German imperial rule is no longer prevalent.

One can view the workings of such limited heritage reclamation as a reprise of the historical image(s) of the city (*Stadtbild*). The constellation of elements that compose that image in its totality lends the character and distinction to the city so important in the formation of place-based identity. The following attempts to articulate larger aspects of the restoration of a historical urban image.

---

16 In speaking with the architects, archaeologists, urban planners, and public advocates of the reconstructed Town Hall Square in Riga and the Lower Palace complex in Vilnius, it became apparent to me that in neither case had the supporters of these projects thought thoroughly about the use of the projected architecture. Symbolic and aesthetic reasoning were largely used in their advocacy of the reconstructions.
17 Donald Tusk (1998) has almost become a pattern book for architects.
18 Interview with the architect Stanisław Michel in Gdańsk, April 2000.

Memorable Silhouettes: Historic Outlines

Urban silhouettes reduce the city into a single comprehensible image; characteristic silhouettes impress themselves upon the mind of the beholder and often become common points of reference for a particular place, ones which are immediately recognizable and intimately familiar to the city's residents (Attoe 1981).

Approaching Riga from the West and nearing the banks of the Daugava, a familiar urban silhouette looms on the horizon. Punctuated by Baroque and neo-Gothic church steeples, it is a typical Northern European skyline rising from a coastal plain. Such typical but individually memorable silhouettes provide orientation, measure and meaning to the urban gestalt. Curiously, even that exceptional peak in Riga's skyline toward the South, the Stalinist 'wedding cake' Academy of Sciences with its multiple pinnacles, fits well into the picture.[19] Although the scale of 20th-century buildings inserted into the city centre is, as the architectural historian Janis Krastins has suggested,[20] too large, the church towers which still frame the Old City maintain its general urban image, evocative of a historic Baltic and Hanseatic that 'locates' Riga in a geopolitical and cultural zone.

A similar image impresses itself upon one in the approach to Gdańsk. The massive tower and nave of St. Mary Cathedral with its many pinnacles and the tall and ornate Rathaus Tower dominate this silhouette. Other church steeples punctuate the skyline. Below these landmark elements Gdańsk has a secondary skyline, one just as important for a perception of the city: the individually designed and often ornate gables of the Gdańsk Burgher houses which dominate the streetscape. To speak with the Gdańsk architect Wiesław Gruszkowski, who had a leading role in the reconstruction of the city after the Second World War, the maintenance of the two contrasting scales was of utmost importance in restoring the historic *Stadtbild* and lending it a distinctive character.[21] It is true that Vilnius, set into the hills along the River Neris, has no singular skyline comparable to Riga or Gdańsk. Rather it offers a multiplicity of shifting views toward variegated cityscapes dotted by church steeples and towers. Yet the palace hill with its reconstructed castle tower presents a strong centring element. From the high castle hill and from other ridges that surround and penetrate into the city one overlooks a city displaying a suggestive unity between natural landscape and the built environment (Markevičienė 1999). The old city from most points of view appears 'couched' in nature.

Although such concise views of Riga, Vilnius and Gdańsk no longer correspond to the actual breadth and extent of these modern cities, which sprawl

---

19 The two colonizers of the region, Merchant-Christianity and Soviet-Russia are well represented in the skyline.
20 Janis Krastins is an internationally renowned art and architectural historian; interview, July 2000, Riga.
21 Interview in Gdańsk, March 2000.

into the landscape and far beyond the historic cores, the outlines of urban structure set against the horizon or their merger into the natural topography allows them to be concisely characterized. The views are integral and memorable. Identity with place is fixed and transported in such memorable views.

The old towns that offer such views retain a sense of scale and integrity. A set of circumstances has contributed to this situation. The lack of resources to build new housing and office space to replace the historic buildings, local protest, and the development of historic preservation within the Soviet Union, combined to counter the grand schemes that characterized Communist building programmes in Riga and Vilnius. In Gdańsk, the commitment to reconstruct the almost totally destroyed historic city was accompanied by the modern impulses to fill the reconstructed Burgher houses with working class apartments and to clear the long, narrow courtyards to let in air and light. The unbroken street façades prevented the historic city from appearing too fragmented.

Still, if historic façades remained or were rebuilt to maintain the historic *Stadtbild*, the interiors behind them were thoroughly transformed under the pressures to provide housing under the Communists. Townhouses and villas and large bourgeois apartments were subdivided into smaller flats to make room for communal living. One has to look behind these facades in a different way and see that they not only offer picture-postcard-perfect images for touristic consumption, they are meaningful historic images through which one identifies a particular city. They fulfil aesthetic and emotional needs, while creating a place for the historical imagination.

The Return of Walls, Gates, and Towers: Boundaries and Structures

In Vilnius, over a long period of time, walls were partially razed and integrated into new buildings, so that the inner structural border of the city disappeared into the mass of buildings. The sole survivor among the numerous city gates is the highly symbolic Ostra Brama, a chapel with an image of the Virgin Mary sacred to Catholics and especially Polish Catholics from the region. This situation is changing. Jonas Glemza head of the Department of Heritage Conservation at the Vilnius Academy of the Arts, and a major actor in preservation politics in Vilnius before and after the fall of the Soviet Union,[22] has a project to mark the whole course of the wall. Curiously, similar projects exist in Gdańsk and Riga. In Gdańsk, there was a plan to dig a trench to expose the partially buried mediaeval wall and then to pave a walkway next to it so that the tourist could circumambulate the central historic district (Główne Miasto). One architect has drawn up plans to mark the course of the northern and western fortifications that had been razed in

---

22 Indeed, former head of ICOMOS for the whole Soviet Union; interview, May 2000 in
    Vilnius.

the 19th century. [23] And in Riga, Peteris Blumis, an architect and former preservationist, defends the construction of a parking garage he designed on the remnants of an old Swedish bastion by noting that it harmonizes with the proportions of the historic fortifications. [24] Blumeris also suggested uncovering other bastions in the parks composing Riga's inner ring. Already during the late Soviet period stone foundations of the Riga city wall had been exposed and battlements were reconstructed. [25] Such reconstructive projects call attention to the importance of a particular type of historic imagery in lending even a city contemporary identity. Reconstructed walls provide clearly defined borders and transitions from the interior to the exterior. The city can be recognized as a bounded place or object. Figuratively speaking, one can more easily take possession of such a bounded city.

Also spatial rhythms and urban scale, peculiar street patterns, and borders established by landscape elements such as rivers or forests (parks) serve to maintain a city's coherent image. Interesting in this regard is that despite all disregard of individual historic buildings, the urban image played an important role in urban reconstruction and preservation even during the era of centralized regulation of building in the Communist era. In the words of Vytautas Jurkstas, a proponent of 'architectural harmonization' in Vilnius during the Soviet period, one had to move toward a study of 'unified urbanistic complexes with distinct individual peculiarities'. [26] It is perhaps then not so surprising that so many of these peculiarities have survived the Soviet period in Vilnius and Riga. This conceptualization of the city may have saved historic macro-structures lost to the piecemeal planning undertaken in a capitalist West and certainly helped preserve the individuality of cities, that core element in local identification.

In the post-Communist era the restoration of such formative historical elements generally involves a reversal of *modern* city planning. A traffic artery that cuts off the southern districts of the historic Gdańsk and a magisterial boulevard that separates Old Riga from the river are now viewed as *foreign* incursions into the city which have led to its fragmentation. Even before the demise of the Soviet Union, the residents of Riga had protested against plans for a subway system into the heart of the Old Town. And in Vilnius, plans by the Soviet government to build a parking lot in the Old Town and to slash a thoroughfare through it from the train station to a major bridge, met with similar protests. The plans were dropped. The city retained an integral and memorable imagery.

This decidedly anti-modern and thoroughly physical comprehension of urban form presents the city as a comprehensible or perceptible place even if it extends to

---

23 Interview with Mirosław Hrynkiewicz. See also Hrynkiewicz (2000).
24 Interview, Blumeris in Riga, June 2000.
25 The Ramera Tower and a fragment of the fortification wall from the 13th to 15th century.
26 I do not, however, suggest that the ugly structures inserted into the Old City of Vilnius using the principles of 'harmonization' were successful.

the horizon. Walls delimit the city and together with the direction, width, and length of streets, they present the image of a particular place and a particular history.

Local Peculiarities: In Place and Out of Place

The employment of distinct building materials and techniques within a defined geographical area indicates the level of development, patterns of cultural influence, and sometimes characterizes a place if we conceive these materials and techniques as 'indigenous'. As Akos Moravansky (2000) has noted, these indicators help define 'material landscapes' both real and imaginary and may even help compose the imagined geography of a nation or a region. The distinctive local character of cities often relies on such associations. One could write an urban history of cities based solely on the use of construction techniques and materials. Red-brick gothic marks Northern European cities; the yellow stucco of large public buildings in the cities of Central Europe is sometimes seen as co-extensive with the Habsburg Empire. Still, in our global age all types of materials are available everywhere; each technique is easily transferable, and air conditioning combined with better insulation allows one to build independent of the local climatic conditions. Thus by referring to materials and techniques, one can now define an indigenous architecture mainly in a historical sense.

Still, one question I posed to residents of Gdańsk, Riga and Vilnius concerned the 'indigenous materials and techniques' that they associated with the architecture of their 'home towns'. The question elicited almost exclusively references to their Old Towns and at most their 19th- and early 20th-century expansions. Any discussion about a place-specificity as defined by materials focused on the 'historical' city or its postmodernist and post-Communist extensions. Residents of all three cities referred to brick. In Gdańsk, brick held a position of primary importance due to its extensive use in public buildings, major monuments and landmarks throughout the centuries. The 'Prussian (brick) gothic' of public administrative buildings still impressed itself upon the city as much as the 'Northern European' manner of construction in an area where natural stone was not readily available.[27] In Vilnius brick was associated with the Gothic era; it called forth an era before the predominance of Baroque and Neo-Classical styles, when a smooth stucco layer was used to finish brick buildings. One could say brick represented different epochs in these two cities.

In Riga beside the 'Hanseatic' brick, one mentioned especially wood, a construction material still quite evident in Vilnius, Riga, Tallinn, and other cities of the northern and eastern Baltic. In general, wood could be said to define the

---

27 It is interesting to note how many times I was told that the granite of the streets derived from the ballast of empty ships coming into the harbour to load grain from the inland of Poland.

vernacular architecture in Riga and Vilnius, but not in Gdańsk. In both Vilnius and Riga wooden architecture is a species of architecture tending toward extinction.

Outside Riga's Old Town in an area of Jugendstil and eclectic apartment houses, a unique building pattern exists in which wood plays a prominent role. Sequences of six-storey apartment houses are abruptly broken by pairs of one-storey wooden houses in Neo-Classical style – remnants of the wooden suburbs of the city built after their predecessors were burnt down in 1812.[28] Courtyards of six-storey apartment houses sometimes still enclose examples of this Baltic vernacular architecture. This stark contrast in building type, scale, style, and materials characterizes Riga and became one reason for designating the city a World Heritage City in 1996. Now these same examples of a local-historic architecture are threatened by free-market values and the increasing value of land in the inner city.

Vilnius has a comparable situation, with wooden architecture scattered throughout the city. A large preserve of wooden architecture is endangered in, for example, the Zverynas suburb. Only in exceptional cases is this architecture being preserved. Many of the wooden buildings in both cities are dilapidated; they are disappearing under the pressures of capitalist investment, lack of a systematic execution of historic preservation laws, and municipal corruption or negligence. In the Moscow suburb of Riga, such examples of wooden architecture are being cleared by such negligence, although Rigans do seem to *identify with* this architecture in a way they would never identify with the ferro-concrete wastelands scattered on the periphery.

The ferro-concrete structures offer an example of negative identification. The post-Stalinist socialist architecture has been devalued and is associated with poor workmanship and a failed political system. The denizens of such complexes remain silent about them when asked about their 'home' towns.[29] The mass housing is the major monument to a Communist past, with which the residents of these cities no longer identify. In all four cities I heard similar and very popular stories about getting lost in an area of mass housing where everything looked the same. The anonymous structures seem less the markers of a particular place than of an era most residents of these cities would like to forget. While walking through such complexes in Gdańsk and Vilnius, after having visited similar settlements in Lviv, Warsaw, Lublin, and on the outskirts of Cracow, I wondered about the sense of place that might be engendered by them. In Gdańsk people spoke with pride about the totally reconstructed Old Town, about Oliwa with its monastery and beautiful church, about Sopot, the renowned 19th-century seaside resort, or even about modern Gdynia, the harbour city the Poles built from scratch in the inter-war years. Wrzeszcz, a district of Gdańsk, was mentioned for its small villa quarter. But if the

---

28 All the wooden buildings in Riga's suburbs were burnt down as a defence measure when Napoleon's forces advanced towards the city.

29 In over 60 interviews with residents of the region, many of whom lived in socialist housing, not once did my questioning about their 'home' town elicit any reference to the towers of reinforced concrete on the peripheries of Gdańsk, Lviv, Riga or Vilnius.

expansive modern settlements such as Przymorze and Zaspa were mentioned at all
– then only disparagingly.

To an extent the same pattern of depreciation was true in Vilnius and Riga. But
when referring to Antakalnis, a suburb of Vilnius to the north and east of the Old
Town between wooded hills and the River Neris, compact socialist housing
interspersed among many individual houses and estates and set near the river or
wooded areas had a positive reputation, as did Zverynas, a district full of wooden
houses and small apartment complexes. Scale and landscape elements played a role
in this positive identification. Each of these older suburbs had their particular
character and particular histories and myths as well. In contrast the large settlement
districts across the river in the northern part of the city remained largely nameless
and without historical or mythic associations.

In Riga the questions about the identity and character of the city elicited
descriptions of its parks, the relationship to the river, and those three areas which
gave it the right to be a World Heritage City: the Old Town, the ring of Jugendstil
architecture, and wooden architecture. One also 'had to see' the district of
Wilhelmine villas on the edge of the city. These elements formed the central shared
image of the city. The slab apartment complexes on the periphery were not
mentioned, with the notable exception of an ethnic-Russian journalist, Katya
Borchova, who spoke of getting to know the *tristesse* of the socialist suburbs in
order to actually get to know the city. Socialist housing complexes, so it seems
from the silence surrounding them, do not *belong* to Gdańsk, Riga and Vilnius
proper. They now have a very subordinate part in establishing the identity and
character of these cities. But again, there are certain exceptions. In the Przymorze
district of apartment blocks in the northern expanses of Gdańsk, I visited the
architect and scholar Jacek Dominiczak. His apartment is located near the large
park and former airport named after Pope John Paul and not far from the reputedly
longest building in the world – an apartment block of the Communist era that
stretches for one full kilometre. Professor Dominiczak, an architectural theorist at
the Technical University of Gdańsk, remained in his socialist apartment; he
removed the wall coverings to reveal bare concrete slabs. The subtle variations in
surface texture, the modulations in tones of grey, and the exposed structure in the
joints between each block work well with unfinished wood and furnishings and
tableware of modern design without ornamentation. Yet few people who have lived
with the deprivations of the notably 'grey' Socialist era share such a modern and
sachlich aesthetic sensibility.

Poor quality materials, slip-shod construction, and a lack of distinctiveness
characterize the housing stock of the Communist era. The results of the socialist
experiment in mass housing and industrialized construction are a deep distrust of
modern architecture in general and a weakened identity with the places where the
apartment complexes have been built.

Belonging and Expanded Horizons: House with an Oriental Roofline

Michael, a student of Dominiczak who I interviewed, had recently moved with his family into a turn-of-the-century German villa (1911) in the Wrzeszcz district of Gdańsk near a forest and the central cemetery. In this historic villa suburb his family shared their home with two other families. Michael exhibited an archaeological interest in his home. He outlined floor plan changes, told me about the original stairways, shutters, and heating system. He showed a high regard for German building technology, materials and small quirky fixtures. An original Nietzsche volume, found in the cellar between heating pipes and the original paving on the street in front of the house were key clues for Michael's understanding of a former German *Großbürgerliche* existence in this contemporary Polish city.

Sensitive to form, Michael complained about a concrete dormer that destroyed the 'oriental' roofline and introduced 'foreign materials' into his present home. He proudly displayed the attempt his family had made to retain some original door fixtures and to emulate curvilinear ceilings in the entranceway. He evinced a respect for the original design of the house and a willingness to try and understand the tradition in which the house was built. The distinctive style of this house was not foreign to Michael, who had been born in Gdańsk. Michael's attachment to his home/house and his identification with it suggests how place-based identities are being formed and how urban heritage has been expanded as the new generation takes possession of the city. Michael pursued the history of his house without ethnic or national qualification and internalized its aesthetic. He recognized the turn-of-the-century villa as a distinctive home worth preserving. He had found a place to live and in his respect for a broader tradition was finding a place in 'Europe'. On a very personal level the identity of second and third generation Poles in Gdańsk, Lithuanians in Vilnius, or Latvians in Riga is thus changing. The attachment to familiar surroundings and an engagement improving and preserving them sets the tone for the individual transformation of identity in place. As the residents of these cities configure their lived environment and identify their heritage with a respect for the history in places that environment begins to belong to them and they begin to belong to that environment. Putting heritage into public place is only an extension of the personal evolution of place-based identities and a sense of belonging in the historically conflicted cities of East-Central Europe. The re-establishment and contestation of such identities and senses of belonging are, I think, also one aspect in the reconstitution of a civic and civil society.

Works Cited

Attoe, Wayne (1981) *Skylines: Understanding and Molding Urban Silhouettes.* New York: John Wiley & Sons.
Boym, Svetlana (2001) *The Future of Nostalgia.* New York: Basic Books.

Čaplinskas, Antanas Rimvydas (2000) *Vilniaus Gatves Istorija Vardynas Žemėlapiai* (Vilnius Streets, History, Street Names, Maps). Vilnius: Charibdė.

Carter, Erica, James Donald and Judith Squires (eds) (1993) *Space and Place: Theories of Identity and Location*. London: Lawrence & Wishart.

Hrynkiewicz, Mirosław (2000) 'Śródmieście i stocznia', *30 dni*, Gdańsk, no. 4 (April), 36-46.

Hrytsak, Yarolslav and Victor Susak (2003) 'Constructing a National City', in John Czaplicka and Blair Ruble (eds), *Composing Urban History and the Constitution of Civic Identities*. Baltimore: Johns Hopkins University Press.

Krastins, Janis (2000) *Rigas Ratslaukams (The Town Hall Square of Riga)*. Riga: Rigas Domes Plsetas.

Lynch, Kevin (1960) *The Image of the City*. Cambridge, MA: MIT Press.

Markevičienė, Jurate (1999) 'Genius Loci of Vilnius', Vilnius: Lithuanian Literature, Culture, History (Summer), 101-124.

Moravansky, Akos (2000) 'Materiallandschaften', Kritische Berichte, 28(2), 20-28.

Outekhine, Ilya (2003) 'Filling Dwelling Place with History: The Case of Communal Apartments in St. Petersburg', in John Czaplicka and Blair Ruble (eds), *Composing Urban History and the Constitution of Civic Identities*. Baltimore: Johns Hopkins University Press.

Rückkehr der Geschichte (1991) special issue of *Transit: Europäische Revue*, no. 2, (Summer).

Sezneva, Olga (2003) 'The Dual History: The Politics of the Past in Kaliningrad, Formerly Königsberg', in John Czaplicka and Blair Ruble (eds), *Composing Urban History and the Constitution of Civic Identities*. Baltimore: Johns Hopkins University Press.

Smith, Graham (1998) 'Nation Re-building and Political Discourses of Identity Politics in the Baltic States', in Graham Smith, Vivien Law et al. (eds), *Nation-building in the Post-Soviet Borderlands. The Politics of National Identities*. Cambridge: Cambridge University Press, 93-118.

Snyder, Tim (2003) *The Reconstruction of Nations: Poland, Ukraine, Lithuania, Belarus, 1569-1999*. New Haven, CT: Yale University Press.

Sparitis, Ojars (2003) 'The Rebirth and Restoration of Administrative, Political, and Cultural Symbols in Riga's Town Hall Square', in John Czaplicka and Blair Ruble (eds), *Composing Urban History and the Constitution of Civic Identities*. Baltimore: Johns Hopkins University Press, 341-371.

Strauss, Anselm L. (1961) *Images of the American City*. New York: The Free Press.

Tusk, Donald (1998) *Był sobie Gdańsk*. Gdańsk: Fundacja 'Dar Gdańska'.

Die wiedergefundene Erinnerung/Die Verdrängte Geschichte in Osteuropa (1992). Berlin: BasisDruck.

Zouain, Georges (2001) 'The Heritage, Art and Economics: Cultural Heritage in the Light of Economic Theory', in *Urban Heritage Landscape: Heritage Management in a Living City*. Karlskrona: Karlskrona Kommun, 29-41.

Chapter 9

Between Doctrine and Belonging: The Official Language of Nation in China

Flemming Christiansen

How does official China construct the national and ethnic belonging of the Chinese? How is the citizens' individual ethnic and national belonging integrated in the ideological project of the Chinese nation? Is national and ethnic belonging a matter of personal preference and lifestyle or a tool for social inclusion or exclusion? Authoritative (official) media use topoi of the nation with great frequency and apparent hyperbole in an official discourse. At the same time, non-official players appropriate this official discourse and reinterpret it, setting new agendas that the official discourse must deal with.

Since 1978 the freedom to publicly formulate political opinions on nation and ethnicity widened dramatically in China. In the early 1990s, the central leadership under Jiang Zemin sought to regain the initiative in these discourses. This accompanied the reinforcement of the Taiwan policy, and coincided with Hong Kong's and Macau's retrocession in 1997 and 1999.

Central authoritative construction of the nation in the 1990s became central to Jiang Zemin's ideological agenda. It countered the populist groundswell of national and ethnic feelings in the 1980s and 1990s expressed in cultural debates that broke into 'no-go areas' of public debate. Television series like *River Elegy* and *A Beijing Man in New York*, together with book-length essays like *China Can Say No*, as well as debates in the less controlled popular and regional printed press, had, for example, created unease among political leaders.

An anonymous essay writer[1] summed up the soul-searching intellectual debates about the nation as 'in reality not concerned with culture, but with politics, not with history, but with the present reality'. Su Xiaokang, the author of *River Elegy*, allegedly used the series to 'boycott Marxism' in a way 'understandable to normal people outside the small circle of intellectuals'. Although some of the debaters and their works were attacked and barred from official media, the genie was out of the bottle.[2] Many contributions to the debates were sophisticated, playing on many

---

1   Ni Ming (Anonymous) 'River Elegy and Saying No' (*Heshang he Shuo Bu*), Baiyun Shuku website (http://www.baiyun.web/library/).

2   For analyses and critiques of *River Elegy*, *China Can Say No*, etc. see Woei Lien Chong (1989-90), Richard Bodman and Pin P. Wan (1991); Cui Wenhua (1988); Hua Yan

layers of symbolism and using suggestive and subliminal effects. *River Elegy*'s description of the lethargic and atrophied cultural origins in the murky waters of the Yellow River as the cause of China's present backwardness and misery provoked strong nationalist sentiments, a mixture of hurt pride and anger at the immediate political past. Most importantly, it essentialized history, race and nation. The opinions among Party leaders varied, and it was difficult to define a clear demarcation line between the intellectuals initiating the debates, their media critics and the politicians.

The focus in this chapter is on how Chinese authorities sustain nationalist ideas, promote them in authoritative media, and seek to rationalize them within the ideology of Chinese Communist Party. The official version of nationalism and Chinese ethnicity seeks to authenticate the Chinese Communist Party, to promote Chinese unification, and to explain China's place in the post-Soviet world order. The first section outlines the institutional and ideological ramifications of the nationalism and ethnicity theme. The second section discusses how the nation is constructed. The third section examines the language of nationalist inclusion. The fourth section considers local belonging is endorsed, and while fifth looks at the construction of the Chinese nation within the world.

Ideological Institutions

Patriotic Ideology

Marxism-Leninism-Mao-Zedong Thought promotes a *Chinese* Communist revolution. From the 1920s, anti-colonialism and anti-imperialism defined China in national terms, and from the early 1940s, the strategy was that a patriotic alliance of progressive groups and individuals concerned with the fate of the Chinese nation should found 'New China'. The coalition of patriots (i.e. the Chinese People's Political Consultative Conference, CPPCC), not the Chinese Communist Party, established the Chinese state. Constitutionally and ideologically, the nation is a core factor in China.

In reality the Chinese Communist Party does control the CPPCC and all other parts of the state apparatus. The Chinese Communist Party deals with patriotic individuals and organizations through its 'United Front Department'. During the Cultural Revolution (1965-1978), the patriotic coalition was regarded as reactionary, but by 1978, patriotism stood out as the only viable source of political legitimacy, and the reformers under Deng Xiaoping re-emphasized the nation. The

---

(1989); Su Xiaokang and Wang Luxiang (1991); Anonymous (1989); Xing Lu (1999). On a Beijing Man in New York and a broader analysis of nationalism themes in the 1980s and 1990s, see Geremie R. Barmé (1995). For an analysis of the complexity and crosscutting themes in the nationalism debate, see Edward Friedmann (1994).

post-1978 era asserted territorial unity and racial integration of the overseas Chinese in the Chinese nation.

The patriotic inclusion of the overseas Chinese, Taiwan, Hong Kong and Macau in the Chinese nation made it necessary to legitimize the state through history and culture. Ideas of Confucianism as a source for Chinese politics emerged as popular. Ethnic Chinese intellectuals across the world joined in the effort to reconstruct China as a nation. The profusion of ideas and the sophistication of the debates stole the ideological initiative from the Chinese Communist Party. Within China, intellectual critics clamoured that the underdog nationalism of the 1980s (like the one expressed in *River Elegy*) merely extolled the greatness of the foreign. They demanded a positive nationalism that sought the best in Chinese cultural origins (Shi Zhong 1997). After 1989, Jiang Zemin emphasized the broad national tenors of Deng's policies, and went along with the popular demand for a positive appraisal of the Chinese nation, in 1994 launching the 'Programme for Patriotic Education'. Measured by a nationalist yardstick, the programme was bland, promoting the teaching of the achievements of the Chinese nation and the public veneration for the flag and the national anthem. The policy reflected established ideological and administrative precepts. Its lack of innovation matched the bureaucratic and dogmatic approaches.[3]

The Media

The Chinese Communist Party's Propaganda Department prescribes how the news and publishing media work. It publishes guidelines for editors, and monitors and censors publications. The main infrastructure for creating normative material consists of *Xinhua News Agency* and the *People's Daily*, both belonging to the Chinese Communist Party. The top leadership of the Chinese Communist Party formulates policy through long processes of drafting, ghost writing, editing and approval of documents and speeches (Schoenhals 1992). Texts written by leaders and journalists alike have normally been through collective rethinking and rewriting before they are made public in an unrestricted format.

The *People's Daily* leading articles are political documents written by or directly reflecting opinions in the central leadership. The *People's Daily* interprets core thematic areas through the use of style and narrative strategies that span chains of stories (Sun 1995). It accordingly sets the terms for public use of language on nationalism and ethnicity by interpreting them within the frameworks of policy and administrative decision making. By regulating the nationalism discourse, the Communist Party also authorizes it. While it cannot fully control the discourse, it can seek to dominate it.

---

3   For a collection of the core documents, see for example *Xinhua Yuebao*, no. 9, 1994, pp. 17-26. See Dong Liwen (1995) for an analysis.

The *People's Daily* as a Source

The official nationalism discourse of the *People's Daily* (*Renmih Ribau*, henceforth also 'RMRB') exists in competition with other discourses on Chinese nationalism (as already mentioned), but it also integrates with other official discourses like Marxism, Leninism and Mao Zedong Thought, foreign policy, international cooperation, cross-straits relations and issues of reform.

The *People's Daily* validates statements: it only carries statements that do conform to the rules of expression; those carried are regarded as authoritative. The rules of expression emerge from the collective practice among the political elite, and their interpretation is largely implicit. The readership is, generally speaking, domestic, but the *People's Daily* also carries statements explicitly aimed at the international community or foreign governments.

The *People's Daily* generates narratives through long chains of editorial items, sometimes even introducing 'competing' narratives related to each other, working on different readerships (Sun 1995). It also creates a shared conceptual and stylistic framework that works across a wide range of news stories and other editorial matter.

How is the nation authenticated by reference to a supra-state idea of China? To what extent does the official discourse acknowledge and address the parts of the nation beyond the territorial Chinese state – the Chinese in Taiwan, Hong Kong, Macau, and overseas? How do sub-state identities in China fare in the authoritative discourse? Are they accepted or rejected as part of the nation? How are, if at all, dialects, local culture and tropes of difference treated by the *People's Daily*?

To answer these questions, more than 300 articles and other editorial items of the *People's Daily* between January 1995 and April 2000 were examined.[4] Each text contains at least one occurrence of a word associated with nationalism discourse. Some are speeches by leaders, others relate to specific events or issues, like the US bombing of the Chinese Embassy in Belgrade, China's accession to the WTO, the retrocession first of Hong Kong and then of Macau, and relations across the Taiwan Strait, but many have little thematic relationship with nation or ethnicity. This ensures that casual references to nationalism in other contexts are included.

---

4   100 articles dating from early 1998 to early 2000 were found through a targeted selection, in the sense that the concept 'nation' (*minzu*) must appear at least once in each of them; among the almost 1,000 hits from a search on the *People's Daily's* search machine, 100 articles were selected at random. All 182 articles between 1995 and 2000 containing the term 'Confucianism' (*rujia*) were likewise selected. A small sample of 27 articles containing the term China (*huaxia*) was also included.

Constructing the Nation: History and Authenticity

The Chinese Communist Party seeks to reconcile two separate histories that provide different forms of political legitimacy. The first is the Chinese Communist Party's own history that claims its moral task in creating the statehood of the People's Republic; the Communist movement sees its roots in the modernizing nationalist ferment of the early 20th century, in the struggle against the encroachment by the colonial powers, and in the social revolution aimed at doing away with the exploiting 'feudal' classes. The second is the projection of the nation back into distant history, declaring its roots in the '5,000-year civilization' of China, whereby the Communist Party alongside the Chinese people becomes a continuation of this tradition.

The present generation is regarded as part of history; history is not just something of the past, but is made today. The link between past and present is not only expressed in the overly frequent use of 'historic' qualifying words like 'moment' or 'contribution', but also in ideological stereotypes from Marxism like 'historical necessity' that reflect historical determinism.

Most references to China's history in the newspaper material are characterized by repetition of a standard narrative or elements of it. One of the articles[5] contains a particularly detailed use of these set phrases:

It is a historical necessity that the Chinese Communist Party represents the forward movement of advanced culture.

China is a country with a history of 5,000 years civilization. In the development history of the Chinese nation, the Chinese people and its superior intelligence have created resplendent culture, science and technology, thus giving shape to an excellent tradition of historical culture and making important contributions to the development of humanity and the progress of the world.

After the Opium War in 1840, China gradually sank into a state of semi-colonialism and semi-feudalism. Generation upon generation of progressive Chinese fought unswerving and exhilarating battles to vigorously develop China. Under the influence of the Russian October Revolution, Marxism began to spread in China and gradually took the leading position among progressive thinkers in China and merged with the workers' movement that arose at that time; large numbers of progressive youths and intellectuals with an incipient Communist thinking turned into Marxists and became the most progressive class in China's history: the Chinese Communist Party was born out of this avant-garde of the proletariat.

---

5   The article entitled 'Push Cultural Construction Forwards', a theoretical discussion written by three officials, of whom Long Xinmin holds a senior position in the Propaganda Department of Beijing's Party organization, was published on 30 March 2000 to introduce Jiang Zemin's theory of 'three represents' (*sange daibiao*).

The link between the two histories is that those who fought to develop China in the face of crisis did not abandon tradition, but continued it, advancing ahead. In this interpretation, modernity did *not* destroy tradition,[6] but continued a 'superior tradition of historical culture'. The Chinese Communist Party, therefore, is centre-stage in the advancement of China, building on the best historical antecedents. Accordingly, 'the Chinese nation's excellent cultural tradition is an organic part of the socialist culture with Chinese characteristics'. This coded formulation indicates that Chinese culture and history from times immemorial are integrated in the Chinese Communist Party's reform project (i.e. socialism with Chinese characteristics).

The white paper on Taiwan, *The One-China Principle and the Taiwan Issue*, claimed that China's 5,000-year history had unity as its mainstay, as 'after each division unity was restored'. This is an outcome of a 'national will' deeply rooted in the hearts of the Chinese, invoked by the 5,000 years of history and culture (RMRB, 22 February 2000, p. 3). Similarly, a Taiwanese delegate to the National People's Congress used an interview to claim that 'the great cause of unification follows the course of history, and political negotiations are the only solution'. He included the Taiwanese compatriots in the nation by claiming that they possessed a 'glorious patriotic tradition' (RMRB, 14 March 2000, p. 6). A top official in a meeting with China's religious leaders in early 2000 explained the Party's efforts for religious freedom. He gave four reasons. One was that religion is an objective product of dialectical materialism, following its own unswerving laws that nobody should tamper with; religion has its origins in the development of society, and it is impossible to do away with it through political means. The second reason was that the party in its basic programme aims to serve the people and to protect the people's fundamental rights; only an equitable and respectful policy towards religion would be favourable to the development of a modern state. The third reason was that the five officially recognized religions of China serve a positive role by propagating a morally sound and patriotic feeling for the nation, serve society, work for the good, and in all respects help humanity in its 'search for the true, the good and the beautiful'. The fourth reason was that religion followed principles of the traditional Chinese culture, for historically China has always 'fused' cultures, so that foreign religions have not only found strong expression in China, but have in various degrees become sinicized. Religious freedom, thus endorsed by the Chinese Communist Party, is part of the effort to justify present policy with history (RMRB, 1 February 2000, p. 1).

The themes of strengthening the nation are emphasized through the memories of China's humiliation between 1840 and 1949, which impose upon the Chinese of today the obligation to resist hegemonic intrusions. The strengthening of China since 1978 has paid off, for China has achieved several 'historical firsts' and 'firsts in the world', as testified in evaluations 'by World Bank specialists' (RMRB, 27 May 1999, p. 9).

---

6   For such views, see for example several contributions to Tu Wei-ming's (1994) volume.

'History' as used in the pages of the *People's Daily* is not a motley font of past events, but a deterministic machine that has produced the present; the heroic efforts of those who fought for the strengthening of China only succeeded because they worked with the grain of history. Nationalism, therefore, is not an issue of restoring the old, but of being proud of and inspired by past achievements. In the present, the historic struggle continues, using the insights of 'socialism with Chinese characteristics' (RMRB, 4 May 1999, p. 9).

Even where an article ventures into one of the homelands of Chinese Moslems, Ningxia, characterized by its mosques, deserts and the 'unrestrained and candid manner of the people', and discovers a 'Yellow River civilization' where irrigation allows 'lush forests and pastures' to form a 'green plain', we are assured that this is Chinese heartland:

> In the distant palaeolithic age of three thousand years before the Common Era, the ancestors of the Huaxia [i.e. Chinese] nation lived in caves in the gullies along these banks; in the eleventh century BCE, the Chief of the Dangxiang [tribe] Li Yuanwu set himself up as a ruler in a capital here, established an administrative system, created a written language, and named his state Xia ... [Their descendents] left behind the resplendent and magnificent Xixia culture. Today, although the pastoralists have already entered modern civilisation, the excellent character and national spirit deposited in thick layers of history are deeply rooted in the hearts of the Ningxia people (RMRB, 30 October 1998, p. 9).

Modernity is not a loss of culture and history, but incorporates it. History, even pre-history, unites the nation in its diverse expressions.

The Academy of Social Sciences was, in 1998, put in charge of a special programme, the 'Chinese Culture Link Programme' that aimed at exploring all aspects of cultural linkage in the Chinese culture. The programme focused on how Chinese cultural understanding and cultural values were shared among Chinese across the world. The aim was to achieve national cohesiveness. The top leader in charge of the Party's united front work (including the connections with the overseas Chinese) Chen Qichen outlined these issues in a speech (RMRB, 31 May 1999, p. 3).

History is construed as a projection of Communist ideology, as a project of building a strong Chinese nation that still continues, aimed at letting the advanced Chinese culture contribute to the world and the development of humankind. This authentication of the nation is radically different from the cultural pessimism of Su Xiaokang's *River Elegy* and the widespread view that the coming of modernity with the Nationalists and later the Communists annihilated traditional and authentic Chinese cultural values.

Constructing the Nation: The Outside World and China

China and the rest of the world exist in a complex relationship. The texts in the collection both emphasize China as a part of the world and as distinctly different; on the one hand existing by its own rationale, on the other evaluated positively by international standards; on the one hand seeking strength to contribute to the world, on the other impeded by foreign powers. A later section will deal with China's position in the world, and here the discussion will be limited to the use of 'others' to construct the nation.

An editor of a literary journal explained a new format and new printing style, claiming that in the past, the 'Central Plain culture made its name by being *tu* (meaning local, crude and earthbound), but in its finer details it did not lack *ya* (elegance)'. Using a refined 'internationally popular "alternative format"', he hoped to 'raise the standard of our Central Plain literature periodical' so that it may become 'a cultural journal addressing the global Chinese language circle' (RMRB, 19 November 1999, p. 11). The editor, of course, played with the words, and did so consciously, realigning the inference between 'local' and 'coarse' and 'global/international' and 'elegant'; bringing out the innate elegance of the local may lift it into world. This example gives a first taste of the intricate system of pointers involved: a continuum of local→national→international, as well as China and the 'global Chinese language circle'.

Foreigners study sinology out of curiosity, while what drives Chinese to study 'national studies' is to 'raise the level of the nation' (RMRB, 18 April 1996, p. 10). Some foreign scholars think that 'corruption in China is an ugly aspect of "patriarchy" that is the most important characteristic of "Confucian culture"' (RMRB, 15 February 1995, p. 10). Abroad there has 'all along existed a so-called "theory of the clash of civilisations," attacking the expansion of Chinese culture' (RMRB, 28 June 1997, p. 10). The Chinese nation stands in sweeping contrast to its perceived opposite, the 'foreign', 'things abroad' and 'Western'. But these opposites interact, for one article discusses how to transform cultural concepts by 'critically taking on the best of our country's traditional culture, while dialectically borrowing from foreign advanced culture'. In this process, 'adverse cultural influences from the West should be criticised' (RMRB, 20 January 1996, p. 6), while some 'foreign moral traditions deserve to be emulated by us, like the notion of fair competition, [and] the enterprising spirit ...' (RMRB, 3 April 1997, p. 11). The 'cultural content of economic activity' must be improved, for example 'cultural content of commodities, retail, service and consumption', so as to make 'China enter international trade exchange, and obtain the fruits of world culture, thus raising the cultural level of the whole nation' (RMRB, 15 February 1995, p. 10).

An in-depth interview in 1998 with the then 89-year old philosopher Zhang Dainian tells the readers how this scholar already in the 1930s promoted the idea of 'creative synthesis' of cultures, taking the best from Chinese and Western cultures: the spirit of vitality, the persevering endeavours, the *noblesse* of peace, the moral and un-materialistic spirit of the Chinese, and the Western science, democracy and rule of law. Zhang thought that one should not return to Confucianism, but should acknowledge some of its good points. The Chinese past, in his view, had many serious deficiencies, like the obstruction of science and technology and the lack of academic freedom. He questioned the present trend to 'turn everything old into something new' and suggested that one should go forward under the guidance of Deng Xiaoping's ideas, catch up with Western science and technology, and at the same time understand and develop China's excellent cultural tradition in order to bring China into a state of prosperity (RMRB, 17 July 1998, p. 12).

In stark opposition to this are formulations like 'under the flood wave of reform and opening, some Western values and morals flowed into China like silt and attacked the traditional moral culture of our country'. 'Some youths do not respect the elderly, but regard them as a "burden" and so on; one obviously cannot say that this hasn't got anything to do with Western values' (RMRB, 20 January 1995, p. 4). Many of the articles voice such differences in culture between China and the West, but the opposites differ from formulation to formulation. The main issues raised in the material is how to combine the two sides, in phrases like 'mutual complementarity of East and West', 'the melting together of Chinese and Western learning'; promoting cultural exchange and 'creating a bridge that Western culture can pass in order to set up home in China' (RMRB, 19 September 1998, p. 5) are ideas put forward to overcome the distance between the two sides. Several articles among the sources are summaries of conferences discussing relevant issues; they universally regard nations (and civilizations) in their stereotyped essence, never probing into the meaning of the abstract terminology. Chinese terms like *Dongfang* (the East), *Zhongguo* (China), *Zhonghua* (China), *woguo* (our country) are juxtaposed *Xifang* (the West), *guoji* (international), *waiguo* (foreign), occasionally specifying individual countries. China is peaceful, morally superior and culturally sophisticated, while the West is competitive (or aggressive), instrumentalist, liberal, and technologically advanced. The most common opposites are China↔the West, and Chinese culture↔Western culture, while 'international' normally is positively related to and includes China, in terms of cooperation, recognition of Chinese achievements, and so on.

The division between the two essentialized parts of the world appears firm, vigorously discussed and intractable. The scope for referring to the Chinese-Western differences is almost unlimited, and the notion that the 'West' is the 'Other' is ubiquitous. Even if the Chinese achieved the fusion of Chinese and Western culture, would the Western 'Other' remain unchanged? The assertion of the 'Other' as a strong oppositional force does not exclude cooperation with it. The own national identity, however, must remain defined in essentialist difference from its 'Other', for otherwise the ideas of cultural fusion and cooperation become meaningless. Hegemonism↔international cooperation as a set of opposites signals the ambivalence of the West. By way of parallel, China's foreign policy, so one article claims, is based on two fundamental moral principles: (a) to oppose hegemonism and protect world peace, and (b) to increase international cooperation and promote common development (RMRB, 28 June 1997, p. 10). The 'Other' is abstract (rather than a specific nation or group of nations); it is vague and subject to interpretation. The flexibility of the 'Other' reflects back on 'self', that accordingly can assume a variety of qualities.

Constructing the Nation: What is China?

From the discussion so far it becomes obvious that concepts of China diverge. At a first glance, they state the obvious: China is a state among states, and defined by its institutions, territory and other official attributes. A majority of articles that refer to China point at or imply the Mainland, the people living in China and the state organs of the PRC.

Another view, however, is superimposed, where 'nation' replaces 'China': 'The Chinese nation must stand upright in the forest of nations' (RMRB, 21 December 1999, p. 1); 'Patriotism has, since its birth, been an excellent tradition of the Chinese nation. The bombing of our embassy by NATO under US leadership and the killing of our compatriots...' (RMRB, 25 May 1999, p. 6); '... the ocean territory of the Chinese nation...' (RMRB, 28 September 1998, p. 5). The usage implies more than casual variation, as the 'Chinese nation' is larger than Chinese statehood itself. The Chinese leadership assumes responsibility for the wider nation, wants to defend it and make it prosper. A crucial nexus underlying this perception is that the 'one-China principle is recognized by most states in the world' and that the 'unification with Taiwan is a matter of China's sovereignty and territorial integrity'. Other formulations include ethnic Chinese overseas in the 'Chinese nation'. In the official discourse, 'statehood' and 'nation' are closely related, but signify different things: the actual institutions of governance of the People's Republic of China and an imagined entity composed of all Chinese as defined by a shared culture.

Inclusion

The Chinese language lacks some of the grammatical markers of deixis available in other languages (like the distinction between definite and indefinite articles), but has alternative ways of expressing direction and inclusion, for example, the use of 'we' and 'us'. In newspaper prose one normally associates the use of 'we' with direct speech in verbatim quotes, leading articles and narratives of events that a journalist experienced first hand. In most cases, 'we' includes the writer and implies difference with the 'you' of the readers. In sports reportage and other instances where partisanship is intended, the 'we' extends to include the reader.

The use of the Modern Standard Chinese word *women* is very close to 'we' in English usage.[7] In many of the sources, 'we' includes the reader, or indicates partisanship ('we' as opposed to 'foreign' or 'international'); this corresponds to English usage. However, the distinction between direct and indirect speech is less clear in Chinese than in many other languages, so 'we' is often used in indirect quotes, where English would use 'they'. In some sources, the use of 'we' slides between different deictic positions. In an article (RMRB, 24 February 1999, p. 11) about the protection of the national heritage from illegal export, 'we' (and 'us', 'our') means 'China as opposed to foreign', 'the Chinese nation', and 'this generation as opposed to the forefathers'. The term is used to include the reader. 'This generation' is linked to the 'forefathers' through a 'heritage of material culture':

> In confronting the issue of cultural artefacts illegally flowing out of the nation's door, we both have the 'Law of the People's Republic of China on the Protection of Cultural Artefacts' and other domestic laws, as well as international treaties. Armed with these laws, we are justified to seek the return of every cultural artefact... During the last century, valuable cultural artefacts of the nation have been stolen and taken out of the country on a large scale.

> Our Chinese nation has a civilisation that stretches back 5,000 years, and if we count from the age of the 'Beijing Man', whose skull was discovered in 1929 by the Chinese archaeologist Mr. Pei Wenzhong, then there was early human activity on Chinese land (*Zhonghua dadi*) around 200,000-700,000 years ago. Generations of forefathers have created and bequeathed to us a resplendent heritage of material culture below and above the ground, thereby enriching our nation's cultural, artistic and scientific endeavours, [a heritage] that is a spiritual treasure for the unity, the cohesion and strengthening of the national self-confidence of our nation.

The 'we' unifies the writer, the reader, the nation, and the generation, and sets these perspectives off against a vague foreign 'Other', that in later passages is substantiated with among other things the 'imperialist invasion' between 1840 and 1945. 'We' is also indirectly linked to the Chinese territory (*Zhonghua dadi*). In the claim for repatriation of cultural artefacts presently displayed in museums abroad, formulations with direct and implied reference to 'foreign' emphasize the contrast with the 'Other', like 'these activities of plunder and sale have caused immeasurable losses to our historical and cultural heritage', and 'we have full support in international law to claim back the artefacts'.

The use of 'we' in what one could term collective indirect speech has the effect of drawing the reader into the collective. Indirect speech with a plural agent (e.g.

---

7   The distinction traditionally made in Northern Chinese dialects between 'zamen' (we, the speaker and the interlocutor, at the exclusion of others) and 'women' (we, the speaker and associates, at the exclusion of the interlocutor) does not exist in Modern Standard Chinese, and only occasionally finds its way into the *People's Daily* when a folksy style is intended.

'they claimed that they had seen...') constructs the illusion of a collective voice speaking. Using 'we' rather than 'they' is a strong stylistic tool with which the authors can create intimacy between the speaker, the author and the reader.

> The university students who had participated in the meeting expressed that hearing the situation reports allows us to better understand the reality of American human rights, that the so-called 'human rights' they eulogise are in reality hegemonism. The recent violent attack by the NATO under the leadership of the USA on our embassy in Yugoslavia further aroused our determination to study with even greater resolution in order to contribute with greater efforts to the strengthening and flourishing of the fatherland; we will definitely follow firm ideals, serve the people, penetrate the masses [of the people], totally commit ourselves to practice ... following the demands raised by General Secretary Jiang [Zemin] and the hopes in four points that comrade Hu Jintao formulated for the young generation at the meeting commemorating the 80th anniversary of the May Fourth Movement [1919] (RMRB, 18 May 1999, p. 5).

The 'we' is suspended between the students and the readers. It strings together contributions to the fatherland and obedience to the Party leadership, that points at its own tradition, symbolized in the May Fourth Movement (i.e. the protest movement against the Versailles Treaty that the Chinese Communists regard as their moment of inception). The 'they' is the hostile American 'Other'.

The bombing of the Chinese Embassy in Belgrade was the backdrop of a different use of 'we' in indirect speech. The speaker, a Chinese politician visiting the wounded from the bombing, addressed them, using 'we' to represent himself and the rest of the Chinese nation, versus 'you', the heroic Chinese diplomats who had suffered hardship, but none the less had remained in their posts in the most adverse of circumstances (RMRB, 15 May 1999, p. 4). Through the 'we' the reader is drawn into the collective gratitude of the nation. A speech commemorating the three people who died in the embassy bombing also uses 'we' (in direct speech) to join speaker and audience in respect for 'them' (*tamen*) (RMRB, 14 May 1999, p. 1).

In several sources 'we' in an indistinct way carries the voice of the core Party leadership. A leading article discussing the White Paper on the cross-Straits policy uses 'we' to address the 'Taiwanese compatriots' (which are in the third person); it is remarkable how the 'we' formulations in the context of this specific article shunned the inclusion of the readers. The use of 'we' referred to the top leaders' views, while avoiding creating an 'us-them' distinction between people in the Mainland and in Taiwan (RMRB, 30 January 2000, p. 1).

An article used 'we' to refer to the leaders of the Union of Taiwanese Compatriots in the Mainland, asserting unity between all Taiwanese compatriots (in Taiwan and the Mainland), and creating distance to the 'regime' in Taiwan:

> More than 20,000 Taiwanese compatriots sacrificed their precious lives in their patriotic movement to resist the reactionary Nationalist rulers. Taiwanese compatriots cannot allow the banner of the 28 February insurrection that was stained by their fresh blood to

be soiled by elements propagating 'Taiwanese Independence'. We hope that the regime in Taiwan will understand the situation and under the principle of one China make a real contribution to the unification of the nation ... The Chinese government has always stuck to the One-China principle, international organisations recognise the One-China principle, and 161 countries in the World recognise that Taiwan is an inalienable part of the Chinese territory. We can absolutely not allow Taiwan to be divided from the nation once more ... Huang Xin made a speech, saying that the publication of the white paper 'The One-China Principle and the Taiwan Question' has given us great encouragement. We hope that the future leaders of Taiwan will be able to take their point of departure in the fundamental interests of the people in Taiwan, returning to the principle and standpoint of one China, and eventually bring about unification through political negotiations across the Strait (RMRB, 27 February 2000, p. 2).

'We' represents the Taiwanese compatriots (people of Taiwanese origin who settled in the Mainland and were officially classified in this way). The 'unity of Taiwanese compatriots' makes it possible to link the February 28 Uprising of 1947 with the claim for national unification. The narrative claims that the insurrection was against the 'reactionary' Nationalist party and for a united Chinese nation, rejecting the common view that the Taiwanese rose against Chinese (Mainland) rule and sought independence.

The overlapping perspectives of the speaker (protagonist in the text), the writer (author of the text), the reader, the Chinese authorities, the Chinese people, the Chinese nation is its historical extension, this generation, and the individual part of the nation all come together in the use of 'we'. It joins together the Taiwan compatriots across the Taiwan Strait and includes them in the Chinese people. It links 'us' as a generation with the generation of forefathers to whom we are indebted for (a) the cultural heritage they bequeathed us and (b) their revolutionary sacrifices in the struggle for the nation.

An example of a highly evocative usage is a narrative of two *People's Daily* journalists' visit to an artist in Macau on the eve of retrocession. The two journalists' report in the first person plural has the voice of shared experience:

He [Mr. Liang] grasped both our hands and said excitedly: 'The retrocession [of Macau to China] is imminent, in only a couple of days I'll have come home!'

'After the lonesome tears of youth on the four seas, I treasure the spring rain in the saintly land'. We hummed one of Old Liang's poems, and he laughed. At the mention of retrocession, the face of this old man, who had walked alongside the nation for almost a century, radiated (RMRB, 18 December 1999, p. 3).

The themes of homecoming, life-long yearning for and artistic preoccupation with the nation create the atmosphere of young people visiting an old distant relative: Macau's retrocession is a family reunion, and the readers are members of the family.

Local Belonging

The *People's Daily* is conspicuously tacit on the local: it is merely an aspect of national culture. The report on a festival in Ningxia (RMRB, 30 October 1998, p. 9), cited above, depicts staged local identity (represented by folk songs, folk customs, and eulogies to the reform and opening as well as to the CCP Central Committee's 'wise policy of making the country prosper and the people live in peace'). Local identity links local and national belonging. By pointing to local customs and popular (*minjian*) culture, the national discourse constructs its own roots in local diversity, and uses this to underpin its authenticity. The description of the festival in Ningxia, the 'Flowers Flying Into the Next Century', referred to local place in a generic sense, the region's position in national history, and references to other Chinese localities. The costumes were 'red, yellow, blue, white and black', which is not a description of any specific costumes, but both symbolizes the exotic and refers to the colours of Ningxia's 'five native products' (wolfberries, licorice root, ink slabs, sheep hides and black moss).[8] The people of Ningxia descended from 'the forefathers of the Huaxia culture', and various dialects including Ningxia and Shanghai (sic) dialects were used to 'recite highlights of Ningxia history'. Within the nationalist discourse, the local is synthesized and general. The depiction of Ningxia could with few alterations depict any place in China.

Localism, accordingly, helps authenticate nationalism, like the construction of history does. Stereotyped and formalized diversity is an aspect of unity. Unlike history, however, localism exists in the present. The nationalist discourse, therefore, relies on the complicity of the 'locals' to enact the local stereotype. This potentially empowers local people to use and influence local belonging to their own advantage while remaining within the wider nationalist discourse.

'Locals' enacting their 'local customs' within a nationalist discourse may not in itself give much political or divisive ethnic leverage. However, the Chinese authorities encourage the use of local bonds with overseas Chinese communities. For many overseas Chinese, the 'ancestral place' is of particular importance, for, being the place of the lineage origin, it represents the claim to Chinese identity by descent. In the 1980s and 1990s, local authorities in the 'home villages' of the overseas Chinese established strong links with overseas Chinese and aimed at attracting them. Ancestral halls were rebuilt, forefathers' graves were restored, and complex relationships emerged between local and overseas Chinese leaders, involving money gifts, honorary positions, informal help and ritualistic exchange of status markers.

Local belonging is a strong autonomous undercurrent, as it pulls in the same direction as official nationalism, helping sway Taiwan-leaning overseas Chinese

---

8   Incidentally (or possibly due to the author's attempt at subliminal symbolic manipulation) the five colours – in that order – were also those of China's now long forgotten national flag between 1912 and 1928.

towards the Mainland, and as it gives content to the claim of Chinese ethnicity to many overseas Chinese who would have to search hard for common points with co-natives in China, were it not for the dialect and the claim to ancestral origin in some place in China. It is an important source of remittances and donations for good causes, and it binds a pool of overseas Chinese who work for China as good compatriots.

The authorities condone local belonging, but do not promote it. The silence in the *People's Daily* on local belonging and identity testifies this. In the official discourse, local belonging only exists as a colourful manifestation and as an authentication of the National.

China in the World

The sources indicate that China must 'catch up' to reach international levels of technological development, and that, due to historical circumstances, it suffers from a 'science and technology gap'. This gap, so the newspaper articles claim, stems partly from the set-backs between 1840 and 1945, when colonial powers dominated China. However, an analysis of China's security situation (RMRB, 27 May 1999, p. 9) sees China as a strategic opponent of Western countries in a global war; the USA's global leadership position means that the USA has hegemonic power and is 'opposed to an independent, democratic and affluent China'. This present obstruction of China's development deepens the science and technology gap. However, China contributes actively to global development.

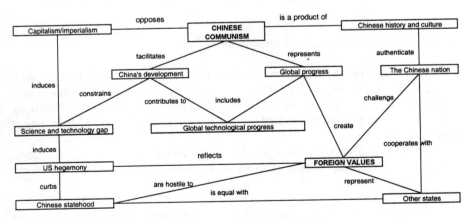

Figure 9.1 A conceptual map of China in the world

In a speech, Jiang Zemin claimed that the 'Chinese nation must direct its attention towards the world', 'it must go with the trend of the time' and so on (RMRB, 21 December 1999, p. 1). In order to do so, China must strengthen its economic and defence power and national cohesion. The world is separate from China, but China must work to enter it.[9] Although China may suffer from a technological deficit, the Chinese state is equal to other states and must seek to strengthen its economy, defence and nationhood. A strong China and a cohesive Chinese nation is a precondition for international cooperation.

We have already seen how the Chinese nation derives its authenticity from Chinese history and culture, and how the Chinese Communist ideology is a product of Chinese history. Communism, especially in the formula of 'socialism with Chinese characteristics', aims at pushing forward global progress, while opposing the capitalist and imperialist forces in the world. Chinese culture differs from (and is superior to) Western value systems, and Communism is part of that culture. These complex relationships are represented in Figure 9.1.

The perception of China's situation in the world is thus strategic, dividing the effort between opposing the hegemon and collaborating on an equal basis. China's deficit in terms of technology, including military hardware, leads to the reinvention of tradition. The notion of 'people's war' as opposed to high-tech war has recently regained its position in Chinese security thinking,[10] and some even see the development of new technology as an opportunity to give 'people's war' a new and more dynamic meaning.[11] The Maoist notion of 'people's war' is a part of the Chinese heritage as well as a fruit of Chinese Communism, and so seems suitable for both the nationalist and the developmental discourse.

This does not reveal much about Chinese strategic thinking, foreign policy, or specific negotiation positions, but does sketch out the lines of reasoning and conceptual constructions which the leadership uses to influence Chinese citizens. The figure suggests the interdependence among the core conceptual positions.

Constructing National and Ethnic Belonging

The readers may or may not believe the authoritative version of the Chinese nation as presented in the pages of the *People's Daily*; they constitute the leadership's effort to gain the initiative in the public discourse on nationalism, depriving popular 'cultural pessimism' and all-out anti-foreignerism of some of their appeal and credibility.

The leadership seeks to place Chinese Communism at the centre of history, legitimizing it through the past. It also aims to define China in terms of territory,

---

9   The Chinese acronymic term for 'WTO accession' (*ru shi*) literally means to 'enter the World'.
10 See remarks by member of the CCPCC Standing Committee, Deputy Chairman of the Central Military Commission and State Councillor Chi Haotian cited in RMRB, 9 January 1998.
11 See works by Professor Zhang Zhaozhong of the National Defence University, summarised in http://www.usembassy-china.org.cn/english /sandt/unresw1.htm.

statehood, race (by including the overseas Chinese), and culture. The territorial unity of the Chinese Mainland, Hong Kong and Taiwan is essential, and constructing the common historical and cultural roots is supplemented with stylistic efforts at uniting them into one big family. Local difference is de-emphasized, and where it occurs, is turned into a colourful variation of the National. Foreign or Western phenomena are constructed to be different from Chinese; however, the demarcation line remains fluid, dividing East and West as well as China and foreign countries. The two sides are both repelled from and attracted to each other, for while the differences are rooted in national essence, the debates in the 1990s call for cultural synthesis and fusion.

When the Chinese Communist Party addresses the issues by leading the debates, financing them, and by calling for patriotic ritual, it is able to achieve more than through restrictive censorship. Setting the agenda and controlling how concepts are used in the public sphere, however, does not mean that strong popular expressions of nationalism and anti-foreignerism are precluded or that spontaneous popular debates are silenced (the 'chat rooms' of China's internet service providers, for example, include rather unrestrained opinions on nationalism). Neither does it silence the many Chinese scholars of 'national learning' across the world who tend to appraise the Chinese nation in a more questioning manner, nor does it put a lid on the identity ferment in Taiwan. The public disregard (in the *People's Daily*) for local identities and cultures does not curb deeply ingrained patterns of social behaviour, assertion of local identities, dialects, and separateness.

Even so, I do believe that it has an impact on people's belonging, for it sets an authoritative schema for rewarding and promoting public behaviour. In the People's Republic of China, official acknowledgement and public affirmation of individuals is celebrated through the individuals' confirmation of the authoritative discourse. By accepting promotion to a particular role, one accepts the official ways of putting things, and uses them actively. By participating in a meeting, one underwrites the official message of that meeting. By wanting to belong to the Chinese nation and be recognized by its authorities, one is drawn into the official understanding of the nation. For many people the advantage of seeking ethnic solidarity, social protection and cementing social relationships can be achieved through accepting the official discourse on the nation. For many the need to reflect on the issue never arises, for it is taken for granted. For others being Chinese is an existential choice, and some may regard the issue as a question of lifestyle or of playing the identity card in business or politics. The authoritative representation of the Chinese nation may not suffice to solve issues of identity conflict in Hong Kong and Macau or among overseas Chinese, and it almost certainly does not for people in Taiwan. It also challenges critical intellectuals and provokes historians in China and abroad. Yet debates on and issues relating to Hong Kong, Macau, Taiwan and overseas Chinese will fuel this ideology-machine for some time to come.

184 The Politics of Multiple Belonging

Works Cited

Anonymous (1989) *'Heshang' pipan. Fu 'Heshang'*. Chengdu: Bashu Shushe.
Barmé, Geremie R. (1995) 'To Screw Foreigners is Patriotic: China's Avant-Garde Nationalists'. *The China Journal*, 34 (July), 209-234.
Bodman, Richard and Pin P. Wan (eds) (1991) *Deathsong of the River*. Ithaca: Cornell University.
Chong, Woei Lien (1989-90) 'Su Xiaokang On His Film "River Elegy"'. *China Information*, 4(3) (Winter), 44-55.
Cui Wenhua (ed.) (1988) *'Heshang' lun*. Beijing: Wenhua Yishu Chubanshe.
Dong Liwen (1995) 'Lun Zhong Gong de aiguozhuyi'. *Gongdang Wenti Yanjiu*, 21(8), 26-39.
Friedmann, Edward (1994) 'Reconstructing China's National Identity: A Southern Alternative to Mao-Era Anti-Imperialist Nationalism'. *The Journal of Asian Studies*, 53(1) (February), 67-91.
Hua Yan (ed.) (1989) *'Heshang' pipan*. Beijing: Wenhua Yishu Chubanshe.
Schoenhals, Michael (1992) *Doing Things With Words in Chinese Politics. Five Studies* (China Research Monograph no. 41). Berkeley: University of California.
Shi Zhong (1997) 'Chinese Nationalism and the Future of China'. *Chinese Law and Government*, 30(6) (Nov.-Dec.), 8-27.
Su, Xiaokang and Wang Luxiang (1991) *Deathsong of the River: A Reader's Guide to the TV Series Heshang*. Ithaca: Cornell University.
Sun, Wanning (1995) 'People's Daily, China and Japan: A Narrative Analysis'. *Gazette*, 54, 195-207.
Tu, Wei-ming (ed.) (1994) *The Living Tree. The Meaning of Being Chinese Today*. Stanford: Stanford University.
Xing Lu (1999) 'Rhetoric of Nationalism and Anti-Americanism: A Burkean Analysis of "China Can Say No"'. *Intercultural Communication Studies*, 8 (2), 163-176.

Chapter 10

Marking Out Boundaries: Politics of Ethnic Identity in Southwest China

Xiaolin Guo

Of China's 1.3 billion population, eight per cent constitute what is officially designated 'minority nationalities' (*shaoshu minzu*), altogether 55 in number; the rest of the population is categorized as Han and makes up one single nationality, irrespective of disparities within and across regions. China is thus a country comprising 56 nationalities. The official designation of minority nationalities is a product of the state integration policy aimed at accommodating a vast expanse of territory and diverse ethnic populations at the time when the People's Republic of China (PRC) was founded. This institution imposed a new order upon society, and redefined relationships between the state and society, between the Han and non-Han populations, and between various ethnic minority communities.

It is hardly debatable that ethnic categories are patterned not in terms of cultural differences and similarities in any objective sense, but rather as a form of cognition, such categories being highly dependent on how cultural differences and similarities are organized by those who subscribe to them (Barth 1969, pp. 14-15). Yet a more dynamic approach to such categories involves looking at the externalities (country- and region-specific) of the subjectively organized cultural differences and similarities. This chapter sets out to explore the role of some political and economic forces in the formation of ethnic boundaries, and to explain how such formation has, in turn, affected the individuals' 'value orientations' (ibid., p. 18), that give expression to cultural differences.

The geographic focus of the present study is southwest China, in particular Yunnan province that borders Sichuan and Tibet in the north and northwest, Guangxi and Guizhou in the east, Burma in the west, and Laos and Vietnam in the south. Among the 55 minority nationalities officially designated in China, 25 are found in Yunnan. The reach of the state into these multifarious societies began with identifying the level of their social development and establishing government administrations. These tasks were facilitated by the official classification of minority nationalities; it henceforth became the basis of the state nationality policy in the decades to come. The policy shifts in the PRC nationality work, as this chapter will show, have had a significant impact on the development of ethnic consciousness and the formation of ethnic boundaries.

Integration and National Politics

> The common core of ideology among the leaders of transformative states has been to create a hegemonic presence – a single authoritative rule – in multiple arenas, even in the far corners of society. The goal has been to penetrate society deeply enough to shape how individuals throughout the society identify themselves, and the organization of the state has been to effect such far-reaching domination (Migdal 1994, p. 24).

In the spring of 1950, merely a few months after the PRC was founded, the central government organized and dispatched a delegation consisting of 120 people to the south-western provinces of Xikang (incorporated into Sichuan in 1955), Yunnan and Guizhou. Their task was to identify the socio-economic conditions and the history of the peripheral societies as well as their linguistic and other cultural particulars, in preparation for a major social transformation which was to proceed in steps according to different levels of social development. Guided by Marxist historical materialism, the ethnic minority societies were ranged and classified in terms of relations of production. Of the five million ethnic minority population in Yunnan at the time, 600,000 were labelled as living in a transitional stage from the 'late primitive society' to 'class society', 50,000 people as belonging to the 'slave society', 1.5 million people as belonging to 'feudal lord system' or a transitional stage from 'feudal lord system' to a 'landlord economy', and the remaining three million people were classified as having already developed a 'landlord economy' (*Yunnan minzu gongzuo* 1994, vol. 1, p. 70).

The establishment of new government in these areas inhabited by ethnic minority populations took the form of regional autonomy, a policy adopted by the Chinese People's Political Consultant Conference in September 1949 and outlined in the 'Common Program' (essentially the new national constitution) which stipulated that regional autonomy be established at three levels: province, prefecture and county. China today has five provincial-level regional autonomies, namely, the Inner Mongolia Autonomous Region established in 1947, Xinjiang Uighur Autonomous Region established in 1955, Guangxi Zhuang Autonomous Region and Ningxia Hui Autonomous Region, both established in 1958, and the Tibetan Autonomous Region established in 1965. Apart from Guangxi, these autonomous regions had previously been administered as the 'Outer' domains of the Qing empire.[1] Sub-provincial regional autonomies currently include 30 autonomous prefectures most of which were established in the 1950s, and 124 autonomous counties, half of which were established in the 1950s and 1960s.

Contrary to what might have been assumed to be otherwise the case, Chinese leaders had pointedly cautioned against the application of the Soviet model in

---

1   During the Qing, the 'Inner' domains which were made up of the former Ming territory were administered by the Han-Chinese officials, whereas the administration of the 'Outer' domains which included the northeast, Mongolia, Tibet and Turkestan (or Xinjiang) was dominated by the Manchu and Mongol banner men (Rawski 1996, p. 833).

delineating regional autonomies in China because the ethnic minority population – six per cent at the time – occupied areas amounting to 60 per cent of the country's territory; besides, in many areas multiethnic population communities were dominant, especially in the southwest (*Guojia minzu shiwu weiyuanhui* 1994, p. 154). The establishment of regional autonomies in China, therefore, must adapt to domestic conditions wherein territory and population composition became the main determinants. In some cases provincial and county borders were redrawn, whereas in others ethnic minority populations were reordered to merge or to divide.

Despite the Stalinist criteria of the 'four commons' – territory, language, economy, and collective consciousness – being stubbornly upheld by the Chinese authorities as an official guideline in defining nationalities, the influence of domestic politics on the outcome of nationality classification should not be in any way underestimated. The identification of the Hui and Manchu nationalities, for instance, contrasted sharply with the identification of many other ethnic minority populations especially those living in southwest China; in the case of the former, the 'four commons' definition was made irrelevant, whereas in the case of the latter the elements that theoretically make up ethnicity were taken into consideration, notwithstanding manipulations motivated by specific political needs in the locality. The contrast suggests that regardless of how big or small they are, and no matter how homogeneous or heterogeneous they appear to be, the officially classified minority nationalities in China are results of accommodation between local interests and national politics.

The Hui, or Muslim Chinese, constitute a cumbersome category.[2] In the early period, political needs very much affected the policy of the CCP (Chinese Communist Party) toward the Hui. The expansion and consolidation of a Communist base in north-western China in the course of the struggle against the KMT (Nationalist Party) and invading Japanese in the 1930s led the CCP leadership to affirm its ardent support for recognition of the Hui nationality and autonomy, despite the prevalent view that the Hui identity was not an ethnic issue but an issue of religion (*Minzu wenti wenxian* 1991, 518; 850). The contribution of the Muslim elite to the Chinese revolution was highly appreciated by the Party, and after 1949 many Hui members of the CCP served at the highest levels of the central government, in particular dominating the State Nationalities Affairs Commission.[3] Owing to their political influence, the Hui were not only recognized by the central government as a nationality despite their dispersed settlements and lack of common cultural traits, but also granted a provincial-level regional autonomy by redrawing the provincial border, making 17 counties and two cities previously under the jurisdiction of Gansu province into a Ningxia Hui Autonomous Region.[4]

---

2   See Dru Gladney (1996).
3   Among the thirteen deputy directors of the State Nationalities Affairs Commission (reorganized in 1954), four were Hui.
4   Ningxia was part of the Gansu province during the Qing. It was made a separate province in 1928 by the KMT government as a strategy to break up the power of

The Manchu identity was more complicated because of the lingering legacies from the imperial and the Republican states. The 1911 Revolution that overthrew the Qing dynasty (1644-1911) bore a distinct anti-Manchu sentiment, and the racial discourse adopted in the course of nation-building in the early Republican period (1912-1949) was primarily responsible for a muted expression of the Manchu identity.[5] The attitude of the CCP leadership toward the Manchus was different, albeit somewhat ambivalent. There were notable signs indicating a preparedness of the CCP leaders to vindicate and historically identify themselves with the Qing rulers.[6] Nevertheless, the Manchus were not as privileged as the Hui because they were not as strategically important as the Hui for the CCP united front. In the 1940s, the official line of the CCP was that the Manchus should not be treated as a separate nationality, for they had penetrated far into China proper for so long and hardly possessed any special ethnic markers (ibid., p. 1218). This policy was revoked in 1952, whereupon a resolution was adopted by the central government that the Manchus be recognized as one of China's nationalities, and regional autonomies (only at sub-provincial levels) be established in areas where Manchu populations were concentrated (*Dangdai Zhongguo minzu gongzuo* 1990, p. 34). It has been argued that the decision to recognize the Manchu nationality was taken by the CCP leadership for political reasons, that is, to repudiate the KMT policy of assimilation of the Manchus (Dreyer 1976, pp. 145-146). Clearly, there was an intention to make a break with the Republican rhetoric proscribing the 'alien' rule of the Qing by the Manchus, as further effort was made by the PRC government to ban uses of terminology such as 'Manchu-Qing regime' tainted by the Nationalist racial discourse from all official documents and the media, except in citations from historical sources (*Dangdai Zhongguo minzu gongzuo* 1990, p. 81).

---

warlordism in the northwest. In September 1954, the Ningxia province was abolished and reincorporated into the Gansu province, following the CCP Central Committee's decision to reorganize the central and regional governments. The newly organized State Nationalities Affairs Commission in which the Hui had a strong representation lobbied for establishment of a Hui autonomous region in the northwest, and the proposal was approved by the CCP Central Committee in 1956 (*Dangdai Ningxia jianshi* 2002, pp. 53-55).

5   As noted, many Manchus were forced to go underground at the time in order to protect themselves, and the Manchu identity is yet to be officially acknowledged on Taiwan (Rigger 1995, p. 212). The predicament of the Manchu identity would explain the silence of the Hakka identity in China and abroad, for which, see Mary Erbaugh (1992), and Flemming Christiansen (1998).

6   In 1950, delegations dispatched to the southwest were specifically instructed to 'apologize to the local peoples on behalf of the central government for the misery inflicted upon them by the old regimes'; since, as the then Premier Zhou Enlai explained, 'we have inherited the entire family estate from our ancestors, we may just as well take the blame for them, too' (Wang 1999, p. 2). On other occasions, the Manchu rulers were hailed by the CCP leadership for their great success in incorporating vast territory into China and for their prolonged rulership (*Guojia minzu shiwu weiyuanhui* 1994, p. 147).

Regardless of the differences in their cultural and historical backgrounds, the recognition of the Hui and Manchu nationalities seemed to be essentially a matter of political concerns at the central level, and the decisions regarding their nationality and administration statuses were taken directly by the central government. By contrast, the nationality identification in many other cases was primarily dominated by local politics and regional stability. This is especially so in the southwest, where the jurisdiction of local government had a notable impact on the eventual assignments of nationality status.

Administrative Divisions and Nationalities

The official nationality identification was a national project, but its organization was province-based in that the personnel carrying out the actual work were mostly assembled within each province. Their work was supervised by policy makers and assisted by specialists like linguists and ethnologists from the national capital. It was a dual process – ethnic identification and identity confirmation – the former being basically research, the latter policy making. Early in 1951, the Yunnan provincial Nationalities Affairs Commission was formally set up embarking upon the official nationality identification. It was at the time emphasized that the purpose of the task was to 'facilitate delimitation of administrative boundaries' (*Dangdai Zhongguo de Yunnan* 1991, vol. 2, p. 228). Initially, the Commission produced a list of 132 ethnic groups, having reduced from several hundred names gathered, in that some 60 were deemed to be branches of the Yi and a dozen or so branches of the Zhuang; by 1953 a dozen or so ethnic groups had been formally identified; in the following year 29 names of nationalities were submitted to the State Council for approval, in that 21 became officially confirmed (*Yunnan minzu gongzuo* 1994, vol. 1, pp. 276-277).[7] The timing of the identification work is said to be vital for the result of nationality confirmation (Du 1999, p. 23). This was indeed the case in the region across the Yunnan-Sichuan border where the volatile political situation in the 1950s played a decisive role in the nationality identifications of the Mosuo and Prmi populations.[8]

Mosuo (Mo-so) is a Chinese name referring to the people who had been recorded living in the region of today's north-western Yunnan and south-western Sichuan as early as 700 AD. Presently, they are recognized as comprising two 'dialect' groups separated by the Jinsha River – the Naxi living on the western side (the area surrounding the ancient town of Lijiang and its vicinities in northwest Yunnan), and the Mosuo on the eastern side (including today's Ninglang county of Yunnan province, Muli and Yanyuan counties of Sichuan province) – but both are

---

7   Four more nationalities – Buyi, Shui, Manchu, and Jinuo – were added later.
8   Unless otherwise noted, information about the Mosuo and Ninglang county (quotations included) appearing in this chapter hereafter is drawn from my own fieldwork from 1992 to 2001.

believed to be of the same people who originally emigrated from the north. The spread of the 'Yellow sect' of Tibetan Buddhism on the eastern side of the Jinsha and the Qing reform to the local chieftainship on the western side made significant impact on the development of religious institutions, social organizations, and economy in these geographically separated communities. While in Lijiang the practice of patriliny has long since replaced matrilineal inheritance, the kinship system of Mosuo society on the opposite side remains predominantly matrilineal to this date.

The decision of lumping the Mosuo with the Naxi would have been based on the assumption that they share a history. If so, the Naxi ought to be part of the Mosuo rather than the other way around.[9] Some attribute the identification of the Mosuo as Naxi to the influence of Marxist doctrines adopted by Chinese ethnologists who 'see the transformation from matrilineal to patrilineal descent as a natural process of social evolution' (McKhann 1995, p. 55). However, in view of the dynamic local politics in that particular period, the static Marxist doctrines would appear to have less influence on the Mosuo nationality status than is credited.

Compared to other ethnic minority peoples in northwest Yunnan, the Naxi in Lijiang have always been seen as having a closer relationship with the central state (White 1998). The Naxi population in general boasts high achievements in scholarship, and has produced many high-ranking officials in Yunnan province. In the 1950s, the aspiring Naxi leaders embarked upon a course to win an official designation of Lijiang Naxi autonomous prefecture; the Mosuo population in Ninglang county under the jurisdiction of Lijiang prefecture was purportedly included in the Naxi nationality (already identified in 1953) to satisfy a population size requirement for the intended administrative set-up. Coinciding with this event was an ethnic insurrection that broke out across the Sichuan-Yunnan border in the predominantly Yi populated areas when the land reform was under way between the winter of 1955 and the spring of 1956. Months later (as early as in September), a crucial step toward regional stability was taken with the inauguration of the Ninglang Yi autonomous county in northwest Yunnan. The establishment of the Yi autonomous county incidentally marked a shift of local power in Ninglang that had been previously dominated by the Mosuo chieftains for many centuries. The marginalization of Mosuo influence in the new administrative set-up centred on the Yi autonomy was also likely to have impacted on the Mosuo nationality status. As the county gazetteer indicates, the Mosuo had been officially recognized as a

---

9   Some research has shown that the name Naxi (Na-khi) had not appeared in any official documents until the Daoguang reign (1821-1850), which indicates that Naxi was not an original name for the people concerned (Tao 1962). Rather it might have been a consequence of the Qing reform (1700s) and subsequent sinicization in Lijiang. As observed, 'The name Mo-so is of Chinese origin and is disliked by the Na-khi, it is looked upon as derogatory' (Rock 1947, vol. 1, p. 4).

nationality in Ninglang county until 1959 (*Ninglang Yizu zizhi xian zhi* 1993, p. 176).

As it happened, having incorporated the Mosuo, the total Naxi population did not in the end reach the desired size that would have entitled it to an autonomous prefecture; a Naxi autonomous county was established in Lijiang instead. The *status quo* of the Mosuo ethnic identity as a branch of the Naxi was, however, maintained. Currently, the population of the officially identified Naxi nationality in Yunnan is estimated at 270,000 of which some 15,000 are Mosuo.

A larger portion of the (matrilineal) Mosuo population (40,000 in total) are concentrated in the south-western Sichuan, and their fate is very different as far as nationality status is concerned. Despite sharing the same religion and being bound by kinship with the Mosuo in northwest Yunnan, the Mosuo in Sichuan were officially identified as Mongolians. Such a move may be interpreted as consistent with the political strategy to fragment the Mosuo population in the presence of the ethnic Yi autonomy, especially given that incorporating the Mosuo in Sichuan into the Naxi nationality would have made little sense in the existence of the provincial border. However, the fundamental element explaining the ultimate outcome seems to lie with the relationship between the local elite and the state, an alliance vital to power consolidation in the areas historically dominated by the aboriginal chieftains. Because such an alliance was formed and played out differently in Yunnan and Sichuan, the results of nationality classification differed. The ascription of the Mongolian nationality to the Mosuo in Sichuan was based on the local elite's claim to be the descendants of Chinggis Khan (*Muli Zangzu zizhixian zhi* 1995, p. 862).[10] The identifications of the Prmi population (or Xifan) in Sichuan (Muli county) as Tibetans, and not as in Yunnan (Ninglang county) as Pumi, provide yet another example.

Prior to the land reform, the local chieftainship in Muli had been held by the Great Lama of the Tibetan Buddhist Church since 1648 (ibid., p. 115). A political united front established with the local chieftainship in the early 1950s enabled the new government to consolidate its presence in society; in exchange, the Great Lama acquired the Tibetan autonomy that he desired. In 1952, Muli was separated from the jurisdiction of Yanyuan county and became a county-level administration itself, thus making Muli Tibetan autonomous county a reality (ibid.). This administrative manoeuvre would have been a main reason why the Prmi population in Muli was classified as Tibetans.[11] The relationship between the Pumi leader in Ninglang and the state was different, but it nonetheless helped him win the necessary support from the state as far as the nationality status of his people was concerned. As a commoner with a humble background, the Pumi hero joined the Communist revolution and stayed loyal to the Party throughout the turbulent years

---

10 In 1253, the grandson of Chinggis, Khubilai, led the Mongol armies past the region on route to conquer the Dali Kingdom; it subsequently became Yunnan province of the Yuan empire.

11 See Stevan Harrell (1996).

of political transition in Ninglang. As a reward, he was made a member of a provincial government delegation to visit Beijing in 1957 and be received by the central leadership. On that occasion, the Pumi leader reportedly discussed the nationality status of his people in person with the Premier; as he requested, formal nationality status was duly granted the Pumi (*Ninglang Yizu zizhixian zhi* 1993, pp. 622-623).

The classification of nationalities across the Yunnan-Sichuan border shows that ethnic identity in China is not really about *who* one was, but rather *where* one was at the time of the official identification. The PRC classification of nationalities in the 1950s served a distinct political agenda and did achieve its intended purposes, that is, reorganizing society and establishing new government at the local levels. This contingent strategy, however, had many consequences in the relationship between the state and ethnic minority societies. Despite the stated intention to make all nationalities equal, the PRC classification of nationalities resulted in a hierarchical relationship between Han and non-Han (minority nationalities). The Han were made dominant not only as the majority population, but also as the elite force in revolution and economic construction, being portrayed as 'advanced' *vis-à-vis* the 'backward' minority nationalities. This polarization has, to a great extent, contributed to political radicalism in the PRC nationality work, manifest in the adoption at one time of the official line that the issue of nationalities was one of class struggle,[12] in encroachment upon regional autonomies,[13] and in attacks on the cultural practices of ethnic minority societies.[14] It also actuated the practice of 'paternalism' in a less rigid political atmosphere.[15] Both radicalism and paternalism in PRC nationality policy have significantly impacted the development of ethnic consciousness.

---

12 It was adopted in 1958 ensuing a series of ethnic insurrection in southwest and northwest China, and used as a pretext to suppress ethnonationalism. The periods during which Yunnan was embraced by escalated ethnic conflicts were 1958-1960 (coinciding with the national movement of the Great Leap Forward) and 1969-1971; in the latter period the conflict was in the disguise of the 'Political Frontier Defence' campaign (Schoenhals 2000).

13 Four of the total eight autonomous prefectures in Yunnan were abolished subsequent to the imposition of military control in 1967.

14 See for example 'Shadian Incident' which resulted from mishandling the Muslim cultural practices by the local authorities (Gladney 1996, pp. 137-140), and the campaign of 'Monogamy' that was carried out in Mosuo society in the name of eradicating the 'primitive remnants' (Guo 1997, pp. 186-187).

15 Paternalism is a term that has been used to describe the United States federal policies towards the American Indians during two centuries after the Revolutionary War, and to refer to 'a determination to do what was best for the Indians according to white norms, which translated into protection, subsistence of the destitute, punishment of the unruly, and eventually taking the Indians by the hand leading them along the path to white civilization and Christianity' (Prucha 1995, p. xxviii). Although the Chinese government never assumed the image of the Great Father like the US government, the image of the Elder Brother assigned to the Han population generates a similar effect.

Preferential Policy and Ethnicity

A major policy shift from radicalism to paternalism in PRC nationality work was marked by the CCP leadership's repudiation, at the beginning of China's economic reform, of the official line that the issue of nationalities was one of class struggle. The rehabilitation of *political* relations between the state and the ethnic minority societies subsequently brought about relaxed *economic* policies toward the minority nationalities. The 1980 fiscal reform granted the five autonomous regions and three provinces (Qinghai, Guizhou and Yunnan that have large ethnic minority populations) an annual 10 per cent increase in financial subsidies to government administrations, in addition to the appropriation of annual funds earmarked for supporting economic development, education and healthcare in areas populated by ethnic minorities (*Dangdai Zhongguo caizheng* 1988, vol. 1, pp. 293-294, 388). In the mid-1980s, the central government launched poverty-alleviation programmes which further increased the level of financial support available to the Western and South-western regions where the ethnic minority populations are concentrated. The economic reform also reinstated a series of preferential treatment policies ranging from food subsidies and family-planning quotas to education and employment opportunities, all granted on the basis of minority nationality status.

The new policy and its implementation stimulated the development of ethnic consciousness, manifested in appeals to the state by the members of the ethnic minority communities for correcting nationality status. While some maintained that they had been given a different nationality status than the one desired, a majority of cases were individuals who had been previously identified or self-identified as Han, including the children of Han and ethnic minority parents, and people who had been considered either assimilated or no longer culturally distinguishable from the Han, like the Tujia and Manchus.

In 1981, the State Council and the State Nationalities Affairs Commission formally put nationality status correction on the agenda. Between 1982 and 1986, in excess of five million people registered for a change; they were largely concentrated in Hunan, Liaoning, Guizhou, and Hebei provinces where applications were predominantly submitted by Tujia and Manchu, as well as Dong and Miao; by 1986, about half of the five million applications for nationality status correction had been approved (*Guojia minwei bangongting* 1996, p. 579). The nationwide work of correcting nationality statuses was formally concluded in 1989. It resulted in unprecedented growth of ethnic minority population by 40.78 per cent between the 1982 population census and the 1990 population census (Deng 1998, p. 28). A number of nationalities doubled their population, including Tujia growing from 2.8 million in 1982 to 5.7 million in 1990, the Manchu from 4.3 million to 9.8 million, and Xibo from 83,629 to 172,847; Dong and She populations grew by 76 per cent and 70 per cent respectively, during the same period (*Zhongguo minzu tongji* 1991).

Compared to these provinces, demands for nationality status correction in Yunnan was not phenomenal. Yet it by no means suggests that the question of

Mosuo identity was in any sense less controversial. Throughout the 1980s, the Mosuo in Ninglang repeatedly appealed to the higher levels of government to reverse their nationality status from Naxi to Mosuo, and the provincial Nationalities Affairs Commission organized an investigation into the matter (*Ninglang Yizu zizhi xian zhi* 1993, p. 176). All signs seemed to suggest that the provincial government was inclined to grant the Mosuo a separate nationality status, but the motion failed to win the support of the central government.[16] Searching for a compromise, the provincial People's Congress carried a resolution in 1990 to recognize the Mosuo as a separate people from the Naxi by granting the title Mosuo *ren* ('people'). The title, however, has little effect outside the province. As a Mosuo county-level official related, his son, upon enrolling at Beijing University, insisted on being registered as Mosuo, but the computer refused to accept the command because the name Mosuo is not an officially designated nationality.

The title of Mosuo *ren* may be comforting but hardly gratifying for the Mosuo officials at the local level, because many benefits to which their locality might become entitled are dependent on a full nationality (*zu*) status. The issue essentially concerns the status of government administration. The Mosuo constitute about 40 per cent of the total population in Yongning, but the township is not entitled to an autonomous status because the Mosuo are officially identified as Naxi.[17] Though ethnic minority autonomous townships are, strictly speaking, not one level of autonomous government like the autonomous regions, prefectures and counties, they are nonetheless entitled to certain privileges. Politically, the autonomous townships are headed by the ethnic minority members, and the government has the authority to regulate with respect to the employment of ethnic minority cadres, the use of ethnic minority languages in government institutions, and the protection of ethnic minority customs; economically, the government of the autonomous townships is granted certain discretionary powers to draw up plans to exploit natural and cultural resources within its jurisdiction, and is offered a favourable arrangement of revenue sharing with the higher level of government (Shen 2001,

---

16 Applications for correcting the nationality status of individuals were handled and approved by the government Nationalities Affairs Commission at the county level; applications for correcting the nationality status of large ethnic communities (as in the case of the Mosuo) were to be submitted to the responsible departments at the provincial level and approved by the State Council (*Guojia minwei bangongting* 1996, pp. 576-577).

17 By the State Council regulations, minority autonomous townships may be established in mono-ethnic population areas as well as in multiethnic population areas, and the nationality to which the autonomy is designated is required to constitute a minimum of 30 per cent of the total population in the community (*Guojia minwei bangongting* 1997, pp. 31-32). China now has more than 1,200 ethnic minority autonomous townships, most of which were established in the 1980s.

pp. 109-111). As far as the Mosuo leaders are concerned, the Naxi nationality gets in the way of their aspirations to achieve prosperity.[18]

For the ordinary Mosuo making a living on land in the villages, the official nationality status is hardly an issue. The Mosuo call themselves Na as a people, and across the communities – Yongning, Zuosuo, or Langqu across the Yunnan-Sichuan border – the Mosuo are differentiated among themselves by reference to places. For the elite individuals, however, Mosuo nationality is a matter of great significance. Although being Mosuo or Naxi makes little difference when it comes to the benefits granted by the preferential policy, such as family-planning quotas (which are in fact far more relaxed in Mosuo villages), it becomes a major issue in the situation where Mosuo have to compete with the Naxi, such as in the area of higher education. Because both Mosuo and Naxi as one nationality have equal access to the same quota assignment, the highly competitive Naxi who enjoy the highest literacy rate within the province inevitably put the Mosuo in a disadvantageous position. According to a Mosuo township official who took the national university entrance exams in the same year as a Pumi friend, the latter had a lower score but was nonetheless admitted to the provincial university and later acquired a job in government in the provincial capital upon graduation, while he himself ended up reading in a vocational school at the prefectural seat and was later assigned a job with the township government in his hometown. The success of his Pumi friend was attributed to the privilege of Pumi being a separate nationality who only have to compete with themselves within a small group (with a total population of 32,000).

The Mosuo assertion of ethnic identity – either by individuals or by the local government – illustrates how directly ethnicity interacts with state policy. The initial identification of ethnic minority societies as worthy of socio-economic development policies associated with an image of inferiority and the ensuing harsh treatment toward the minority nationalities during the years when radical ideology was dominant disaffected the ethnic minority populations to whom the nationality status became a term of abuse. The awakening of ethnic consciousness and the assertion of minority nationality status in the 1980s were a spontaneous response from the ethnic minorities to the rectified national policy toward the minority nationalities. The response itself was *political* but the driving force behind it was largely *economic*, the centre of which is the link between nationality status and preferential treatment. Both in the case of Mosuo who sought a separate nationality status and in the case of the Tujia who finally decided to differentiate themselves from the Han, there is little difference as far as motivation is concerned.

The growing sense of ethnicity heightened the rights consciousness among the minority nationalities, manifest in their demand on the state for special treatment,

---

18 A designation of a Naxi autonomous township has never been on the agenda, because difficulties may involve the ongoing lobbying for a Mosuo nationality, the recognition of Mosuo *ren* by the provincial government, and the Naxi community included in the same township but differentiated from the Mosuo.

with the elite members at the forefront. The legitimacy of their demand has been placed upon the official discourses pertaining to the inferior social development of ethnic minority societies, thus turning the table on the state. As the head of the poverty-alleviation office of Ninglang Yi autonomous county government openly claimed, 'We start from a very low point' (invoking the 'slave society' classification of the Yi in the 1950s), 'and without financial support from the state, the goal of poverty-alleviation cannot be reached by the year 3000, never mind the year 2000'. This line of argument has been effective in drawing financial support from the state.

The preferential policy and its implementation have not only impacted on the relationship between the state and the ethnic minorities, but also substantially influenced how the ethnic minorities see themselves as a group *vis-à-vis* others who have the same or a different nationality status. The variation in the perception of ethnic boundaries is not so much an effect of the official classification of minority nationalities *per se*; rather it is an outcome of the delimitation of administrative divisions that provided the impetus for the nationality classification in the first place. The interplay of these elements has important implications for understanding the development of ethnonationalism in China.

Ethnic Boundaries Consolidated

Classification of minority nationalities in China is a process through which the state reorganizes society. Indeed, 'If society is the outermost limits with which people identify, then it is the state that initially determines those limits or social boundaries' (Migdal 1994, p. 23). The state designation of nationality status in China, especially in the ethnically diverse southwest, has contributed to conscious construction and reconstruction of cultural traits in conformity with the state designated nationality status by the ethnic leadership within its jurisdiction. Such practice has, in turn, reinforced cultural images of oneself in relation to the others, and inadvertently it has facilitated consolidation of ethnic boundaries defined by the administrative divisions.

Since the Prmi were classified into separate nationalities in Sichuan and Yunnan, both sides have actively promoted different cultural characters – the government officials in Muli Tibetan autonomous county (Sichuan) having 'gone to great lengths to reinforce the identity of the county' with Tibetan language and culture, while efforts are being made by the Pumi leaders in Ninglang county (Yunnan) to 'research and publicize the glories of the Pumizu as a separate and ancient culture' (Harrell 1996, pp. 288-292). Across the provincial border between Yunnan and Guangxi, divided ethnic consciousness has developed among the Zhuang population. Prior to the PRC state nationality classification, neither the Zhuang in Guangxi nor the Zhuang in Yunnan had used the name Zhuang for themselves; instead they identified themselves with different communities in which they resided. The PRC classification of nationality provided these culturally diverse peoples with a common identity. However, because of the differences in local politics regarding ethnicity on either side of the border, a perception has developed of the 'Yunnan Zhuang' as culturally diverse and the 'Guangxi Zhuang' as culturally united (Kaup 2002). The contrasting ethnic consciousness has subsequently estranged the Zhuang people across the provincial border, to the extent that neither side is considered to have anything to contribute to the interests of the other. The distinct apathy is rooted in the territory-bound loyalty 'as a result of the structure of resource distribution along administrative boundaries' (ibid., p. 881). The same explanation would be applicable to the construction of cultural traits among the Pumi-Tibetans across the Yunnan-Sichuan border.

China's micro-level political economy is characterized by the designation of discrete levels of government administration as the loci of policy implementation and economic planning. In government operations, financial subsidies are distributed from higher to lower levels (province to prefecture, prefecture to county, and county to township), and tax exemption and reduction decisions are made at each level of government with the approval of its immediate superior. While ethnicity is crucial in policy making, the actual implementation – distribution of resources and execution of economic plans – in the locality is rarely focused on any particular ethnic population, especially in the areas populated by numerous and diverse ethnic groups, like Yunnan where no county or township is populated by a mono-ethnic population (even in the designated ethnic minority autonomies), and large nationalities like Yi, Hui, Bai, Miao and Dai are found in almost every county and city. Even with funds earmarked for the ethnic minority autonomous counties and townships, benefits are intended for the community rather than a specific ethnic group. In Ninglang Yi autonomous county, populated by a dozen minorities (in that the Yi make up about 60 per cent of the county's population) while certain poverty-alleviation and social relief programmes are primarily designed to benefit the Yi population whose living conditions in the mountains are generally more severe than those of other communities, other ethnic minorities are by no means excluded (except for the Han).

Such a framework of resource distribution would indeed make it difficult for the Mosuo in northwest Yunnan to reconcile themselves with the Naxi identity designated by the state. Given the jurisdiction of their residence, the Mosuo are predisposed to remain loyal to the government of Ninglang Yi autonomous county, since it took the Mosuo appeals for a separate nationality status to the higher levels of government and allocated funds to the township where a large Mosuo population reside to help make ends meet. Unlike the Pumi-Tibetans, the Mosuo in Ninglang have consistently resisted the state-designated nationality status, and every effort is made to distance themselves from the Naxi in Lijiang by enhancing the Mosuo cultural practices of Tibetan Buddhism and matrilineal kinship.[19] The contrast

---

19 The Naxi in Lijiang are equally keen to differentiate themselves from their matrilineal cousins on the opposite side of the Jinsha River, but for different reasons. See

between the Mosuo and the Pumi-Tibetans across the provincial border in their attitudes toward the state-designated nationality status indicates that the designated nationality status is likely to be accepted when the community interests are not jeopardized by it; in the opposite case, it is likely to be disputed. The contestation and consolidation of the ethnic boundaries in these cases highlight a central role of the administrative divisions that have, in a way, served to break up potential formations of ethnicity-based alliances. However, contrastive cases do exist.

Unlike the Zhuang across the Yunnan-Guangxi border and the Pumi-Tibetans across the Yunnan-Sichuan border, the ethnic boundaries perceived by the Yi do not coincide with administrative divisions. The population of the Yi nationality, amounting to 6.5 million, are concentrated in the region straddling the border between Guizhou and Yunnan, and the border between Yunnan and Sichuan. Like the Zhuang, the Yi are culturally diverse people. While the Yi in northwest Yunnan have little to identify themselves with the Yi in central-north Yunnan, who are regarded by the former as too 'sinicized', they consider the Yi in southwest Sichuan as one family, bound by kinship and class system.[20] This part of the Yi territory, known as Cold Mountains (Liangshan), had never been ruled by any unified political power in history; presently, the Yi population in Sichuan is largely included in the Liangshan Yi autonomous prefecture (known as the 'great Cold Mountain') established in 1952, whereas the Yi on the south of the border belong to the Ninglang Yi autonomous county (known as the 'small Cold Mountain') established in 1956. The practice of endogamy has enabled the Yi kinship ties to penetrate the government administrations on both sides,[21] and the flexibility in making economic plans granted to the ethnically autonomous governments has promoted economic cooperation across the provincial border, especially in forestry. The criss-crossing political system (regional autonomy granted by the state) and social organizations have fostered strong ethno-nationalism in the area. Though armed ethnic uprising against the state, like the one in 1955-1956, has not recurred in this area over the past four decades, a strong Cold Mountain Yi united front is a reality, upheld by the local elite on either side, who share considerable political and economic interests.

The contrast between the Yi and Zhuang perception of ethnic boundaries suggests that regional autonomies play a decisive role in the development of ethno-nationalism. However, the results can be strikingly different: while the creation of the Zhuang autonomous region in Guangxi is seen to have prevented the spread of ethno-nationalism (Kaup 2002), the designation of the Yi autonomies in Yunnan and Sichuan appears to have facilitated the growth of ethno-nationalism.

---

discussion on the impact of the state discourse on the Naxi perception of themselves as the 'advanced' *vis-à-vis* others as the 'backward' (White 1998).

20 The Yi in northwest Yunnan originally emigrated from Sichuan.

21 In the Yi marriages, blood relations and class differences are observed; partners of matching ranks are often sought across the provincial border, and government officials are no exceptions.

Reasons for this discrepancy are related to the local history of ethnic relations (in particular with the Han) and the relationship between the ethnic elite and the state.[22] The role of social organizations is also important, in view of how the Yi across the Yunnan-Sichuan border are united as one, and how the Yi in northwest Yunnan and the Yi in central-north Yunnan stay separated. The fluctuation of the ethnic boundaries as perceived by the various minority nationalities, however, does not in any way reflect a uniformly bounded Han category.

The Residual Category

The Han population are not subject to the official nationality classification, but this does not make the category of Han – as pitted against the non-Han (minority nationalities) – less problematic. If, as maintained, minority is 'primarily understood to be a group that does not share the ethnic or national characteristics of the majority of the population' (Heberer 1989, p. 7), it may be assumed that there are such things as 'the ethnic or national characteristics of the majority of the population'. This definition, however, runs into problems when characterizing the majority population in China because, apart from a wide range of differences in settlement, dialect, diet, and livelihood among the people who are categorized as Han, the relevance of 'Han-ness' or, in other words, Han consciousness, is felt very differently between the cosmopolitan cities and the peripheral provinces (Blum 2000, p. 59). In this sense, the Han population in China is best defined as a residual category that comprises the people who do not bear any distinct ethnic markers and who are not identified as minority nationalities. Such an approach helps gain insights into the Han identity in Yunnan differing from the rest of China, as a result of the geographic distance that separates the peripheral province from the core regions, and as a result of the relationship between the Han and the non-Han populations within the province.

The Han in Yunnan constitute two thirds of the total population in the province. A cluster of place names with which many Yunnanese Han identify – Nanjing, Yingtianfu, Liushuwan, Gaoshikan – traces the history of Han immigration from China's eastern province of Jiangsu into Yunnan to the Ming dynasty (1368-1644). Yingtianfu is where the Hongwu Emperor founded the Ming dynasty, and it became the dynasty's first capital, Nanjing. Liushuwan and Gaoshikan are two place names believed to have been the locations of the Ming military barracks (Hao 1998, p. 159); from there, the Ming army was dispatched to Yunnan in 1381, jointly with troops from Jiangxi and Hunan provinces, to subdue a resistance force still loyal to the Mongol prince. Once Yunnan was pacified, the conquering army was garrisoned across Yunnan; the total number was estimated at a quarter of a million, one third being on active military duty while two thirds were engaged in

---

22 The Zhuang have a strong representation in the central government which in effect had a great influence on the establishment of the Zhuang Autonomous Region.

farming (Liu 1991, p. 249). In the ensuing years, the Ming emperor ordered that the dependants of the garrison troops from the central China plains be escorted to Yunnan (You 1994, p. 354), making the garrison settlement permanent. The generations of descendants thereafter became residents of Yunnan. Following the military settlement, civilian immigrants (farmers and artisans) from the central plains arrived in Yunnan, thus significantly altering the ratio of the Han to non-Han population in the frontier areas. Prior to the Ming era, the Han population in Yunnan had been small and has for the most part become assimilated into the aboriginal population; the Han emigration during the Ming era for the first time transformed the non-Han population in Yunnan into a minority. The Han population further expanded during the succeeding Qing period, as trade with China proper increased and the exploitation of resources in Yunnan intensified.[23]

In the modern period, the Han population who came to settle down in Yunnan was of a very different pattern. Cadres from the north and university students having retreated to Kunming during the Sino-Japanese war constituted a major force carrying out the social transformation in Yunnan during the 1950s; depending on their professional and personal circumstances, many of them continued to work and live in Yunnan afterward. The construction period in the 1960s drew additional Han population to Yunnan. Dozens of 'Production-Construction Corps' state farms were created along the borders with Vietnam and Burma to provide border security as well as employment for university graduates and unemployed urban youth from central and eastern China; the national defence-related 'Third Front Construction' project brought additional technicians and workers to Yunnan from north and northeast, followed by youths (middle school graduates) dispatched from Beijing, Tianjin and Shanghai. With the exception of these youths, most of whom had returned to their places of origin by 1980, the Han population – cadres, technicians and workers – who arrived in Yunnan after 1950 became permanent residents, many of them having by now reached retirement.[24] These categories of 'frontier support personnel' were largely employed in the state sector; and strictly speaking, they were not exclusively Han, as the Hui among other nationalities were included.

While the first generation of immigrants in the modern period rarely became full Yunnanese as far as their accent and food culture are concerned, their children and grandchildren are largely Yunnan-ized. Having grown up and received their education in Yunnan, the mostly city dwelling second and third generations of immigrants are distributed across a variety of professions in public as well as private sectors. Despite their diverse 'homes of origin', they now all identify themselves as Yunnanese in the way they speak and the way they relate to others. Many Yunnanese Han tend to describe themselves as 'honest' and 'unsophisticated' – characteristics often attributed to the ethnic minorities –

23 Miners from China proper alone was estimated at close to 100,000 (Cang 1997, pp. 61-62).
24 Many of the central government's enterprises had been transferred to provincial level management by the 1970s.

vis-à-vis the Shanghaiese or Cantonese. When travelling outside the province, they are frequently mistaken for minority nationalities on the basis of their Yunnan accent, or simply because they come from Yunnan. The cultural image of the Yunnanese as perceived by others has sometimes contributed to the identification of the Yunnanese Han with the ethnic minorities to mark the difference between themselves and others outside Yunnan. Within the province, however, the Yunnanese Han are markedly distinguished from the ethnic minority population in a series of institutionalized arrangements with respect to preferential treatment.

The Han population in Yunnan, to a large extent, shares with the minority nationalities the same economy which has benefited from the central government's financial subsidies allocated to the region. However, in the local context, benefits enjoyed by the Han and minority nationalities are sharply differentiated, and the Han communities are generally excluded from benefits earmarked for minority nationalities; even when the Han population only makes up a minority in a community, it is not treated as a minority. The exclusion of the Han population from the preferential treatment and the image of 'backwardness' associated with China's periphery have jointly contributed to the predicament of Han consciousness in Yunnan. In the recent development of cultural regionalism as observed in China's interior and western provinces where the local governments have fervently pursued 'cultural authenticity' as a way to attract capital investment and develop tourism (Oakes 2000), the provincial government of Yunnan – being aware of its lack of advantage in competing with central China to develop 'Han culture' – opted for the development of cultural pluralism focusing on the 'colourful' ethnic minorities, while exploring a new identity with the Southeast Asian culture (*Yunnan shengwei xuanchuanbu* 1999). Drawing closer to the Southeast Asian culture in the new-found economic environment of the 21st century, the Yunnanese Han may be seen to further distance themselves from the Han population in the rest of China, hence making the category of Han even fuzzier.

Conclusion

The classification of minority nationalities in the 1950s was central to the integration of peripheral societies into the Chinese state. In the given political environment, the scheme was not so much aimed at differentiating peoples of diverse ethnic backgrounds as at reinventing society. The need to create and maintain regional stability made nationality work a priority in government administrations, and it was under these circumstances that the classification of minority nationalities was launched. Because local discrepancies in ethnic population, community organization, state-society relations, and interethnic relations all, in one way or another, had potential influence on regional stability, the official designation of nationalities ultimately came to reflect how these elements interacted and how conflicting interests were accommodated. The merger and separation of the ethnic groups across the Yunnan-Sichuan border, as discussed in this chapter, bear out such complexity.

Regional autonomy and administrative divisions not only had considerable influence on how minority nationalities were classified, they were also potentially effective in delineating ethnic boundaries. The Zhuang across Guangxi and Yunnan embody a case of contrasting ethnic consciousness and divided interests between the people who share the same nationality status. This phenomenon has a bearing on the structure of resource distribution to which administrative divisions are essential. The cultural differences and similarities perceived and promoted by the Pumi and Tibetans across the Yunnan-Sichuan border in conformity with the state designation of nationality status illustrate further the compatibility between community interests shaped by administrative divisions and ethnic identities. The perception of ethnic boundaries by the people making up one particular group vis-à-vis others has a direct impact on the expression of ethno-nationalism in the locality and significant implications for integration.

By classifying minority nationalities, the PRC state created a hierarchical relationship between the Han and non-Han. Regional disparities, however, make the Han a peculiar category, meaningful only in opposition to the designated minority nationalities as a whole. The self-perception of the Yunnanese Han is, by and large, a reflection of the implementation of the state nationality policies. Hence, as the chapter has come to emphasize, ethnic categories, Han or non-Han, are subject to manipulation, not only by the policy makers, but also by the intended, or indeed the unintended beneficiaries of the policy. The forces behind manipulations are political as well as economic, and the interaction between them results in shifting ethnic boundaries.

Works Cited

Barth, Fredrik (1969) 'Introduction', in Fredrik Barth (ed.), *Ethnic Groups and Boundaries: The Social Organization of Culture Difference*. Bergen-Oslo: Universitets Forlaget, pp. 9-38.

Blum, Susan D. (2000) *Portraits of 'Primitives': Ordering Human Kinds in the Chinese Nation*. Lanham, CO: Rowman & Littlefield Publishers.

Cang, Ming (1997) *Yunnan minzu qianxi wenhua yanjiu* [Studies of Ethnic Population Migration and Culture in Yunnan]. Kunming: Yunnan minzu chubanshe.

Christiansen, Flemming (1998) *'Hakka: The Politics of Global Ethnic Identity Building'*. Aalborg: Aalborg University, Center for International Studies (*SPIRIT* Discussion Paper), pp. 1-21.

Dangdai Ningxia jianshi [Short History of Contemporary Ningxia] (2002). Beijing: Dangdai Zhongguo chubanshe.

Dangdai Zhongguo caizheng [Contemporary China: Finance] (1988) Vols. 1-2. Beijing: Zhongguo shehui kexue chubanshe.

Dangdai Zhongguo de Yunnan [Contemporary China: Yunnan] (1991) Vols. 1-2. Beijing: Dangdai Zhongguo chubanshe.

Dangdai Zhongguo minzu gongzuo dashiji 1949-1988 [Chronology of PRC Nationality Work] (1990). Beijing: Minzu chubanshe.

Deng, Hongbi (1998) *Zhongguo shaoshu minzu renkou zhengce yanjiu* [Research on China's Ethnic Minority Population Policy]. Chongqing: Chongqing chubanshe.

Dreyer, June Teufel (1976) *Minority Nationalities and National Integration in the People's Republic of China*, Cambridge, Mass.: Harvard University Press.

Du, Yuting (1999) 'Qiu Zhongguo minzuxue zhihun' [Searching for the Spirit of Chinese Ethnology], in Hao Shiyuan (ed.), *Tianye diaocha shilu* (Fieldwork Recording). Beijing: Shehui kexue wenxian chubanshe, pp. 17-30.

Erbaugh, Mary S. (1992) 'The Secret History of the Hakkas: The Chinese Revolution as a Hakka Enterprise'. *The China Quarterly*, No. 132 (December), pp. 936-68.

Gladney, Dru C. (1996) *Muslim Chinese: Ethnic Nationalism in the People's Republic.* Cambridge Mass.: Harvard University Press.

Guo, Xiaolin (1997) *Rice Ears and Cattle Tails: A Comparative Study of Rural Economy and Society in Yunnan, Southwest China.* Vancouver, BC: University of British Columbia (Doctoral Dissertation).

Guojia minwei bangongting (1996) Guojia minwei wenjian xuanbian 1985-1995 [Selected Documents of State Nationalities Affairs Commission], Vols. 1-2. Beijing: Zhongguo minhang chubanshe.

Guojia minwei bangongting (1997) Zhonghua renmin gongheguo minzu zhengce fagui xuanbian [Selection of the PRC Nationality Polices and Laws]. Beijing: Zhongguo minhang chubanshe.

Guojia minzu shiwu weiyuanhui (1994) Zhongguo gongchandang zhuyao lingdaoren lun minzu wenti [CCP Key Leaders on Issues of Nationalities]. Beijing: Minzu chubanshe.

Hao, Zhengzhi (1998) *Hanzu yimin rudian shihua: Nanjing Liushuwan Gaoshikan* [The History of Han Immigration to Yunnan: From Gaoshikan-Liushuwan of Nanjing]. Kunming: Yunnan University Press.

Harrell, Stevan (1996) 'The Nationalities Question and the Prmi Problem', in Melissa J. Brown (ed.), *Negotiating Ethnicities in China and Taiwan*, Chinese Research Monograph. Berkeley: Institute of East Asian Studies, University of California, pp. 274-296.

Heberer, Thomas (1989) *China and Its National Minorities: Autonomy or Assimilation?* Armonk, New York: M. E. Sharpe.

Kaup, Katherine Palmer (2002) 'Regionalism versus Ethnonationalism in the People's Republic of China'. *The China Quarterly*, No. 172 (December), pp. 863-884.

Liu, Wenzheng (1991) *Dianzhi* [History of Yunnan]. Kunming: Yunnan jiaoyu chubanshe.

McKhann, Charles (1995) 'The Naxi and the Nationalities Questions', in Stevan Harrell (ed.), *Cultural Encounters on China's Frontiers.* Seattle: University of Washington Press, pp. 39-62.

Migdal, Joel S. (1994) 'The State in Society: An Approach to Struggle for Domination', in Joel S. Migdal, Atul Kohli and Vivienne Shue (eds), *State Power and Social Forces: Domination and Transformation in the Third World.* Cambridge: Cambridge University Press, pp. 7-34.

Minzu wenti wenxian huibian 1921-1949 [Collection of Documents on Issues of Nationalities], (1991). Beijing: Zhonggong Zhongyang dangxiao chubanshe.

Muli Zangzu zizhixian zhi [Gazetteer of Muli Tibetan Autonomous County] (1995). Chengdu: Sichuan renmin chubanshe.

Ninglang Yizu zizhi xian zhi [Gazetteer of Ninglang Yi Autonomous County] (1993). Kunming: Yunnan minzu chubanshe.

Oakes, Tim (2000) 'China's Provincial Identities: Reviving Regionalism and Reinventing "Chineseness"'. *The Journal of Asian Studies*, Vol. 59, No. 3 (August), pp. 667-92.

Prucha, Francis Paul (1995) *The Great Father: The United States Government and the American Indians* [Volumes 1 and 2 – unabridged]. Lincoln: University of Nebraska Press.

Rawski, Evelyn S. (1996) 'Presidential Address: Reenvisioning the Qing: The Significance of the Qing Period in Chinese History'. *The Journal of Asian Studies*, Vol. 55, No. 4 (November), pp. 829-50.

Rigger, Shelley (1995) 'Voices of Manchu Identity, 1635-1935', in Stevan Harrell (ed.), *Cultural Encounters on China's Ethnic Frontiers*. Seattle: University of Washington Press, pp. 186-214.

Rock, Joseph F. (1947) *The Ancient Na-Khi Kingdom of Southwest China*, Vols. 1-2, Harvard-Yenching Institute Monograph series, Vol. IX. Cambridge, Mass.: Harvard University Press.

Schoenhals, Michael (2000) 'The Yunnan "Political Frontier Defence" of 1969-1971', paper presented at the conference *Ethnicity, Politics and Cross-Border Cultures in Southwest China: Past and Present*, Lund University.

Shen, Lin (2001) *Zhongguo de minzuxiang* [China's Ethnic Minority Autonomous Townships]. Beijing: Minzu chubanshe.

Tao, Yunkui (1962) 'Guanyu moxie zhi mingcheng fenbu yu qianyi' [On the Name of Mosuo and Their Distribution and Migration], bibliographic details unknown, copy in the Harvard-Yenching Institute Library.

Wang, Lianfang (1999) *Yunnan minzu gongzuo huiyi* [Recollection of Nationality Work]. Kunming: Yunnan renmin chubanshe.

White, Sydney D. (1998) 'State Discourse, Minority Policies, and the Politics of Identity in the Lijiang Naxi People's Autonomous County', in William Safran (ed.), *Nationalism and Ethnoregional Identities in China*. London: Frank Cass, pp. 9-27.

You Zhong (1994) *Yunnan minzu shi* [History of Yunnan Ethnic Minorities]. Kunming: Yunnan daxue chubanshe.

Yunnan minzu gongzuo sishinian [Forty Years of Nationality Work in Yunnan] (1994), Vols. 1-2. Kunming: Yunnan minzu chubanshe.

Yunnan shengwei xuanchuanbu (1999) *Zouxiang 21 shiji de Yunnan minzu wenhua* [Yunnan Ethnic Cultures at the Turn of the 21st Century]. Kunming: Yunnan renmin chubanshe.

Zhongguo minzu tongji 1949-1990 [China's Nationalities Yearbook] (1991). Beijing: Zhongguo tongji chubanshe.

PART IV

MULTICULTURAL BELONGING

Chapter 11

No Joking Matter: The Multiple Identities of Belgium

Georges van den Abbeele

for Anne Morelli

For several years now, a popular joke has been circulating within and without Belgium. While many versions of the joke exist, they all follow the same basic pattern: a crowd of 'Belgians' is called to order for some reason (military induction, medical examination, or whatever), then asked to divide into two groups: Flemings on one side, Walloons on the other. After much shifting and shouting, one, two, or more individuals still surprisingly remain in the middle (clinging to the Belgian flag in some versions). When asked who they are, they reply that they are 'Belgians', when asked their names, they reply with varying manifestly foreign names: Mario Maccaluso, Simon Levy, Mohammed Ben Stiton, etc, etc.[1] The point of the joke is not only to make fun of the obsessively split character of the Belgian state between its two primary language groups, but also the very limits of that hyperbolic dichotomization, i.e. the fact that after all the uproar, perhaps not all Belgians understand themselves as either Flemish or Walloon. As in all humour, there is inevitably a trace of anxiety. There is a certain comfort in the notion that the Belgian state is no more than an administrative fig leaf for two discrete and distinguishable communities whose identity is readily mapped in ethnic and geographic as well as linguistic terms. Belgium, though small enough as nation states go, would in reality be not one but two nations joined at the hip in Brussels and readily separated if only the right, politically adroit, surgeon would come along. Such is, of course, not the case, or it would have already happened.

Instead, what is troubling about the Belgian situation is its manifest lack of fit with the standard models of nationalism theory. There is no apparent ground of homogeneity that binds its citizens into a strong sense of communal identity based

---

1   I read a darker side to the joke. When my father was arrested by the Gestapo in the summer of 1944, his interrogation began – in a perverse acknowledgement of the Geneva protocol – by his being asked to declare his 'nationality' as either Flemish or Walloon. He soon found out to his dismay that the answer 'Belgian' was unacceptable to the Nazi authorities.

on national belonging. No common language, ethnicity or shared history. No imagined community through print culture (Anderson 1983), modernization (Gellner 1983) or invented tradition (Hobsbawm 1990). Yet to deny the nationhood of Belgium on these grounds is by the same token to deny the viability of a significant percentage of the world's nations. To ask the question 'What is Belgium?' is not only a personally compelling question for an expatriate Belgian national like myself, but also, and more profoundly, a way to interrogate the assumptions we all too readily make as theorists or historians of that phenomenon we term 'nationalism' and its correlate, 'national identity'. Rather than viewing such heteroclite state formations as peripheral or marginal cases for theorists of nationalism to explain away under the rubric of exceptionalism, it is time that we begin to rethink what nationalism might mean in contexts where identity appears as overtly fragmentary, multiple and overdetermined. To be sure, the canonical examples of coherent nation states – France, Britain, Germany – have revealed themselves in recent years to be less than homogeneous, if not founded upon the repression of distinct linguistic, ethnic, cultural or regional differences. The deconstruction of these classic nation states suggests both the perils of modelling the concept of nationalism upon solely Western European examples (although that model is not even true for all of Western Europe!) and the limits of understanding nationalism and national identity as dependent upon homogeneity of language, culture or ethnicity. Alternatively, can we in any way think of the heterogeneous nation state in positive terms, especially when its problems – such as in the very different cases of a Belgium, a Yugoslavia, or a Congo – are explained away quickly and tersely in terms of their 'failure' as nations? In fact, the really interesting question is not why such nation states are (rather unsurprisingly) prey to extreme dissension and/or violence but rather why despite everything they continue to exist, even to prosper and command both the political loyalty and emotional attachment of their citizenry. The Swiss may also be less of an exception than we (or they) think.

Belgium would seem to present a classic case of a nation founded upon identities that are not only multiple but also in historical terms strikingly changeable (Zolberg 1974; Murphy 1988; Stengers 1990, 2000). Moreover, there are several distinct dimensions to the question of multiple identities in Belgium that seriously complicate the viability of the most basic terms used to assign identity. These include language, class, religion, ethnicity, emigrant or immigrant status, as well as region itself, which can be construed either in purely geographical terms or in those of political administration. Now, according to the reigning mythology, Flanders is defined politically by the five northern provinces of Belgium, geographically discernible by the low-lying plains of the region ('vlaanderen' means flatlands) and inhabited by Dutch-speaking people, staunchly Catholic in creed, commercially oriented and affluent. Wallonia, by the same bipolar logic, is the region defined politically by the five southern provinces, geographically by its rolling hills and valleys ('les vallons'), and demographically by socialist-leaning French speakers who tend to be poor, working class and secular. Such stereotypes are at best approximative, to be sure, yet this imaginary division of the nation – so reminiscent in its stark dualism of those South American Indian myths famously studied by Claude Lévi-Strauss in the heyday of French structuralism – could easily be said to have constituted the 'myth' of Belgium for well over a century and a half. The progressive need of the Belgian state to appease these perceived regional '*moities*' has also led over the years to a series of constitutional crises and revisions culminating in the current rashly decentralized and virtually dysfunctional shell of a nation that still manages (who knows for how long!) to call itself 'Belgium'. Only in recent years, with the federalist agenda complete, have doubts about the process begun to appear, ironically with the very weakness of a central government that is both corruption-ridden and almost unbelievably incapable of protecting its own citizenry from harm (as sadly shown by the awful sequence of scandals that has unraveled from the mysterious assassination in 1991 of socialist politician, Albert Cools, to the Dutroux paedophile murders, to the dioxin contamination of the nation's food supply in the spring of 1999).[2] The irony of ironies is that the last round of national elections merely replaced one inept regime advocating decentralization (under Dehaene) with a so-called 'rainbow' coalition government (under Verhofstadt) advocating even greater decentralization, this time under the banner of neoliberalism.[3] Will the Belgians ever learn? Despite the powerful political pull of regional identity in the 'unmaking' of the Belgian nation state, it is fairly easy to debunk the essentialist portrayal of those identities. The touted geographical partition between northern *vlaanderen* and southern *vallons* is scarcely perceptible to a modern traveler driving along the nation's highways, the much more dramatic switch being the one between the open western plains and the densely forested eastern Ardennes area. Linguistically, the razor-sharp distinction between the two primary languages represents a process of historical refinement and repression in which, ironically, the greatest casualties have been the regional dialects themselves with Old Walloon having virtually disappeared into Standard French and the many varieties of Flemish likewise subsumed into 'Algemeen Nederlands' – not just practically through print culture and the school system but by official proclamation in 1973 (Deprez 1985, 1998). These are classic examples of identity formation established through the institutions of print culture and public education (pace Anderson).

---

2   For those who do not follow events in Belgium, an excellent overview of the many recent scandals there can be found in Dirk Barrez (1997).

3   Not to be confused with Jesse Jackson's attempts in the 1980s to establish a progressive, multicultural political movement in the United States, the Belgian 'rainbow' coalition of 1999 was an unlikely alliance of liberals, socialists and ecologists (indeed every political party except the previously ruling Social-Christians and the extreme right-wing Vlaams Blok) merely for the sake of unseating the Dehaene government and not presenting any positive agenda of its own. As for the Vlaams Blok, it has the amazing audacity to advance a radical separatist agenda that would abolish the Belgian state while blaming that already decentralized and administratively crippled entity for the country's high crime rate. State decentralization thus functions viciously as both solution and problem.

What is somewhat unusual, though (or rather unparadigmatic for nationalism theory) is that both of the national languages in their standardized form are derived from beyond the nation's borders, as if to realize on a mass scale what has been termed the 'monolingualism of the other' (Derrida 1996). In this land of strife over language use and privilege, no one's language is strictly his or her own.

It is, of course, not at all true that only two languages are spoken in Belgium, or that everyone speaks just one language. A sizeable German community resides in eastern Belgium, and individual Belgians often pride themselves on their multilingual fluency (with a working knowledge of at least four languages not uncommon among the educated elite). Moreover, the provincial, political boundaries that divide the autonomous regions of Flanders and Wallonia do not, at every point, precisely follow the linguistic border between Dutch and French speakers. Towns such as Fourons/Voeren, politically under Flemish rule, insist on their right not only to speak French but to use French in all official dealings and documents with the provincial and regional government. From 1970 to 1993, a series of revisions have radically altered the Constitution of Belgium, amputating central state power to the extreme while also begrudgingly avowing the difficulty of sundering the nation along regional lines by establishing an unusual set of parallel institutions whose exact powers and responsibilities remain to be clarified. On the one hand, three autonomous 'regions' were established: Flanders, Wallonia, and the city of Brussels (which is officially bilingual). On the other, three linguistic 'communities' were declared: Netherlandophone, Francophone and Germanophone. The exact nature of the relation between the 'regions' and the 'communities' is, unsurprisingly, an area of tremendous legal haranguing and bargaining (Dieckhoff 1996). One result of this multi-tiered federalism is that 'the normal rule for resolving conflict among juridical norms, that is to say, the primacy of the higher norm over the lower one, has been rendered inapplicable' (Columberg 1998). In any case, what the asymmetry between administrative regions and linguistic communities implicitly acknowledges is that the language one speaks and the region one inhabits may not be coterminous. Yet the infamous Belgian law of 24 July 1961 (*Moniteur Belge – Belgisch Staatsblad* 131, 182, p. 6140), which forbids census takers from asking anyone his or her linguistic preference (Levy 1962) may ultimately doom the so-called linguistic communities to irrelevance. Indeed, serious demographic surveys to establish actual linguistic use in given areas have been precluded by this Belgian equivalent of 'Don't ask, don't tell'. Alexander Murphy (1988, p. 5) concludes: 'The only available statistics are population figures for the official language regions'. The result, he continues, has been to regionalize linguistic use, and thus to encourage the development of a pseudo-ethnic identity for each of the two major (monolingual) regions. In other words, since Limburg is a Flemish province, all of its citizens are presumed to be not only ethnically Flemish but also speakers of Dutch – indeed those citizens must communicate with the provincial and regional governments in Dutch. Only when entire townships such as Voeren/Fourons have risen up in protest has some attention been focused on the problem, but one can only imagine how many families, individuals or small communities have been affected adversely by the regionalization of linguistico-ethnic identity. The utter lack of flexibility in the application of the Belgian language laws was evidenced again in the spring of 1998, when the very Flemish mayor of the incontestably Flemish township of De Panne (on the Belgian seacoast at the opposite end of the country from Voeren/Fourons) ran into trouble with the Flemish Ministry of the Interior for his having written a circular letter in French to the francophone inhabitants of his community, thereby committing the political sin of recognizing and thereby potentially legitimating the existence of French speakers within Flanders.

To have reduced linguistic and ethnic identity to only two (or three) exclusivist categories is the sad error of Belgian political process. The 'single language, single culture' trope of doctrinaire, canonical nationalism forces the issue of separatism by understanding a linguistically and culturally heterogeneous nation to be the mere sum of a couple of smaller, more homogeneous ones. Regional (hence proto-national) monolingualism, rather than any comprehensive attempt at bilingualism, has repeatedly been the choice of the Belgian political elites, scandalously without ever even once having posed the question to the Belgian citizenry itself in the form of a national referendum of any kind (Columberg 1998). One can only wonder what it would have been like to de-regionalize language identity and tolerate, even encourage, the multiple and mixed identities found in many Belgians: bilingual, trilingual, and multilingual speakers; Flemish Walloons and Francophone Flemings, Jewish Belgians, Maghrebian Belgians, Italian Belgians, African Belgians, etc.; individuals whose official 'identity' is apparent neither by name nor accent nor physique. A place in Belgium does exist where such multiple identities do occur, and on a massive scale: the capital city of Brussels. A key source of contestation in the Belgian linguistic debates, Brussels has experienced unprecedented growth in the last half century, not only as the officially bilingual capital of Belgium but as a hub of international trade and diplomacy, culminating in the establishment of the European Union itself as a reputedly Brussels-based operation. The stunning urban growth of what has become a leading world city was fueled, of course, by intense immigration, both internally by Francophone Flemings seeking to maintain their language habits, and externally by Italians, Iberians, Maghebians, Turks, Congolese and other sub-Saharan Africans, and more recently by Southeast Asians and Eastern Europeans (Denis 1992, pp. 319-26). Since a good many of these immigrants spoke a similar romance language or knew French via colonial experience, they enhanced the francophone tendency of Brussels – a situation rendered provocative by the capital city's geographical immersion within Flemish-speaking territory. A spillover of sorts has happened over the years as the suburbs of metropolitan Brussels – known as the Rand – have spread out into the Flemish countryside populating it with many French-speaking inhabitants. This situation of *'verfransing'* has been viewed with dismay by Flemish nationalists, who have responded with a variety of efforts that have become increasingly confrontational, from anti-immigrant legislation to even stricter interpretation of the language laws. On 16 December 1997, the Flemish

Minister of Internal Affairs, Leo Peeters, issued a circular requiring inhabitants of the Brussels suburbs previously allowed unrestricted linguistic 'facilities' in French to request French documents each and every time they had official business with the communal, provincial or regional governments. A storm of protest against a policy perceived as an attempt to limit and eventually eliminate those linguistic facilities led to a predictably ineffectual protest by the francophone community and a dramatic intervention by the European Commission of Juridical Matters and Human Rights, who itself cited the Belgian state for failing to respect the rights of 'linguistic minorities' (Columberg 1998). That characterization was rejected in advance by the Flemish Parliament, which had already stipulated in a July 1997 decree that the term 'national minority' may not be applied to either French or Dutch speakers, regardless of their location in Belgium. The issue remains unresolved, and in June 2001, the European Council sent another Swiss official, Lili Nabholz-Haidegger, to revisit Brussels and vicinity. A month prior to Columberg's visit in 1998, another flare-up occurred as the European Court ruled negatively on Belgium for dragging its feet in responding to the EU directives to allow resident non-nationals to vote in local elections. Here, suspicion reigned in Flemish political circles that allowing non-Belgians to vote would give undue advantage to the francophone element since those non-Belgians, as per the large immigrant population in Brussels, would be more likely to speak French than Flemish (Columberg 1998). Finally, the decision of the Flemish Parliament to hold its sessions in Brussels and to declare Brussels the 'capital of Flanders', also manifests the Flemish concern to maintain control over Brussels at all costs. After all, Brussels is the obvious crown jewel in the Belgian economic treasure chest, and, of course, it is the much vaunted 'capital of Europe' as well. The on-going situation remains tense enough for a best-selling novel to appear describing a civil war between language groups in the city, characterized in the opening pages as 'Babel and Sarejevo put together' (Neirynck 1996).

The most extreme Flemish nationalists, as satirically rendered by the character of Erwin in Neirynck's novel, lay claim not only over Brussels itself but also, more ambitiously, over parts of north-western France (Nord, Pas-de-Calais), citing their historic inclusion within the ancient County of Flanders. Such claims based on historical demarcation are, of course, cynically self-serving, for if Flanders were to be coterminous with the mediaeval fiefdom of that name, one would by the same logic need to exclude three of the five Belgian provinces that make up the modern region of Flanders: Limburg would belong to the Dutch region around Maastricht; Antwerp and Flemish Brabant (which geographically envelops the city of Brussels) would belong to the old Duchy of Brabant. Wallonia has even less of a claim to historical validation, since the territories that currently make it up belonged variously to the County of Hainaut, the Duchy of Luxemburg (still in existence!) and the Bishopric of Liège. This has, of course, never prevented nationalist or separatist tendencies on the Walloon side, from the endless flirtation with France about possible annexation to the imperialist dreams of reviving the old Burgundian realm that inspired the Second World War followers of the fascist, Léon Degrelle (Conway 1993).

Such historical investments in the myths of regional identity are parried by the ever-increasing portion of the Belgian population that has little or no historical connection to the country, namely immigrants, yet for whom Belgium itself is the sole viable category of national belonging. Hence the joke that serves as the pretext to this discussion. Curiously, it is they whose other possible sense of identity is established by their belonging to a diasporic community who are most eager to see the survival of the nation state where they currently reside (as exiles to a greater or lesser extent) – and this despite their lesser status in that nation state. Nonetheless their importance can be gauged by the fact that fully ten per cent of Belgium's total population hold foreign passports. Adding naturalized citizens and second-generation immigrants to this number, Morelli and Schreiber (1998) estimate that a good quarter of the country can be considered recent immigrants. That non-native population, they argue, may in this way be very much the nation's best hope:[4]

> Aliens by far outnumber citizens who are nostalgic for a single, united Belgium. They fail to identify with or simply refuse to take on identities that are emerging in a federal Belgium where ethno-linguistic categories seem to be supplanting the main political cleavages. While it is quite possible to 'feel Belgian', it is rather difficult to 'feel Flemish' or to 'feel Walloon' especially if one realizes that the mere luck of the draw upon arrival accounted for the fact that one's father got a job in a Walloon mine whereas one's uncle ended up in a Flemish one. Hence, a recent song written by Salvatore Adamo for Belgium's national soccer team calls for national unity. Yvonne Somadossi, a journalist, is baffled by the quarrels between Flemings and Walloons. Franca Massa, the daughter of an Italian miner and wife of Jacques Santkin, a former Walloon minister, declares that Belgians of Italian descent fail to understand the hostility between Flemings and Walloons, ...When asked about his identity, a young man of Vietnamese descent replied: 'I, myself, am very patriotic about Belgium; now I feel fully Belgian and I am a Royalist' (p. 252).

The significance of this immigrant experience of 'identifying' with Belgium rather than with one of its regions, in my view, lies less in their numbers, impressive as

---

4   Not much can be said, on the other hand, for the emigrant population of Belgium. Despite waves of emigration since the 16th century, nothing resembling the establishment of a Belgian diasporic community has ever been so much as whispered. The subject appears not even to have merited much scholarly inquiry until the 1998 publication of Anne Morelli's *Les émigrants belges*. If anything, this work reveals the peculiarity of the Belgian emigrants' disappearance from history, their identity as Belgian appearing to vanish as quickly abroad as they are irremediably forgotten back home. Is it the weakness of national identity that makes it so impossible to maintain it abroad? Do multiple internal identities in a nation obstruct the formation abroad of strong diasporic communities linked with that nation? I think it would be quite easy here to adduce both supporting and counter examples without resolving such questions.

they are, than in its symptomatic value, as a kind of sociological equivalent to the geopolitical impasse that is Brussels. In other words, the immigrants' overt hesitation to identify with either Flanders or Wallonia, their preference for an entity called 'Belgium', may point to a wider paradigm within Belgian society as a whole. Public opinion polls have revealed overwhelming majorities (90 per cent or greater!) both on the Walloon and on the Flemish side opposed to the concept of separatism and at least a third of the population again on both sides who 'primarily identifies with Belgium' and opposes the federalising revisions of the constitution (Dieckhoff 1996, p. 16; Maddens, Beerten and Billiet 1998, pp. 206-7). Separatist views have been held by only the feeblest of minorities, loud and effective though they may have been. Indeed, as Dumeni Columberg points out in his 1998 report, the development and implementation of the language laws, including the establishment of the language border as a fixed, permanent feature of the Belgian landscape, have been the work of political elites: never has there ever been a national referendum on any aspect of language law in Belgium. Belgium is certainly a small country, not appreciably bigger than the greater Los Angeles metropolitan area in southern California. Unsurprisingly, Belgians frequently cross the linguistic divides of their country in their everyday lives. Mixed marriages are not uncommon and rare is it that one does not have relatives in the other camp. The inability to choose is surely not the sole affair of the immigrant population although they may live that debacle with greater intensity.

Even the recent electoral successes of the Vlaams Blok party are paradoxical grist for the mill to the extent that the foregrounding of the party's anti-immigrant agenda over its traditionally separatist platform is what has attracted voters (Betz 1994, pp. 136-39). Not unaware of this development, the Vlaams Blok has even begun to target francophone voters in Brussels itself (Bouveroux 1998). And reprehensible as such xenophobia may be, it is also a sign *a contrario* of the continuing existence of a specifically Belgian identity, since the concern in anti-immigrant rhetoric is that of an external threat to that identity rather than the problem of internal factionalism.

Occasionally too, something happens that incontrovertibly qualifies as a 'national' event, one that could be said to instantiate the existence of Belgium itself as a coherent community; i.e. as a nation. Something called 'Belgium' certainly took place, for example, in the so-called 'White March' of 20 October 1996. Over 300,000 people (a good three per cent of the entire national population) marched silently through the streets of Brussels to mourn the tragic deaths of several young girls who had been the victims of the notorious and evil Marc Dutroux paedophile ring, but also to express their outrage at the incomprehensible ineptitude and corruption of a government who had released the killer from previous incarceration and then negligently, incompetently allowed two of his child victims to die after he had been rearrested. The outrageousness of the crime and the horrifying behaviour of the government officials involved, from blundering police officers to corrupt judges to indifferent political leaders, drove Flemings, Walloons, citizens of Brussels and immigrants from every part of the country and every walk of life to descend on their capital city in a powerful expression of unity for a nation reputedly incapable of such sentiments.

Should one disregard the White March as an exceptional moment triggered by a truly unprecedented and horrific set of events? Or is it the dramatic sign of a truly popular sentiment that exceeds classic models of socio-political determination, i.e. that rare moment of spontaneous public expression or 'enthusiasm' which Jean-Francois Lyotard, following Kant, calls a 'sign of history (*Geschichtszeichen*)' (Lyotard 1983, 1986; Kant 1795)? It would seem that there are a few too many 'exceptions' when one begins discussing the situation of Belgium: the polylingual state as an exception to classic nationalism; Brussels, Fourons/Voeren, De Panne, Mouscron, etc. as 'exceptions' to the purity of linguistic regionalism; the significant immigrant populations as an exception to citizenship; the White March as an exception to normal political process, etc. There is a point at which one feels caught up within the epicycles of late Ptolemaic cosmography in attempting to explain (away) Belgium. Perhaps these exceptional moments are indeed the sign of a certain Belgian identity that manages somehow to express itself over and beyond the ingenious 'compromises' the Belgian political class prides itself on brokering (Moulin 1975; Van Hassel 1975). The popular rejection of such compromises in the name of some more vibrant hybridity may in fact be what is quintessentially Belgian. Indeed, such expressions seem to be more rather than less common in the wake of the federalizing process. I think of the Independent Media Center in Belgium (http://belgium.inymedia.org), exuberantly plurilingual in its internet format, which announced in a sardonic April Fool's joke in 2001 that it had decided to split into two entities (a Flemish and a Walloon one) on the model of so many other Belgian institutions. Or there is that intriguing volume titled *Belgique toujours grande et belle* (Pickels and Sojcher 1998) that features, as the back cover reveals, '126 artists, intellectuals and other singular personages from the Belgian Melting Pot' musing on the particular ways they still feel Belgian – sometimes precisely because of the indeterminacy of belonging to so apparently weak and limited a nation state. The unusual use of the term, 'melting pot', applied to Belgium, is also significant here to the extent that it translates a burgeoning discontent with the reigning ideologies of regionalism and separatism. Flemish novelist Kristien Hemmerechts sums up both points quite well:

> None of us wishes the break-up of Belgium, but neither does any of us want to march behind a Belgian flag. No, we want Belgium to survive so that we are not obliged to march behind a flag, not a tricolor flag [that of Belgium] and certainly not one sporting a lion [that of Flanders]. This is what makes for all the charm of being Belgian: it doesn't represent much, it's the negation of having a nationality so to speak (Hemmerechts 1998, p. 119).

Finally, I think of what is widely considered to be the greatest Belgian novel of the 20th century, *Het Verdriet van België* (*The Sorrow of Belgium*), written in

Dutch by a Flemish writer, Hugo Claus, who lives permanently in southern France. Among the many intriguing aspects of this long and complex novel, which describes a young boy's coming of age in Nazi-occupied Flanders, is the Frenchified vocabulary used by the most ardent 'Flamingant' nationalists in defence of their collaborative ventures with the German authorities. The 'sorrow' that is 'Belgium' – and it is most significant that the title refers to 'Belgium' even though the entire narrative takes place in Flanders alone – is that of its irremediably border status between the Latin and German worlds (language, culture, religion), and even of its having historically often been between French and German armies. Symptomatically, the young Paul de Man (1941) wrote an extraordinary piece for *Le Soir* under the German occupation where he discusses the existence of a surprising number of common words and phrases that cross the linguistic divide between Liège and Limburg provinces, as if to offer philological support for his uncle, Henri de Man, who, as prime minister from 1940-1942, resisted German (and Flemish and Walloon!) efforts to divide Belgium in two (de Man 1942a). Even the vexed question of collaboration in occupied Belgium depends very much on the angle from which one looks at it. In any case, there have been and still are, despite all odds, partisans of an entity called 'Belgium', perhaps even a preponderance of the country's population though it be scarcely perceptible in its decision-making bodies. Certainly, this apparent disconnect between Belgian popular sentiment and Belgian political process, what the Swiss judge Columberg intimates as a virtual disenfranchisement of the Belgian citizenry, is worth serious additional study and empirical research. If the kind of popular reclamation of politics dramatized by the White March is a harbinger for the future, then the ironic outcome of the federalization of Belgium may in fact be, as some have predicated, a 'tightening rather than weakening [of] the bonds between the regional and the national levels' (Hedetoft 1995, p. 164).

There is, however, one peculiar, additional ingredient in the Belgian situation that merits commentary, if for no other reason than the fact that it finds impressive echoes elsewhere. That element is the fervent internationalism of Belgium – and most notably among its political elites since Paul-Henri Spaak (Huizinga 1961; Spaak 1969)[5] – even as federalism has run its course. Indeed, strong support for the European Union (and all its predecessors going back to the Coal and Steel Consortium of the early 1950s) prevails across all the regions and communities of Belgium even if they disagree on all else. Only recently, here again, has the relation between regionalism and internationalism come to be seen as non-

---

5   The earliest formulation of this internationalism as a specific form of Belgian nationalism appears in the works of Henri de Man (1942a, 1942b, 1946). De Man repeatedly sees European unification as the key ironically to maintaining a strong and independent Belgium (as opposed to its fragmentation along ethno-linguistic lines). It is, of course, equally ironic that it was none other than his chief political rival, Spaak, who most aggressively pursued de Man's theoretical vision of a Europe 'beyond nationalism' into the practical reality of the various consortia and 'common markets' (i.e. de Man's 'Zollverein') that ultimately led to the advent of the European Union.

contradictory. Internationalism could indeed be said to be the common national agenda of the bickering Belgian regions that see a strong European Union as precisely the best way to achieve regional autonomy at the expense of the intermediate nation state. A weak sense of Belgian national identity can be supplemented by a strong sense of European identity, which in turn does not exclude a strong sense of regional identity. This logic has now surfaced elsewhere in the European Union, with a number of regions viewing an unparalleled opportunity to undercut or circumvent the nation that houses them.

But does the so-called 'Europe of Regions' promoted by EU planners really bespeak the irrelevance of nation states? I believe the Belgian case (among others), as I have analyzed it, suggests that it may not be the 'nation' that is so much in trouble as the 'state', especially given the peculiar entity that the European Union is. The EU is not itself a state, much less the superstate many predicted (with either joy or dread), and all movements in that direction have been repeatedly, effectively blocked by member states. On the other hand, the kinds of limited authority the EU has and will have is very much a work in progress, and I think we have all learned in recent years to be much more cautious in our predictions about the EU's future. It does seem at this point that the general tendency of the organization will be to maintain a good sense of autonomy and identity for the larger, more powerful nation states (Germany, France) as well as smaller but relatively homogeneous and coherent entities (such as Denmark and the Netherlands). On the other hand, nation states that are already faced with a high degree of heterogeneity (in language, ethnicity, economic well-being, etc.) risk in a number of cases becoming seriously compromised (Spain, Italy, Belgium).[6]

What is undermined in these instances, though, is less a concept of nation than the specific powers and duties of the state, with whatever centrifugal tendencies internal to the nation encouraged by the mere existence of a supranational entity. In Spain, a strongly centralized state for decades forcibly suppressed the multiple identities that make up that nation. Its replacement by a more democratic and federalist regime then suddenly allowed the explosive expression of those long-suppressed aspirations. In Italy and Belgium, however, the state has already long been eroded by the governing practice of compromising between multiple internal

---

6   The case of the United Kingdom in its recent devolution presents an interesting variant of this situation since the sense of state imperilment seems not to obtain. No doubt this stems from the legacy of imperial administration whereby Scots, Welsh and Irish were long governed from London virtually as colonized nations (the core of what would become in the 18th and 19th centuries the British Empire). The kingdom of the British Isles was very much 'united' under 'God's Firstborn', the English, whom it has been argued were the first people to develop a true sense of nationalism (Greenfeld 1992). The historically independent administration of Scotland and Wales, and their longstanding identity as non-English, thus make their emergence as separate political and state entities both culturally plausible and bureaucratically manageable, whereas the less hierarchical and/or clearly defined relations between regional entities in countries like Belgium or Italy make any renegotiation of their union a cause for crisis.

identities. Belgium, in particular, conjures up the terrible image of a nation without a state: administratively inept, endemically corrupt, and most worrisome, capriciously violent (whether by the arrogant impunity of organized criminals or by the forces of authority itself – as attested by such well-documented brutality as that of the Belgian paratroopers in Somalia or the 1998 death of a young Nigerian 'economic' refugee, Sémira Adamu, at the hands of the gendarmes who were 'escorting' her out of the country).

The question raised, in sum, is that of the relation between the cultural sense of identity as a willed autonomy of self-expression, on the one hand, and the legitimizing conditions of a working polity, on the other. At some point, the political expedience of decentralization would seem to run up against popular demand for a functioning state, as in the case of the Belgians' White March. Rather than idealizing the confluence of cultural identity with state institutions (say in the image of the 'daily plebiscite' which Ernest Renan (1882) idealized as the very picture of nationhood), perhaps the state/nation needs to be better understood and theorized as the political entity wherein the culturally and socially multiple, or even diasporic, identities it embraces are both represented and transcended, 'mediated' to use that old Hegelian word, such that justice is properly adjudicated to all, including those least empowered and assimilated, yet perhaps most dependent and invested in the state (Nancy 1981). We need to take the joke about who the 'true' Belgians are seriously.

Works Cited

Anderson, Benedict (1983) *Imagined Communities: Reflections on the Origin and Spread of Nationalism*. London: Verso.
Barrez, Dirk (1997) *Het land van de 1000 schandalen*. Roeselare: Roularta.
Betz, Hans-Georg (1994) *Radical Right-Wing Populism in Western Europe*. New York: St. Martin's Press.
Bouveroux, Jos (1998) 'Nationalism in Present-Day Flanders', in Kas Deprez and Louis Vos (eds), *Nationalism in Belgium: Shifting Identities, 1780-1995*. New York: St Martin's Press, 209-218.
Claus, Hugo (1983) *Het Verdriet van België*. Amsterdam: De Bezige Bij.
Columberg, Dumeni (1998) *La situation de la population francophone vivant dans la périphérie bruxelloise*. Projet de rapport, Commission des questions juridiques et des droits de l'homme, Conseil d'Europe.
Conway, Martin (1993) *Collaboration in Belgium: Léon Degrelle and the Rexist Movement, 1940-1944*. New Haven: Yale University Press.
de Man, Paul (1941) 'En marge du dialecte liégeois'. *Le Soir*, 22 April 1941; reprinted in Werner Hamacher et al. (1988), *Wartime Journalism, 1939-1943*. Lincoln: University of Nebraska Press.
de Man, Henri (1942a) 'Belgien als Europäisches Problem', in Michel Brélaz (ed.) (1989), *Henri de Man: le 'Dossier Léopold III' et autres documents sur la période de la seconde guerre mondiale*. Geneva: Antipodes, 272-276.

de Man, Henri (1942b) *Réflexions sur la paix*. Brussels: Toison d'Or.

de Man, Henri (1946) *Au delà du nationalisme*. Geneva: Cheval ailé.

Denis, Jacques (ed.) (1992) *Géographie de la Belgique*. Brussels: Crédit Communal.

Deprez, Kas (1985) 'The Dutch Language in Flanders', in T. Hermans (ed.), *The Flemish Movement: A Documentary History, 1780-1990*. London: Athlone, 416-429.

Deprez, Kas (1998) 'The Language of the Flemings', in Kas Deprez and Louis Vos (eds), *Nationalism in Belgium: Shifting Identities, 1780-1995*. New York: St Martin's Press, 96-109.

Derrida, Jacques (1996) *Le monolingualisme de l'autre: ou la prothèse d'origine*. Paris: Galilée.

Dieckhoff, Alain (1996) 'Présentation', in *Belgique: la force de la désunion*. Brussels: Editions complexe, 9-17.

Gellner, Ernest (1983) *Nations and Nationalism*. Ithaca, NY: Cornell University Press.

Greenfeld, Liah (1992) *Nationalism: Five Roads to Modernity*. Cambridge, MA: Harvard University Press.

Hedetoft, Ulf (1995) *Signs of Nations: Studies in the Political Semiotics of Self and Other in Contemporary European Nationalism*. Aldershot: Dartmouth Publishing Company.

Hemmerechts, Kristien (1998) 'Belgique/België', in Antoine Pickels and Jacques Sojcher (eds), *Belgique toujours grande et belle*. Brussels: Complexe, 118-119.

Hobsbawm, Eric J. (1990) *Nations and Nationalism since 1870: Programme, Myth, Reality*. Cambridge: Cambridge University Press.

Huizinga, Jakob Herman (1961) *Mr. Europe: A Political Biography of Paul Henri Spaak*. New York: Praeger.

Kant, Immanuel (1795) *Der Streit der Fakultäten*. Königsberg: Nicolovius.

Levy, Paul M. G. (1962) 'La mort du recensement linguistique'. *Revue nouvelle* 37(9), 145-154.

Lyotard, Jean-Francois (1983) *Le différend*. Paris: Minuit.

Lyotard, Jean-Francois (1986) *L'enthousiasme: la critique kantienne de l'histoire*. Paris: Galilée.

Maddens, Bart, Roeland Beerten, and Jaak Billiet (1998) 'The National Consciousness of the Flemings and the Walloons. An Empirical Investigation', in Kas Deprez and Louis Vos (eds), *Nationalism in Belgium: Shifting Identities, 1780-1995*. New York: St Martin's Press, 198-208.

Moniquet, Claude (1999) *Les dossiers noirs de la Belgique*. Neuilly: Michel Lafon.

Morelli, Anne and Jean-Philippe Schreiber (1998) 'Are Immigrants the Last Belgians?' in Kas Deprez and Louis Vos (eds), *Nationalism in Belgium: Shifting Identities, 1780-1995*. New York: St Martin's Press, 249-257.

Morelli, Anne (ed.) (1998) *Les émigrants belges*. Brussels: EVO.

Moulin, Léo (1975) 'The Politicization of the Administration in Belgium', in Mattei Dogan, (ed.), *The Mandarins of Western Europe: The Political Role of Top Civil Servants*. New York: Sage, 163-186.

Murphy, Alexander (1988) *The Regional Dynamics of Language Differentiation in Belgium*. University of Chicago: Geography Research Paper, no. 227.

Nancy, Jean-Luc (1981) 'La juridiction du monarque hégélien', in Philippe Lacoue-Labarthe and Jean-Luc Nancy (eds), *Rejouer le politique*. Paris: Galilée, 51-90.

Neirynck, Jacques (1996) *Le siège de Bruxelles*. Paris: Desclée de Brouwer.

Pickels, Antoine and Jacques Sojcher (1998) *Belgique toujours grande et belle*. Brussels: Complexe.

Renan, Ernest (1882) 'Qu'est-ce qu'une nation?' translated by Martin Thomas 'What is a Nation?', in Homi K. Bhabha (ed.) (1990) *Nation and Narration*. London: Routledge, 8-22.

Spaak, Paul-Henri (1969) *Combats inachevés*. Paris: Fayard.

Stengers, Jean (1990) 'Belgian National Sentiment', in Marina Boudart, Michel Boudart and René Bryssinck (eds), *Modern Belgium*. Palo Alto, CA: Society for the Promotion of Science and Scholarship, 86-97.

Stengers, Jean (2000) *Histoire du sentiment national en Belgique des origines à 1918*. Brussels: Racine.

Van Hassel, Hugo (1975) 'Belgian Civil Servants and Political Decision Making', in Mattei Dogan (ed.), *The Mandarins of Western Europe: The Political Role of Top Civil Servants*. New York: Sage, 187-195.

Zolberg, Aristide R. (1974) 'The Making of Flemings and Walloons: Belgium, 1830-1914'. *Journal of Interdisciplinary History*, 5(2), 179-235.

Chapter 12

Writing Indigenous Belonging: Ownership in the Construction of Identity in Japan

Annette Skovsted Hansen

Introduction

This chapter explores how indigenous peoples' sense of belonging in the 20th century was affected by the way in which outsiders wrote indigenous identities during the previous centuries. The basic question is why indigenous peoples seem to have difficulties in being accepted as indigenous – by non-indigenous and indigenous groups alike – if they are lawyers or doctors, dress in suits, and do not speak an indigenous language. The question comes to mind, because few people would question that Japanese and Danes, who eat, dress, work, and speak differently from 150 years ago, still belong to the Japanese and Danish nations, respectively. I argue that the transnational indigenous movement has to struggle to achieve acceptance of their peoples as indigenous regardless of profession and lifestyle due to the fact that the written documents of the 19th century recorded changes in the lives and behaviour patterns of indigenous populations as assimilation into identities of nation states.

   Written indigenous identities of the 19th century have created a dilemma for many 20th-century indigenous movements, because the movements, on the one hand, rely on 19th-century written records for concrete information on their cultural heritage, but, on the other hand, have to contend with images of essentially static communities. Indigenous peoples have formed transnational alliances and networks to achieve common goals *vis-à-vis* national governments. Many of the claims and rights granted by national governments during the United Nations International Decade for Indigenous Peoples (1994-2003) have been so-called cultural rights. Museum sites and cultural centres for performances and exhibits of indigenous arts are among the palpable results. However, increasingly, economic and political rights to self-determination, influence, and compensation for knowledge have appeared on the agenda. The Inuit of Canada have spearheaded efforts to ensure indigenous peoples' rights to be educated and employed in as many diverse fields as they please without thereby being considered less indigenous (Alaska Native Knowledge Network; Sjöberg 1995).

In order to illustrate my point about the role of written language in determining ownership of identity in the case of indigenous peoples, I have chosen to describe the process of defining the Ainu of Japan during the 19th century. I call this group of people the Ainu of Japan, because I will argue that, today, what is referred to as Ainu identity by Ainu as well as non-Ainu Japanese to a large extent is based on reports and choices made by Japanese, European and North American writers in the 19th century. It is an identity propagated to show the benefits and legitimacy of the Ainu to be part of the Japanese nation. Non-Ainu writers chose to depict 'Ainu culture' as essentially static. Most observers measured all subsequent change in the behaviour, rituals and habits within Ainu communities as the extent to which the Ainu had been assimilated by Japan and become Japanese. Ainu and Japanese identity were deemed mutually exclusive. To the extent Ainu had become Japanese, they had ceased to be Ainu.

The Ainu Movements

The Ainu have, however, not simply been passive recipients, but have actively made choices in response to Japanese nation-building. In the first written history of Japan from 720 CE, the ancestors of the Japanese of today described their contemporary Ainu neighbours to the north as fierce in battle and barbarian in the Chinese sense of the word, which applied to any Other. From the 17th to the 19th century, many Ainu chose to work in fisheries administered by the Matsumae clan, while others chose to continue feeding themselves as hunters and gatherers. As circumstances changed during the 19th century, the trend continued where some Ainu chose to get directly involved in Japanese enterprises and others chose to keep apart. As keeping apart from Japanese influence became increasingly difficult in the 20th century, some Ainu tried to assimilate and others chose to fight to stay apart from the idea of a homogeneous mainstream Japan (Oguma 1998; Sjöberg 1995).

The Ainu movements have reflected the diversity among the Ainu. The Ainu who have chosen to assimilate have not been involved in the movements and have even expressed regret that the movements exist. The Ainu who have chosen to unite in movements to achieve group goals have also not always agreed on the means and the goals. This has led to multiple movements. Some of the points of contention concern the weighting of the goals of economic welfare, political influence, and survival of a common cultural heritage. Assimilation through economic and social welfare programmes has been a policy of changing Japanese governments, but also the aim of Ainu Kyōkai, initially operated as an extension of the social section of the Hokkaidō government (*Dōchō*), and its successor Utari Kyōkai. Others argue that the stigma invoked to receive welfare simply regenerates stigma, which prevents assimilation and the elimination of discrimination (Siddle 1997; Baba 1980).

Ainu actions of the 20th century have not been unified, but have all been related to developments in Japan and the world. Combined with the surge in Japanese literature on the homogeneity of the Japanese populations and the 'fear of discovery' of the Ainu who had 'succeeded in passing', the social activism and focus on civil rights of the 1960s and 1970s inspired a continuation of multiple responses and choices. In 1987, the Japanese Prime Minister Nakasone officially stated that Japan was a homogeneous nation. This statement evoked international, non-Ainu Japanese, and Ainu responses on behalf of the Ainu and other minorities in Japan. This coincided with an increased focus on indigenous peoples throughout the world, which resulted in the proclamation of 1993 as the United Nations International Year for Indigenous Peoples (Siddle 1997; Yearbooks of the United Nations 1993-2000; Sjöberg 1995).

The Ainu of Japan have been very active in the transnational indigenous networks. In 1997, a revision of the 'The Law for the Protection of the Former Natives of Hokkaidō' from 1899 was enforced. Several Ainu movements had complained that the law of 1899 was discriminatory, because its premise was that the Ainu needed economic protection. As the name indicates, the new law, 'Law concerning Promotion of Ainu Culture and Dissemination and Enlightenment of Knowledge about Ainu Traditions', only addresses issues of cultural rights. The new law defines culture as language, dance, weaving, architecture, and woodcarving. According to Sjöberg, the Ainu, today, 'make use of information gathered about them not only to reconstruct, reorganize, and reinvent their values and beliefs but to gain an understanding of why their ancestors acted as they did and how they became marginal in their own domains'. Other Ainu are critical of the focus on cultural rights, because they feel Japanese governments avoid addressing issues of discrimination in other spheres (Sjöberg 1995).

The Who, Why and How of Writing Ainu Identities in the 19th Century

The information about Ainu culture available to the Ainu of today comes from an Ainu oral tradition as well as from written sources. Non-Ainu Japanese, non-Japanese, and Ainu all contributed to the written image of the Ainu. The descriptions of the Ainu appeared first in history books, travelogues, and reports written by Japanese and non-Japanese visitors to Ainu communities during the 18th and 19th centuries. Several Japanese settlers, who came to trade and farm in Hokkaidō, compiled word lists and included descriptions of their Ainu neighbours in prefaces or introductions. Towards the end of the 19th century, Japanese and non-Japanese anthropologists contributed their observations along with those of Christian missionaries who worked among the Ainu. Seemingly, few Ainu wrote. However, there were exceptions. In 1904, Frederick Starr was in Hokkaidō to take a group of Ainu to the St. Louis Exposition. Starr mentioned how the missionary Reverend Batchelor had taught and encouraged an Ainu by the name of Tuperek to write a collection of Ainu folktales (Starr 1904, p. 92).

According to Reverend Batchelor, who had worked as a missionary among the Ainu in Hokkaidō since 1879, the teacher Mr. Takekuma was the first Ainu who wrote a book about his people. Mr. Takekuma entitled the book *Ainu monogatari* [The Story of the Ainu] and had it published in 1918. The main thrust of Takekuma's argument was the many changes and adoptions of Japanese practices among the Ainu. His point of departure in the chapter on Ainu education was that Ainu history suffered because of the lack of an Ainu script. In chapter 5, he emphasized how little was known about Ainu technology prior to the adoption of Japanese tools. The conclusions of the first attempt at an interpretation of the Ainu by an Ainu are not easy to distinguish from non-Ainu interpretations, with which he was familiar (Takekuma 1918).

The different accounts represented various types of messages. The people who compiled dictionaries expressed their desire to encourage and/or facilitate contact, exchange, shared village life, and trade. Travelogues constituted a very popular genre of literature in the late 19th century, not least in Europe and the United States. They described adventures, which bore witness to the endurance and courage of the author and to the strangeness of peoples all over the world. Japanese newspapers and popular magazines published descriptions of Ainu and cities organized expositions with Ainu families aimed to inform about an exotic Other within Japan. Anthropologists sought to collect as much data as possible about all the different groups of people in the world, especially those thought to be in danger of 'disappearing'. Whereas all of the above are interpretative descriptions, the initial voices of the Ainu through folktales were read as remnants or artefacts (Siddle 1997; Lie 2001; Sjöberg 1995, p. 384).

Besides the information on Ainu culture of the 19th century, the wordlists and dictionaries also provided models for transcribing Ainu languages, on the basis of which some Ainu movements have developed Ainu language textbooks. The reason for the predominance of non-Ainu texts establishing Ainu identity is the fact that Ainu languages were spoken, not written, until the 19th century. The first written records of Ainu languages were vocabulary lists prepared by Japanese interpreters employed by Matsumae fisheries in Hokkaidō and Ainu interpreters of Russian. Subsequently, Ainu transcribed oral traditions by employing the orthography from the vocabulary lists. Later Ainu observers interpreted their own history and society in texts where they drew on the transcribed oral traditions for style and grammar choices.

The people involved in compiling dictionaries and vocabulary lists of Ainu words in the 19th century had to choose a script for phonetic renditions of the words. The Christian missionaries, such as Dening and Batchelor, and interpreters of Russian and Dutch, such as Uehara and Siebold, chose the Latin alphabet and many Japanese, such as Watanabe Zenji chose one of the two Japanese syllabaries, *katakana* or *hiragana*. By 1900, a certain standard of style and orthography of Ainu languages existed. Jinbō Kotora, a Professor of Science, spent three years in Hokkaidō from 1888-1891 where he came in contact with the Ainu during his tour of inspection. He began his text by stating how the Ainu use many Japanese words just as there are English words in everyday Japanese. He also mentioned traces of Ainu words in classical Japanese, and Japanese influence on Ainu grammar. He then underlined the fact that Ainu is written horizontally as opposed to Japanese. These observations testified to an actual practice of writing Ainu (Fritze 1893, p. 45; Fischer 1896, p. 231; Watanabe 1890; Dixon 1883; Hansen 2000; Jinbō 1900, p. 1).

One contributor to the miscellaneous column for the *Journal of Linguistics* in Japan wrote in 1900 that the Ainu '[l]earn kana, the Japanese phonetic script, at school and rōmaji [Roman alphabet] from Christianity. A British woman Bryant assembles the girls and women in the village every evening and teach them kana and rōmaji, they read the sacred books, which Rev. Batchelor has translated into the indigenous language with rōmaji. [...]. The young girls all write rōmaji and freely read the sacred books in rōmaji, [...]' (*Gengogaku Zasshi* 1900, p. 61).

Under miscellaneous in the sixth issue of *Gengogaku Zasshi* from 1903, Yasugi Sadatoshi (1876-1966), who is today considered a pioneer in Russian language research in Japan, introduced his publication of three stories written with Roman letters in the local Ainu language of Saru. He explained how he recorded the stories during two to three talks in Ainu language ('Saru dialect') and then requested Professor of Science Jinbō Kotora to correct them. He acknowledged that Rev. Batchelor had already made many contributions of Ainu legends to the Japanese *Transactions of the Asia Society* and stated how he followed the orthography as established by Rev. Batchelor (Yasugi 1900b, p. 33).

The European, US and non-Ainu Japanese compilers of dictionaries in the 19th century contributed to the creation of a whence-lacking Ainu written language, which Ainu language text books, records and newsletters continue to draw on today.

Inability to Change

Besides contributing to the Andersonian sense of imagined community, the act of writing has two main functions in the construction of identities of nation states as well as of indigenous peoples. Written language is used 1) to record observations of characteristics to be associated with an identity and 2) to trace change and continuities over time. Individual representatives of literate groups wrote down observations they made when they encountered or studied indigenous groups. These observations were made during periods ranging from a few hours to a few years, which resulted in descriptions, which were oblivious to change over time. As a result most of the initial observers identified the indigenous groups as static. Later observers recorded changes – as either positive or negative – and attributed these to contact with literate or more advanced groups. If the observers considered changes, such as the introduction of national education, agriculture, fishing, and healthcare, positive, they celebrated these changes as assimilation. Whereas they often attributed negative changes such as the prevalence of alcoholism to the lack of adaptability and inherent shortcomings of the indigenous peoples. Most observers regarded these changes as either a positive or a negative impact on essentially passive indigenous groups (Anderson 1991; Ohnuki-Tierney 1998; Walker 2001).

Exactly the fact that most observers used words, such as 'savage', 'primitive', 'vanishing', 'disappearing', and 'extinction' and their Japanese equivalents served to invoke an image of the Ainu as static and unable to change and remain Ainu. The observers themselves got this impression of 'stasis' for two main reasons 1) the practical circumstances, under which observations were made and 2) a romantic interest in that which was thought to be 'vanishing'. Most non-Ainu observers were among the Ainu for periods ranging from some hours until one year. These time spans seldom allowed for the observation of change over time. The essentially objectified characteristics also contributed to the static image. Many observers focused on household structures, the structure of the homes, fishing and hunting techniques, religious rituals, dress-making, the outward appearances, and facial expressions (Howard 1893; Suzuki 1908; Yoshino 1998).

In this context, it might be useful to employ Yoshino Kosaku's distinction between objectified identity and identity based on 'abstract notions'. In Yoshino's interpretation, 'institutions, rituals, customs, and artistic production' form the basis of objectified identity, whereas 'cultural ethos, national character, and patterns of behaviour and thought' are classified as more abstract notions (Yoshino 1998, p. 16). If the selection of 'significant' characteristics primarily qualify as 'objectified identity', changes over time would be apparent. In order for the identity to survive, it needs to be defined in such a way that it allows for change, which can be documented in writing. For example, the fact that one defining characteristic of the Japanese identity is the innate ability of Japanese people to choose and improve borrowings from abroad. In J.C. Hepburn's words of 1886, the Japanese is 'a people, peculiarly impressible, inquisitive, and ready to imitate and adopt whatever may conduce to their own aggrandizement'. Thereby, change is necessary not only for Japan as a nation state, but also for the survival of the identity that signifies whether somebody is Japanese or not. However, if the identity is defined as static or 'primitive', any change will qualify as a loss of rather than an advance for the identity (Hepburn 1886, p. xi).

According to several observers, the basic problem remained the inability of the Ainu and other indigenous peoples to develop. In 1872, the German General Consul to Japan, Max von Brandt (1835-1920) gave a speech in Berlin where he observed that '[t]he Ainos, in spite of this contact (having fought the Japanese over land), continuing for thousands of years, have adopted nothing from the Japanese; they are, what they were, a race standing at the lowest stage of culture, and probably also not capable of civilization' (Refsing 2000, vol. I, p. 34). Where Brandt referred to the stages of culture, R.G. Watson, a former British Chargé d'Affaires in Japan, recorded that '[...]although the Ainos were an interesting and harmless people, they had never shown any capability of development. Many of them had entered the houses of foreigners as servants, and been honest and faithful, but had not evinced any of the cleverness or ingenuity of the Japanese, or any talent for adapting themselves to a higher order of things than that to which they were accustomed' (Watson 1873, p. 241). Watson compared the non-Ainu Japanese to the Japanese and found them lacking in basic survival instincts, such as cleverness, ingenuity, and a talent for adapting.

The first missionary of the British Church Missionary Society, Reverend Walter Dening, who had previously worked in Madagascar, furnished his positive opinion of the Japanese attempts at civilizing the Ainu. He blamed the lack of success entirely on the Ainu.

> Let me say here that all attempts on the part of the Japanese to civilise the Ainos have been utterly fruitless, although, in some instances, the most strenuous efforts have been made. Not long ago a number of Aino lads were taken to Tokio and educated. When it was supposed they knew enough to make them useful to their fellow countrymen, they were sent back to Ishikori, one of the provinces of this island, with the exception of one lad. I learnt, when at Satsuporo, they have all returned to their old mode of living, and are making no efforts whatever to elevate their fellow countrymen (Dening 1877, p. 219).

Not all observers agreed. Scheube had carefully studied many of the interpretations and accounts about the Ainu and expressed his disagreement with the conclusion that the Ainu should be a 'vanishing people'. '[The opinion] has been voiced repeatedly and from several quarters that the Ainu are among the primitive peoples that cannot endure contact with an alien higher culture and would consequently perish. In my opinion unjustly'. Scheube's image of the Ainu was very nuanced and allowed for both change, contradictions and differences (Scheube 1881, p. 244).

Scheube was not the only one who regarded the Ainu ability to survive in a positive light. In the writings of the observers, the ability to survive as a separate people was closely linked to the ability to adapt and change. In 1883, the German geologist, David August Brauns, wrote that 'The intelligence of the Ainu is by no means slight; they acquire the Japanese language easily, rapidly accustom themselves to all innovations that do not conflict with their religious ideas, are occasionally able to apply them in improved ways, and they give precise answers to all questions' (Brauns 1883, p. 181).

Regardless of Ainu intelligence and ability to develop, Dr. Adolf Fritze from Freiburg expected that the Ainu would share the experience of other indigenous peoples elsewhere: 'I, myself, believe that the Ainu are civilisable, however so were the Tasmanians, and yet they perished'. For Fritze the issue was not purely one of aptitude, but more importantly one of time, place, and relations among different peoples (Fritze 1893, p. 47). In 1899, Archibald Gowan Campbell, who travelled on bicycle, explained why the Meiji government did not respect the rights of the Ainu, by stating that the Ainu 'being an utterly unprogressive race and a hindrance in the way of the go-ahead Japanese settlers, their rights are not respected by the Imperial Government'. Yet, under a photograph of Penri, the chief of Piratori village next to the text, Campbell wrote that the Ainu 'are gradually being influenced by Japanese progress' (Campbell 1899, p. 49).

As for the romantic interest in the 'savage', the German traveller Georg Schlesinger explained that anyone who wanted a romantic experience of danger, seclusion, or discomfort in Japan would have to travel among the Ainu. The French Dr. Michaut, who wrote under the pseudonym Vacarimasen, a transliteration of the Japanese word for 'I do not understand', stated that 'Great interest is attached to this Ainu people, which is rapidly decreasing and is destined to an impending death. Just as everything that ends, it deserves attention'. By emphasizing his commitment to pay attention to everything that ends, Michaut testifies to the romantic attraction of that which is lost (Schlesinger 1880, p. 449; Vacarimasen 1892, p. 2).

Other observers focused on lack of change and what they referred to as the 'primitive' as part of a romantic project of experiencing an untouched version of the past of their own ancestors. In 1893, Benjamin Douglas Howard (1836-1900), who had left London in 1889 to study the Russian penal system in Siberia and lived among the Ainu in Sakhalin for one year, wrote that '[t]heir qualities were in some respects so superior, that I sometimes felt while living with them, that by some supernatural process I had been set back thousands, perhaps millions of years amongst my earliest and most remote ancestors[...]'(Howard 1893, p. 179). The sense of loss and urgency in reaching the 'vanishing' traces of a past was combined with a sense of responsibility to record what may no longer be recorded a few years later. Thereby the authors implied that the Ainu communities were changing.

Regardless of whether the sense of imminent loss was purely romantic or part of a larger scheme of civilizing the less civilized, the image of the Ainu as 'vanishing' was central to the interpretations of Ainu in the latter half of the 19th century. Furthermore, the image of the Ainu as an indigenous Other with a future not as a distinct group, but as an integral part of Japan was necessary for the politics of Japanese nation-building.

Change as Japanization

Often the construction of identity is not controlled or even initiated by the people, nation, or other group being identified. The Other does not only play the role of mirror, but can also play an active role as constructor by coining terms and gathering and presenting observations at a time when the people in question are not themselves actively involved in the politics of belonging. Issues of belonging have been closely connected to the building and preservation of nations over the past two hundred years. The interest of nation states in defining indigenous identities was twofold. One was to describe indigenous populations as subordinate to justify the inclusion of the territory of these groups within the geopolitical boundaries of nation states. Secondly, the idea of the nation was plotted in on a time line made up of developmental stages. In the climate of evolution theory, the nation had to progress through stages of development. By placing the indigenous peoples at a 'primitive stage', the nation states could define themselves as advanced. As comparatively advanced, the governments of nation states could then justify their assimilation policies as essentially altruistic. Assimilation was presented as an effort to help the indigenous peoples' progress on the time line of development and civilization (Morris-Suzuki 1998).

At the outset of the 19th century, the number of Russian ships increased near the island of Ezo, an island located immediately north of the main island of Japan. This island was later renamed Hokkaidō by the Japanese Meiji government (1868-1912). The Japanese Tokugawa government (1603-1867) initiated an assimilation policy *vis-à-vis* the Ainu from 1799-1821 in response to what was perceived as a Russian interest in territories inhabited by the Ainu. The reasoning behind this policy was that if the Ainu could be argued to be Japanese then their territory would by extension be considered legitimate Japanese territory. The Tokugawa government resumed this policy in 1853 and in 1869 the Meiji government granted the Ainu population legal status as Japanese commoners (Karino 1996, pp. 152-156, 172; Oguma 1998).

The goal of the Japanese Meiji government *vis-à-vis* the Ainu was assimilation for three purposes. One was to legitimate the incorporation of Ainu territory within the borders of the Japanese nation. The second was to make the Ainu population assist in building the agricultural expansion of Hokkaidō. The third was to annihilate differences and create the notion of one homogeneous nation. From 1868, one of the most pressing concerns of the Japanese Meiji government was to renegotiate the unequal treaties with the United States of America and European nations. The so-called Western powers maintained that they would only commit to equal treaties with civilized and developed nations. In the pursuit of proving that Japan was civilized, the construction of Ainu identity served yet another function. By describing the Ainu as 'primitive' Japanese, the rest of Japan would appear comparatively civilized (Morris-Suzuki 1998).

The 19th century concepts of civilization and development were based on an idea of progressive time. Fukuzawa Yukichi, who as a young scholar had been among the participants in the Tokugawa mission to Europe in 1861 and later became both an entrepreneur and an educator, argued that Japan was behind the West, but ahead of the rest of Asia in terms of civilization and development into a modern nation. Fukuzawa wrote *An Outline of a Theory of Civilization* in 1875 where he argued that all nations had to go through three stages and that '[...] people all over the globe have universally accepted the designations "civilized," "semi-developed," and "primitive." Why does everybody accept them? Clearly because they are demonstrable and [ir]refutable'. He defined the three stages of development as primitive, semi-developed, and civilized, in that order. At the stage of civilization, he maintained that people:

[...] neither yearn for the old nor become complacent with the new. Not resting with small gains, they plan great accomplishments for the future and commit themselves wholeheartedly to their realization. Their path of learning is not vacuous; it has indeed, invented the principle of invention itself. Their business ventures prosper day by day to increase the sources of human welfare. Today's wisdom overflows to create the plans for tomorrow (Fukuzawa 1973 [1875]).

Fukuzawa emphasized that these stages were relative 'if we compare the Japanese with the Ezo [now Ainu], then both China and Japan can be called civilized'. This was a perfect example of what Morris-Suzuki has argued to be the use of the geographical periphery in the formulation of national identity. Because of the role assigned the Ainu as Japanese periphery as backward in time, they could be used to set central Japan in a positive light (Fukuzawa 1973 [1875], pp. 13-14; Morris-Suzuki 1998, pp. 28-31).

Records written by non-Ainu Japanese observers traced the success of the assimilation policy. In the interest of this enterprise, the visibility of Ainu traditions was important. These traditions were to work as a measure by which the assimilation of the Ainu would be obvious. Japanese writers recorded the general tendency of change among the Ainu as a reflection of the extent to which they had been in contact with *wajin* – non-Ainu Japanese. The contact with the *wajin* included the fact that many Ainu had engaged in trade with the *wajin* since the 15th century and had been employed in the *wajin* fishing industry in Hokkaidō since the 17th century (Howell 1995, p. 39). In 1903, the anonymous author of the article 'Ainu Natives' mentioned the long-standing employment of Ainu in the Japanese fisheries in Hokkaidō and the general interaction with Japanese during the Tokugawa period. He claimed that the ways of the old Ainu were gradually disappearing (Anonymous 1903).

Takaki Senshi (1994) has called this phenomenon *nihonjinka*, Japanization. Japanization was seen as a 'civilizing' influence and the Japanese saw non-assimilated Ainu at the time as 'uncivilized'. Japanization became another term for the process of civilization or modernization of the Ainu. Scheube used the concept in 1881 and Starr in 1904. Scheube recognized the influence of the new road to Sapporo as an instrument of Japanization, as he wrote '[The Ainu] on the west coast along the road to Sapporo that the government constructed a few years ago, where civilisation, albeit slowly, spreads across the land, are on average the most civilised, i.e. Japanised' (Scheube 1881, p. 245). However, he was generally sceptical of the sincerity of the Japanese civilization efforts. Scheube stated very clearly that he understood why the Japanese civilization of the Ainu was not working. First and foremost because the Japanese with whom the Ainu came into contact were not themselves civilized.

It is [...] not a great surprise that civilization has not gained entrance among the Ainu yet. What sort of people is it with whom the Ainu have until the present day, primarily, come into contact? Predominantly, Japanese fishermen thousands of whom the abundance of fish along the west coast lure from Hakodate and the main island. These men are coarse fellows who often squander their fast earnings just as fast on debauchery on the spot. Indeed, these people do not stand much above the Ainu in their breeding and lifestyle. Furthermore, [there are] Japanese traders who are only intent on exploiting their compatriots, as well as the natives. It is obvious that these elements cannot be civilizers. They are more likely to exert an unfavourable influence on the Ainu (Scheube 1881, p. 245).

Not only for the sake of the survival of the Ainu as a separate identity from the Japanese, but also in the interest of exhibiting 'Ainu culture', evidence of Japanization was problematic at times. Starr vividly described how it was with hesitation that they accepted a Japanized Ainu, Tuperek's request to join the group of Ainu to be at the St. Louis Exposition in 1904. Starr's concerns included that the thirty-year-old Tuperek, who worked at a newspaper in Tokyo, 'is shrewd and knows something of white men as well as Japanese' and that 'he dresses in Japanese costume and shaves'. What spoke in Tuperek's favour was 'the heavy stubble on his face and the straight eyes'. Besides Tuperek argued that '[a]s for his appearance, he knew that it was against him but he still had an Ainu costume and his beard would soon grow' (Starr 1904, pp. 92-93). Starr had an exclusive interest in the visible and objectified identity of the indigenous person.

In the 19th century, not all observers believed that the Ainu had a good chance of assimilating to become Japanese. The American Romyn Hitchcock explained in the *Annual Report of the U.S. National Museum* of 1891 that:

We have a remarkable instance of the close association of two distinct races, one superior and powerful, the other degraded and weak, working together day by day, living in contiguous villages, intermarrying more or less, and yet, after a century of such intimacy, as distinct in their character, habits of life, superstitions and beliefs as though they had never come together. The Ainu has not as much as learned to make a reputable bow and arrow, although in the past he has had to meet the Japanese, who are famous archers, in many battles. It is a most remarkable example of persistence of distinct types together, when the conditions are apparently favourable for the absorption of one by the other. The Ainus, being unable to affiliate more closely with the Japanese, remain distinct and apart, and are therefore doomed to extinction from the face of the earth (Hitchcock 1891, p. 433).

Hitchcock was not alone in concluding that the contact between the Ainu and the Japanese would result in the 'extinction' of the Ainu.

Dr. Adolf Fritze, who had read several travel descriptions of the Ainu before he arrived among them, stated that

I do not believe that under such circumstances it is possible to answer in the affirmative the question about the continued ability of the Ainu to exist. Their, after all rather strong, constitution may allow them to offer resistance for a while and a fraction of them will be absorbed in the Japanese, in any case. I believe, however, that in general we must write the Ainu on the list of primitive peoples on the point of dying out. This is a fact to be deeply deplored by anybody who has had personal contact with these endearing people (Fritze 1893, p. 47).

Fritze was not the only one who expressed regret in the face of what he and others considered the inevitable fate of the Ainu.

Mabel Loomis Todd was a member of the Amherst College expedition, which travelled to northern Japan to see a total eclipse of the sun in 1896. She gave the following verdict:

> One result only is inevitable from the collision of two races, where one is mentally inferior and the other is masterfully conscious of itself. Although the latest census gives the number of Ainos as about seventeen thousand – a slight gain over the previous year – the impression seems to be generally prevalent that they are steadily dying out. Half-breeds, Aino and Japanese, rarely survive the second or third generation. The race evidently lacks force, and will be entirely unable to hold its own in the march of nations. The bears are decreasing in number; tattooing, using poisoned arrows, and other characteristic customs, are forbidden by law, and will soon be only matters of tradition. The gradual extinction of an entire race will be one of the pathetic features of further development of the Hokkaido (Todd 1897, p. 350).

Todd seemed less sentimental about the future of the Ainu and focused on outside factors of development that affected the livelihood of the Ainu, for example, the decrease in the number of bears for hunting and the laws instituted by the Japanese prohibiting Ainu practices, such as tattooing and the use of poisoned arrows.

Seven years later, in 1903, the anonymous contributor of the article 'Ainudojin' [The Indigenous People, the Ainu] concluded that the Ainu had indeed become like the Japanese through contact.

> Their customs have almost become the same as those of the wajin, because these indigenous people have long been employed at the wajin fishing stations, they have been in contact with wajin, they have received some education, they have been influenced by systems of self-government, conscription, and political representation, and the ways of the old people have gradually disappeared (Anonymous, *Shinshōsetsu* 1903).

This anonymous writer to the *Journal of New Fiction* testified to the natural Ainu selection of Japanese ways.

Many observers interpreted language change and language choices as signs of Japanization. Parallel to the original question of this chapter, the Japanese language had many loan words from Chinese and English. Some people criticized these borrowings, but apart from a few advocates of substituting English for Japanese, nobody saw the changes in the Japanese language as a sign that it would no longer be used at all. However, in the case of the Ainu language, non-Ainu Japanese observers, such as the authors of the miscellaneous articles in the Japanese *Journal of Linguistics*, in 1900, explained the changes in the Ainu languages as lack of usage and the gradual adoption of Japanese. The same year Jinbō Kotora wrote '[i]n order to avoid errors in my copying, I studied Ainu language, but it is now already eight or nine years since I was there, the Ainu language has already passed through many changes'. Jinbō referred to changes in the Ainu language, not a change from Ainu to Japanese (Jinbō 1900, p. 2).

In 'Ainugo no genzai', the author described how the Ainu language was only spoken in the home by old people and women. All young men made many mistakes when speaking Ainu, but often spoke and understood better Japanese than people from the interior of northern Japan. The reason why young women were not yet as good at Japanese as the young Ainu men was attributed to the lack of development of the education of girls. As for the future, the author stated that very soon the Ainu language would not be necessary. He believed that Japanese would be used freely inside and outside the home. Another statement was that '[...]the Ainu themselves are throwing out their Ainu language and assimilating to kokugo [Japanese]'. If this was right, it was an expression of Japanization of language use, by abandoning Ainu language as one characteristic of identity (*Gengogaku Zasshi* 1900, pp. 58-60). This is significant, because language today is used as one of the key criteria for measuring how many Ainu exist.

Conclusions

The transnational indigenous movement relies on the written records about indigenous communities of the 19th century for content in support of a pride in indigenous heritage. By relying on these records for practical reasons, they also find that national governments can relate to their arguments for reclaiming so-called cultural rights for their peoples, as well as some degree of compensation often in the form of welfare. The 1997 law on indigenous cultural rights in Japan is a good example of a law which reflects an interest in preserving remnants of a culture. However, when it comes to claiming a pride in 'modern' achievements and the possibility of active change within the indigenous communities, the struggle becomes different. One of the reasons for this is the fact that the writers of indigenous identity established a paradigm of change being assimilation into an identity of a nation state. In the 19th century, Ainu identity was written not to ensure the survival of Ainu identity, but rather to ensure the survival of Japan as an independent nation state in the face of perceived military threats from Russia and of unequal treaties with the United States and other Western powers. The written, remembered, and remembering Japanese language allowed 19th century Japanese scholars, such as Fukuzawa Yukichi, to self-identify as 'civilized', Japan to establish itself as a civilized and developed nation, and changing Japanese governments to interpret Ainu identity.

The person who writes determines the perspective applied in the initial records as well as on subsequent changes. In the case of indigenous peoples without writing systems of their own, the initial written records often described them as 'static' and 'primitive'. The fact that stasis and 'primitiveness' were defining features allowed for the interpretation of all subsequent change as assimilation into the homogeneous identity of the nation state and a proportional loss of indigenous identity. Non-Ainu Japanese initially wrote Ainu identity as part of the process of constructing the Japanese identity. Therefore, the perspective on Ainu identity was essentially non-Ainu. Seen from Tokyo, Europe or the US, the Ainu identity was static and all change qualified as successful assimilation. Change within a community is often attributed to contact with an Other. However, the change can be interpreted either as active adaptation, as in the case of the Japanese, or as passive assimilation into another identity, as in the case of the Ainu of Japan. I have argued above that the fact that changes within the Ainu community was interpreted as assimilation rather than development was, mainly, because the Ainu lacked a written language of their own, when their identity was first outlined in writing.

In the 21st century, many members of indigenous populations identify with – and by extension belong to – at least three groups of people: a specific indigenous group, a nation state, and a modern globalizing world. Japanese people with Ainu ancestry can celebrate their roots, call themselves Japanese, and participate in a global network of indigenous peoples through modern technology, such as the internet and air travel. The static depictions of Ainu by 19th century written records are valuable sources on a 19th century Ainu past seen from a non-Ainu perspective. However, they can be combined today in a meaningful way with indigenous Ainu oral traditions, and a modern 20th century Ainu past. Regardless of the language in which they write or speak, Ainu can lend their perspective to issues of belonging – multiple or singular – and influence change in their communities. Transnational belonging opens up the possibility of rewriting indigenous identities to allow for a contemporary indigenous person, who combines indigenous belonging with changing employment, dress and language.

Works Cited

Alaska Native Knowledge Network (www.ankn.uaf.edu).

Anderson, Benedict (1991) *Imagined Communities: Reflections on the Origin and Spread of Nationalism*. Revised edition. London and New York: Verso.

Anonymous (1903) 'Ainudojin' [The Indigenous People Ainu]. *Shinshōsetsu* (September), 262-263.

Baba Yūko (1980) 'A Study of Minority-Majority Relations: The Ainu and the Japanese in Hokkaido'. *Japan Interpreter* 13 (1) (Summer), 60-92.

Brandt, Max von (1874) 'The Ainos and Japanese', in Kirsten Refsing (ed.) (2000), *Early European Writings on Ainu Culture: Travelogues and Descriptions*. Volume 2. Richmond, Surrey: Curzon Press and Edition Synapse.

Brauns, David August (1883) 'Die Ainos der Insel Yezo', in Kirsten Refsing (ed.) (2000), *Early European Writings on Ainu Culture: Travelogues and Descriptions*. Volume 3. Richmond, Surrey: Curzon Press and Edition Synapse.

Campbell, Archibald Gowan (1899) 'Among the Hairy Ainus of Yezo', in Kirsten Refsing (ed.) (2000), *Early European Writings on Ainu Culture: Travelogues and Descriptions.* Volume 4. Richmond, Surrey: Curzon Press and Edition Synapse.

Dening, Reverend Walter (1877) 'A Visit to the Ainos', in Kirsten Refsing (ed.) (2000), *Early European Writings on Ainu Culture: Travelogues and Descriptions.* Volume 2. Richmond, Surrey: Curzon Press and Edition Synapse.

Dixon, James Main, M.A. (1883) 'The Tsuishikari Ainos', in Kirsten Refsing (ed.) (2000), *Early European Writings on Ainu Culture: Travelogues and Descriptions.* Volume 3. Richmond, Surrey: Curzon Press and Edition Synapse.

Fischer, Adolf (1896) 'Auf Yezo: Unter den Ainos, den Ureinwohnern Japans', in Kirsten Refsing (ed.) (2000), *Early European Writings on Ainu Culture: Travelogues and Descriptions.* Volume 4. Richmond, Surrey: Curzon Press and Edition Synapse.

Foundation for Research and Promotion of Ainu Culture (www.frcap.or.jp).

Fritze, Dr. Adolf (1893) 'Ein Besuch bei den Aino', in Kirsten Refsing (ed.) (2000), *Early European Writings on Ainu Culture: Travelogues and Descriptions.* Volume 3. Richmond, Surrey: Curzon Press and Edition Synapse.

Fukuzawa Yukichi (1973[1875]) *An Outline of a Theory of Civilization.* Translated by David A. Dilworth and G. Cameron Hurst, Monumenta Nipponica Monographs. Tokyo: Sophia University.

Gengogaku Zasshi [Journal of Linguistics] 1 (6) (1900).

Gladney, Dru C. (1998) *Making Majorities: Constituting the Nation in Japan, Korea, China, Malaysia, Fiji, Turkey, and the United States.* East-West Center Series on Contemporary Issues in Asia and the Pacific. Stanford, CA: Stanford University Press.

Hansen, Annette Skovsted (2000) *The Institutionalization of Language in Nineteenth Century Japan: When Language became a Manifestation of National Identity, a Commodity, and a Full-Time Profession.* Unpublished Ph.D. dissertation.

Hepburn, J.C. (1886) *A Japanese English and English Japanese Dictionary.* Tokyo. Reprint edition 1996.

Hitchcock, Romyn (1891) 'The Ainos of Yezo, Japan', in Kirsten Refsing (ed.) (2000), *Early European Writings on Ainu Culture: Travelogues and Descriptions.* Volume 3. Richmond, Surrey: Curzon Press and Edition Synapse.

Howard, B. Douglas (1893) 'Life with Trans-Siberian Savages', in Kirsten Refsing (ed.) (2000) *Early European Writings on Ainu Culture: Travelogues and Descriptions.* Volume 3. Richmond, Surrey: Curzon Press and Edition Synapse.

Howell, David L. (1995) *Capitalism from Within: Economy, Society, and the State in a Japanese Fishery.* Berkeley, Los Angeles, and London: University of California Press.

Jinbō Kotora (1900) 'Ainu no nihongo' [The Japanese Language of the Ainu]. *Gengogaku Zasshi* [Journal of Linguistics], 1 (6) (July), 1-5.

Kano Yokichi (1917) '"Ainu" no kodai fūzoku no kenkyū ni tsuite' [About the study of the ancient culture of Ainu], in *Shokumin kōhō* [Colonial Public News] (January), 127. Reprinted in Shokumin kōhō hensan iinka (ed.) (1976), *Shokumin kōhō*, vol. 16. Tokyo: Ikkōsha.

Karino Yōichi (1996) 'Meijiishin no chiiki to minshū' [Regions and People of the Meiji Restoration]. *Meijiishinshikenkyū*, Volume 4. London and New York: Furukawa Hirobumikan, 157-176.

Lie, John (2001) *Multiethnic Japan.* Cambridge, MA and London: Harvard University Press.

Morris-Suzuki, Tessa (1998) *Re-Inventing Japan: Time, Space, and Nation.* An East Gate Book. Armonk, NY and London, England: M.E. Sharpe.

Oguma, Eiji (1998) 'Nihonjin no kyôkai: Okinawa, Ainu, Taiwan, Chôsen shokuminchi shihai kara fukki undô made' [The Boundaries of the Japanese: Okinawa, Ainu, Taiwan, and Korea from Colonial Control to Reversion Movement]. Tokyo: Shinyôsha.

Ohnuki-Tierney, Emiko (1998) 'A Conceptual Model for the Historical Relationship Between the Self and the Internal and External Others: The Agrarian Japanese, the Ainu, and the Special-Status People', in Dru C. Gladney (ed.), *Making Majorities: Constituting the Nation in Japan, Korea, China, Malaysia, Fiji, Turkey, and the United States.* East-West Center Series on Contemporary Issues in Asia and the Pacific. Stanford, CA: Stanford University Press.

Refsing, Kirsten (ed.) (2000) *Early European Writings on Ainu Culture: Travelogues and Descriptions.* Volumes 1-5. Richmond, Surrey: Curzon Press and Edition Synapse.

Scheube, B. (1881) 'Die Ainos', in Kirsten Refsing (ed.) (2000), *Early European Writings on Ainu Culture: Travelogues and Descriptions.* Volume 3. Richmond, Surrey: Curzon Press and Edition Synapse.

Schlesinger, Georg (1880) 'Die Insel Yezo und die Ainos', in Kirsten Refsing (ed.) (2000), *Early European Writings on Ainu Culture: Travelogues and Descriptions.* Volume 2. Richmond, Surrey: Curzon Press and Edition Synapse.

Siddle, Richard (1997) 'Ainu: Japan's Indigenous People', in Michael Weiner (ed.), *Japan's Minorities: The Illusion of Homogeneity.* London and New York: Routledge.

Siebold, Heinrich von (1881) 'Ethnologische Studien über die Aino auf der Insel Yesso', in Kirsten Refsing (ed.) (2000) *Early European Writings on Ainu Culture: Travelogues and Descriptions.* Volume 2. Richmond, Surrey: Curzon Press and Edition Synapse.

Sjöberg, Katarina (1995) 'Practicing Ethnicity in a Hierarchical Culture: The Ainu Case', in R.H. Barnes, Andrew Gray and Benedict Kingsbury (eds), *Indigenous Peoples of Asia.* Monograph and Occasional Paper Series, Number 48. Ann Arbor, MI: Association for Asian Studies.

Snow, Captain H. J., F.R.G.S. (1887) 'Notes on the Kuril Islands', in Kirsten Refsing (ed.) (2000), *Early European Writings on Ainu Culture: Travelogues and Descriptions.* Volume 2. Richmond, Surrey: Curzon Press and Edition Synapse.

Starr, F. (1904) *The Ainu Group at the St. Louis Exposition.* Chicago: The Open Court Publishing Company.

Suzuki, Haruura (1908) 'Ainu no jijitsudan' [A Discussion of the Truth about the Ainu]. Shinshôsetsu [New Fiction] (October), 81-96.

Takaki Senshi (1994) 'Ainuminzoku e no dôkaseisaku no seiritsu' [The Establishment of Assimilation Policies vis-à-vis Ainu Peoples], in Rekishigaku Kenkyūkai (ed.), *Kokumin kokka o tou* [Asking about the Nation-State]. Tokyo: Aoki shoten, 166-183.

Takekuma Tokusaburō (1918) *Ainu monogatari* [The Story of the Ainu]. Reprinted in Ogawa Masahito and Yamada Shinichi (1998), *Ainu minzoku kindai no kiroku* [Modern Archives of the Ainu People]. Tokyo: Sōfūkan.

Todd, Mabel Loomis (1897) 'In Aino-Land', in Kirsten Refsing (ed.) (2000), *Early European Writings on Ainu Culture: Travelogues and Descriptions.* Volume 4. Richmond, Surrey: Curzon Press and Edition Synapse.

Vacarimasen (1892) 'Un coin du Japon: Les Ainos', in Kirsten Refsing (ed.) (2000), *Early European Writings on Ainu Culture: Travelogues and Descriptions.* Volume 3. Richmond, Surrey: Curzon Press and Edition Synapse.

Walker, Brett L. (2001) *The Conquest of Ainu Lands: Ecology and Culture in Japanese Expansion 1590-1800*. Berkeley, Los Angeles, and London: University of California Press.

Watanabe Zenji (1890) Hokkaidō dojin tsūgo [Hokkaido Native Common Language]. Tokyo: Hatsugadō.

Watson, R. G. (1873) 'Notes of a Journey in the Island of Yezo in 1873, and on the Progress of Geography in Japan', in Kirsten Refsing (ed.) (2000), *Early European Writings on Ainu Culture: Travelogues and Descriptions*. Volume 2. Richmond, Surrey: Curzon Press and Edition Synapse.

Yasugi Sadatoshi (1900a) 'Ainugo danpen' [Ainu Language Fragments]. *Gengogaku Zasshi* [Journal of Linguistics] 1 (6) (July), 39-44.

Yasugi Sadatoshi (1900b) 'Miscellaneous News'. *Gengogaku Zasshi* [Journal of Linguistics] 1 (6) (July), 33-38.

Yearbook of the United Nations (1993-1996). Dordrecht: Martinus Nijhoff Publishers.

Yearbook of the United Nations (1997-2000). New York, NY: United Nations Publications.

Yoshino Kosaku (1992) *Cultural Nationalism in Contemporary Japan: A Sociological Inquiry*. London and New York: Routledge.

Yoshino Kosaku (1998) 'Culturalism, Racialism, and Internationalism in the Discourse on Japanese Identity', in Dru C. Gladney (ed.), *Making Majorities: Constituting the Nation in Japan, Korea, China, Malaysia, Fiji, Turkey, and the United States*. East-West Center Series on Contemporary Issues in Asia and the Pacific. Stanford, CA: Stanford University Press.

Chapter 13

The Pan-Ethnic Movement of Taiwanese Aborigines and the Role of Elites in the Process of Ethnicity Formation

Michael Rudolph

Introduction

When we try to understand processes of ethnicity formation in Taiwan,[1] we have to distinguish between two periods: the period of authoritarian rule and its aftermath until 1990; and the period of *Taiwanization* and democratization since 1990.[2] This distinction seems necessary because the conditions under which the formation of ethnicity and its manifestation could take place in Taiwan were very different during these two periods: in the first period ethnicity was suppressed by the Nationalist Party-state that proclaimed ethno-cultural homogeneity of all Chinese in order to have a legitimization to recover the mainland. In the second period, ethnicity was fostered and enhanced by the government that now – after a sweeping internal transformation of its 'human resources' from Mainlander- to Hoklo-domination – subscribed to building up a multicultural society *vis-à-vis* the mainland and its claims of ethno-cultural homogeneity of all Chinese.[3] The former

---

1   This chapter draws on my PhD research (1994-1996) that examined: (1) Taiwan's aborigine movement, where I looked at the actions and ideologies of aborigine elites who participated in the movement or in certain currents of it; (2) segments of Taiwanese Han-society who supported the aborigine movement, i.e., opposition party, clerical and academic circles, and after the early 1990s also government institutions; (3) the aborigine population in rural areas, which consists of at least twelve different ethnic groups, for whose rights and living conditions aborigine elites 'fought', but whose voices were only seldom heard (Rudolph 2003a).

2   The *'Taiwanization'* (*bentuhua*) that took place in the course of the increasing quest of Taiwan's population for political and cultural independence from the mainland can also be translated as *'nativization'*.

3   Hoklo-Chinese constitute the majority of the island's population (75 per cent). The so-called 'Mainlanders', who emigrated from the mainland with Chiang Kai-shek after 1945 and suppressed Taiwan's population in the following four decades until the lifting of martial law in 1987, make up only 14 per cent of Taiwan's population. Another group of Han Chinese who settled on Taiwan before the arrival of the Mainlanders are the

discourse of homogeneity was now replaced by a discourse of ethnic heterogeneity and – in order to enhance a feeling of togetherness in the new frame of reference – a discourse of hybridity. This process can be particularly well observed in the development of the aborigine movement in Taiwan and the efforts of aborigine elites[4] to adapt their cultural representations to the changing paradigms.

From the founding of the first aborigine rights group in 1984 until the establishment of the Council of Aboriginal Affairs under the central government in 1996,[5] the pan-ethnic movement of Taiwanese aborigines (*Yuanzhumin*)[6] was always among the smallest of all social and ethnopolitical movements evolving during Taiwan's political transformation process. This is not astonishing if one considers that Austronesians only constitute about 1.6 per cent of Taiwan's total population and that they consist of at least nine different cultural groups, each speaking a different language.[7] Nevertheless, it has turned out to be one of the most vigorous and successful movements with a growing degree of attention and support from Taiwanese society – much more than for instance the movement of the

---

4   Hakka (9 per cent). The only non-Han on Taiwan are the aborigines (*Yuanzhumin*), who today comprise no more than 1.6 per cent of the population (about 350,000 people).

4   The terms 'aborigine elite' (*Yuanhumin jingying*) and 'aborigine intellectuals' (*Yuanzhumin zhishi fenzi*) are commonly used in Taiwan. The Taiwanese anthropologist Xie Shizhong (1987a) has made a first classification of 'aborigine elites'. He distinguishes between three kinds of elite: (1) the 'traditional aborigine elite' like chiefs and shamans; (2) the 'political aborigine elite' (*Yuanzhumin zhengzhi jingying*), loyal to the Nationalist Party, not recruited through the modern educational system, and only partially coinciding with the traditional elite; and (3) the 'intellectual aborigine elite' (*Yuanzhumin zhishi jingying*), that split into two main, mutually antagonistic, 'subgroups' in the early 1980s, i.e., the young 'political aborigine elite' (*Yuanzhumin zhengzhi jingying*) loyal to the China Nationalist Party (KMT), and the 'resistance aborigine elite' (*Yuanzhumin kangzheng jingying*) that was organized in the pan-ethnic movement (Xie 1987a, p. 75; Xie 1992a, p. 54). In general, only the members of the 'resistance aborigine elite' are referred to as 'aborigine intellectuals' or members of the 'intellectual aborigine elite' (Wei Yijun 1997, p. 5).

5   The Council has the status of a ministry. In 1998 it employed a 120-strong staff and was subdivided into four sections.

6   The term 'Yuanzhumin' (Engl: 'original settlers') was chosen in 1984 by the 'resistance aborigine elite' to substitute the official term '*shanbao*' (Engl: 'mountain compatriots'). It took ten years until this new ethnonym was officially recognized by the second constitution amendment on 28 June 1994, and two more until the government yielded to pressure from Yuanzhumin legislators to establish a central-level committee representing *Yuanzhumin*. I principally agree with Xie Shizhong (1994) who suggests that the term '*Yuanzhumin*' should only be used to mean 'aborigines with awakened consciousness'. Nevertheless, for the sake of simplicity, I here use '*Yuanzhumin*' to refer to 'Taiwanese aborigines' in a general sense.

7   Anthropoligical findings suggest that originally there lived more than 25 different Austronesian groups on the island. Most assimilated into Han society during the last two centuries. The cultures and languages of the Ami (120,704 individuals), Atayal (75,995), Paiwan (60,764), Bunun (35,041), Puyuma (7,989), Cao (7,140), Rukai (6,815), Saisiat (3,884) and Yami (3,497), however, still exist (Rudolph 2003a).

Hakkas that has lost attention and momentum since its emergence in 1988 in spite of the comparatively larger number of Hakkas in Taiwan (approximately nine per cent). However, as testified by the results of aborigine elections[8] as well as by the low participation in demonstrations for the ethnonym '*Yuanzhumin*', for dedicated central government institutions charged with aborigine affairs, and for cultural and political autonomy, the main motor of the aborigine movement was a small elite that was in general only able to rally meagre support from the majority of members of aborigine society.[9] This chapter investigates the reasons why ethnicity in Taiwan's aborigine society had its origins mainly in the elite strata and not in other parts of aborigine society. What motivated members of aborigine elites to engage in ethnic politics and identity construction in Taiwan at a time of changing political paradigms, while common people in the villages hardly showed any ambitions to fight for more cultural recognition?

Aborigine Elites' Interaction During Authoritarian Rule

The role of elites in the process of ethnicity formation has been thoroughly dealt with in the instrumentalist branch of ethnicity research. Paul Brass (1991) suggests that 'ethnic self-consciousness, ethnically-based demands, and ethnic conflict can occur only if there is some conflict either between indigenous and external elites and authorities or between indigenous elites'. For Brass, ethnicity is 'created and transformed by particular elites in modernizing and in post-industrial societies undergoing dramatic social change' in a 'process that invariably involves competition and conflict for political power, economic benefits, and social status between competing elites, class, and leadership groups both within and among different ethnic categories' (Brass 1991, p. 25). For an initial understanding of the origins of the pan-ethnic movement of Taiwanese aborigines and the role of different elites, two studies are of special interest, not only because of their different perspectives, but also because of the high degree of involvement of the authors of both accounts.

The first work was composed by Xie Shizhong, today professor in the Department of Anthropology of Taiwan National University, who may be called an advocate of engaged anthropology in Taiwan and who has been in close contact with the movement since its early days (Xie 1987c). In *Stigmatised Identity – Ethnic Change of Taiwan Aborigines* (Xie 1987a),[10] Xie contends that in the mid-1980s two different types of identity prevailed in aborigine society: the stigmatized identity resulting from inadequate government policy, discrimination and

---

8   Aborigines have quotas for own representatives in the parliament (Rudolph 1996).
9   An exception was the movement for land return (*huan wo tudi yundong*) in 1988, 1989, and 1993. Numbers of participants in each of the demonstrations reached from one to two thousand (Rudolph 1996).
10   On the movement, see also the article published by Xie later that year (Xie 1987b).

marginalization on the one hand, and the pan-ethnic identity as a reaction of intellectuals on this stigmatization on the other hand. The stigma felt by most aborigines because of their cultural background as 'savages', 'mountain people', and poorly educated 'Chinese' was not only expressed in strong inferiority feelings towards the outside, but also in passing behaviour when exposed to Han society, as well as in different kinds of anomie, like alcohol abuse, prostitution, and a high divorce rate. From an investigation by the Taiwanese anthropologist Fu Yangzhi (1994) we know that – analogous to the attitudes in Han society – there existed a strong feeling within aborigine society that the predicament of aborigines reflected a lack of industriousness on the part of the 'mountain people' rather than social injustice.[11] Pan-ethnic identity on the other hand found its strongest expression in the foundation of the Alliance of Taiwan aborigines in 1984.[12] Being in close contact with the younger generation of Taiwan's anthropologists including Xie himself, members of the Alliance of Taiwan aborigines were not only well informed about anthropological conceptions of ethnic groups, but also aware of the cultural rights and autonomy rights of aborigine people in other countries. On anthropological advice they created the new pan-ethnic name 'aborigines' (*Yuanzhumin*), that was supposed to replace the government's term 'mountain compatriots' and the commonly used terms 'savages' and 'mountain people', and defined a set of symbols and special rights that should apply to all Taiwanese aborigines equally, including rights to ancestral land, use of vernacular languages in schools, revitalization of individual aborigine names as well as autonomous cultural and political institutions. In order to let all this become reality, they organized petition movements and demonstrations that not only turned against the Nationalist Party-led government and ethno-centric Han society, but also against those members of aborigine elites who had moderated the Nationalist Party's assimilation policy in aborigine society for four decades.[13] Eager to replace them,

---

11 Fu Yangzhi (1994) found this attitude not only among most middle- and lower-class aborigines, but also among most middle-class Han including 'medium-level' intellectuals (not to speak of lower-class Han).
12 According to Xie, pan-ethnic identity was constituted of exogenous as well as of endogenous factors. Exogenous factors included the dissatisfaction with a number of discriminatory ethnonyms like the commonly used term 'savages', the official term 'mountain compatriots' used by the Taiwanese government until 1994, as well as the academic term 'high mountain tribe' (today, this term is still used by the PRC). A further exogenous factor was the indifferent attitude and the ideology of the government in terms of *Yuanzhumin* administration. Endogenous factors included the common historical experience of the last 400 years (i.e., the decline from the status of dominating to dominated under the Han and the Nationalist Party's government), the similar cultural background (all groups belong to the Austronesian language group), the cultural crisis experienced by the members of these ethnic groups (i.e, the rapid dying of their languages and cultures) as well as the development of a new critical consciousness within a growing number of *Yuanzhumin* intellectuals in the course of political change in Taiwan during the 1980s (Xie 1987a).
13 Xie Shizhong (1987a, 1987b).

elite members of the Alliance of Taiwan aborigines have regularly participated as non-party candidates in public elections since 1986, albeit without success. In all their actions, they were strongly supported by the Taiwanese opposition party, the Democratic Progress Party (DPP),[14] which considered the aborigine issue as a good opportunity to attack the inadequate ethnic and cultural policies of the Nationalist Party. Other important support came from critical scholars of Han-society, who expressed their worry that poor minority policies would not only have negative impact on aborigine society itself, but also on Taiwanese society as a whole as well as on Taiwan's international reputation. And, last but not least, aborigine elites also got strong support from the Presbyterian Church of Taiwan that had one third of its 210, 000 followers in aborigine areas.

A second work on the aborigine movement with a very different focus has been presented by the Canadian Michael Stainton (1995), who himself played a catalytic role in the movement as a missionary, activist and teacher of aborigine youths in the Aborigine Presbyterian Church of Taiwan from 1980-1991. As Stainton contends in a voluminous MA dissertation he wrote after his return to Canada in 1995, the aborigine movement was more or less a creation of the Presbyterian Church of Taiwan, which initiated the activism as a reaction to the tyranny it endured from the side of the Nationalist Party government after the publication of the 'three statements' in the 1970s. Though the Alliance of Taiwan Aborigines always seemed to be the main actor to the outside, it only played a minor role as an executor: to the extent that the aborigine movement had an organization, it was the Presbyterian Church, which provided an ideology (built on metaphors like 'chosen people' and 'promised land'), a multi-level organizational network (for instance Urban Rural Mission-training in Japan and Canada), trained and paid workers (both clergy and staff at the national offices) and financial access to Taiwanese donors and foreign grants through the World Church Council Program to combat racism. As Stainton shows in his MA dissertation, the Alliance of Taiwan Aborigines, while led by secular activists as well as people related to the Presbyterian Church of Taiwan, was financially and logistically dependent on the Presbyterian Church of Taiwan for all its successful mobilization.

From Xie's and Stainton's accounts, we learn about the existence of at least three different kinds of aborigine elites that were involved in identity construction in aborigine society during the years of the evolution of the movement.

The first was the old political elites loyal to the Nationalist Party, that had been co-opted to accomplish the Nationalist Party's project for assimilation of the aborigines and whose policy of non-recognition of cultural differences constantly nurtured the stigma of aborigines. The main 'capital' of these elites, whose members had not been brought up within the modern educational system, had been

---

14 Taiwan's first political opposition party – the Democratic Progress Party – was founded in 1986 before martial law was lifted. Until its legalization in 1989, the DPP was only tolerated by the Nationalist Party-led government.

their biculturalism. Their own feelings of stigma were compensated for by their high positions in Han-society.

The second was the intellectuals in the Alliance of Taiwan Aborigines, who criticized members of the elite associated with the Nationalist Party for their assimilation policy, and who led the pan-ethnic movement in Taibei. Most of them derived from Taiwan's general educational system. For these young members of the educational elite whose access to higher school education had been facilitated by a bonus system for students with 'mountain area status', biculturalism was much more a hindrance than a 'capital'. Since the early 1970s, the membership of the educational elite in aborigine society had steadily grown.[15] Many wished to join political elites after finishing college or university, but faced a dead end because the state pretended until 1990 that there existed cultural homogeneity in Taiwan and so had not created new opportunities for bicultural aborigines with their particular talents and weaknesses. The leaders of both the pan-ethnic movement in the cities and the 'tribalist movement' that split away in 1989 were graduates from the Department of Political Science of Taiwan National University. As becomes clear from Xie's accounts, the impetus for these intellectuals to offer resistance was largely born out of dissatisfaction to be – in spite of their equivalence in terms of education – discriminated against on ethnic grounds; their opposition thus also resulted from the failure to assimilate to the dominant society.[16] Nevertheless, neither of these educational elites succeeded in building up grassroots in the tribal areas. As Xie (1992) contends in an article entitled 'Elites Without People', the main reasons for the inability of these elites to spread their influence all over aborigine society were the Nationalist Party's strong control over the people, the dispersal of aborigines all over Taiwan, the differences in interest and attitudes of different cultural groups as well as the differing world views of elites and people.[17]

---

15 Although the proportion of aborigines with higher school education was always five times lower than in Han society, their number doubled between 1978 and 1985, rising from 0.92 per cent to 2 per cent. By 1988 it had risen to 2.5 per cent of the aborigine population in Taiwan (Institute of Ethnology, Academia Sinica 1992, pp. 24f). The number of preachers and social workers in the Presbyterian Church of Taiwan, 390 in 1983, had by 1993 risen to 500 (Yuanxuan 1993, p. 33).

16 Wang Fu-chang (1989) has described a similar process in his analysis of the development of Taiwanese political opposition in Taiwan. Wang contends that Taiwanese Han intellectuals experienced a twofold process of assimilation and discrimination when they competed with Mainlander Han elites in a system biased towards Chinese culture. This finally caused them to stand up against the Mainlander regime. Though Xie, who strongly supported the aborigine movement, also warns that world views and symbols of the elites might be not intelligible for ordinary people from aborigine society, he does not go deeper into this argument.

17 As results from my own fieldwork from 1994-1996 indicate, the incompatibility of *Yuanzhumin* ideology with the perceptions of ordinary people became one of the most important reasons for the gap between 'elites and people' that kept on existing in the period after authoritarian rule.

The aborigine church elite was the third type of elite involved in identity construction in aborigine society. It worked closely together with the educational elite from the campuses. Its members derived from the educational system of the Presbyterian Church of Taiwan – a system that was not acknowledged by the state and thus isolated – and were assigned to stimulate ethnic consciousness on the local level, a task that was not easy because of the Nationalist Party's strong control in the villages. As we learn from Stainton, the re-conceptualized Bible exegesis in the liberation theology of the Presbyterian Church of Taiwan provided the main impetus as well as the psychological basis for resistance in the case of these intellectuals. Used as a 'codification' which represented the social reality of aborigine people, the Bible permitted the reader to stand outside the hegemonically determined common sense of the believer's own existence as a member of a devalued and violated ethnie, and allowed him or her to critically examine that situation. Another, rather pragmatic, motivation for this elite to oppose assimilation of aborigines to Han society was connected to their wish to survive as a religious group. In some areas where aborigines lived in close contact with Han Chinese, more than 80 per cent of the aborigines had already become Buddhist or members of Taiwan folk religion, compared to the fact that 80 per cent of the aborigines in general were Christians.[18]

As the aborigine church elite was deeply rooted among people in the tribal areas, it was much more successful in mobilizing large segments of aborigine society than the elite of the Alliance of Taiwan Aborigines. Particularly in the 'Return-our-Land movement' launched in 1988 and 1989 as a reaction to high taxation of aborigine church land by the state since 1981, it was possible to mobilize large numbers of protesters. However, strong control from the side of the Presbyters, who were mostly loyal to the Nationalist Party, prevented activist ministers from spreading Presbyterian Church of Taiwan-style liberation theology in their parishes. Thus, the influence of the aborigine church elite was mainly confined to institutions like colleges or administrative units of the Presbyterian Church of Taiwan.

Aborigine Elites' Interaction in Times of Multiculturalism

After 1990, however, a significant change took place in the attitudes and the impetus of aborigine elites. The most salient difference compared to the preceding period was an increasing cooperation between former Nationalist Party-loyal aborigine elites and resisting aborigine elites. Particularly in the period of the modification of Taiwan's constitution (the constitution that had originally been set up when the Nationalist Party was still on the mainland and that was supposed to represent all Chinese), these elites worked closely together: their common aim now was to assure aborigines' representation in the new constitution. Another

18 Xu Muzhu (1990, p. 137).

remarkable change took place in the claims that were made: the focus now shifted from land rights to recognition of the *Yuanzhumin* name and the status of the *Yuanzhumin*. Further, there was a change in the way the claims were made. Where the aborigine elites had referred to aborigine culture mainly to point out the reasons for the structural backwardness of aborigine people *vis-à-vis* their Han-oppressors – there were frequent references to the 'culture of poverty' of Taiwan's aborigines or the 'moral superiority of Christian aborigine Culture' – it now served to emphasize the 'authenticity' and the 'subjectivity' of Taiwan's aborigines as a distinct ethnic group, while Christianity increasingly lost its former importance as a cultural marker.

The changes described above were brought about by a major shift in Taiwan's wider political landscape in 1990. The pace of liberalization that had been slow during the first three years following the lifting of martial law in 1987 was accelerated when Li Denghui – a descendant of those Han who had their roots in Taiwan – was officially confirmed in his office as President of the Republic of China (ROC) in May 1990.[19] Where the government in the past had been dominated by Mainlander Han who were also in control of the military, the Taiwanese Han – mainly Hoklo – within the Nationalist Party now soon gained superiority in the party as well as in the military. Their relation to mainland China was not as unquestioned as it had been under the former Mainlander government elites. Neither the claim to recover the mainland nor the claim of sovereignty over all of China was now held up anymore. On the contrary, the Presbyterian Li Denghui soon became suspected of siding with the Democratic Progress Party (DPP) – Taiwan's political opposition party that promoted the island's independence and that shortly after its official approval in 1989 already occupied one third of the seats in the national parliament and controlled three of the island's eleven county governments. In order to make Taiwan politically and culturally distinct from the mainland, the so-called 'mainstream faction' of the Nationalist Party around Li Denghui agreed with the Hoklo-dominated Democratic Progress Party on a multicultural policy in a multi-ethnic Taiwan – a clear affront to their opponents in the non-mainstream faction of the Nationalist Party who had denied the existence of different 'ethnic groups' in Taiwan for four decades.[20] According to the new political discourse after 1989, Taiwan's population was not composed of a homogeneous Chinese race (*zhonghua minzu*) anymore, but of 'four big ethnic groups' (*Taiwan si da zuqun*), i.e. Hoklo, Hakka, Mainlanders and aborigines, that in the course of time had merged into a 'new Taiwanese' as a result of cultural

---

19 Two years passed until Li Denghui, who had succeeded president Jiang Jingguo after his death in late 1988 as vice-president, was officially approved by the parliament.

20 The term 'ethnic group' (*zuqun*) had not been used in Taiwan's political vocabulary before 1989 (Chang 1996). When the term became popular in Taiwan in 1989/1990, it was totally unfamiliar to people in mainland China.

cross-fertilization and intermixture.[21] The concept was not only suitable for creating a new sense of commonness among the members of Taiwan's different ethnic groups, but also defied the mainland's claims on Taiwan in historical and in cultural terms. With the ingredient 'Taiwanese aborigines' – a people that had been classified as part of the 'Austronesian language group' by Japanese and Western linguists and anthropologists – Taiwan's history could now be projected between eight and ten thousand years into the past, even longer than that of the mainland. Furthermore, Taiwan's Austronesian heritage also served as a proof that Taiwan – in cultural and genetic terms – had its own particularity and was much more connected to the pacific region than to any region to the west of Taiwan.[22] In order to create the basis that was necessary for the further development of a 'Taiwan living community' and a 'new Taiwanese', the government in 1992 started a long-term community renaissance policy. In this project that was also strongly supported by the Democratic Progress Party, all communities in Taiwan – ethnic, rural and urban communities, most of which where either Hoklo, Hakka or Aborigine – where asked to participate actively in local cultural life, to organize rites and festivals, and to engage in the preservation of local culture and the collection of oral history. It was in this context that more and more members of the former resistance aborigine elites began to take over the role of administrators of tribal culture. Aborigine literature in Chinese language and aborigine art now blossomed in the big cities, and travels and study-stays were organized in the tribal areas. Apart from these activities, many young people returned to the tribes to engage in either state- or church-financed cultural revitalization projects, as for instance the reconstruction of traditional buildings and cultural sites, education in

---

21 How much the Nationalist Party's mainstream faction – relieved of the Mainlanders within the Nationalist Party after the splitting away of the China New Party (CNP) in 1993 – supported this discourse was demonstrated by Li Denghui, who in 1994 adopted the notion of the 'Taiwan living community', a notion that was originally created by Taiwan's opposition party and that was slightly altered by Li. The term used by the DPP was 'Taiwan community of fate', referring to the common experiences of the different peoples of Taiwan who were 'thrown together by fate'. As the promotion of the 'Taiwan living community' was not the only pro-Taiwan notion made by Li at that time (another important slogan was '[Let's] manage great Taiwan and establish a new Chinese cultural centre'), authorities in Beijing harboured the suspicion that Li was a 'traitor to the Chinese nation'.

22 Of course, the 'Austronesiation' that seized Taiwan after the early 1990s did not stay unnoticed in the PRC. The new kind of nationalist discourse in Taiwan that referred to the hybridity of Taiwan's inhabitants and that hence stayed caught in the category of 'race', was now again countered with arguments stressing 'racial origins'. For instance, an article with the title 'Testification of the genealogical (*xueyuan*) origin of Taiwan's *Yuanzhumin*' in the foreign edition of *People's Daily* on 16 February 1996 pointed to new archaeological findings, according to which the ancestors of the *Yuanzhumin* had originally come from the mainland and partly even from north China to Taiwan and hence must have been Chinese. The author of the article contends enthusiastically that these findings should also have 'direct impact on the important national question of reunification of Taiwan and China' (Wang Xiaohui 1996, p. 5).

mother languages, rehabilitation of traditional aborigine names, etc. With the organizational help of the Presbyterian Church of Taiwan, the intellectuals from the Alliance of Taiwan Aborigines and aborigine church leaders after 1991 on a regular basis participated in the meetings of the Working Group of Indigenous Affairs (WGIP) in Geneva, a measure that increased the pressure on Taiwan's government to improve the Taiwanese aborigines' situation in general, but that also caused increasing protest from the side of the PRC, because aborigines after all were representatives of the ROC, a state that had ceased to exist in 1949 according to the official discourse of mainland China's government.[23] Simultaneously, the demonstrations for aborigine political and cultural rights in Taiwan continued. As a reaction to the obvious attitudinal change in Han society toward aborigines and aborigine rights, now even the members of the old political elite loyal to the Nationalist Party joined the petitions for issues like autonomous zones, rehabilitation of traditional aborigine names and the re-education of children in their mother-languages. At least in Taiwan's political and intellectual world, ethnic and cultural difference now no longer had a negative image; instead, it was looked upon as an important heritage and enrichment of Taiwanese culture. The 'cultural headhunting raid'[24] staged by a couple of well-known aborigine intellectuals at the first Aborigine Culture Congress in 1994, that was supposed to urge the government to comply with the activists' claims and got a lot of positive feedback and recognition within Han society, must be seen in this context. Another related phenomenon was Tian Guishi's homepage 'The Facial Tattoo of Tayal'[25] on the internet, where users worldwide were confronted with impressive and exotic pictures – photographs of old men and women with greenish-blue tattoos on their chins and foreheads, in the case of the men rather decently done, but somewhat more shocking in the case of the women, whose lower part of the face is sometimes totally covered by tattoos.[26]

---

23 Allio (1998, pp. 59f.).
24 The incident happened on the first day of the conference: a group of ten aborigine activists in traditional costumes suddenly interrupted the official programme, marched on to the stage, and openly announced the 'cultural headhunting raid proclamation'. In general, this was a catalogue of demands in which aborigines requested to be taken more seriously with respect to their sovereignty. The participating cadres were asked to intensify their cooperation on correcting names as well as on the implementation of aborigines' institutions and autonomous zones; and the anthropologists who had been the main planners of the congress were blamed not only for wasting too much time on academic questions, but also for their Han-centred world view, demonstrated by the under-representation of aborigines at the congress. The first official recognition of the ethnonym 'Yuanzhumin' occurred during the speech Li Denghui gave on the last day of the congress. For a more detailed description of the event, see Rudolph 1996.
25 http://hledu.nhltc.edu.tw/ tayal/.
26 In one of the attached Chinese language articles Tian – himself a member of the Taroko, a subgroup of the Atayal – explains the myth of the origin of the custom; in another article he explains the qualifications men and women needed to demonstrate in order to receive the tattoo and acquire the right to marry: men had to prove their skills in hunting

The View from the Countryside

Cultural representations of this kind, however, could hardly attract ordinary people still living in the tribes. They had their own attitudes toward the new development. Some findings from my field research in villages of the Taroko (a subgroup of the Atayal) and the Paiwan between 1994 and 1996 with the aim to evaluate the acceptance of the aborigine movement may serve as an example.[27] In the case of the Taroko, for instance, few villagers perceived the former tattooing practices – an integral part of the Taroko's former headhunting habit – as an admirable part of Taroko culture. Rather, they looked upon it as a stigma and a symbol of 'savageness'. Those who still wore tattoos were kept hidden or at least out of the view of outsiders. Even less did people wish to talk about headhunting. Instead, I was often told the story of Ji Oang, the Taroko woman who brought Christianity to the Taroko under the Japanese, and the plight and the suffering of indigenous missionaries like Wilang Takao, who was said to have endured severe punishment for his efforts to evangelize aborigines in times of Japanese colonial rule. Despite all the cruelty of the Japanese, most people said that they would not blame them because after all the Japanese had liberated the Taroko from headhunting even before the consolidation of Christianity.

As with the attitudes concerning the headhunting past of the Taroko, the conceptions of origin often formed a contrast to the convictions among elites. Only a few villagers were inclined to consider themselves as 'Austronesians' as proclaimed by their elites, i.e. as members of peoples totally different from the Han. They had already got used to the belief that they were of common origin and descent with the Han people (including the affiliation to a 5,000-year-old mainland culture), of which Nationalist Party-dominated education had assured them for decades, in spite of the daily allusions to their backwardness, exemplified by their 'dialects', and different life and housing styles. They had strongly internalized the political view proclaimed by the Nationalist Party until the early 1990s, according to which some day in the future the mainland would be recovered and ruled again. In some cases, I was told how 'one' (i.e., the Chinese) had been mistreated by the Japanese during the 'eight-year anti-Japanese war', and how it was 45 years since 'one' (i.e. the ROC) had come to Taiwan. At the same time, the political situation of the aborigines in Taiwan was not very well known. Few people knew that the only central government institution for minorities was

---

and in battle, while women were expected to have high skills in weaving. Males who were successful several times in headhunting were authorized to add special tattoos to their breast, feet and forehead. Among the stories reported is also that of 90-year-old Biyang Lahang, who had observed the bloody scenes of headhunting with her own eyes and who could account for the way the heads were treated after headhunting.

27 That members of the *Yuanzhumin* movement were only poorly supported by the larger aborigine society was also certified by the election results for *Yuanzhumin* legislators in December 1995. All politicians elected belonged to the aborigine political elite loyal to the Nationalist Party (Rudolph 1996).

dedicated to Tibetans and Mongolians and that there was no similar institution for Taiwan's aborigines – one of the improprieties the elites where fighting against.

From the perspective of the villagers, it seemed totally useless and even against one's own interests to rehabilitate traditional first and family names, as had been allowed by the government in January 1995 after many years of engagement by the elites.[28] Even for outsiders they would then be discernible as Taroko, a prospect that did not seem very attractive to them after the long period of discrimination. Likewise, the people could not see a crisis of their mother language in the same sense as this was perceived by the elites. The Taroko language was widely used, but many people also believed that they could live without it. English was believed to be more important.[29] The attitudes concerning the possession of mountain reservation land were similar; it was believed to be of equal importance to gain some surplus money – for instance by selling this land illegally to the Han – so that one could afford an estate or a home in the city. Autonomous zones did not seem very attractive from this point of view; it was even suspected that this was only a means to get aborigines 'locked up in a cage so that people could look at them like monkeys in the zoo'. But not only the Taroko villagers regarded the activities of the elites to revitalize and protect culture with suspicion. In the Paiwan village where I lived after my stay with the Taroko, I realized that the scepticism against official rehabilitation of traditional first and family names was especially strong. Due to the rudimentary persistence of certain structures of the former nobility and class society (which was partially a consequence of how the government had utilized people with former nobility status), non-noble members of this society naturally regarded the possibility of name rehabilitation with very mixed and ambivalent feelings. An official rehabilitation of one's status-revealing first and family names would inevitably cause a relapse into one's former inferior status.[30] Thus, they often even refused to tell me their 'bad-sounding' Paiwan names. In contrast, the former 'nobles' with their 'nice-sounding' names tried to make use of the favourable situation, emphasizing the superiority of their class in government-

---

28 Although the office for population registration of the Ministry of Interior had 'mobilized all forces to encourage aborigines to rehabilitate their original names' (for example by making advertisements on all state TV channels and by permitting aborigines to go through formalities without official identity papers), only 154,000 of 380,000 aborigines had made use of the possibility of name rehabilitation by July 1997. As Lin Jiangyi, director of the *Yuanzhumin* educational board, emphasizes, even younger aborigines (including his own children) do not dare to reveal their *Yuanzhumin* status while their social ties and relations in their living environment have not yet been fixed (*Taiwan Aktuell*, No. 201, 16 July 1997).

29 It was looked upon with suspicion that many members of aborigine elites who claimed that their 'mother language was the root of a particular culture and thus should be practised more often in everyday life' sent their own children to Han schools in the plains.

30 The intellectuals justified their behaviour by emphasizing the importance of opposing these structures, which could take on excessive forms during periods of authoritarian rule.

sponsored nativist publications, schoolbook materials and in newly established 'culture protection committees'.

Conclusion

As the account above showed, motivations and incentives for intellectual and political elites in Taiwan's aborigine society to participate in political activism and identity construction were much higher than for ordinary people in this society. Both in the period of authoritarian rule in Taiwan and in the period of *Taiwanization* and multiculturalism that started after 1990, political activism of elites was linked to competition either between members of aborigine elites or – in the latter case – between aborigine and Han elites. Where members of bicultural aborigine elites in the first period had struggled for the rare positions as mediators between Han and aborigine society, they soon recognized their new opportunities in the period of Taiwanese nativism and sought mutual solidarity in order to enlarge their common territory *vis-à-vis* ethnic Han elites. This aim could best be reached by emphasizing the aborigines' particularity. In both periods, competition and conflict between different elites and struggle for political power played an important role, as Paul Brass has suggested in his instrumentalist approach. Nevertheless, it also became clear that there was still another important motivation for educated aborigines to engage themselves in politics. The activism must also be seen as a reaction to the strong feelings of stigma that had been imposed on aborigine identity for many decades and that now could be overcome with the help of techniques provided by anti-systemic and system-critical forces inside and outside Taiwan. In a study on Burakumin identity in Japan, George De Vos and Hiroshi Wagatsuma (1966) suggest that political activism may be an alternative way to compensate for social stigma and simmering discontent with discrimination.[31] Hence, discontent with discrimination on the basis of collective social stigma must not be underestimated as a reason why aborigine elites took to political activism. The contact of a growing number of aborigines with higher school education as well as with certain elite groups outside of aborigine society stimulated the formation of conscientiousness. Societal groups with a strong catalytic function in the first period were intellectuals within the Taiwanese opposition party Democratic Progress Party, Taiwan's anthropologists, foreign missionaries and the Presbyterian Church of Taiwan. In the second period, these

---

31 De Vos and Wagatsuma state: 'As a result of involvement, the individual may participate in politically deviant behaviour rather than resort to individual extra-legal deviancy. Far left political movements are socially integrative insofar as they seek means of effecting change without a denial of self-identity (...). The individual who takes political action is mobilizing his energy toward a cause rather than falling back from it in either resignation or apathy, as is the case with a great majority of the Burakumin' (De Vos and Wagatsuma 1966, p. 259).

influences were reinforced by a further factor outside Taiwan, i.e. the link to the Fourth World Movement that was provided through the church and the anthropologists. By this linkage and by adoption of the strategies of this movement, Taiwan's aborigines were able to become an influential pressure group within Taiwanese society.

The attitudes of ordinary people towards aborigine identity, however, were very different. Though the style of interaction with Han culture varied according to the social system of every ethnic group, people in general did not like to emphasize their aborigine origin or cultural background in front of outsiders; sometimes they even refused to admit it. Instead, they were very eager to adapt their actions and attitudes to the 'Taiwanese standards' as they perceived them – for example emulating Taiwan's middle and lower social strata. On one hand, this behavioural pattern enhanced the adoption of cultural conceptions and consumption styles.[32] On the other hand, it caused a rejection of one's own aborigine culture, including language, traditional names and certain traditions that were perceived as symbols of aborigine savageness and backwardness, like headhunting, tattooing, and traditional style buildings. Most salient was the dislike of being defined as a member of a cultural group not belonging to the ethnic Chinese. Further attitudes that pointed to a low degree of identification with aborigine culture were the indifferent attitudes of ordinary people toward aborigine land or toward the intrusion of industries that caused the destruction of environment and living sites, but that created working places and brought surplus money through the (illegal) selling and letting of aborigine land.

These observations suggest that different self-perceptions and behavioural patterns of aborigine elites and ordinary people developed because different segments of aborigine society attached themselves to different groups of reference and value orientations within Han society. As the work of culture preservation and revitalization pursued by aborigine elites was frequently morally and financially supported by *Taiwanization* circles, environmental protection groups and so on, aborigine elites also often identified or at least sympathized with their world views; by establishing the concept of '*Aboriginality*' (Stainton 1995), they finally achieved a high amount of recognition in Taiwanese society; in contrast, common people felt much more attracted by the value-orientations of a consumption-oriented Han middle class. Differently from the elites who could rely on their upper class mentors, they did not get any support from the side of middle class and middle educated Han. Instead, they were often discriminated against because of their low degrees of qualification and their different mentality (for instance their 'low working morale'). As I said in the beginning, most aborigines and Han shared the conviction that the aborigines' integration would be successful with 'only a little bit more effort from their side' (Fu Yangzhi 1994). To free oneself from one's inferior status and to be engaged in such well-respected jobs as in the police or in the army, a high degree of conformity was necessary. For those who longed for

---

32 This also included the adoption of certain Han stereotypes of aborigine identity in the tourism sector, see Xie (1992b).

social mobility within Han society, the identity symbols propagated by the intellectuals hence did not make much sense and were often perceived as an impediment.

In sum, there is much evidence that people within both segments of aborigine society harboured a strong inclination to assimilate with Han society or at least to adapt themselves to the expectations within Han society.[33] Nevertheless, contrary to the elites, ordinary people from the villages neither had the tools to develop alternative ways to handle their feelings of stigma and inferiority, nor did they feel any support or incentives to expose their feelings of discontent toward the members of the Han middle class, where most people believed that the aborigines' predicament was due to the lack of diligence of aborigines rather than a result of social injustice.

Works Cited

Allio, Fiorella (1998) 'The Austronesian Peoples of Taiwan: Building a Political Platform for Themselves'. *China Perspectives*, 18 (7), 52-60.

Brass, Paul (1991) *Ethnicity and Nationalism: Theory and Comparison*. London: Sage Publications.

Chang Mao-kuei (1996) 'Political Transformation and the "Ethnization" of Politics in Taiwan', in A. Schneider and G. Schubert (eds), *Taiwan an der Schwelle zum 21. Jahrhundert - Gesellschaftlicher Wandel, Probleme und Perspektiven eines asiatischen Schwellenlandes*. Hamburg: Institut für Asienkunde, 135-152.

De Vos, George and Hiroshi Wagatsuma (ed.) (1966) *Japan's Invisible Race*. Berkeley, CA: University of California Press.

Fu Yangzhi (1994) (in Chinese) 'Explaining the Predicament of Taiwan's Aborigines – Comparison of Han and Aborigines Perceptions). *Bulletin of the Institute of Ethnology Academia Sinica*, 77. Taibei: Academia Sinica, 35-87.

Huang Yinggui, Jiang Bin, Chen Maotai, Shi Lei and Qu Haiyuan (1993) (in Chinese) 'Respect the Yuanzhumin's Autonym', in Zhang Maogui, *Zuqun guanxi yu guojia rentong*. Taibei: Yeqiang chubanshe, 191-197.

Institute of Ethnology, Academia Sinica (1992) (in Chinese) *An Evaluation of the Assistance Measures towards Mountain Compatriots*. Taibei: Executive Yuan.

Li Yiyuan (1992) (in Chinese) *Portraits of Culture: Observations of Religion and Ethnic Culture*. Taibei: Yunchen Wenhua Chubanshe.

Rudolph, Michael (1996) (in German) '"Taiwanese? What's That?" – Taiwan's Aborigines between Discrimination and Self-Organization', in A. Schneider and G. Schubert (eds), *Taiwan an der Schwelle zum 21. Jahrhundert.-Gesellschaftlicher Wandel, Probleme und Perspektiven eines asiatischen Schwellenlandes*. Hamburg: Institut für Asienkunde, 285-308.

---

33 This is also testified by the relatively high degree of intermarriage of aborigines and Han: data provided by Li Yiyuan (1992, pp. 253f) indicate that the proportion of aborigine women marrying Han men in 1984 almost reached 40 per cent.

Rudolph, Michael (2003a) (in German) *Taiwan's Multi-Ethnic Society and the Movement of Aborigines – Assimilation or Cultural Revitalization?* Muenster/Hamburg/London: LIT Verlag.

Rudolph, Michael (2003b) 'The Quest for Difference vs the Wish to Assimilate: Taiwan's Aborigines and their Struggle for Cultural Survival in Times of Multiculturalism', in P. R. Katz and M. A. Rubinstein (eds), *Religion and the Formation of Taiwanese Identities*. New York: Palgrave Macmillan, 123-156.

Stainton, Michael (1995) *Return our Land: Counterhegemonic Presbyterian Aboriginality in Taiwan*. MA Thesis, York University.

Wang Fu-chang (1989) *The Unexpected Resurgence: Ethnic Assimilation and Competition in Taiwan, 1945-1988*. PhD Thesis, University of Arizona.

Wang Xiaohui (1996) (in Chinese) 'Confirming the Blood Relationship Origin of Taiwan's Aborigines'. *Renmin Ribao* (Haiwaiban) 16 February 1996, 5.

Wei Yijun (1997) (in Chinese) *Another World Approaches: Realising the Theory in Taiwan's Aborigine Movement*. MA Thesis, Qinghua Daxue, Taibei.

Xie Shizhong (1987a) (in Chinese) *Stigmatized Identity – Ethnic Change of Taiwan Aborigines*. Taibei: Zili wanbao she.

Xie Shizhong (1987b) (in Chinese) 'Towards Theories of the Origin and Development of Aborigine Movements: The Cases of North America and Taiwan'. *Bulletin of the Institute of Ethnology Academia Sinica*, 64. Taibei: Academia Sinica, 139-177.

Xie Shizhong (1987c) (in Chinese) 'Ethnographic Morals and the Dilemma of the Social Anthropologist: The Example of Research on Taiwan's Aborigine Movement'. *ConTemporary*, 20, 20-30.

Xie Shizhong (1992a) (in Chinese) 'Preliminary Discussion of the Relation between the Symbol "Yuanzhumin" and the Elite Phenomenon'. *Daoyu bianyuan*, 5, 52-60.

Xie Shizhong (1992b) (in Chinese) 'Tourism, the Shaping of Tradition, and Ethnicity: A Study of Daiyan Identity of Wulai Atayal'. *Kaogu renleixue kan*, 48, Taibei 12/1992, 113-129.

Xie Shizhong (1994) (in Chinese) 'Where Are the Songs and Dances from the Mountains Put on Stage?' *Zili zaobao* 19 December.

Xu Muzhu (1990) (in Chinese) 'The Ethnic Identity Movement of Taiwanese Yuanzhumin: A Prelimineary Discussion of the Psycho-cultural Approach', in Xu Zhengguang and Song Wenli (eds), *Taiwan xinxing shehui yundong*. Taibei: Juliu tushu gongsi, 127-156.

Yuanxuan (Yuanzhumin Mission Committee of the Presbyterian Church of Taiwan General Assembly) (1993) (in Chinese) 'Special Issue on Occasion of the 40th Anniversary of the Yuanzhumin Mission Committee of the Presbyterian Church of Taiwan General Assembly and on Occasion of the Year of Indigenous People'. Taibei: Yuanxuan.

Chapter 14

Identity Matters:
The Case of the Singaporean Chinese

Benedicte Brøgger

The interplay between identity as an existential *and* a political concern will be the theme explored in this chapter.[1] In recent anthropology there has been a renewed focus on the interplay between human agency and structural and institutional factors, not least when it comes to questions of identity. The influence of institutional factors, like one's position in the political economy or belonging to a nation state, is important, but identities are also worked out within the framework of specific cultural meanings (Ong 1999). These may be the source of immediate existential concerns that may, or may not, concord with the macro level conceptualizations. A person's identity might change even within the span of one lifetime, as a result of the combined influences of economic and political changes as well as personal choices and taste (Carstens 1993). Reflection about one's identity may be seen as perpetually multiple and open-ended, rather than singular and final. This is in contrast to basic assumptions about identity in Western thought. Post-structuralist analyses of the 'post-modern condition' of paradox and ambiguity have led to critique of a very basic assumption, namely the status of the 'I' in Western thought (Kondo 1990). The critique is not directed against such a notion *per se*, but against regarding this idea of the self as a universally valid category. The Western 'I' is perceived as an entity that is autonomous, bounded and distinct (Cushman 1991). How this distinct whole then becomes one with other wholes, groups and societies, then becomes a perennial analytical problem (Strathern 1994). In a Chinese context on the other hand, the perspective is that notions of self are ego-centred and relational at the same time (Hsu 1948; Fei 1992; Bell 2000). The ego is seen as the centre of a highly particular and individual network of people, and it is the qualities of these relationships that define who one is. Identity must accordingly be understood as a dynamic process in the midst of changes and adjustments at many levels (Lim 1983; Wee 1988), and we may speak of multiple identities. This implies that one may regard oneself as belonging to

---

1   The empirical data in this chapter is based on fieldwork in Singapore from January 1996 through June 1997. An earlier version of the paper was presented at the *SPIRIT* workshop *Multiple and Diasporic Identities: Ethnic and National Belonging*, in Aalborg 15-16 September 2000.

different collectives for different purposes and occasions, without the agony of having to draw absolute and consistent boundaries between oneself and others.

Even if the contrast between Western and Chinese notions of identity are useful for illuminating general differences, a closer look at either category reveals that they are far from coherent. The concepts have different historical trajectories and raise different images. For example, I regard myself as a Norwegian, but rarely, if ever, do I regard myself as a Westerner. Westerner is not a concept that provides me with any sense of identity or belonging. On the other hand, based on experience from fieldwork among Chinese in both Malaysia and Singapore, it appears that the category Chinese is important for definition of self. Even so, there are many different interpretations as to what it means to be Chinese, as will be demonstrated below.

The perspective in the chapter is bottom-up and the empirical material is from Singapore. Most of the empirical detail will be from the presentation of self by one individual. His utterances about himself in different situations will be placed in the context of wider discourses and from this it will become clear that he is operating within a few and quite distinct discursive fields shaping his sense of self,[2] discourses that are of considerable political importance.

Identity, Multiple and Southeast Asia

Identity is related to two separate but interrelated facts: the first is a person's sense of selfhood, a 'me' that is different from all other 'me-s'. It is pointed out that people all over the world have a sense of inner coherence and continuity, no matter how ideas of selves are otherwise expressed and experienced (Ewing 1990). The second are processes of identification, which implies some 'us' (or 'them'), a collective identity. We are born alone and die alone, but to live the in-between, we are greatly dependent on others. How one is identified by others is as important as how one identifies oneself, and people are neither socially determined nor completely at will to decide for themselves (Cohen 1994). Identity has both an individual and a collective component, commonly referred to as inner self and social person (Jacobson-Widding 1983).

The matter of multiplicity in this case refers to the social self. Through identification with different groups, a person has several more or less overlapping social selves. In areas where people interact with others who look more or less similar, speak the same language, celebrate the same rituals, use the same calendar and eat more or less the same food, there is no need to develop a range of selves

---

2   I will not go into the matter of identification by others, the 'who are you?' but limit the presentation to his identification of himself – his search for an answer to the question 'who am I?' The identification by others is a natural next step, but for the purpose of this chapter I will limit the focus to his own words about himself and the situations in which these occurred.

that can be drawn upon in different situations. Reliance on multiple identities becomes a way of life in situations where people constantly and continuously have to engage with others who look different, speak and act differently, as a way of handling different demands and contexts. The tourist, the cosmopolitan or the average TV viewer may get many and occasionally profound impressions about life elsewhere, but such people do not have to deal with diversity in the practicalities of their own daily living. Therefore, the term multiple identities should be reserved for the cases were people, forcibly or voluntary, depend on their ability to interact in a multicultural setting. This is for example the case with refugees, long-term migrants and members of diasporic communities, as well as citizens of multiethnic states.

Only when diversity is acknowledged as a constitutive feature of one's identity may we speak of multiple identities. This raises another important issue. How does this apply to construction of national identity that demands clear-cut definitions of who is within and who is outside the national order? In the West, the notion of the bounded self matches the notion of the bounded society. It has for example been argued that the discovery of the problematic 'postmodern condition' of multiculturalism, discontinuities and ambiguity is itself distinctly Western and quite ethnocentric. In most parts of the world existence has always been postmodern in this sense, and the surprise at the multiplicity of identities truly reveals the Western assumptions (Wikan 1996). In the grand tale of the nation state that has dominated in the West, a perception that we are all more or less alike was needed in order to fix the boundaries between 'us', the members of the nation, and 'them', members of other nations. The fact that many people do not quite fit has been undercommunicated. This is particularly salient in Southeast Asia. Here people have dispersed and gathered, spread by emigration, wars and famines, attracted by riches and fertility of land and sea for thousands of years (Wang 1997). In these countries (Thailand, Malaysia, Indonesia, Singapore, Brunei, the Philippines, Myanmar, Laos, Cambodia and Vietnam) diversity is a way of life. One may only consult government statistics and a few books from each country to find this vividly displayed. There is fundamental disagreement as to the division of the population into ethnic groups, and the number of people belonging to each group. As part of the nation-building processes after the Second World War, governments have tried to order their populations into neat categories, much as the colonial powers did before them, and they have to some extent succeeded (Kahn 1998). The classical definition of a nation is a territory, a polity and a people (Gellner 1990); in Southeast Asia the situation is a territory, a polity and many peoples. Questions about cultural integrity lie at the heart of Southeast Asian politics. In this region the matter of identity is an issue of considerable political importance. The answer to the question 'who am I?' is as much a matter of politics as it is an existential concern. For example, the idea of the autonomous 'I' is essential for understanding treasured Western political ideals like human rights, democracy and citizenship. In Southeast Asia the situation is far from that neat.

Hence the particular ways that multiple identities, moulded, are shaping the particulars of the socio-political order and vice versa.

In Singapore, the situation is even more precarious that in other Southeast Asian countries. Three factors may be pointed at as especially important. First, Singapore does not have the benefit of a long and glorious mythical history, celebrated in history and ritual. It first came into being as a British colony in 1819, and has a population mainly composed of immigrants. Even today, many are still only second and third generation locals, and have their parents' and grandparents' stories of other places and belongings fresh at heart. Second, Singapore gained full sovereignty in 1965 only as an unexpected result of high-level political manoeuvres during its short-lived union with Malaysia. A Singaporean Chinese who witnessed the processes at close range explained that, 'when we were thrown out of the union, they expected us to come crawling back on our knees after a few years'. He said that the Malaysians had not expected Singapore to survive on its own, and neither had the Singaporeans, at first. Even today there was a common concern that Singapore's survival was precarious.

Finally, what Singapore does have to show for itself is an economic prosperity unparalleled in the region. These factors not only reflect political concerns, they resonate with existential concerns as well, as will be demonstrated in the case of Andrew below.

Singapore

In 1965, the new political leadership set about transforming Singapore, not only politically and economically, but also culturally, into a nation state. Development of a distinct nation state was important for several reasons. In the global political climate of the 1960s, Singapore's neighbours, and the superpowers, feared that Singapore would develop into Southeast Asia's Cuba, a bridgehead for China's expansion in the region. As long as Singapore was part of the federated states of Malaysia, this potential threat could be checked. When Singapore unexpectedly appeared as a sovereign state, other solutions had to be found. A nation state with primary loyalty toward itself could to some extent allay the fears. There were also domestic reasons for such a policy. Singapore has a population of three million. 2.7 million of these are Singapore residents (citizens and permanent residents), the rest, about 300,000, are mainly foreign workers. In 1990 the Chinese constituted 77.7 per cent of the resident population, the Malays 14.1 per cent, the Indians 7.1 per cent and others 1.1 per cent, and the numerical dominance of the Chinese has been a fact since nearly 1819. Mutual hostility and mistrust between the different ethnic groups have on a few occasions erupted into violence. To develop Singapore into an economically and politically viable entity required some kind of cooperation between the different ethnic groups. The idea of a common interest could clearly be recognized by all in the common denominator of 'Singaporeans'. Culturally, Singapore was to become a nation state for all its citizens regardless of ethnic belonging. With this the old social contract between political authority and subjects changed. Rights and duties that had earlier been defined according to particularistic ethnic status were exchanged for universal citizenship status, Singaporean. Political and legal rights, which had so far been denied most of the locals, were now extended to all as political and legal subjects. The ideal of a unified nation was an important motivator for developing Singapore culturally, but there was no one 'putative folk culture' on which Singaporean nationalism could draw. The idea of Singapore the nation could not be legitimized through any form of unifying 'ethnic' nationalism of shared origins, customs and language. This had its reason not only in the ethnic composition of the population, but in the political struggles of those years as well. What emerged was a distinct form of civic nationalism, which 'consists of various groups and individuals who have formed a united whole and who deserve citizenship by virtue of their behaviour, their demonstrated loyalty and adherence to values and codes of the nation' (Chirot 1997).

The universal civic nationalism was coupled with a policy of 'multiculturalism' whereby the customs and traditions of each ethnic group were to be respected and each group was to be represented in the affairs of the state (Benjamin 1976). Even if legally and politically Singaporeans, the various communities even today do not regard themselves as sharing the same culture. The cultural, historical and social links to part of India for the Indians, to parts of China for the Chinese and to Malaysia and Indonesia for the Malays means that the Singaporean population has orientations and loyalties which stretch far beyond the national borders. The differences are superseded by identification with Singapore. Therefore there is not one dominant national identity. Rather there are complex identities drawing on a variety of sources and relevant in different situations. There are two main categories for identification – Singaporean and Chinese/Malay/Indian/something else. This is so much inscribed in everyday practice today that a standard question among strangers is 'what are you?' (PuruShotam 1998). Within the Chinese group, there is a range of opportunities for more specific definitions. The boundaries between Chinese, Malay and Indian as cultural categories were clearly drawn and this resulted in a weaker identification with the identity as Singaporean, which was supposed to encompass all three.

In Singapore the problem appears to be how to strike a balance between a national Singaporean and an ethnic identity in a situation where the former as yet has little substance and the latter is both politically problematic and ambiguous. What does unite the Singaporeans is the tale of the economic success of the country (Chua 1998).

Andrew

At the time we got to know each other, Andrew[3] was in his mid-20s. He wore his hair short, and usually dressed casually in jogging shoes, chinos and loose T-shirts over his large and bulky frame. He held a front line job in an international company, not so much due to his educational merits as to his language fluency. He spent what spare time he had with (mostly male) friends, whom he was in frequent contact with through his mobile phone. He spent as little time as possible at home, a flat on the northern part of Singapore, where he lived with his parents, two younger siblings and a dog. He was a devoted swimmer. He often came to swim in the pool in the complex where I lived, as the friend of a person living there. We somehow started to talk, and the small talk developed into long conversations and occasional excursions. Usually our conversations started as I asked him questions about something I had seen or heard but not understood since the last time we spoke, and as often they ended with him talking about himself. The data analyzed here is therefore based on his own statements about himself, not on my observation of his social relationships. In so far as one accepts that language has the power to shape, if not the world, so at least the understanding of the world, these conversations served to constitute him discursively, for me, and it appeared, to himself. He once said he rarely talked about such matters with others. Our conversations represented a possibility for him to explore different aspects of self. His ponderings were always related to what happened in his life at any given time. Throughout the nearly one and a half years we met nearly weekly; he presented himself in different ways, most often related to whatever he was engaged in at the moment. There were a few main dilemmas that cropped up in the conversations time and time again, dilemmas that were clearly of great concern to him, but not to him alone. They were related to similar concerns expressed by others and in other contexts, so that we are not merely left with the idiosyncrasies of an individual, but rather with grander themes with which collectives are involved, and as such they are of considerable political importance.

Andrew's grandparents emigrated from China to Singapore before the Second World War, whereas he and his parents have lived there all their lives. His parents have lived through the hard times of Singapore and seen it emerge as a rich, modern, industrialized nation. Andrew on the other hand belongs to what in Singapore is defined as the 'post-independence generation', the generation that was born after 1965; those who have never experienced the hardship, riots and economic insecurity. Andrew grew up in a well-functioning modern state, has had his education in the free government schools, which, as could be seen from the content of textbooks and syllabus, represent a distinctly Singaporean outlook. Even though he has visited China, he was clear that he did not want to live there. He was born and raised in Singapore, and at one level clearly identified himself as

---

3   Andrew Tan was not his real name and other aspects of his background have been changed in order to anonymize him.

Singaporean. How he expressed his sense of self as well as national belonging is therefore particularly interesting.

'I Do Not Belong Here'

It was getting close to evening when Andrew stopped under a palm tree on Kusu, the little island where we had spent the day. He looked at the cityscape on the other side of the Singapore Strait and said, 'I do not belong here' and paused. 'The soil here is Malay', he continued, 'even if we Chinese have been here a long time, we never know how long it is going to last. What will happen when Lee Kuan Yew passes away?' I tried to continue the talk with him, but it was as if his energies were spent with this utterance, and we walked toward the ferry mainly in silence.

We had spent the day discussing the Chinese earth god. Andrew's few sentences emerged as an unexpected conclusion. We visited Kusu because I had been struck by the fact that the Chinese in Singapore, unlike so many other overseas Chinese communities (Willmott 1960; Soh 1990; Gupta 1993), did not have a shrine of a pioneer deity or at least a Toh Peh Kong, god of prosperity. I suspected that the two temples of Kusu, one devoted to Toh Peh Kong, the other to a local deity called Dato Kong, housed some sort of pioneer deities. Kusu lies half an hour by ferry just south of the main island. It is situated close to another island, St. Johns Island, where the immigrants were quarantined. I therefore suspected that Kusu could be an appropriate site to search for a pioneer deity. Andrew wanted to come with me because he wanted to pray in the temples. His dog had disappeared and he wanted to know if it would come back. The day had been futile. Andrew had received an answer that he interpreted to mean that his dog would never return. He was sad. I had not found out much about the earth god. The conclusion he drew was quite revealing. A very personal comment, the connection between his sense of belonging, the Malay soil and Lee Kuan Yew, was nevertheless an eloquent summary of the dilemma facing the Chinese, as Chinese, in Singapore.

All the difference was submerged under the common denominator 'Chinese', when Andrew referred to 'we Chinese' in relation to the Malay soil. Soil is an important Chinese concept (Fei 1992), part of a peasant ideology that has been transported and transplanted even in the overseas merchant communities. Soil and belonging are synonymous. No wonder belonging became difficult for Andrew when he perceived the soil as Malay and hence not something with which he could identify. Andrew's perception of the soil as Malay was in line with what others said, as I discovered when I continued to gather information about Dato Kong. Several people told me that Dato Kong was the god of the undeveloped soil, of the trees and the jungles. Since Singapore hardly had any undeveloped soil he was not much sought any more, they added. Interestingly enough, Dato Kong was described as a Malay god. (A fact which Malays indignantly denied. They said that Malays are Muslims and hence there can be no Malay god of this kind.) 'Dato' means Lord in Malay, 'Kong' means the same in Chinese dialect. The temple at

Kusu was a blend of Chinese and Malay elements. It was a Malay *Kramat*, or grave, and the person buried there turned out to be a Sheik Abdul Rahman, an important wadi who lived at the end of the 19th century. The colours, layout and practices of the temple were Chinese and there was a group of Chinese businessmen who had financed the temple. This information fitted how Andrew perceived Singapore – its soil was Malay. The Chinese had some place there too, but it was precarious, connected to Lee Kuan Yew, founder of modern Singapore. The soil is where the ancestors are, and from where prosperity springs forth. And ancestral belonging in China, the ancestral earth, is still of importance to create a specific Chinese identity. At the level of his collective identity as a Chinese, he had no sense of territorial belonging – the soil was Malay.

A Chinese, a Teochew, and More

At one level 'Chinese' signifies a unified identity, as exemplified above when Andrew spoke of 'we Chinese'. At another level, even that identity becomes multiple. Many of the Singaporean Chinese still brought their children to the ancestral town in China at least once, to 'get them to understand where they come from, find their roots' as one man said it. They brought their children, not to China, but to particular places in China. Children were brought to their ancestors' village, district, province. They were brought to meet people of their surname, people speaking a specific Chinese dialect. At this level we can therefore talk of a Chinese as having multiple identities, because he can claim identification with people with ancestors from the same village, district, province or with people of the same dialect or with people of the same name. The different sources of belonging differentiate the Chinese into groups. Particular soil is an important symbol for connecting to others, for creating a sense of 'us' in opposition to a variety of 'them', while still keeping within the broader framework of being a Chinese.

Andrew spoke Teochew at home and clearly defined himself as a Teochew from the Guangdong province. He was a connoisseur of Teochew food, which he placed above the cuisine of the other dialect groups. He knew the Teochew restaurants in Singapore, and often went to his favourite dining spots. He had been back and visited the graves of his ancestors and the house of his paternal relatives in Guangdong. Andrew's mother was Cantonese and he spoke some Cantonese too. He said that he felt some identification with people from this dialect group too, although he did not elaborate on which situations or occasions. At first he did not show any particular concern with his surname, Tan. It was only when he learnt that I was going to visit his surname association that he started talking about it. It was, after all, one of the most common Chinese surnames, a fact he told me with some pride. They were many, a strong group, he said when he brought me a copy of the genealogy of his father's lineage, taken from the souvenir magazine of his clan association. The clan association has members from all Chinese dialect groups as they traced their common connections back to the place where the very first ancestor lived. Andrew said he never visited the surname association now, but indicated that it might change when his parents passed away and became ancestors. Thus, Andrew was not just a Chinese, he was a specific kind of Chinese. There are many Chinese 'us' and 'them' for different purposes and situations.

A Singaporean

On other occasions, Andrew fully embraced his identity as a Singaporean. This became most clear when he talked about the situation in his workplace. He was working in an international company. His colleagues came from a wide range of Asian countries, and there were also Britons and Americans working in the company. His boss, with whom he had much difficulty, was German. He had only vague ideas about Northern Europe, and as I came from Scandinavia, he assumed that I could help him sort his boss out. He wanted help to find a way to establish a better working relationship with his boss. What was interesting in his deliberations of his situation at work was the fact that he continuously referred to the fact that he was Singaporean. He insisted that Singaporeans were efficient workers who knew how to get things done, whereas the German seemed to think that all Asians were lazy and inept workers. This irked him and hurt his pride in being a Singaporean. He was not just any Asian or any Chinese, he was a Singaporean, citizen of a country known for efficiency and economic success. This pride in being Singaporean was apparent in other situations as well. For instance, when the World Bank failed to recognize Singapore as a developed country, and the country continued to be placed in the category of newly industrialized economy, he was indignant (as were many other Singaporeans). He compared this event with events at his workplace in order to illuminate the case against his German boss. Even if Andrew was a Chinese, he was also very much a Singaporean.

A Modern Young Man

Being Singaporean had other connotations for Andrew as well. The country is modern and developed, and the honour of that achievement Andrew awarded to Lee Kuan Yew, Singapore's former prime minister. And if there was one thing that Andrew wanted, it was to appear as modern and sophisticated. For me, this was first of all symbolized in his choice of name. At our first meeting, he presented himself as Andrew. On a later occasion I commented upon the fact that he had chosen a very English-sounding name. He then looked at me, quite surprised, and said that he didn't know that it was particularly English. I listed up for him different spellings of the name and told him a little about its history. He pondered this for a while, then just shrugged and repeated that he liked the sound of the name and that was why he had chosen it. His personal name was one chosen by himself. It has been customary among Chinese to change their names in different life phases, so the pattern of name change is nothing new, but the fact that he had chosen a Western name is significant. Many of his age group did, and many did not, and it was not altogether clear to me why some did and some did not. Andrew could not explain.

Andrew later volunteered his Chinese personal name, but said that he only used it with his family and closest friends. By changing names he was able to oscillate between different situations and to 'wear different hats', as he said, using a common expression that was popular in Singapore. As Andrew, his favourite pastime was to hang out with friends in popular youth-hangouts; he listened to pop-music, craved for the newest high-tech gadgets (even if he could not afford them) and for all practical purposes appeared as a modern youth who could have come from anywhere in the world. Points of identification were provided by the powerful fashion industry, music industry and technology industry, which shaped his expectation of what being a modern young man was all about. This was partly connected with his identity as a Singaporean, but most of all was connected with his age and his circle of friends, mainly Chinese. With them, whether he was Chinese or Singaporean was of little importance. His sense of belonging sprang from his identification with people from his age group.

Rituals and Their Power to Create a Sense of Belonging

Andrew's deliberations over his identities were mostly of an existential kind. It revealed to him, and me, who he was to himself. Such deliberations do not happen in a vacuum. In a multiethnic state they are intimately linked to politics, and have political consequences, whether these are intended or not intended. In order to approach the political aspects of identity we need to understand how senses of belonging are created and sustained. There are a range of institutions that serve this purpose, educational institutions, political bodies, family, religious and cultural institutions and the media. This has been powerfully demonstrated for instance in studies of ethnicity and nationalism (see for example Shils 1981; Anderson 1983; Gellner 1990; Hobsbawm 1992; Eriksen 1993). One other institution is often overlooked in modern, industrialized societies, but is in fact of particular importance when it comes to mobilizing people, imprinting on them experiences that can serve to tighten (or loosen) their ties with others. That is – rituals.

Rituals have been analyzed from a wide range of perspectives and no doubt serve a number of purposes. A major focus has been rituals' power to reproduce and strengthen people's sense of attachment to a place and/or a group. Rituals, with their rich symbolism, can be understood as the celebration of unity of a group of people (Durkheim 1995). Whereas Durkheim demonstrates his point by detailed descriptions of the rituals of Australian aborigines, the concept which best captures the experience of unity is suggested by Turner when he speaks of 'communitas'. He opposes 'communitas' to 'societas' (Turner 1974). The latter is the pace and organizations of everyday life, whereas the former is the experience of being lifted out of the ordinary, of being transported into a different reality. This experience cannot last for long, but the effects of the experience linger and are carried over into the mundane matters of 'societas'.

Through the lens of rituals an analyst can get a look at different groups, the order of society as well as cultural ideas corresponding to order. Both Durkheim and Turner were concerned with rituals as they unfold event by event. Other studies point to different degrees of involvement from the participants, depending on their social position, their role in the ritual and the identification with important objects and traditions of knowledge (Geertz 1973; Kapferer 1984, 1998; Baumann 1999). Paul Connerton has demonstrated how what he calls commemorative rituals serve as a mnemonic device for a group of people, by recreating and making alive past events and persons, in such a way that the group celebrating feels that it is intimately linked with these mythical or historical events and persons (Connerton 1989). The Chinese cultural world is rich with commemorative rituals.

In Singapore the Chinese celebrate only a few major rituals, including Chinese New Year, *Qing Ming* (in some respects comparable with All Soul's Day), the Autumn festival (in some respects comparable with Thanksgiving) and the Hungry Ghost festival (in a few aspects comparable with the American Halloween or the Norwegian Christmans ritual of *Julebukk*). In addition to these public rituals there are a host of everyday ritual practices that serve the same commemorative function, in addition to the even wider diversity of individual ritual and religious observances. Rituals may entail 'communitas', but not for everyone; they may produce a sense of convergence between cultural beliefs and the social order, but at different levels. In Singapore, the observance of rituals is one way to express a sense of belonging, of identification, and as such the form and degree of participation of ritual and ritual activities will illuminate the connection between identity as a major existential *and* a political concern.

Ritual Reproduction of Andrew's Chinese Identity

Andrew claimed that he was not very active in the daily ritual celebrations in his home; those were the duty of his mother. Yet, he dutifully followed his parents on major ritual festivals. The New Year celebration is the celebration of the union (and reunion) of the family, and the *Qing Ming* is the time for care of the ancestors. Both of these rituals serve to strengthen ties between people, and at the same time they serve to commemorate the history of these ties. For instance, it was through the visit to the ancestral gravesite in China that Andrew felt he had a connection with a certain place in Guangdong, a connection that was strengthened by the ritual observances of *Qing Ming*. At a more general level it was through knowledge of the history of his surname that he gained a sense of belonging to a great Chinese family, originating from the great Yellow Emperor, a family that to him had a real presence. When he described how he did not like to eat the food that was offered to the ancestors during the New Year celebration, he vividly illustrated his physical experience of the ancestors' presence. The food was offered to the ancestors, and when the ancestors had eaten their share, it was served to the living. Andrew said he did not like to eat the food because he could taste its lack of spiritual matter, (which had nourished the ancestors).

Andrew's sense of belonging was also decisive when he chose not to participate, or chose to share in only some aspects of a celebration. The Hungry Ghost festival is in a sense the opposite of the New Year celebration and *Qing Ming*. The two latter sustain the ancestors, and feed the living. The Hungry Ghost festival involves sacrifices to evil spirits, the hungry ghosts. These are the ghosts of those who do not get sustained by their descendants, or who have no descendants. Andrew was not particularly concerned with this last ritual. After all, he said, his ancestors were well taken care of. The Autumn festival is a commemorative ritual, celebrating the reinstatement of a Han Chinese emperor, after a successful uprising against the Mongol Yuan dynasty in the 12th century; it still served to kindle feelings of political protest. The slogan 'destroy the Qing, restore the Ming', refers to the political quest to overthrow the Manchu rule under the Qing dynasty, and return the Han Chinese to power. The slogan was quoted by people who expressed political protest against the Singaporean government through their participation in the celebration. Andrew, even though he knew the historical heritage of the ritual, was happy merely to enjoy the joyous atmosphere of the celebration. He said that the political stuff was not for him. On this occasion, the Chinese and Singaporean aspects of the ritual were intertwined. All in all, different aspects of his Chineseness and Singaporeanness were reproduced when he participated in different rituals.

Singaporean Rituals

Compared to the richness of rituals among the Chinese, the simplicity of the rituals of the Singapore state is striking. The most general is the celebration of the national day on 31 August. The national day celebration dates from 1965. It has as yet not managed to establish itself as a natural and self-evident ritual. Singapore's 'myth of origin' was consciously created around two dates: the day of independence from the union with Malaysia (31 August 1965), and the year when the treaty between the British and a Malay sultan was signed, creating Singapore as a British trading port (1819). This moment of origin was chosen by the new political leaders, and was carefully designed to avoid conflict between the ethnic groups about 'who came first' (Rajaratnam 1990). These are moments of origin with which few feel any identification. The focal point of the national celebration is the military parade and culture shows, which take place in the national stadium and are broadcast live. The national day is a holiday, but there is not much activity in the streets on this day. Like many others, Andrew just stays at home.

There are the nationalist rituals every day at school, which include hoisting of the flag, singing of the national anthem and recitation of the national pledge, but, at least from what I saw from my own children, this was experienced more as a routine than a ritual. Apart from this, the state was conspicuously secular, on the verge of puritan minimalism, in comparison with the noisy, colourful and symbolically rich celebrations of the Chinese. This was not without its reasons, well illustrated with the problems with developing a national costume. This case indicates some of the obstacles that the state faces in its quest to establish a culturally meaningful national Singaporean identity in the presence of the strong ethnic identities of its diverse population. In early 1966 the 'Malchindeuro' emerged on the drawing board. Its name was drawn from the three languages and names for ethnic dresses; it cuts was a blend, a Chinese style jacket with European trousers, Malay sarong and an Indian-style shirt. The public quickly dismissed it. In 1967, the 'Cheongarong' was launched; with a Chinese diagonal collar, Malay skirt sarong and a detachable sash to represent an Indian sari. Again without success. New attempts were left until the 1980s, when one particular design had to be shelved to 'avoid upsetting ethnic sensitivities'. Finally, in 1989 there was at least agreement that a national Singaporean costume should contain an orchid motif (Ng 1996). On formal occasions that did not require a tie, people would sometimes meet in orchid patterned shirts as a way to 'state our patriotism for Singapore', as a man said. People were genuinely Singaporeans. The patriotism however, did not stand in the way of expression of ethnic sentiments.

Ritually speaking, unity was expressed for different collectives on different occasions, but for the Chinese the policy of multiculturalism served to strengthen their ties with their own history and hence their multiple identities as Chinese, not their sense of belonging in Singapore. Their diasporical identity is continued, barred from setting roots in any soil. The situation is a double bind and affects the state of Singapore on the macro-level, as much as it affects Andrew on the micro-level.

Conclusion

Andrew is an example of how people cope with multiple identities, not as extremes, but as continuously blending one into the other. Each identity is connected to different collectives and frames of reference which can be drawn on when need be, yet some are more deep-felt than others.

Between the Singaporean Chinese and their government there seems to be a modicum of agreement; at least they are somehow Chinese, and they are somehow Singaporean. Even if their sense of belonging and rootedness is connected with the fact that they are Chinese, their livelihoods and their citizenship are linked to the existence of Singapore. The living standards, the infrastructure, the education and social security is unparalleled in most places in the world. Like Andrew, most of them have nowhere else to go and most of them really do not want to go anywhere else. They want to be Singaporeans. On the other hand, the Malays and the Indians are Singaporean too, but they are also different. Singapore is not Chinese, it is multiethnic, in principle and in practice, but as long as this Singaporeanness has to be filled with some cultural content, identification as Chinese becomes important. For Andrew, being Chinese was related to being a person at all, whereas for the Singaporean government, creating Singaporeans was a prerequisite for the existence of the state. Hence, the existential dilemmas of one become the political concerns of the other and vice versa. These people are, therefore, together with their government, engaged in an act of creation and recreation of identity in which they are mutually dependent.

Works Cited

Abu-Lughod, Lila (1993) *Writing Women's Worlds. Bedouin Stories.* Berkeley, Los Angeles and London: University of California Press.

Anderson, Benedict (1983) *Imagined Communities. Reflection on the Origin and Spread of Nationalism.* London: Verso.

Baumann, Gerd (1999) *The Multicultural Riddle: Rethinking National, Ethnic, and Religious Identities.* New York: Routledge.

Bell, Duran (2000) 'Guanxi: A Nesting of Groups'. *Current Anthropology* 41(1), 132-138.

Benjamin, Geoffrey (1976) 'The Cultural Logic of Singapore's "Multiracialism"', in Riaz Hassan (ed.), *Singapore Society in Transition.* Kuala Lumpur: Oxford University Press, 42-77.

Carstens, Sharon A. (1993) 'Chinese Culture and Polity in Nineteenth-Century Malaya: The Case of Yap Ah Loy', in Mary Heidhues and David Ownby (eds), *'Secret Societies' Reconsidered. Perspectives on the Social History of Modern South China and Southeast Asia.* Armonk: M.E. Sharpe, 120-152.

Chirot, Daniel (1997) 'Conflicting Identities and the Dangers of Communalism', in Daniel Chirot and Anthony Reid (eds), *Essential Outsiders. Chinese and Jews in the Modern Transformation of Southeast Asia and Central Europe.* Seattle and London: University of Washington Press, 3-32.

Chua, Beng Huat (1998) 'Radical Singaporeans: Absence after the Hyphen', in Joel S. Kahn (ed.), *Southeast Asian Identities. Culture and the Politics of Representation in Indonesia, Malaysia, Singapore and Thailand.* Singapore: Institute of Southeast Asian Studies, 28-50.

Cohen, Anthony P. (1994) *Self Consciousness. An Alternative Anthropology of Identity.* London and New York: Routledge.

Connerton, Paul (1989) *How Societies Remember.* Cambridge: Cambridge University Press.

Cushman, Paul (1991) 'Ideology Obscured. Political Uses of the Self in Daniel Stern's Infant'. *American Psychologist*, (March), 206-219.

Durkheim, Emile (1995) *The Elementary Forms of Religious Life.* New York: Free Press.

Eriksen, Thomas H. (1993) *Ethnicity and Nationalism: Anthropological Perspectives.* London: Pluto Press.

Ewing, Katherine (1990) 'The Illusion of Wholeness: Culture, Self and the Experience of Inconsistency'. *Ethos*, 18, 251-78.

Fei, Xiaotong (1992) *From the Soil. The Foundations of Chinese Society*. Berkeley and Los Angeles: University of California Press.

Geertz, Clifford (1973) *The Interpretation of Cultures. Selected Essays*. New York: Basic Books.

Gellner, Ernst (1990) *Nations and Nationalism*. Oxford: Basil Blackwell.

Giddens, Anthony (1991) *Modernity and Self-Identity: Self and Society in the Late Modern Age*. Cambridge: Polity Press.

Gupta, Smita (1993) 'Marginality and Segregation – A Concept of Socio-Political Environment in Urban Setting'. *Man in India*, 73(1), 41-47.

Hobsbawm, Eric J. (1992) *Nations and Nationalism Since 1780: Programme, Myth, Reality*. Cambridge: Cambridge University Press.

Hsu, Francis L. K. (1948) *Under the Ancestors' Shadow: Chinese Culture and Personality*. New York: Columbia University Press.

Jacobson-Widding, Anita (1983) 'Introduction', in Anita Jacobson-Widding (ed.), *Identity. Personal and Socio-Cultural*. Stockholm: Almqvist & Wicksell International, 13-32.

Kahn, Joel S. (1998) 'Southeast Asian Identities: Introduction', in Joel S. Kahn (ed.), *Southeast Asian Identities. Culture and the Politics of Representation in Indonesia, Malaysia, Singapore and Thailand*. Singapore: Institute of Southeast Asian Studies, 1-27.

Kapferer, Bruce (1984) 'The Ritual Process and the Problems of Reflexivity in Sinhalese Demon Exorcism', in John MacAloon (ed.), *Rite, Drama, Festival, Spectacle*. Philadelphia, PA: Institute for the Study of Human Issues (Papers from the 76th Burg Wartenstein Symposium), 179-207.

Kapferer, Bruce (1998) *Legends of People, Myths of State: Violence, Intolerance, and Political Culture in Sri Lanka and Australia*. Washington, D.C.: Smithsonian Institution Press.

Kondo, Dorinne K. (1990) *Crafting Selves. Power, Gender and Discourses of Identity in a Japanese Workplace*. Chicago, IL: The University of Chicago Press.

Lim, Linda Y. C. (1983) 'Chinese Economic Activity in Southeast Asia: An Introductory Review', in Linda Y. C. Lim and Peter L. A. Gosling (eds), *The Chinese in Southeast Asia: Ethnicity and Economic Activity*. Singapore: Maruzen Asia, 1-29.

Ng, E. (1996) 'The Orchid Blooms'. *Life Style*, 2, 28-29.

Ong, Aihwa (1999) *Flexible Citizenship: The Cultural Logics of Transnationality*. Durham, NC: Duke University Press.

PuruShotam, Nirmala (1998) 'Disciplining Difference: "Race" in Singapore', in Joel S. Kahn (ed.), *Southeast Asian Identities. Culture and the Politics of Representation in Indonesia, Malaysia, Singapore and Thailand*. Singapore: Institute of Southeast Asian Studies, 51-94.

Rajaratnam, S. (1990) 'The Hookafusalem Bird'. *Straits Times*, Singapore (3 April).

Shils, Edward (1981) *Tradition*. Chicago, IL: University of Chicago Press.

Soh, Wei Nee (1990) 'Chinese Clan Associations and Religious Activities in Penang'. Contribution to *Southeast Asian Ethnography*, 9, 67-89.

Strathern, Merilyn (1994) 'Parts and Wholes: Refiguring Relationships', in Robert Borofsky (ed.), *Assessing Cultural Anthropology*. New York: McGraw-Hill, 204-216.

Turner, Victor (1974) *Dramas, Fields, and Metaphors: Symbolic Action in Human Society*. Ithaca, NY: Cornell University Press.

Wang, Gungwu (1997) *Global History and Migrations*. Boulder, CO: Westview Press.

Wee, Vivienne (1988) What does 'Chinese' Mean? An Exploratory Essay. Singapore: Department of Sociology.

Wikan, Unni (1996) 'The Nun's Story: Reflections on an Age-old, Postmodern Dilemma'. American Anthropologist, Vol. 98 (2), 279-289.

Willmott, Donald E. (1960) The Chinese of Semarang: A Changing Minority Community in Indonesia. Ithaca, NY: Cornell University Press.

Index

Note: bold page numbers indicate figures & illustrations; *n* in brackets refers to notes.

aborigine people 18, 191, 239-54
  discrimination against 251, 252
  languages of 134
  use of term 242
  see also aborigines *under* Taiwan;
    indigenous people
Academie Francaise model 133
Activists Beyond Borders (Yeck/Sikkin)
  61
Adamo, Salvatore 213
Adamu, Sémira 66, 218
Africa
  belonging in 141
  identity with 136-7
  migrants from 67, 70, 79
  nationalism in 31-2
Afro-Caribbean identity 135-7
Ainu people 17-18
  activism of 222-3
  assimilation of 229-34
  discrimination against 223
  diversity in 222
  perceived stasis in 225-8, 233-4
  writings of 223-5, 232-3
Ainudojin (1903 article) 232
Albanian migrants 65-6
Alevis 80, 86, 87-8
allegiance 38
  oaths of 12-13, 42
Amit, Vered 52
Amsterdam Treaty 64, 67, 71
Anderson, Benedict 39, 132, 134, 225
Ankara 62-3, 77
anti-colonialism 168
Apartheid 110
Arabic language 131
archaeology 155, 177
architecture 148, 154, 155-65, 252
Armenians 79
arranged marriage 13
Asia
  diversity in 50

East 4, 102
  multiculturalism in 13
  nationalism in 31-2
Southeast 5, 134, 201, 211
  multiple identity in 257-8
  see also individual countries/regions
assimilation 1, 11, 12, 47, 68, 200, 221,
  229-34, 242
  aversion to 113, 119, 123-4
asylum 62
  seekers 65-6
Atatürk, Mustafa Kemal 77
Atatürk's Thought (association) 77-8
Australia 13, 47
  aborigines in 8
autonomy 14, 190-1, 196-8, 202
  cultural/political 241
  of networks 102
  regional 186-9, 217

Bahasa Indonesian language 135
Bakhtin, Mikhail 128
Balkans 62
Baltic states 137, 140-1, 149-50, 162
  architectural style 163
  see also Riga
Barcelona Conference (1995) 70
Batchelor, Rev 224, 225
Beijing 200
Beijing Man 177
Belarus 127, 131
Belgium 3, 15, 17, 66, 67
  emigrants from 213(*n*)
  government of 209, 214-15, 217-18
    regional 212
  homogeneity in 31, 207-8
  immigrants in 213-14, 215
  internationalism of 216-17
  language laws 210, 211, 214
  linguistic regions 208, 209-10, 214
  multiple identity in 207-20
  national belonging in 212-13, 215

Belgrade, Chinese embassy in 178
belonging
    ascriptions/constructions of 24, 25-6,
        118-19
    feelings of 24, 25, 28
    fluidities of 26, 52, 88, 127-8
    global 32-5
    indigenous 221-37
    individual/group 17, 18
    language *see under* language
    local 3-4, 180-1
    meanings of 15
    moral ambiguity of 27-9
    multiple 9, 11, 36, 97
        patterns/contexts of 12-13
        political nature of 7, 14
    and nationalism/regionalism 1-5, 30-
        2, 147, 154
        official construction of 167-84
    semiotics of 34-5
    sources of 24-5, 28
    transnational 65
    see also identity
Benedict, Ruth 51
Bengal 132-3
Benhabib, Seyla 28
Bennett, Louise 136-7
Berlin 77, 78
    Wall 15
Bhabha, Homi 128, 130
Billig, Michael 11, 35(n10)
'black box' organization 105-6
Blackheads, House of (Riga) 157-8, **157**
Blumis, Peteris 161
Bologna 99
'boomerang effect' 61, 69
Borchova, Katya 164
borders
    national 1, 10-11, 24, 216
        irrationality of 27-8
        porosity of 23, 26, 40
    theories of 128-9
Bosnia 131
Bosscher, Annette 71
Bourdieu 111
Brandt, Max von 226
Brass, Paul 241, 251
Brauns, David August 227
Breger, Rosemary 110
Britain
    diversity in 50-1

    homogeneity in 31
    migrants in 72, 79
    nationalism in 217(n)
brotherhoods, Turkish 86, 87
Brussels 66, 67, 211, 212, 214, 215
Budapest 154
Buddhism 190, 191

Campani, Giovanna 95
Campbell, Archibald Gowan 227-8
Canada 5, 47, 55, 133, 243
    French language in 142
    Inuit of 134, 221
capitalism 53
Carter, Erica 147
Castles, Stephen 5, 11
catering industry 114
Catholic Church 208
    marriage laws 110
Central Plain culture 174, 200
Chatterjee, Partha 132-3
Chen Qichen 173
children 133
Chin, Jeff 138
China 32
    imperial period 17
    labour market in 94
    local belonging in 3-4, 180-1, 183
        ethnic identity 185-204
        kinship systems 198
        regional autonomies 186-9, 190-1,
            192, 197-9
        state policies 189-99, 201-2
    migrants from 5, 9, 14, 16, 39, 67
        economic activities of 102, 106
        family values 114-18
        links with China 101, 103-5
                    cultural 112-14
        marriage practices 109-24
                    discrimination in 118
        role of press in 103-4, 115-18, 174
        social status in 120-2
        see also Han; Singapore *and under*
            Italy
    Ming period 199-200
    Muslims in (Hui) 4, 173, 187, 189,
        192(n14), 197, 200
    national identity in 13-15, 32, 167-84
        role of culture in 169, 172, 173,
            174-5, 177, **181**, 183

role of history in 171-3, 180-1,
  182-3
role of institutions 168-9
role of language in 17, 174, 175,
  176-9, 180
role of media in 169-73, 176, 180,
  181, 182
Nationalities Affairs Commission
  193, 194, 194(n16)
Qing period 186, 188, 190(n), 200
science & technology gap in 175,
  181-2, **181**
Southwest 185-204
and Taiwan 167, 169, 170, 172, 178-
  9, 183
transnationalism 5
welfare system 193
in the world 174-6, 181-2, **181**
Chinese Communist Party 168-9, 171-2,
  178, 180
and ethnic minorities 187, 188
Chinese New Year (*Qing Ming*) 265-6
Chinese People's Political Consultative
  Conference (CPPCC) 168
Chirot, Daniel 4-5
Christianity *see* church
church 9
  marriage laws 110
  state relations 40
  support for minority groups 70, 243,
    245, 247, 251-2
churches, re-consecration of 150
Cissé, Madjiguène 65
citizenship 3, 12, 93, 105, 257
  and globalization 5-6, 39
  and multiculturalism 8, 45, 54
  multiple 33, 38
  and nationality 28, 28-9(n), 30(n), 31
  rights 32, 68, 84, 96, 102
  of diaspora 138-9
  transnational 5, 11, 85
Citizenship & Migration (Castles &
  Davidson) 5
civic responsibility 28, 90
civil rights 223
class systems 198, 252-3
Claus, Hugo 215-16
Cohen, Robin 78
Cold War 9, 15, 40
colonialism 5, 132, 171, 172, 249, 258

see also anti-colonialism; post-
  colonialism
Columberg, Dumeni 214, 216
Commission for Racial Equality (CRE)
  68
communications technology 66, 80, 88
Communism, Chinese 182-3
communitarianism 47-9, 55, 56
communities 2-3, 46, 52, 97
  economic activities of 96, 98-9
  imagined 39, 208, 225
  pluri-ethnic 37
  political activities of 97
  rights 47, 48
  social mobility within 94, 96, 102,
    103, 105
  sub-cultural/sub-ethnic 9
  see also under transnationalism
Confucian tradition 116, 123, 169, 174-5
Connolly, William 55-6
Cook, Robin 8
Cools, Albert 209
cosmopolitanism 7, 10, 49, 51-2
  and migration 35(n11), 36
Cracow 154, 163
cultural diversity *see* multiculturalism
cultural exclusivism 31
cultural relativism 51
Cultural Revolution 168
cultural theory 128-9
culture 27, 216
  and concept of nation 29-30, 169,
    172, 173, 175
  exchange/synthesis of 174-5
  and identity 6, 81, 111, 129-30
  local/ethnic 180-1, 192
  separatedness of 16
Cunning of Recognition, The (Povinelli)
  47
Czaplicka 29
Czechs 141-2

Danese, Gaia 69
Dante 132
Davidson, Alistair 5, 11
Dawson, Andrew 93
De Vos, George 251
de-territorialization 26, 37, 39, 55, 89
Degrelle, Léon 213
Delors, Jacques 71

democracy 28, 81, 90, 133, 138, 239, 257
  linguistic 142
Deng Xiaoping 168, 175
Dening, Rev Walter 227
Denmark 3, 9, 38
devolution 147, 217(*n*)
dialects 14, 95, 177(*n*), 180, 209, 261
Diana, Princess 15
diaspora 36, 79-80, 85, 141, 143, 213
  Chinese 16
  and multiple identity 257, 267
  nationalism of 78, 79
  Russian 127, 130-1, 137-41
dictionaries 224-5
diversity 45-57, 180
  levels of 50-1
  liberal conception of 46-50
  and multiple identity 257
  non-ethnic factors 55-6
Dominiczak, Jacek 164
Donald, James 147
Durkheim, Emile 264, 265
Dutroux, Marc 214

ecological issues 56
education 70, 100-1, 221, 250(*n*29)
  cultural role of 30, 56, 82, 97, 112, 119
  ethnic discrimination in 195, 242, 243-4
  and language development 133, 233, 247-8
  religious 78
elites
  aboriginal 151, 240, 241-8, 250(*n*29), 252
  global movement of 6, 10, 26, 32, 129
employment 13, 16, 62, 221
endogamy 116, 198
English language 131, 133, 141
entrepreneurship 98, 99, 100
Essential Outsiders (Chirot & Reid) 4-5
Estonia 138-9
ethnic associations 101
ethnic cleansing 31, 151, 152
ethnic 'dilution' 122
ethnicity
  and belonging 1-5, 23, 81-2, 88-9, 167, 169
  boundaries of 6, 8-9, 53-4, 185-204

formation 239, 241
  and multiculturalism 6-7, 31-2, 51
  and national identity 6, 8-9
  political claims based on 14
  transnational 61-75
  and religion 47
  state classification of 185, 189-96
  results of 197-9
ethno-nationalism 196, 198, 202, 264
Europe 3, 14, 102
  belonging in 16, 39, 40, 72
  Central 9, 10
    heritage reclamation in 147-66
    nation statehood in 2, 12
  Eastern 10, 62
    language belonging in 127-45
  'fortress' 67
  multiculturalism in 13, 45
  national language development in 131-3
  and Turkey 79, 80, 88
  see also individual countries/regions
European Commission 64, 67, 69
  Unit D/4 70-1, 71(*n*5)
European Court of Human Rights 86
European Court of Justice 71, 86
European Union (EU) 4, 9, 10, 11, 212, 216(*n*)
  diversity in 55
  enlargement of 127, 133, 138
  migrants' activism in 16, 62, 67-9, 73, 83-4
    funding for 69-72, 83
  Migrants' Forum 65, 67-8, 73
  migration within 67-8
  transnationalism in 62-7
Europeanization 35, 41, 56
Europhobia 68
evolution theory 229
exceptionalism 2
exclusion *see* inclusion
exiles 14, 81

Falun Gong movement 14
family
  and marriage 114-18, 121
  migration 99
Favell, Adrian 69
Fazilet party 78, 81
federalism 215, 216, 217
feudal system 186

fishing industry 230-1
Flanders 208
Flemings/Flemish 17, 207, 211-12, 215-
  16
  hostility towards Walloons 213
Florence 99, 101
folk customs 130, 134, 140, 180, 190,
  223, 232
  rituals 264-5
  stigmatized 249
food, as cultural signifier 114, 121, 134,
  266
Fourons/Voeren 210, 215
Fourth World Movement 252
France 63-4, 132, 217
  migrants in 79, 88, 99, 102
    activism of 66-7, 69
Frazer, George 46
French language 208, 209, 210, 211, 212
Fritze, Dr. Adolf 227, 231-2
Fu Yangzhi 252
Fuentes, Carlos 129-30, 143
Fukuzawa Yukichi 229-30

Gdańsk 17, 147-55
  history 151-3
  identity politics in 153-5
  reconstruction of 158-65
Gediminas, Grand Duke 149
Gellnerian ideals 2, 14
Gemeinschaft 28
Germany 217
  Chinese immigrants in 117, 120-1
  East 15
  migrants' groups in 68
  Turkish immigrants in 9, 16, 33, 79,
    88
    contribution to economy 89(n)
    transnationalism of 77-91
Giddens, Anthony 30
globalization 1-2, 3
  and belonging 5-15, 18, 24, 32-5,
    143-4
  and diversity 45, 53
  and heritage reclamation 162
  history/nature of 40-1
  and language 131
  movement against 8
  nation state undermined by 6, 26, 32,
    41, 54
  and transnational capitalism 5

government, world 26
Grin, Francois 144
Gruszkowski, Wieslaw 159
Guanxi Zhuang region 186, 196, 198
Guizhou province 186, 193
gypsies 55

Habermas, Jürgen 49
Hakka people 188($n5$), 239-40($n3$), 240-
  1, 246, 247
Han Chinese 14, 15, 185, 192, 193, 195,
  199-201, 202
  history of 199-200
  Taiwan 239($n1$), 239-40($n3$), 241,
    245, 249, 251, 252-3
Hanson, Marcus Lee 54
Harlig, Jeffrey 143
headhunting 249, 252
Hemmerechts, Kristien 215
Hepburn, J.C. 226
Herder, Johann Gottfried 25, 132
heritage 177
  reclamation of 147-66
    changing of place/personal names
      150, 250-1
    historic context 151-3
    materials/construction 162-4
    trends 153-5
    urban skylines 159-60
heterogeneity 217
Hill, Rosanna 110
Hispanic Americans 12
Hitchcock, Romyn 231
Hokkaidō 223, 224, 229, 230
Holland 68, 72, 88, 120-1
homeness 35, 37
  and 'house' 38-40
homogeneity 1, 3, 6-7, 13, 29-31, 35, 40,
  86
  assumed 55
  and globalization 41
  imposed 4, 26, 239
  lack of 207-8
  of mainstream society 47
Hong Kong 14, 167, 169, 170
  emigration from 5
housing 62, 70
Howard, Benjamin Douglas 228
Hui *see* Muslims *under* China
human rights 61, 66, 178, 257
  abuses 14, 103, 152

Convention on 86
European Court of 86
organizations 8, 10
Hungary 128
hybridity 128-30
  linguistic 139, 143

identity 3
  collective 93-4, 96
  construction 38, 193-6, 209, 221-37,
    233, 241
  European 72
  fixation 37-8
  fragmented 81-2, 208
  and homogeneity 30-2
  hybrid 10, 37, 52, 54-5
  and marriage 112-14
  multiple 13, 138, 207-20, 255-8
    case study 260-8
  and nationalism 79, 80-1
  nested 10
  pan-ethnic 242-4
  politics 11, 23, 27, 40, 54-5, 147
    and heritage reclamation 153-5
  reclaiming 147-66, 250-1
  and social status 120-2
  see also belonging
Imams 81
immigrants *see* migrants
immigration 78-9
  control/laws 10, 50, 211
  emigrant countries' intervention in 78
imperialism 3, 172, 177
inclusion/exclusion 123
  language of 176-9
  and multiculturalism 8
  processes/policies of 3, 41
India 132-3
  migration from 79, 259
indigenous peoples 3, 18, 47, 55, 61
  and change 225-8
  identity construction of 221-37, 240,
    250
  and multiculturalism 245-8
  see also aborigines
Indochina 5
Indonesia 134-5
Inner Mongolia Autonomous Region 186
instrumentalist school 131
integration 68
  and marriage 111, 122-4

policies 185, 186-9
interculturalism 55
intermarriage 16, 109-24, 134
  concept of 110-11
  in identity construction 118-22
  role in integration 122-3
internationalism 216-17
Inuit people 134, 221
Ireland, Patrick 63-4
Islam 9, 38
  activism of 4, 62, 72, 78, 81, 86-8
Italy 63, 132, 217-18
  Chinese community in 16, 93-107
    access to resources 101
    characteristics of 96-7
    economic activities of 96, 98-9,
      100, 102-3
    education in 100-1
    history of 95-6
    role of press in 103-4
    social mobility 94, 96, 102, 103,
      105
    strategies of 100-3
  migrants' rights groups in 65-6, 69

Jacoby, Russell 54
Jamaica 136-7
Japan 14-15, 187, 221-37, 243, 249, 251
  Ainu people *see* Ainu people
  fishing industry in 230-1
  local belonging in 3-4
  nation-building in 222, 223, 228-31
  national identity of 226
Jews 79, 150, 151-2, 211
  marriage laws 110
Jiang Zemin 167, 181-2
Jinbō Kotora 224-5, 232-3
Jugenstil architecture 154, 163
Jurkstas, Vytautas 161

Kaiser, Robert 138
Kampuchea 112, 117
Kannan, Chirayil 122
Kastoryano, Riva 63
Keck, Margaret 61
Kemalism 78, 82
kinship systems 105, 198
Kirschbaum, Stanislav 141-2
KMT (Nationalist Party) 187, 188
Kosaku, Yoshino 226
Kurds 62-3, 80, 84

activism in Turkey 78, 82
dual minority status of 85-6
Kymlicka, Will 47, 48

labour 13, 16, 62, 221
Laitin, David 140
Lamont, Michèle 111, 124
land reform 190-1, 241(*n*9)
language 54, 80, 106, 174, 175
    belonging 2, 9, 11, 18, 27, 39, 55,
        127-45, 142, 208
        in Belgium 208-11, 214
        and education 133, 233, 247-8
        inclusive aspect of Chinese 176-9
        in indigenous peoples 222, 223-5,
            232-3, 240, 250
        process of 130-3
    censorship 188
    dialects 14, 95, 177(*n*), 180, 209
    and intermarriage 113, 120-1
    laws 133, 138-41
    national 187
        development of 131-3
        split 207
    Patois 127, 135-7, 143
    politicization of 17, 133-5, 138-41
        Western reaction to 141-2
    written 222, 223-5
Laponce, Jean 143
Larsen, Neil 1128
Latin America 133
    cultural identity in 129-30
    indigenous peoples in 61
    nationalism in 31-2
Latvia 139
    see also Riga
Lausanne, Treaty of (1923) 86
Lévi-Strauss, Claude 46, 209
liberalism
    and multiculturalism 6-7, 8, 46-50
    and nationalism 28
Lichtenberg, Judith 27-30, 34
Lijiang 189, 190
Lille 65, 66-7, 72
Limberg 210, 212, 216
Lithuania *see* Vilnius
Liverpool 121
localism 2, 180-1, 183
Lower Palace, Vilnius 155-7, **156**, 159
Lukes, Steven 48
Luxemburg 212

Lviv 154
Lyotard, Jean-Francois 215

Ma Mung, Emmanuel 99
Maastricht 212
Maastricht Treaty 62
Macau 14, 167, 169, 170, 179
McLuhan, Marshall 132
Malaya 5, 18
Malaysia 258, 261-2, 266
Mali 70
Man, Henri de 216
Man, Paul de 216
Manchu identity 187, 188-9, 193
Mao Zedong 168, 170, 182
market forces 40
marriage 16, 96
    agganged 13
    announcements 115-18
    laws 110
    mixed 117, 119, 122-4, 214
    see also intermarriage
Marx, Karl 6, 129
Marxism 128, 167
    Chinese 168-9, 170, 186
May Fourth Movement 178
media
    and globalization 40
    and national identity 167, 169-73,
        179, 180
    and transnationalism 63, 64, 66,
        87(*n*), 88
memory 25, 29, 39, 54
Merton, Robert K. 110, 122
Mexico, immigrant labour from 42
Michaut, Dr. 228
Mickiewicz, Adam 153
Middle East 131
    nationalism in 31-2
migrants 9
    activism of 8, 16, 62-7, 81, 83-5, 89
        EU lobbies 67-9, 84
        funding for 69-72
    allegiance to new country 12-13, 200-
        1, 213-14, 215
    civic belonging of 10
    illegal 62, 65
    links with country of origin 80
    networks 9, 52, 68-9, 80, 93-5
    rights 47, 48, 62, 64, 84

second/third generation 54, 72, 99,
    100-1, 106
  marriage 109-24
  social class of 53-4
  stigmatized 41
  transnationalism 62-4
  see also refugees
Migrants' Forum 65, 67-8, 73, 83
migration 3, 62
  and belonging 23, 33
  and colonialism 5
  family 99
  and globalization 6, 35-6
  intra-national 37, 200-1
Migration Policy Group 69, 72
Milan 99
Millî Görüş 78, 81, 87
Ming period 199-200
missionaries 224, 249, 251
modernity 173
modernization 3
Moldova 140
Mölln 77
Mongolia 186, 191
monuments 149, 158
Moravansky, Akos 162
Morocco 68, 70
Moslems *see* Islam
Mosuo identity 189-92, 194-5, 197-8
Muli 191
multiculturalism 3, 31-2, 35
  aims of 49-50
  and belonging 23, 37-8, 53
  democratic 56
  diversity in 45-50
  and indigenous peoples 245-8
  as political issue 6, 7-10, 16
multilingual states 133, 141, 143, 207-20
multiplicity 5
museums 149-50
Mutabaruka (dub poet) 136-7
myth
  and language 132
  and national identity 31, 34, 79-80,
    209
  of return 38, 41, 179

names 18, 150, 250-1, 262-4, 265-6
Naples 10, 99, 102-3, 104-5
nation state 1-2, 26-32, 37, 183
  and civilizations 9

competition within 3
identity construction in 167-84
imagined oneness of 31-3, 46, 170,
    176, 179, 208, 213
and language belonging 133-5
migrants identify with 12-13, 80-1,
    200-1, 213-14, 215
minority identity in 63-4
undermined by European institutions
    73, 84-5
undermined by globalization 6, 26,
    32, 41, 54
undermined by transnationalism 89
national anthems 169
national identity
  and belonging 1-5, 23, 26, 32-3
  cosmopolitan 10
  and racism 24, 25-6
  separated from ethnicity 6, 8-9
nationalism 15, 167-8
  civic 33
  ethnic 196, 198, 202, 264
  and localism 180-1
  theory 207-8, 210
nationality 3
NATO 153, 176
naturalization 138, 139
Naxi identity 189-92, 194, 195, 197
Nazi occupations 149-50, 151, 215-16
nested identity 10
Netherlands 68, 72, 88, 120-1
Nettle, Daniel 131
networks 9, 52, 68-9, 113
  autonomy of 102
  kinship 105, 198
  transnational 80, 83-5, 101
neutral space 128-9, 130
Nigeria 141
Ninglang county 189, 190, 191-2, 196
Ningxia region 173, 180, 186, 187
Non-governmental organizations
    (NGOs) 6, 103
  anti-globalizing 8
  migrants' rights 61, 65, 67, 69, 70,
    71-2, 71(*n*6), 101
Norway 131
Nurcu movement 87(*n*)

Öcalan, Abdullah 63
OECD 69
Omar ibn al-Khattab 131

Ong, Aihwa 5
oral tradition 223, 224, 234
Øresund project 9
orthography 224, 225
Ostra Brama chapel 160
Other 9-10, 25, 46, 48, 178
    dialogue with 129-30, 143
    indigenous 228, 234
    monolingualism of 210
    Oriental 4
Ouhua Shibao 104
Ouzhou Shibao Nouvelles d'Europe
    109(*n*), 115

Palestinians 79
Paris 66, 67, 99, 102, 117
passports 32, 33
Patois 127, 135-7, 143
patriarchy/patriliny 116, 123, 174, 190,
    192, 193, 262
patriotism 4, 168-9, 172, 176, 183
Peeters, Leo 212
People's Daily 169, 170-3, 177(*n*), 179,
    180, 181, 182
pluralism 48, 201
Pocock, J.G.A. 133
Poland 127, 149, 151
    see also Gdansk
political membership 73
politics of belonging 1
Portes, Alejandro 63
post-colonialism 5, 79, 128
    and language development 132-3
post-Communism 133, 137-41
    and heritage reclamation 147-66
postnational model 63-4, 73
potmodernism 7, 23, 40, 48-9, 51-2
Povinelli, Elizabeth 47
Prague 154
Pramoedya Ananta Toer 134-5
Prantl, Heribert 65
Prato 97, 98-100, 101-2
PRC *see* China
primordialism 23, 23-4(*n*), 26, 131
Prodi, Romano 49
property prices 5
Pumi ethnic group 191-2, 195, 196, 197-
    8, 202
Putin, Vladimir 133

Qing Ming 265-6

Qing period 186, 188, 190(*n*), 200, 266
Québec 142

race segregation 110
racism 2, 15, 41, 46, 47, 48, 77
    actions against 68, 69, 71, 83
    and belonging 24
    in colonial regimes 5
    and diversity 50
    European Year of 70
    institutional 103, 104
    and marriage 111, 118
Rapport, Nigel 52, 93
refugees 9, 35(*n*11), 54, 69, 152(*n*)
    multiple identity of 257
    organizations 8
regionalism 1-5, 30-2, 147, 154, 216
    cultural 201
regions
    autonomy of 186-9, 217
    diversity of 3-4
    identity of 147, 201, 208-9, 210, 211-
        13
Reid, Anthony 4-5
relativism 49
religion 12, 81, 187, 261-2
    ethnicity defined by 47, 80
    movements 14
    and state 40, 86-8
religious belief 40
Renan 30
repatriation 24
republicanism 66, 68, 86
Richard, Madeline A. 122-3
Riga 17, 147-55, **157**
    civic belonging in 150-1
    history 151-3
    identity politics in 153-5
    reconstruction of 157-8, 159-65
rituals 264-6
River Elegy (Su Xiaokang) 167-8, 169,
    173
Roland, statue of 149, 158
Romaine, Suzanne 131
Rome 104
    Treaty of 64
rootedness 34, 36, 111, 112-14, 124
Rorty, Richard 35(*n*10), 49
Ruble 29
Rüsen, Jörn 153
Rushdie affair 62-3

Russia
  diaspora from 127, 130-1, 137-41,
    153
  language laws in 133, 138
  see also Soviet Union

Sadatoshi, Yasugi 225
Said, Edward 9
St Louis Exposition 223, 231
sans papiers movement 64-7, 73
Sassen, Saskia 54, 61
Satanic Verses, The (Rushdie) 62-3
Scandinavia, migrants from 68
Schengen agreement (1990) 10, 64
Scheube, B. 227, 230-1
Schlesinger, Georg 228
science & technology gap 175, 181-2,
  181
SCORE (Standing Conference on Racial
  Equality in Europe) 68
Second World War 151, 152, 157
Senegal 70
separatism 214, 215
Sichuan 189, 191, 196, 198
Sikkin, Kathryn 61
Silent Immigration (Campani et al) 95
Singapore 2, 18, 255-69
  and China 258, 260-8
  history 258, 265-6
  identity case study 260-8
  nationalism in 259
  rituals in 264-7
Slovaks 141-2
Slowacki, Julius 153
social fragmentation 45-6
social mobility 94, 96, 102, 103, 105
Solidarity (Solidarnosc) 65, 148, 149
Somadossi, Yvonne 213
South Africa 110
sovereignty 3
  threats to 6, 8
Soviet Union 9, 17, 128, 130, 151-2,
  157, 161
  former 133, 137-41, 147-66
  see also Russia
Soysal, Yasemin 61, 63
Spaak, Paul-Henri 216
space
  national *see* territoriality
  neutral 128-9, 130
Spain 217

Squires, Judith 147
Stainton, Michael 243, 252
Stalinism 187
Starr, Frederick 223, 230, 231
Starting Line Group (SLG) 65, 67, 68-9
statues 149, 158
Steinberg, Stephen 53-4
stereotyping 4-5, 119, 209
Su Xiaokang 167-8, 169, 173
sub-ethnic groups 121
subculturalization 9
subsidiarity 71
supranationality 2, 85
Sweden 9
Switzerland 31, 63-4, 133, 208

Taiwan 14, 18, 112
  aborigines of 239-54
    activism of 240-8
      assessed 249-51
    church activities 243, 245, 247,
      248, 251-2
    culture of 249, 252
    education issues 242, 243-4
    elites' activities 151, 240, 241-8,
      250(*n*29), 252
    language of 247
    and multiculturalism 245-8
    state relationship with 239, 240,
      242
    stigmatization of 241-2
  and China 167, 169, 170, 172, 178-9,
    183
  Han Chinese in 239(*n*1), 239-40(*n*3),
    241, 245, 252-3
  homogeneity in 239-40, 244, 246
  Nationalist Party of 239, 242-4, 245-
    7(*n*21), 248, 249
Taiwan, Presbyterian Church of 243,
  245, 248, 251
Takaki Senshi 230
Tapia, Stephanie de 80
tarikat 86, 87
Taroko people 249-51
Tarrow, Sidney 61, 66
tattoos 249, 252
territoriality 26, 29, 80, 88, 187
textile industry 98, 102
Theory of Civilization, Outline of
  (Fukuzawa) 229-30
Tiananmen Square protest 15

Tibet
  autonomy of 186, 196-8, 202
  exiles from 14
Tibetan Buddhism 190, 191
Todd, Mabel Loomis 232
toleration 45, 46
Toronto 5
tourism 9, 36, 150, 154, 160, 201, 252(*n*)
trade unions 70, 101
transborder projects 9, 11
transnationalism 5-12, 16, 26, 33, 36,
    234
  claims-making 61-75
    funding for 70-2
    sans papiers movement 64-7
  communities 88-9
    activism of 83-5
    emergence of 79-82
    structure of 82
  and diversity 55
  of elites 10, 26
  institutions 6, 10
  and language 131
  literature on 62, 63-4
  see also under Turkish migrants
Trieste 66
Tujia ethnic group 193, 195
Tully, James 49
Turkey 90
  activities in transnational community
    82, 87(*n*)
  and Europe 79, 80
  homogenization in 86
  migrants from 9, 16, 33, 67, 68
    transnationalism of 77-91
      networks 83-5
      redefined 85-9
    see also under Germany
  political organizations in 77-8, 81, 87
  religious issues in 86-8
Turkish migrants, *see also* Kurds
Turkistan 128
Turner, Victor 264-5
Tuscany 95, 102
Tuva 128

Uighur activists 14
Ukraine 139-40
UNESCO 48
unilingual states 130, 143
Unit D/4 70-1, 71(*n*5)

United Nations 69, 143
  on indigenous peoples 221, 223
United States 14, 40
  belonging in 41-2, 111
    hyphenated model 11-13, 31, 39-
      40
  black organizations in 8, 42
  diversity in 50, 55
  hegemony 178, **181**
  identity formation in 12
  paternalism of 192(*n*15)
universalism 147
urban development 155
urban skylines 159-60
Uyghur people 135

Vancouver 5
Verdriet van België, Het (Claus) 215-16
Versailles Treaty 178
Vilnius 17, 147-57
  history 151-3
  identity politics in 153-5
  reconstruction of 155-7, 158, 159-65
Vlaams Blok party 214
Voeren/Fourons 210, 215
Volk myth 132

Wagatsuma, Hiroshi 251
Wallonia 208-9, 212
Walloons 17, 207, 208-9, 211
  hostility towards Flemings 213
Warsaw 154, 163
Watson, R.G. 226-7
welfare state 13
Welsh language 134, 142
Wenzhou region, migrants from 94, 96,
    100, 117
White March 214-15, 216
Wilson, Andrew 139-40
word lists 223-5
World Bank 172
world government 26
World Trade Organization (WTO) 106,
    170

xenophobia 48, 50, 52, 53, 214
  action against 69, 83
Xibo ethnic group 193
Xie Shizhong 241-2, 243, 244
Xikang province 186
Xinhua News Agency 169

Xinhua Shibao 103
Xinjiang Uighur region 186

Yack, Bernard 31, 33(*n*)
Yasher, Deborah 61
Yellow River 168, 173
Yi ethnic group 189, 190, 191, 196, 197,
    198-9
Yuanzhumin see aborigines *under*
  Taiwan
Yunnan province 185-204
    Han population 199-201, 202
    history of 199-200

Zhang Dainan 174-5
Zhejiang, migrants from 94, 96, 98, 99,
    102
Zhongyi Bao 103
Zhuang ethnic group 189, 196, 198, 202